Barron's 巴朗SAT Ⅱ

数学2（第12版）

Subject Test Math Level 2（12th edition）

［美］库（Richard Ku） 编著

世界图书出版公司
北京·广州·上海·西安

图书在版编目（CIP）数据

Barron's 巴朗SAT Ⅱ 数学2：第12版 = Barron's SAT Subject Test Math Level 2（12th edition）：英文 /（美）库（Richard Ku）编著. —影印本. —北京：世界图书出版公司北京公司，2017.2（2019.6重印）

ISBN 978-7-5192-2409-7

Ⅰ.①B… Ⅱ.①库… Ⅲ.①中学数学课—高等学校—入学考试—美国—教学参考资料—英文 Ⅳ.①G634.603

中国版本图书馆CIP数据核字（2017）第034762号

书　　名　Barron's 巴朗 SAT II 数学2（第12版）
BARRON'S BALANG SAT II SHUXUE 2（DI 12 BAN）

编 著 者　［美］库（Richard Ku）
责任编辑　武传霞

出版发行　世界图书出版公司北京公司
地　　址　北京市东城区朝内大街137号
邮　　编　100010
电　　话　010-64038355（发行）　64037380（客服）　64033507（总编室）
网　　址　http://www.wpcbj.com.cn
邮　　箱　wpcbjst@vip.163.com
销　　售　新华书店
印　　刷　三河市国英印务有限公司
开　　本　880 mm × 1230 mm　1/16
印　　张　22.75
字　　数　620千
版　　次　2017年4月第1版　2019年6月第4次印刷
版权登记　01-2016-9695
国际书号　978-7-5192-2409-7
定　　价　58.00元

目 录

第三部分　测试题

Contents

PART 3
MODEL TESTS

Introduction 绪论

The purpose of this book is to help you prepare for the SAT Level 2 Mathematics Subject Test. This book can be used as a self-study guide or as a textbook in a test preparation course. It is a self-contained resource for those who want to achieve their best possible score.

Because the SAT Subject Tests cover specific content, they should be taken as soon as possible after completing the necessary course(s). This means that you should register for the Level 2 Mathematics Subject Test in June after you complete a precalculus course.

You can register for SAT Subject Tests at the College Board's web site, *www.collegeboard.org*; by calling (866) 756-7346, if you previously registered for an SAT Reasoning Test or Subject Test; or by completing registration forms in the SAT Registration Booklet, which can be obtained in your high school guidance office. You may register for up to three Subject Tests at each sitting.

Important Reminder

Be sure to check the official College Board web site for the most accurate information about how to register for the test and what documentation to bring on test day.

Colleges use SAT Subject Tests to help them make both admission and placement decisions. Because the Subject Tests are not tied to specific curricula, grading procedures, or instructional methods, they provide uniform measures of achievement in various subject areas. This way, colleges can use Subject Test results to compare the achievement of students who come from varying backgrounds and schools.

You can consult college catalogs and web sites to determine which, if any, SAT Subject Tests are required as part of an admissions package. Many "competitive" colleges require the Level 1 Mathematics Test.

If you intend to apply for admission to a college program in mathematics, science, or engineering, you may be required to take the Level 2 Mathematics Subject Test. If you have been generally successful in high school mathematics courses and want to showcase your achievement, you may want to take the Level 2 Subject Test and send your scores to colleges you are interested in even if it isn't required.

OVERVIEW OF THIS BOOK 本书概论

A Diagnostic Test in Part 1 follows this introduction. This test will help you quickly identify your weaknesses and gaps in your knowledge of the topics. You should take it under test conditions (in one quiet hour). Use the Answer Key immediately following the test to check your answers, read the explanations for the problems you did not get right, and complete the Self-Evaluation Chart that follows the explanations. These explanations include a code for calculator use, the correct answer choice, and the chapter number of the relevant topic in the Part 2 "Review of Major Topics." For your convenience, the Self-Evaluation Chart is also keyed to these locations.

The majority of those taking the Level 2 Mathematics Subject Test are accustomed to using graphing calculators. Where appropriate, explanations of problem solutions are based on their use. Secondary explanations that rely on algebraic techniques may also be given.

Part 3 contains six model tests. The breakdown of test items by topic approximately reflects the nominal distribution established by the College Board. The percentage of questions for which calculators are required or useful on the model tests is also approximately the same as that specified by the College Board. The model tests are self-contained. Each has an answer sheet and a complete set of directions. Each test is followed by an answer key, explanations such as those found in the Diagnostic Test, and the Self-Evaluation Chart.

A summary of formulas is given after Model Test 6. These are organized by the chapters of the review section.

OVERVIEW OF THE LEVEL 2 SUBJECT TEST SAT Ⅱ 数学2概述

The SAT Mathematics Level 2 Subject Test is one hour in length and consists of 50 multiple-choice questions, each with five answer choices. The test is aimed at students who have had two years of algebra, one year of geometry, and one year of trigonometry and elementary functions. According to the College Board, test items are distributed over topics as follows:

- Numbers and Operation: 5–7 questions
  Operations, ratio and proportion, complex numbers, counting, elementary number theory, matrices, sequences, series, and vectors
- Algebra and Functions: 24–26 questions
  Work with equations, inequalities, and expressions; know properties of the following classes of functions: linear, polynomial, rational, exponential, logarithmic, trigonometric and inverse trigonometric, periodic, piecewise, recursive, and parametric
- Coordinate Geometry: 5–7 questions
  Symmetry, transformations, conic sections, polar coordinates
- Three-dimensional Geometry: 2–3 questions
  Volume and surface area of solids (prisms, cylinders, pyramids, cones, and spheres); coordinates in 3 dimensions
- Trigonometry: 6–8 questions
  Right triangles; laws of sines and cosines; radian measure; Pythagorean identities, and double-angle identities
- Data Analysis, Statistics, and Probability: 3–5 questions
  Measures of central tendency and spread; graphs and plots; least squares regression (linear, quadratic, and exponential); probability

CALCULATOR USE 计算器的使用

As noted earlier, most taking the Level 2 Mathematics Subject Test are familiar with the use of a graphing calculator. In addition to performing the calculations of a scientific calculator, graphing calculators can be used to analyze graphs and to find zeros, points of intersection of graphs, and maxima and minima of functions. Graphing calculators can also be used to find numerical solutions to equations, generate tables of function values, evaluate statistics, and find regression equations. The author assumes that readers of this book plan to use a graphing calculator when taking the Level 2 test.

> **Note**
>
> To make them as specific and succinct as possible, calculator instructions in the answer explanations are based on the TI-83 and TI-84 families of calculators.

You should always read a question carefully and decide on a strategy to answer it before deciding whether a calculator is necessary. A calculator is useful or necessary on only 55–65 percent of the questions. You may find, for example, that you need a calculator only to evaluate some expression that must be determined based solely on your knowledge about how to solve the problem. In both the Diagnostic Test and Model Tests, an asterisk (*) in the Answers Explained sections indicates questions on which a graphing calculator is necessary or useful.

Most graphing calculators are user friendly. They follow order of operations, and expressions can be entered using several levels of parentheses. There is never a need to round and write down the result of an intermediate calculation and then rekey that value as part of another calculation. Premature rounding can result in choosing a wrong answer if numerical answer choices are close in value.

On the other hand, graphing calculators can be troublesome or even misleading. For example, if you have difficulty finding a useful window for a graph, perhaps there is a better way to solve a problem. Piecewise functions, functions with restricted domains, and functions having asymptotes provide other examples where the usefulness of a graphing calculator may be limited.

Calculators have popularized a multiple-choice problem-solving technique called backsolving, where answer choices are entered into the problem to see which works. In problems where decimal answer choices are rounded, none of the choices may work satisfactorily. Be careful not to overuse this technique.

The College Board has established rules governing the use of calculators on the Mathematics Subject Tests:

- You may bring extra batteries or a backup calculator to the test. If you wish, you may bring both scientific and graphing calculators.
- Test centers are not expected to provide calculators, and test takers may not share calculators.
- Notify the test supervisor to have your score cancelled if your calculator malfunctions during the test and you do not have a backup.
- Certain types of devices that have computational power are **not permitted**: cell phones, pocket organizers, powerbooks and portable handheld computers, and electronic writing pads. Calculators that require an electrical outlet, make noise or "talk," or use paper tapes are also prohibited. A list of allowable calculators can be found on the College Board's web site *collegereadiness.collegeboard.org/sat/taking-the-test/calculator-policy*.
- You do not have to clear a graphing calculator memory before or after taking the test. However, any attempt to take notes in your calculator about a test and remove it from the room will be grounds for dismissal and cancellation of scores.

TIP

Leave your cell phone at home, in your locker, or in your car!

HOW THE TEST IS SCORED 如何评分

There are 50 questions on the Math Level 2 Subject Test. Your raw score is the number of correct answers minus one-fourth of the number of incorrect answers, rounded to the nearest whole number. For example, if you get 30 correct answers, 15 incorrect answers, and leave 5 blank, your raw score would be $30 - \frac{1}{4}(15) \approx 26$, rounded to the nearest whole number.

Raw scores are transformed into scaled scores between 200 and 800. The formula for this transformation changes slightly from year to year to reflect varying test difficulty. In recent years, a raw score of 44 was high enough to transform to a scaled score of 800. Each point less in the raw score resulted in approximately 10 points less in the scaled score. For a raw score of 44 or more, the approximate scaled score is 800. For raw scores of 44 or less, the following formula can be used to get an approximate scaled score on the Diagnostic Test and each Model Test:

$S = 800 - 10(44 - R)$, where S is the approximate scaled score and R is the rounded raw score.

The self-evaluation page for the Diagnostic Test and each Model Test includes spaces for you to calculate your raw score and scaled score.

STRATEGIES TO MAXIMIZE YOUR SCORE 提分策略

- **Budget your time.** Although most testing centers have wall clocks, you would be wise to have a watch on your desk. Since there are 50 items on a one-hour test, you have a little over a minute per item. Typically, test items are easier near the beginning of a test, and they get progressively more difficult. Don't linger over difficult questions. Work the problems you are confident of first, and then return later to the ones that are difficult for you.
- **Guess intelligently.** As noted above, you are likely to get a higher score if you can confidently eliminate two or more answer choices, and a lower score if you can't eliminate any.
- **Read the questions carefully.** Answer the question asked, not the one you may have expected. For example, you may have to solve an equation to answer the question, but the solution itself may not be the answer.
- **Mark answers clearly and accurately.** Since you may skip questions that are difficult, be sure to mark the correct number on your answer sheet. If you change an answer, erase cleanly and leave no stray marks. Mark only one answer; an item will be graded as incorrect if more than one answer choice is marked.

- **Change an answer only if you have a good reason for doing so.** It is usually not a good idea to change an answer on the basis of a hunch or whim.
- **As you read a problem, think about possible computational shortcuts to obtain the correct answer choice.** Even though calculators simplify the computational process, you may save time by identifying a pattern that leads to a shortcut.
- **Substitute numbers to determine the nature of a relationship.** If a problem contains only variable quantities, it is sometimes helpful to substitute numbers to understand the relationships implied in the problem.
- **Think carefully about whether to use a calculator.** The College Board's guideline is that a calculator is useful or necessary in about 60% of the problems on the Level 2 Test. An appropriate percentage for you may differ from this, depending on your experience with calculators. Even if you learned the material in a highly calculator-active environment, you may discover that a problem can be done more efficiently without a calculator than with one.
- **Check the answer choices.** If the answer choices are in decimal form, the problem is likely to require the use of a calculator.

STUDY PLANS 学习计划

Your first step is to take the Diagnostic Test. This should be taken under test conditions: timed, quiet, without interruption. Identify areas of weakness using the cross-references to the Part 2 review. Use the review to strengthen your understanding of the concepts involved.

Ideally, you would start preparing for the test two to three months in advance. Each week, you would be able to take one Model Test, following the same procedure as for the Diagnostic Test. Depending on how well you do, it might take you anywhere between 15 minutes and an hour to complete the work after you take the test. Obviously, if you have less time to prepare, you would have to intensify your efforts to complete the six Model Tests, or do fewer of them.

The best way to use Part 2 of this book is as reference material. You should look through this material quickly before you take the model tests, just to get an idea of the range of topics covered and the level of detail. However, these parts of the book are more effectively used after you've taken and corrected a model test.

PART 1
第一部分
Diagnostic Test
诊断测试

ANSWER SHEET

答题卡

Diagnostic Test

诊断测试

1. Ⓐ Ⓑ Ⓒ Ⓓ Ⓔ	14. Ⓐ Ⓑ Ⓒ Ⓓ Ⓔ	27. Ⓐ Ⓑ Ⓒ Ⓓ Ⓔ	40. Ⓐ Ⓑ Ⓒ Ⓓ Ⓔ
2. Ⓐ Ⓑ Ⓒ Ⓓ Ⓔ	15. Ⓐ Ⓑ Ⓒ Ⓓ Ⓔ	28. Ⓐ Ⓑ Ⓒ Ⓓ Ⓔ	41. Ⓐ Ⓑ Ⓒ Ⓓ Ⓔ
3. Ⓐ Ⓑ Ⓒ Ⓓ Ⓔ	16. Ⓐ Ⓑ Ⓒ Ⓓ Ⓔ	29. Ⓐ Ⓑ Ⓒ Ⓓ Ⓔ	42. Ⓐ Ⓑ Ⓒ Ⓓ Ⓔ
4. Ⓐ Ⓑ Ⓒ Ⓓ Ⓔ	17. Ⓐ Ⓑ Ⓒ Ⓓ Ⓔ	30. Ⓐ Ⓑ Ⓒ Ⓓ Ⓔ	43. Ⓐ Ⓑ Ⓒ Ⓓ Ⓔ
5. Ⓐ Ⓑ Ⓒ Ⓓ Ⓔ	18. Ⓐ Ⓑ Ⓒ Ⓓ Ⓔ	31. Ⓐ Ⓑ Ⓒ Ⓓ Ⓔ	44. Ⓐ Ⓑ Ⓒ Ⓓ Ⓔ
6. Ⓐ Ⓑ Ⓒ Ⓓ Ⓔ	19. Ⓐ Ⓑ Ⓒ Ⓓ Ⓔ	32. Ⓐ Ⓑ Ⓒ Ⓓ Ⓔ	45. Ⓐ Ⓑ Ⓒ Ⓓ Ⓔ
7. Ⓐ Ⓑ Ⓒ Ⓓ Ⓔ	20. Ⓐ Ⓑ Ⓒ Ⓓ Ⓔ	33. Ⓐ Ⓑ Ⓒ Ⓓ Ⓔ	46. Ⓐ Ⓑ Ⓒ Ⓓ Ⓔ
8. Ⓐ Ⓑ Ⓒ Ⓓ Ⓔ	21. Ⓐ Ⓑ Ⓒ Ⓓ Ⓔ	34. Ⓐ Ⓑ Ⓒ Ⓓ Ⓔ	47. Ⓐ Ⓑ Ⓒ Ⓓ Ⓔ
9. Ⓐ Ⓑ Ⓒ Ⓓ Ⓔ	22. Ⓐ Ⓑ Ⓒ Ⓓ Ⓔ	35. Ⓐ Ⓑ Ⓒ Ⓓ Ⓔ	48. Ⓐ Ⓑ Ⓒ Ⓓ Ⓔ
10. Ⓐ Ⓑ Ⓒ Ⓓ Ⓔ	23. Ⓐ Ⓑ Ⓒ Ⓓ Ⓔ	36. Ⓐ Ⓑ Ⓒ Ⓓ Ⓔ	49. Ⓐ Ⓑ Ⓒ Ⓓ Ⓔ
11. Ⓐ Ⓑ Ⓒ Ⓓ Ⓔ	24. Ⓐ Ⓑ Ⓒ Ⓓ Ⓔ	37. Ⓐ Ⓑ Ⓒ Ⓓ Ⓔ	50. Ⓐ Ⓑ Ⓒ Ⓓ Ⓔ
12. Ⓐ Ⓑ Ⓒ Ⓓ Ⓔ	25. Ⓐ Ⓑ Ⓒ Ⓓ Ⓔ	38. Ⓐ Ⓑ Ⓒ Ⓓ Ⓔ	
13. Ⓐ Ⓑ Ⓒ Ⓓ Ⓔ	26. Ⓐ Ⓑ Ⓒ Ⓓ Ⓔ	39. Ⓐ Ⓑ Ⓒ Ⓓ Ⓔ	

Diagnostic Test 诊断测试

The diagnostic test is designed to help you pinpoint your weaknesses and target areas for improvement. The answer explanations that follow the test are keyed to chapters of the book. To make the best use of this diagnostic test, set aside between 1 and 2 hours so you will be able to do the whole test in one sitting. Tear out the preceding answer sheet and indicate your answers in the appropriate spaces. Complete the problems as if this were a regular testing session. Review the suggestions on pages 3–4.

When finished, check your answers against the Answer Key at the end of the test. For those that you got wrong, note the chapters containing the material that you must review. If you do not fully understand how to get a correct answer, you should review those chapters also.

Finally, fill out the Self-Evaluation Chart on page 30 in order to pinpoint the topics that gave you the most difficulty.

50 questions: 1 hour

Directions: Decide which answer choice is best. If the exact numerical value is not one of the answer choices, select the closest approximation. Fill in the circle on the answer sheet that corresponds to your choice.

Notes:

(1) You will need to use a scientific or graphing calculator to answer some of the questions.
(2) You will have to decide whether to put your calculator in degree or radian mode for some problems.
(3) All figures that accompany problems are plane figures unless otherwise stated. Figures are drawn as accurately as possible to provide useful information for solving the problem, except when it is stated in a particular problem that the figure is not drawn to scale.
(4) Unless otherwise indicated, the domain of a function is the set of all real numbers for which the functional value is also a real number.

Reference Information. The following formulas are provided for your information.

Volume of a right circular cone with radius r and height h: $V = \frac{1}{3}\pi r^2 h$

Lateral area of a right circular cone if the base has circumference C and slant height is l:

$S = \frac{1}{2}Cl$

Volume of a sphere of radius r: $V = \frac{4}{3}\pi r^3$

Surface area of a sphere of radius r: $S = 4\pi r^2$

Volume of a pyramid of base area B and height h: $V = \frac{1}{3}Bh$

TIP

For the Diagnostic Test, practice exercises, and Model Tests, an asterisk in the Answers Explained section indicates that a graphing calculator is necessary or useful.

USE THIS SPACE FOR SCRATCH WORK

1. A linear function, f, has a slope of -2. $f(1) = 2$ and $f(2) = q$. Find q.

(A) 0

(B) $\frac{3}{2}$

(C) $\frac{5}{2}$

(D) 3

(E) 4

2. A function is said to be even if $f(x) = f(-x)$. Which of the following is *not* an even function?

(A) $y = |x|$
(B) $y = \sec x$
(C) $y = \log x^2$
(D) $y = x^2 + \sin x$
(E) $y = 3x^4 - 2x^2 + 17$

3. What is the radius of a sphere, with center at the origin, that passes through point (2,3,4)?

(A) 3
(B) 3.31
(C) 3.32
(D) 5.38
(E) 5.39

4. If $f(x) = \dfrac{5x+2}{-3x+1}$, what value does $f(x)$ approach as x gets arbitrarily large?

(A) -15

(B) $-\frac{5}{3}$

(C) -1

(D) $\frac{3}{5}$

(E) 2

5. If $f(x) = x^2 - ax$, then $f(a) =$

(A) a
(B) $a^2 - a$
(C) 0
(D) 1
(E) $a - 1$

6. The average of your first three test grades is 78. What grade must you get on your fourth and final test to make your average 80?

(A) 80
(B) 82
(C) 84
(D) 86
(E) 88

7. $\log_7 9 =$

(A) 0.89
(B) 0.95
(C) 1.13
(D) 1.21
(E) 7.61

8. Which of the following is perpendicular to the line $y = -3x + 7$?

(A) $y = \dfrac{1}{-3x+7}$

(B) $y = 7x - 3$

(C) $y = \dfrac{1}{3}x + 5$

(D) $y = -\dfrac{1}{3}x + 7$

(E) $y = 3x - 7$

9. How many integers are there in the solution set of $|x - 2| \le 5$?

(A) 0
(B) 7
(C) 9
(D) 11
(E) an infinite number

10. If $f(x) = \sqrt{x^2}$, then $f(x)$ can also be expressed as

(A) x
(B) $-x$
(C) $\pm x$
(D) $|x|$
(E) $f(x)$ cannot be determined because x is unknown.

11. If $x + 1$ is a factor of $x^3 - 5x^2 + kx + 2$, then $k =$

(A) –4
(B) –2
(C) 0
(D) 2
(E) 4

USE THIS SPACE FOR SCRATCH WORK

DIAGNOSTIC TEST

12. George invests $1,000 into an account that he hopes will earn 12% interest annually. How many years (rounded to the nearest year) will it take his investment to double in value?

(A) 4
(B) 6
(C) 7
(D) 8
(E) 12

13. A linear function has an x-intercept of $\sqrt{3}$ and a y-intercept of $\sqrt{5}$. The graph of the function has a slope of

(A) −1.29
(B) −0.77
(C) 0.77
(D) 1.29
(E) 2.24

14. If $f(x) = 2x - 1$, find the value of x that makes $f(f(x)) = 9$.

(A) 2
(B) 3
(C) 4
(D) 5
(E) 6

15. The plane $2x + 3y - 4z = 5$ intersects the x-axis at $(a,0,0)$, the y-axis at $(0,b,0)$, and the z-axis at $(0,0,c)$. The value of $a + b + c$ is

(A) 1
(B) $\frac{35}{12}$
(C) 5
(D) $\frac{65}{12}$
(E) 9

16. Given the set of data 1, 1, 2, 2, 2, 3, 3, 4, which one of the following statements is true?

(A) mean ≤ median ≤ mode
(B) median ≤ mean ≤ mode
(C) median ≤ mode ≤ mean
(D) mode ≤ mean ≤ median
(E) The relationship cannot be determined because the median cannot be calculated.

USE THIS SPACE FOR SCRATCH WORK

USE THIS SPACE FOR SCRATCH WORK

17. If $\frac{x-3y}{x}=7$, what is the value of $\frac{x}{y}$?

(A) $-\frac{8}{3}$

(B) -2

(C) $-\frac{1}{2}$

(D) $\frac{3}{8}$

(E) 2

18. Find all values of x that make $\begin{vmatrix} 2 & -1 & 4 \\ 3 & 0 & 5 \\ 4 & 1 & 6 \end{vmatrix} = \begin{vmatrix} x & 4 \\ 5 & x \end{vmatrix}$.

(A) 0
(B) ±1.43
(C) ±3
(D) ±4.47
(E) 5.34

19. Suppose $f(x)=\frac{1}{2}x^2-8$ for $-4 \le x \le 4$. Then the maximum value of the graph of $|f(x)|$ is

(A) –8
(B) 0
(C) 2
(D) 4
(E) 8

20. If $\tan\theta=\frac{2}{3}$, then $\sin\theta=$

(A) ±0.55
(B) ±0.4
(C) 0.55
(D) 0.83
(E) 0.89

21. Suppose the graph of $f(x)=-x^3$ is translated 4 units right and 2 units down, resulting in the graph of a new function g. What is the value of $g(-2)$?

(A) –218
(B) –10
(C) 6
(D) 214
(E) 218

DIAGNOSTIC TEST

USE THIS SPACE FOR SCRATCH WORK

22. $i^{2014} =$

(A) i^{13}
(B) i^{203}
(C) i^{726}
(D) i^{1993}
(E) i^{2100}

23. The statistics below provide a summary of IQ scores of 100 children.

Mean: 100
Median: 102
Standard Deviation: 10
First Quartile: 84
Third Quartile: 110

About 50 of the children in this sample have IQ scores that are

(A) less than 84
(B) less than 110
(C) between 84 and 110
(D) between 64 and 130
(E) more than 100

24. If $f(x) = \sec x$, then

(A) $f(x) = f(-x)$

(B) $f\left(\frac{1}{x}\right) = -f(x)$

(C) $f(-x) = -f(x)$

(D) $f(x) = f\left(\frac{1}{x}\right)$

(E) $f(x) = \frac{1}{f(x)}$

25. The polar coordinates of a point P are $(2,240°)$. The Cartesian (rectangular) coordinates of P are

(A) $\left(-1,-\sqrt{3}\right)$
(B) $\left(-1,\sqrt{3}\right)$
(C) $\left(-\sqrt{3},-1\right)$
(D) $\left(-\sqrt{3},1\right)$
(E) $\left(1,-\sqrt{3}\right)$

26. The height of a cone is equal to the radius of its base. The radius of a sphere is equal to the radius of the base of the cone. The ratio of the volume of the *cone* to the volume of the *sphere* is

(A) $\frac{1}{12}$

(B) $\frac{1}{4}$

(C) $\frac{1}{3}$

(D) $\frac{1}{1}$

(E) $\frac{4}{3}$

27. In how many distinguishable ways can the seven letters in the word MINIMUM be arranged, if all the letters are used each time?

(A) 7
(B) 42
(C) 420
(D) 840
(E) 5,040

28. Which of the following lines are asymptotes of the graph of $y = \frac{x}{x+1}$?

I. $x = 1$
II. $x = -1$
III. $y = 1$

(A) I only
(B) II only
(C) III only
(D) I and II
(E) II and III

29. What is the probability of getting at least three heads when flipping four coins?

(A) $\frac{3}{16}$

(B) $\frac{1}{4}$

(C) $\frac{5}{16}$

(D) $\frac{7}{16}$

(E) $\frac{3}{4}$

USE THIS SPACE FOR SCRATCH WORK

30. How many four-digit personal identification numbers are possible if no digit can be used twice and no number can begin with 0?

(A) 210
(B) 4,536
(C) 6,561
(D) 10,000
(E) 362,880

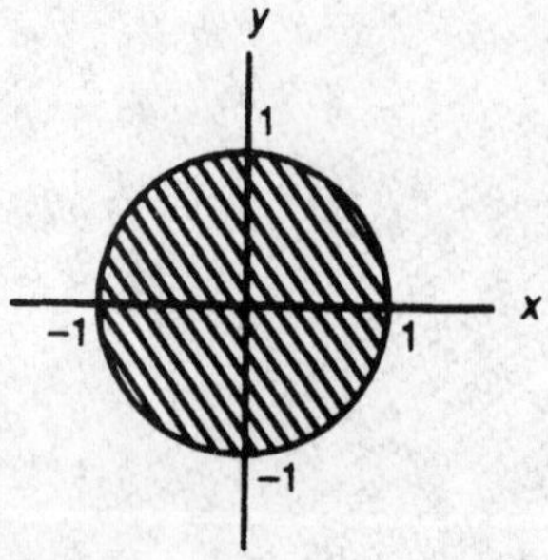

31. In the figure above, *S* is the set of all points in the shaded region. Which of the following represents the set consisting of all points $(2x,y)$, where (x,y) is a point in *S*?

(A)
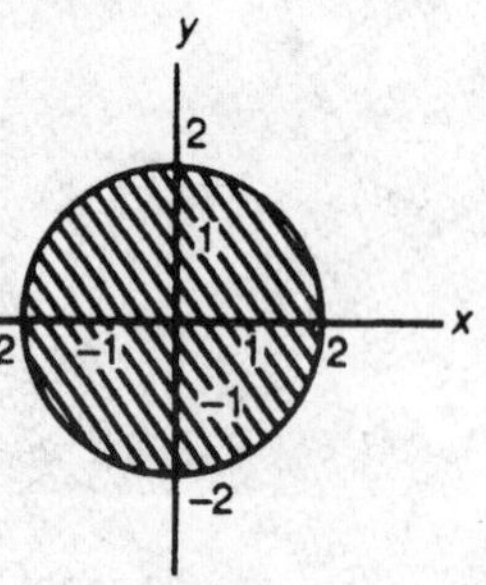

(B)
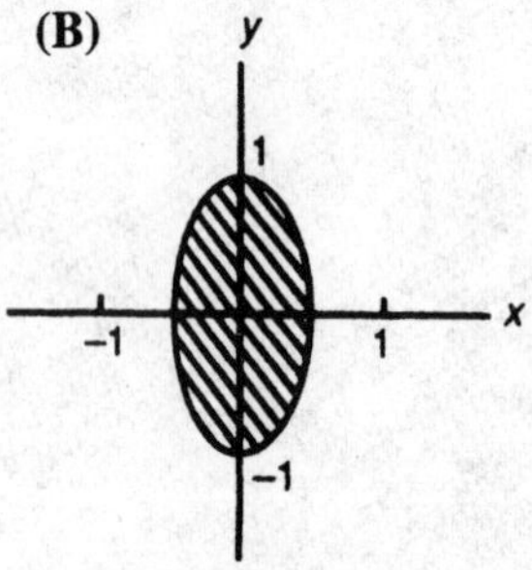

(C)
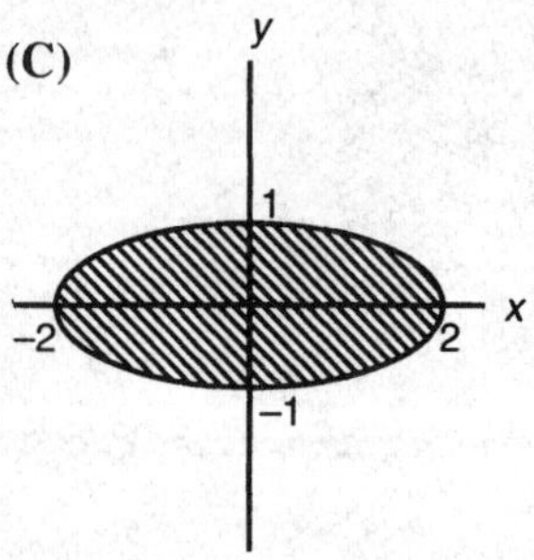

(D)
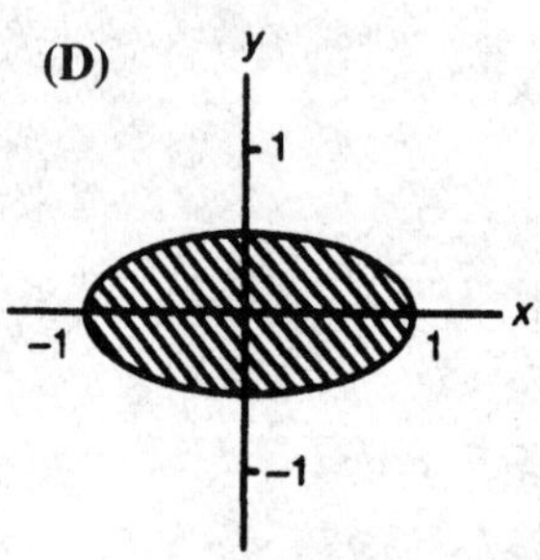

(E)
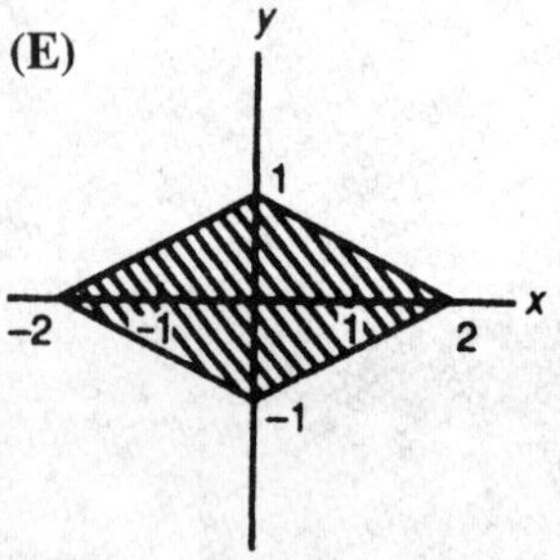

USE THIS SPACE FOR SCRATCH WORK

USE THIS SPACE FOR SCRATCH WORK

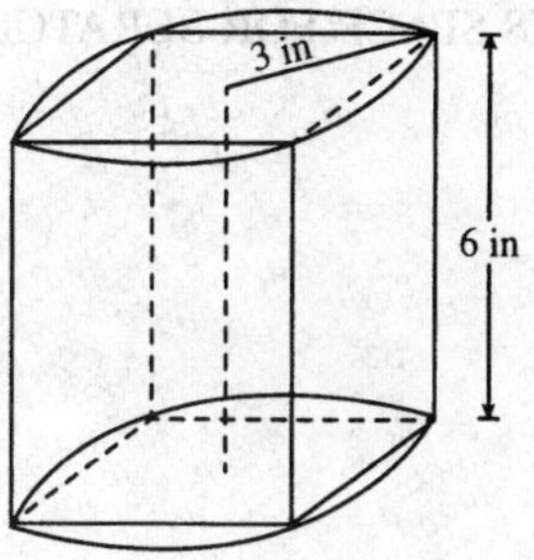

32. If a square prism is inscribed in a right circular cylinder of radius 3 and height 6 as shown above, the volume inside the cylinder but outside the prism is

(A) 2.14
(B) 3.14
(C) 61.6
(D) 115.6
(E) 169.6

33. What is the length of the major axis of the ellipse whose equation is $10x^2 + 20y^2 = 200$?

(A) 3.16
(B) 4.47
(C) 6.32
(D) 8.94
(E) 14.14

34. The fifth term of an arithmetic sequence is 26, and the eighth term is 41. What is the first term?

(A) 3
(B) 4
(C) 5
(D) 6
(E) 7

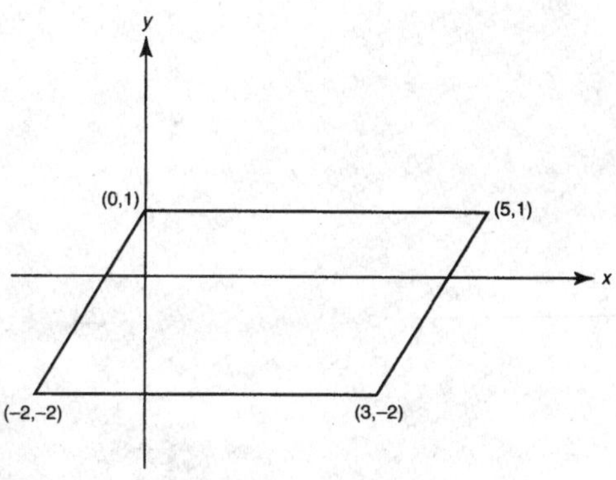

35. What is the measure of one of the larger angles of the parallelogram above that has vertices at (–2,–2), (0,1), (5,1), and (3,–2)?

(A) 117.2°
(B) 123.7°
(C) 124.9°
(D) 125.3°
(E) 131.0°

DIAGNOSTIC TEST

36. If $\cos x = -0.25$, then $\cos(\pi - x) =$

(A) -0.25
(B) -0.75
(C) 0
(D) 0.75
(E) 0.25

USE THIS SPACE FOR SCRATCH WORK

37. The parametric equations of a line are $x = 3 - t$ and $y = 1 + t$. The slope of this line is

(A) -3
(B) -1
(C) $-\frac{1}{3}$
(D) 1
(E) 3

38. If $f(x) = 2x^2 - 4$ and $g(x) = 2^x$, the value of $g(f(1))$ is

(A) -4
(B) 0
(C) $\frac{1}{4}$
(D) 1
(E) 4

39. If $f(x) = 3\sqrt{5x}$, what is the value of $f^{-1}(15)$?

(A) 0.65
(B) 0.90
(C) 5.00
(D) 7.5
(E) 25.98

40. If $2\sin^2 x - 3 = 3\cos x$ and $90° < x < 270°$, the number of values that satisfy the equation is

(A) 0
(B) 1
(C) 2
(D) 3
(E) 4

41. Thirty percent of the 20 people in the Math Club have blonde hair. If 3 people are selected at random from the club, what is the probability that none has blonde hair?

(A) 0.1
(B) 0.25
(C) 0.32
(D) 0.40
(E) 0.50

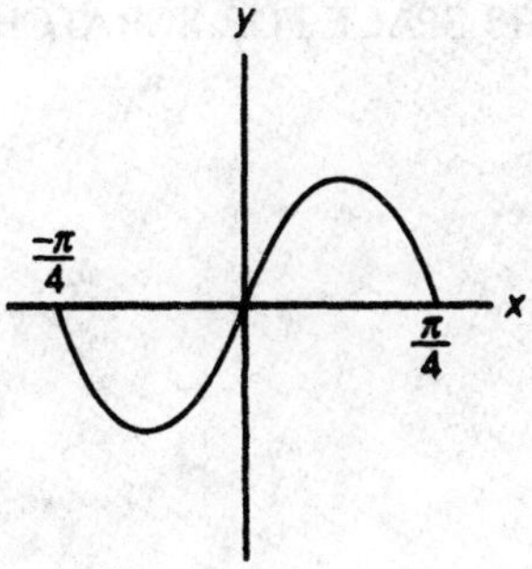

USE THIS SPACE FOR SCRATCH WORK

42. Which of the following could be the equation of one cycle of the graph in the figure above?

I. $y = \sin 4x$

II. $y = \cos\left(4x - \frac{\pi}{2}\right)$

III. $y = -\sin(4x + \pi)$

(A) only I
(B) only I and II
(C) only II and III
(D) only II
(E) I, II, and III

43. Observers at locations due north and due south of a rocket launchpad sight a rocket at a height of 10 kilometers. Assume that the curvature of Earth is negligible and that the rocket's trajectory at that time is perpendicular to the ground. How far apart are the two observers if their angles of elevation to the rocket are 80.5° and 68.0°?

(A) 0.85 km
(B) 4.27 km
(C) 5.71 km
(D) 20.92 km
(E) 84.50 km

44. The vertex angle of an isosceles triangle is 35°. The length of the base is 10 centimeters. How many centimeters are in the perimeter?

(A) 16.6
(B) 17.4
(C) 20.2
(D) 43.3
(E) 44.9

USE THIS SPACE FOR SCRATCH WORK

45. If the graph below represents the function $y = f(x)$, which of the following could represent the equation of the inverse of f?

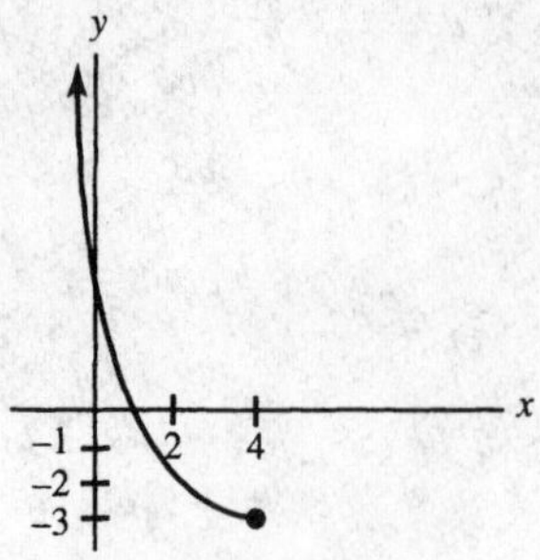

(A) $x = y^2 - 8y - 1$
(B) $x = y^2 + 11$
(C) $x = (y - 4)^2 - 3$
(D) $x = (y + 4)^2 - 3$
(E) $x = (y + 4)^2 + 3$

46. If $k > 4$ is a constant, how would you translate the graph of $y = x^2$ to get the graph of $y = x^2 + 4x + k$?

(A) left 2 units and up k units
(B) right 2 units and up $(k - 4)$ units
(C) left 2 units and up $(k - 4)$ units
(D) right 2 units and down $(k - 4)$ units
(E) left 2 units and down $(k - 4)$ units

47. If $f(x) = \log_b x$ and $f(2) = 0.231$, the value of b is

(A) 0.3
(B) 1.3
(C) 13.2
(D) 20.1
(E) 32.5

48. If $a_{n+1} = a_{n-1} + 2\,a_n$ for $n = 2, 3, 4, \ldots$, and $a_1 = 1$ and $a_2 = 1$, then $a_5 =$

(A) 7
(B) 11
(C) 17
(D) 21
(E) 41

49. Suppose $\cos\theta = u$ in $0 < \theta < \frac{\pi}{2}$. Then $\tan\theta =$

(A) 1

(B) $\frac{1}{\sqrt{1-u^2}}$

(C) $\frac{u}{\sqrt{1-u^2}}$

(D) $\sqrt{1-u^2}$

(E) $\frac{\sqrt{1-u^2}}{u}$

50. A certain component of an electronic device has a probability of 0.1 of failing. If there are 6 such components in a circuit, what is the probability that at least one fails?

(A) 0.60
(B) 0.47
(C) 0.167
(D) 0.000006
(E) 0.000001

USE THIS SPACE FOR SCRATCH WORK

DIAGNOSTIC TEST

STOP

If there is still time remaining, you may review your answers.

ANSWER KEY
答案
Diagnostic Test
诊断测试

1. **A**	14. **B**	27. **C**	40. **D**
2. **D**	15. **B**	28. **E**	41. **C**
3. **E**	16. **C**	29. **C**	42. **E**
4. **B**	17. **C**	30. **B**	43. **C**
5. **C**	18. **D**	31. **C**	44. **D**
6. **D**	19. **E**	32. **C**	45. **C**
7. **C**	20. **A**	33. **D**	46. **C**
8. **C**	21. **D**	34. **D**	47. **D**
9. **D**	22. **C**	35. **B**	48. **C**
10. **D**	23. **C**	36. **E**	49. **E**
11. **A**	24. **A**	37. **B**	50. **B**
12. **B**	25. **A**	38. **C**	
13. **A**	26. **B**	39. **C**	

ANSWERS EXPLAINED 答案解析

The following explanations are keyed to the review portions of this book. The number in brackets after each explanation indicates the appropriate chapter in the Review of Major Topics (Part 2). If a problem can be solved using algebraic techniques alone, [algebra] appears after the explanation, and no reference is given for that problem in the Self-Evaluation Chart at the end of the test.

An asterisk appears next to those solutions for which a graphing calculator is necessary or helpful.

1. **(A)** $f(1) = 2$ means that the line goes through point (1,2). $f(2) = q$ means that the line goes through point $(2,q)$. Slope $= \frac{\Delta y}{\Delta x} = \frac{q-2}{2-1} = -2$ implies $-2 = \frac{q-2}{1}$, so $q = 0$. [2]

* **2.** **(D)** Even functions are symmetric about the y-axis. Graph each answer choice to see that Choice D is not symmetric about the y-axis.

An alternative solution is to use the fact that $\sin x \neq \sin(-x)$, from which you deduce the correct answer choice. [1]

> **TIP**
>
> Properties of even and odd functions:
> Even + even and even × even are always an even function.
> Odd + odd is always an odd function, but odd × odd is an even function.
> Odd × even is always an odd function.

* **3.** **(E)** Since the radius of a sphere is the distance between the center, (0,0,0), and a point on the surface, (2,3,4), use the distance formula in three dimensions to get

$$\sqrt{(2-0)^2 + (3-0)^2 + (4-0)^2} = \sqrt{29}$$

Use your calculator to find $\sqrt{29} \approx 5.39$. [15]

4. **(B)** The polynomials in the numerator and denominator of this rational function have the same degree. Therefore, as x gets arbitrarily large, $f(x)$ approaches the ratio of the leading coefficients, $-\frac{5}{3}$. [9]

5. **(C)** $f(a)$ means to replace x in the formula with an a. Therefore, $f(a) = a^2 - a \cdot a = 0$. [1]

* **6.** **(D)** Since the average of your first three test grades is 78, each test grade could have been a 78. If x represents your final test grade, the average of the four test grades is $\frac{78+78+78+x}{4}$, which is to be equal to 80. Therefore, $\frac{234+x}{4} = 80$.

$234 + x = 320$. So $x = 86$. [21]

7. **(C)** Use the change-of-base theorem and your calculator to get:

$\log_7 9 = \frac{\log_{10} 9}{\log_{10} 7} \approx \frac{0.9542}{0.8451} \approx 1.13$. In some of the newer TI-84$^+$ calculators, you may enter the base, resulting in a single calculation. [8]

8. **(C)** The slope of the given line is –3. Therefore, the slope of a perpendicular line is the negative reciprocal, or $\frac{1}{3}$. [2]

* 9. **(D)** Plot the graph of $y = \text{abs}(x - 2) - 5$ in the standard window that includes both x-intercepts. You can count 11 integers between –3 and 7 if you include both endpoints.

The inequality $|x - 2| \leq 5$ means that x is less than or equal to 5 units away from 2. Therefore, $-3 \leq x \leq 7$, and there are 11 integers in this interval. [11]

10. **(D)** $\sqrt{x^2}$ indicates the need for the *positive* square root of x^2. Therefore, $\sqrt{x^2} = x$ if $x \geq 0$ and $\sqrt{x^2} = -x$ if $x < 0$. This is just the definition of absolute value, and so $\sqrt{x^2} = |x|$ is the only answer for all values of x. [11]

11. **(A)** If $x + 1$ is a factor of $x^3 - 5x^2 + kx + 2$, then dividing $x^3 - 5x^2 + kx + 2$ by $x + 1$ leaves a remainder of 0. Use synthetic division:

$$\begin{array}{r|rrrr} -1 & 1 & -5 & k & 2 \\ & & -1 & 6 & -k-6 \\ \hline & 1 & -6 & k+6 & -k-4 \end{array}$$

Since $-k - 4 = 0$, $k = -4$. [4]

* 12. **(B)** George's investment doubles to \$2,000. Therefore, $2{,}000 = 1{,}000(1 + 0.12)^t$, or $2 = 1.12^t$. Take the log of both sides to get $t = \log_{1.12} 2 = \frac{\log 2}{\log 1.12} \approx 6.12$. [8]

* 13. **(A)** $y = mx + b$. Use the x-intercept to get $0 = \sqrt{3}m + b$, and the y-intercept to get $\sqrt{5} = 0 \cdot m + b$. Therefore, $0 = \sqrt{3}m + \sqrt{5}$ and $m = -\frac{\sqrt{5}}{\sqrt{3}} \approx -1.29$. [2]

14. **(B)** $f(f(x)) = 2(2x - 1) - 1 = 4x - 3$. Solve $4x - 3 = 9$ to get $x = 3$. [1]

15. **(B)** Substituting the points into the equation gives $a = \frac{5}{2}$, $b = \frac{5}{3}$, and $c = -\frac{5}{4}$, so $a + b + c = \frac{35}{12}$. [15]

16. **(C)** Mode = 2, median = $\frac{2+2}{2} = 2$, mean = $\frac{2+6+6+4}{8} = \frac{18}{8} = 2.25$.

Thus, median ≤ mode ≤ mean. [21]

17. (C) Multiply $\frac{x-3y}{x}=7$ through by x to get $x-3y=7x$. Subtract x from both sides to get $-3y=6x$. Divide through by $6y$ so that $\frac{x}{y}$ will be on one side of the equals sign. This gives $\frac{x}{y}=-\frac{3}{6}=-\frac{1}{2}$. [algebra]

∗ 18. (D) Enter the 3 by 3 matrix into the graphing calculator and evaluate its determinant as 0. The 2 by 2 matrix on the right side of the equation has the determinant x^2-20. Solve this for x to get ±4.47. [18]

∗ 19. (E) Plot the graph of $y = \text{abs}((1/2)x^2 - 8)$ in a [–4,4] by [–10,10] window and observe that the maximum value is 8 (at $x = 0$).

An alternative solution is to recognize that the graph of f is a parabola that is symmetric about the y-axis and opens up. The minimum value $y = -8$ occurs when $x = 0$, so 8 is the maximum value of $|f(x)|$. [3]

∗ 20. (A) Tan is positive in the first and third quadrants, so θ is a first or third quadrant angle. The sine of a first quadrant angle is positive, but the sine of a third quadrant angle is negative. Press $\sin(\tan^{-1}(2/3)) \approx 0.55$. The correct answer choice is therefore ±0.55. [7]

∗ 21. (D) The function is $g(x) = f(x-4) - 2 = -(x-4)^3 - 2$. Enter $g(x)$ as Y_1 in the graphing calculator and find $g(-2) = 214$. [12]

22. (C) Powers of i repeat in fours. Therefore, two powers of i are equal if their remainders are equal upon division by four. When 2014 is divided by 4, the remainder is 2. When 726 is divided by 4, the remainder is also 2. [17]

23. (C) Fifty children is half of 100 children, and half of the data points lie between the first and third quartiles. [21]

∗ 24. (A) Plot the graph of $y=\frac{1}{\cos x}$ and observe that it is symmetric about the y-axis. Hence $f(x) = \sec x$ is an even function and $f(x) = f(-x)$. An alternative solution is to recall that $\cos x$ is even, so its reciprocal is also even. [1]

25. (A) From the figure below $\left(-1,-\sqrt{3}\right)$. [14]

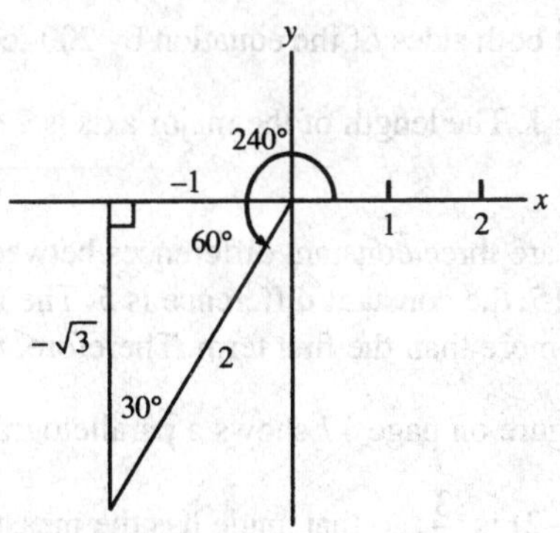

26. **(B)** Since $r = h$ in the cone,

$$\frac{\text{Volume of cone}}{\text{Volume of sphere}} = \frac{\frac{1}{3}\pi r^2 h}{\frac{4}{3}\pi r^3} = \frac{\frac{1}{3}\pi r^3}{\frac{4}{3}\pi r^3} = \frac{1}{4}. \text{ [15]}$$

* **27.** **(C)** The word MINIMUM contains 7 letters, which can be permuted 7! ways. The 3 M's can be permuted 3! ways, and the 2 I's can be permuted in 2! ways, so only $\frac{1}{3!2!} = \frac{1}{12}$ permutations look different from each other. Therefore, there are $\frac{7!}{12} = 420$ distinguishable ways the letters can be arranged. [16]

28. **(E)** Vertical asymptotes occur when the denominator is zero, so $x = -1$ is the only vertical asymptote. Since $\frac{x}{x+1}$ gets closer to 1 as x get larger, the horizontal asymptote is $y = 1$. [9]

* **29.** **(C)** Since each of the 4 flips has 2 possible outcomes (heads or tails), there are $2^4 = 16$ outcomes in the sample space. At least 3 heads means 3 or 4 heads.

$\binom{4}{3} = 4$ ways to get 3 heads. $\binom{4}{4} = 1$ way to get 4 heads and $\frac{4+1}{16} = \frac{5}{16}$. [22]

* **30.** **(B)** There are 9 digits that could go in the first position. For each of those, there are 9 that could go in the second position; 8 that could go in the third position, and 7 that could go in the fourth position. Therefore there are $9 \times 9 \times 8 \times 7 = 4{,}536$ four-digit numbers. [16]

31. **(C)** Since the y values remain the same but the x values are doubled, the circle is stretched along the x-axis. [12]

* **32.** **(C)** Volume of cylinder $= \pi r^2 h = \pi \cdot 9 \cdot 6 = 54\pi$. Volume of square prism $= Bh$, where B is the area of the square base, which is $3\sqrt{2}$ on a side. Thus, $Bh = (3\sqrt{2})^2 \cdot 6 = 108$. Therefore, the desired volume is $54\pi - 108$, which (using your calculator) is approximately 61.6. [15]

33. **(D)** Divide both sides of the equation by 200 to write the equation in standard form $\frac{x^2}{20} + \frac{y^2}{10} = 1$. The length of the major axis is $2\sqrt{20} \approx 8.94$. [13]

34. **(D)** There are three constant differences between the fifth and eighth terms. Since $41 - 26 = 15$, the constant difference is 5. The fifth term, 26, is four constant differences (20) more than the first term. Therefore, the first term is $26 - 20 = 6$. [19]

* **35.** **(B)** The figure on page 17 shows a parallelogram. The tangent of the acute angle with vertex $(-2,-2)$ is $\frac{3}{2}$, so that angle has the measure $\tan^{-1}\left(\frac{3}{2}\right) = 56.3°$. The larger angle is the supplement, or 123.7°. [6]

36. (E) If $\cos x$ is negative, then x must be in QII or QIII. If x is in QII, then $-x$ is in QIII, so $\pi - x$ is QI. If x is in QIII, then $-x$ is in QII, so $\pi - x$ is in QIV. Therefore, $\cos(\pi - x) = 0.25$. You could also key in $\cos^{-1}(-0.25)$ and then key in $\cos(\pi - \text{Ans})$ to get 0.25. [7]

∗ 37. (B) Solve $x = 3 - t$ for t to get $t = 3 - x$, and substitute this in $y = 1 + t$ to get $y = 1 + 3 - x = -x + 4$. The slope of this line is -1. [10]

38. (C) $f(1) = 2 - 4 = -2$, and $g(-2) = 2^{-2} = \frac{1}{4}$. [1]

39. (C) $f^{-1}(15)$ is the value of x that makes $3\sqrt{5x}$ equal to 15. Set $3\sqrt{5x} = 15$, divide both sides by 3 to get $\sqrt{5x} = 5$. Therefore $5x = 25$, and $x = 5$. [1]

∗ 40. (D) With your calculator in degree mode, plot the graphs of $2(\sin(x))^2 - 3$ and $y = 3\cos x$ in a [90,270] by [−3,0] window and observe that the graphs intersect in 3 places.

An alternative solution is to distribute and transform the equation to read: $2\cos^2 x + 3\cos x + 1 = 0$. This factors to $(2\cos x + 1)(\cos x + 1) = 0$, so $\cos x = -\frac{1}{2}$ or $\cos x = -1$. For $90° < x < 270°$, there are three solutions: $x = 120°, 240°, 180°$. [7]

∗ 41. (C) Thirty percent of 20 is 6. Therefore, 14 people in the Math Club don't have blonde hair. There are ${}_{14}C_3$ ways of choosing 3 of these 14 people and ${}_{20}C_3$ ways of choosing 3 of 20 people. The ratio of these two numbers is $\frac{364}{1140} = 0.32$, the probability of choosing 3 people who don't have blonde hair. [22]

∗ 42. (E) Plot the graphs of all three functions in a $\left[-\frac{\pi}{4}, \frac{\pi}{4}\right]$ by [−2,2] window and observe that they coincide.

An alternative solution is to deduce facts about the graphs from the equations. All three equations indicate graphs that have period $\frac{\pi}{2}$. The graph of equation I is a normal sine curve. The graph of equation II is a cosine curve with a phase shift right of $\frac{\pi}{8}$, one-fourth of the period. Therefore, it fits a normal sine curve. The graph of equation III is a sine curve that has a phase shift left of $\frac{\pi}{4}$, one-half the period, and reflected through the x-axis. This also fits a normal sine curve. [7]

DIAGNOSTIC TEST

DIAGNOSTIC TEST

∗ **43.** **(C)** The problem information is illustrated in the figure below.

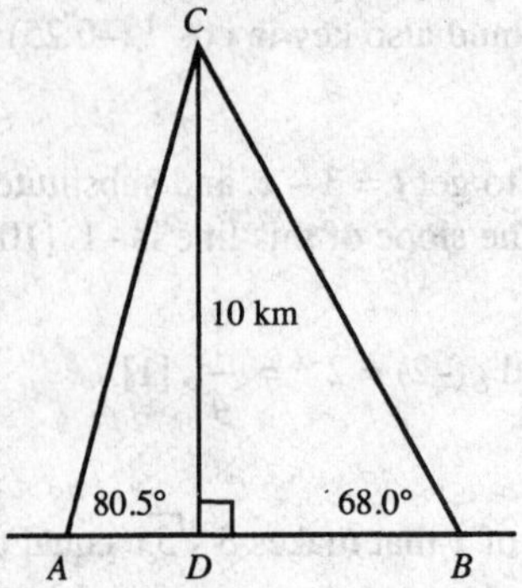

Points A and B represent the two observers. Point C is the rocket, and point D is the base of the altitude from the rocket to the ground. We know that $\tan 80.5° = \frac{10}{AC}$ and $\tan 68.0° = \frac{10}{CB}$. Therefore, $AB = AC + CB = \frac{10}{\tan 80.5°} + \frac{10}{\tan 68.0°} \approx 5.71$ km. [6]

∗ **44.** **(D)** Drop the altitude from the vertex to the base. The altitude bisects both the vertex angle and the base, cutting the triangle into two congruent right triangles. Since $\sin 17.5° = \frac{5}{\text{leg}}$, $\text{leg} = \frac{5}{\sin 17.5°} \approx \frac{5}{0.3007} \approx 16.628$ cm and the perimeter = $2(16.628) + 10 = 43.3$ cm. [6]

45. **(C)** The given graph looks like the left half of a parabola with vertex (4,–3) that opens up. The equation of such a parabola is $y = (x - 4)^2 - 3$. The vertex of the inverse is (–3,4), so its equation is $x = (y - 4)^2 - 3$. [3]

46. **(C)** Complete the square of $x^2 + 4x + k$ by adding and subtracting 4 to get the translated function of $y = (x + 2)^2 + (k - 4)$. Translate $y = x^2$ left 2 units and up $(k - 4)$ units. [12]

∗ **47.** **(D)** $f(2) = \log_b 2 = 0.231$. Therefore, $b^{0.231} = 2$, and so $b = 2^{1/0.231}$, which (using your calculator) is approximately 20.1. [8]

48. **(C)** $a_3 = a_1 + 2a_2 = 1 + 2 = 3$; $a_4 = a_2 + 2a_3 = 1 + 6 = 7$; $a_5 = a_3 + 2a_4 = 3 + 14 = 17$. [19]

49. **(E)** Since $0 < \theta < \frac{\pi}{2}$, the figure below shows θ in Quadrant I with $\cos \theta = u$.

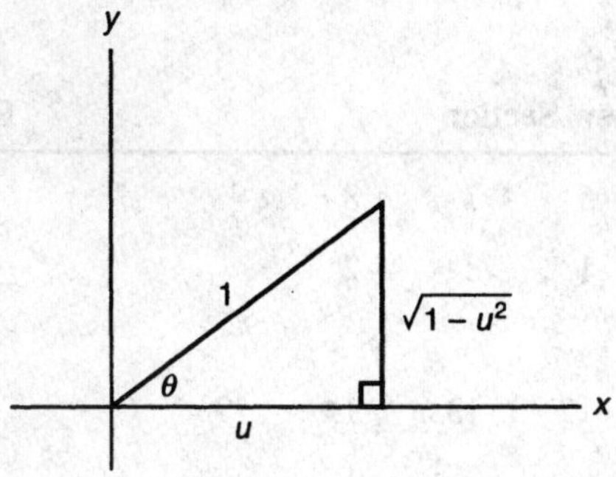

From the figure, $\tan \theta = \frac{\sqrt{1-u^2}}{u}$. [7]

*** 50.** **(B)** The probability that at least one component fails is 1 minus the probability that all succeed. Since the probability of one component succeeding is 1 minus 0.1, or 0.9, the probability that all succeed is $(0.9)^6 = 0.53$, and $1 - 0.53 = 0.47$. [22]

DIAGNOSTIC TEST

Self-Evaluation Chart for the Diagnostic Test 自评表

Subject Area	Questions and Review Section							Number Right	Number Wrong	Number Omitted
Algebra and Functions	1	2	4	5	7	8				
(22 questions)	2	1	9	1	8	2		____	____	____
	9	10	11	12	13	14	17			
	11	11	4	8	2	1	—	____	____	____
	19	21	24	28	37	38	39			
	3	12	1	9	10	1	1	____	____	____
	45	47								
	3	8						____	____	____
Trigonometry	20	35	36	40	42	43				
(8 questions)	7	6	7	7	7	6		____	____	____
	44	49								
	6	7						____	____	____
Coordinate and Three-	3	15	25	26	31	32				
Dimensional Geometry	15	15	14	15	12	15		____	____	____
(8 questions)										
	33	46								
	13	12						____	____	____
Numbers and Operations	18	22	27	30	34	48				
(6 questions)	18	17	16	16	19	19		____	____	____
Data Analysis, Statistics,	6	16	23	29	41	50				
and Probability	21	21	21	22	22	22		____	____	____
(6 questions)										
TOTALS								____	____	____

Evaluate Your Performance on the Diagnostic Test 自评

Rating	Number Right
Excellent	41–50
Very good	33–40
Above average	25–32
Average	15–24
Below average	Below 15

CALCULATING YOUR SCORE 估分

Raw score R = number right – $\frac{1}{4}$(number wrong), rounded = ______________

Approximate scaled score $S = 800 - 10(44 - R)$ = ______________

If $R \geq 44$, $S = 800$.

DIAGNOSTIC TEST

PART 2
第二部分
Review of Major Topics
考点复习

This part reviews the mathematical concepts and techniques for the topics covered in the Math Level 2 Subject Test. A sound understanding of these concepts certainly will improve your score. The techniques discussed may help you save time solving some of the problems without a calculator at all. For problems requiring computational power, techniques are described that will help you use your calculator in the most efficient manner.

Your classroom experience will guide your decisions about how best to use a graphing calculator. If you have been through a secondary mathematics program that attached equal importance to graphical, tabular, and algebraic presentations, then you probably will rely on your graphing calculator as your primary tool to help you find solutions. However, if you went through a more traditional mathematics program, where algebra and algebraic techniques were stressed, it may be more natural for you to use a graphing calculator only after considering other approaches.

Functions
第1章 函数

- → DEFINITIONS
- → COMBINING FUNCTIONS
- → PIECEWISE FUNCTIONS
- → INVERSES
- → ODD AND EVEN FUNCTIONS

A **function** is a process that changes a set of *input* numbers into a set of *output* numbers. A particular input number will always produce the same output number. However, a particular output number could be the result of applying the function to different input numbers. Functions are usually specified by equations such as $y = \sqrt{2x-1}$. In this equation x represents an input number while y represents the (unique) corresponding output number. Functions can also have names: in the example, we could name the function f. Then the process could be described as $f(x) = \sqrt{2x-1}$, whereby f takes the input number x, multiplies it by 2, subtracts 1, and takes the square root to produce the output $y = f(x)$.

Taken as a group, the input numbers are called the **domain** of the function, while the output numbers are called the **range**. Unless otherwise specified, the domain of a function is all real numbers for which the equation produces outputs that are real numbers. In the example above, the domain is the set $x \geq \frac{1}{2}$ since $2x - 1$ cannot be negative if y is to be a real number. In this case, the range is the set of all non-negative numbers.

The domain of a function can also be established as part of the definition of a function. For example, even though the domain of the example function f is $x \geq \frac{1}{2}$, one could, for example, specify the domain $x > 5$. Unless a domain is explicitly stated, the domain is assumed to be all real values that produce real numbers as outputs.

TIP

Typically, a value of x that must be excluded from the domain of a function makes the denominator zero or makes the value of an expression under a square root less than zero.

A function with a small finite domain can be described by a set of ordered pairs instead of an equation. The first number in the pair is from the domain and the second is the corresponding range value. Consider, for example, the function f consisting of the pairs (0, 2), (1, 1), (2, 3), and (3, 8). In this example, the "process" is not systematic: it simply changes 0 to 2 ($f(0) = 2$); 1 to 1 ($f(1) = 1$); 2 to 3 ($f(2) = 3$); and 3 to 8 ($f(3) = 8$). The domain of this function consists of 0, 1, 2, and 3, while the range consists of 2, 1, 3, and 8. Functions like this are typically used to illustrate certain properties of functions and are discussed later.

A function is actually a special type of **relation**. A relation describes the association between two variables. An equation such as $x^2 + y^2 = 4$ is one way of defining a relation. All ordered pairs (x, y) that satisfy the equations are in the relation. In this case, these pairs form the circle of radius 2 centered at the origin. Note that in a relation, unlike a function, a particular input number might be paired with more than one output number.

Circles are examples of relations that are not functions because some x values (0 in the example) have two y values associated with it) (2 and –2), which violates the uniqueness of the output for a given input. Other than circles, relations that are not functions include ellipses, hyperbolas, and parabolas that open right or left, instead of up or down—in other words, the conic sections discussed in Chapter 13.

Like functions, relations can also be defined using specific ordered pairs. The set $R = \{(1, 1), (1, 2), (2, 1), (2, 2)\}$ is an example of a relation that is not a function because the x value 1 has two y values associated with it (1 and 2).

A graph is the graph of a function if it passes the Vertical Line Test. Since a vertical line represents an x value, a graph passes this test if no vertical line intersects the graph in more than one point.

Given two functions, f and g, six new functions can be defined:

Sum function	$(f+g)(x) = f(x) + g(x)$
Difference function	$(f-g)(x) = f(x) - g(x)$
Product function	$(f \cdot g)(x) = f(x) \cdot g(x)$
Quotient function	$\left(\dfrac{f}{g}\right)(x) = \dfrac{f(x)}{g(x)},\ g(x) \neq 0$
Composition of functions	$(f \circ g)(x) = f(g(x))$ $(g \circ f)(x) = g(f(x))$

➡ Examples

If $f(x) = 3x - 2$ and $g(x) = x^2 - 4$, write an expression for each of the following functions:

(A) $(f+g)(x)$

$$(f+g)(x) = f(x) + g(x)$$
$$= (3x-2) + (x^2-4) = x^2 + 3x - 6$$

(B) $(f-g)(x)$

$$(f-g)(x) = f(x) - g(x)$$
$$= (3x-2) - (x^2-4) = -x^2 + 3x + 2$$

TIP

$(f \circ g)(x)$ and $(g \circ f)(x)$ *need not be* the same!

(C) $(f \cdot g)(x)$

$$(f \cdot g)(x) = f(x) \cdot g(x)$$
$$= (3x-2)(x^2-4)$$
$$= 3x^3 - 2x^2 - 12x + 8$$

(D) $\left(\dfrac{f}{g}\right)(x)$

$$\left(\frac{f}{g}\right)(x) = \frac{f(x)}{g(x)} = \frac{3x-2}{x^2-4} \text{ and } x \neq \pm 2$$

(E) $(f \circ g)(x)$

$$(f \circ g)(x) \quad = f(g(x)) \quad 3(g(x)) - 2$$
$$= 3(x^2-4) - 2 = 3x^2 - 14$$

(F) $(g \circ f)(x)$

$$(g \circ f)(x) \quad = g(f(x)) = (f(x))^2 - 4$$
$$= (3x-2)^2 - 4 = 9x^2 - {}_{\text{ı}}2x$$

The inverse of a function f, denoted by f^{-1}, is a relation that has the property that $(f^{-1} \circ f)(x) = (f \circ f^{-1})(x) = x$ for all x in the domain of f. The next two examples show how to find the inverse of a function and verify that it is the inverse.

➡ Examples

(G) Given $f(x) = 3x + 2$. Find $f^{-1}(x)$.

First write y in place of $f(x)$ and interchange x and y. Then solve for y and call the result $g(x)$:

$$x = 3y + 2 \text{ so } y = g(x) = \frac{x-2}{3}.$$

g is the candidate for f^{-1}.

(H) $f(x) = 3x + 2$. Is $g(x)=\dfrac{x-2}{3}$ the inverse of f?

$$(g \circ f)(x) = g(f(x)) = g(3x+2) = \frac{3x+2-2}{3} = x, \text{ and}$$

$$(f \circ g)(x) = f(g(x)) = 3\left(\frac{x-2}{3}\right) + 2 = x. \text{ Therefore, } g = f^{-1}.$$

The inverse of a function is not necessarily a function.

➡ Examples

(I) $f(x) = x^2$. Find f^{-1}.

Write y in place of $f(x)$ and interchange x and y. Then solve for y and call the result $g(x)$:

$$x = y^2 \text{ so } y = g(x) = \pm\sqrt{x}.$$

Since a given input x produces two output values, $\sqrt{x}$ and $-\sqrt{x}$, g is not a function.

(J) Find the inverse of $f = \{(1,2),(2,3),(3,2)\}$.

Interchange x and y to get $f^{-1} = \{(2,1),(3,2),(2,3)\}$. Since the input 2 produces two outputs (1 and 3), f^{-1} is not a function.

If the inverse of a function is not a function, as in Example I, it can be made into a function by limiting the domain of the original function. In the example, the domain of f could have been limited to $x \geq 0$ or $x \leq 0$. Then the inverse would have been $\sqrt{x}$ or $-\sqrt{x}$, respectively.

If a point with coordinates (a, b) belongs to a function, then the point with coordinates (b, a) belongs to its inverse. Therefore, the graphs of inverses are reflections about the line $y = x$. This is illustrated for $f(x) = x^2$ in the figure below. The inverse in this figure is graphed as a dashed curve. You can see that the inverse is not a function because it doesn't pass the Vertical Line Test. Thus a function does not have an inverse if there is a horizontal line that hits its graph in more than one point.

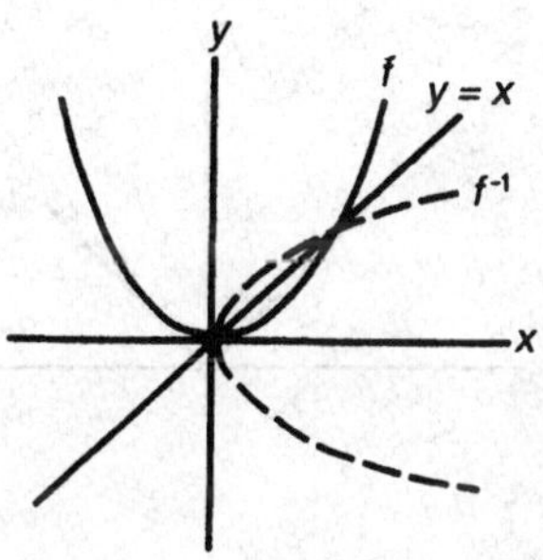

Since the domains and ranges of inverses are switched, the range of a function can be found by finding the domain of its inverse.

➡ Example

(K) Find the range of the function $f(x)=\dfrac{1}{x+4}-2$.

Using the method described in the previous examples, find the inverse to be $f^{-1}(x) = \dfrac{1}{x+2} - 4$.

Since $x = -2$ is not in the domain of f^{-1}, the value -2 is not in the range of f, so the range of f^{-1} is all real numbers except -2.

A function f is called **even** if $f(-x) = f(x)$ for all x in its domain. For even functions, outputs are equal for opposite inputs. In fact, the designation "even" comes from power functions of the form $f(x) = x^n$, where n is an even integer. The graphs of even functions are symmetric about the y-axis.

A function f is called **odd** if $f(-x) = -f(x)$ for all x in its domain. For odd functions, outputs are opposite for opposite inputs. Again, the designation "odd" comes from power functions $f(x) = x^n$, where n is an odd integer. The graphs of odd functions are symmetric about the origin.

Unlike integers, functions need not be even or odd. A function such as $f(x) = x^2 + x + 1$ is neither even nor odd.

Even and odd relations are similarly defined. A relation is called even if $(-x,y)$ is in the relation whenever (x,y) is, and it is called odd if $(-x,-y)$ is in the relation whenever (x,y) is. Relations, unlike functions, can be both even and odd. The unit circle $x^2 + y^2 = 1$ is an example of such a relation.

The sum of even functions or relations is even, and the sum of odd functions is odd. The product of two even or odd functions is even, while the product of an even function and an odd function is odd.

Examples

(L) $f(x) = x^2$ and $f(-x) = (-x)^2 = x^2$. Therefore, f is even.

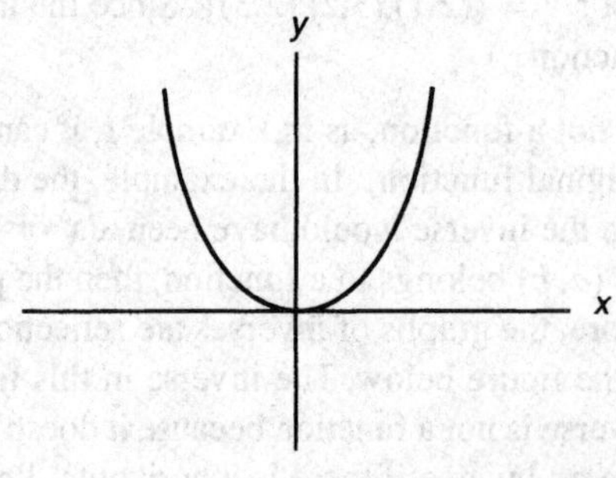

(M) $f(x) = |x|$ and $f(-x) = |-x| = |-1 \cdot x| = |-1| \cdot |x| = |x|$. Therefore, f is even.

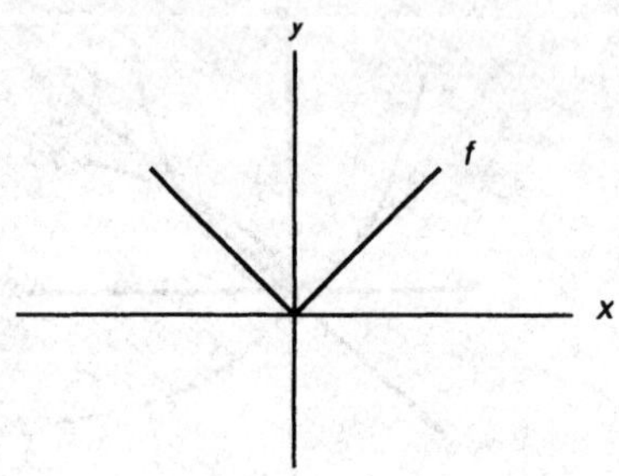

(N) $f(x) = \cos x$ is an even function because $\cos(-x) = \cos x$.

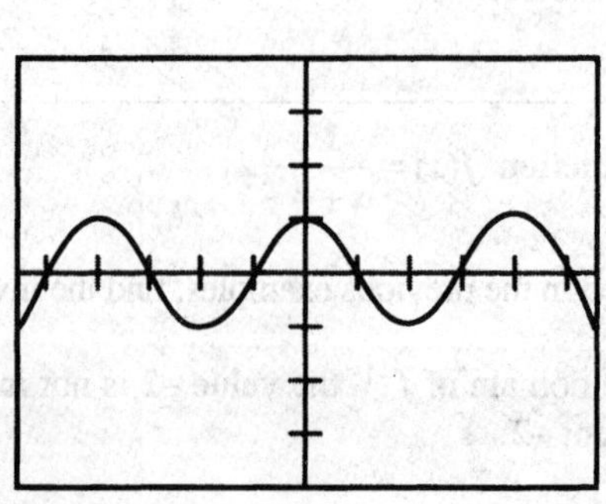

(O) $f(x) = x^3$ **and** $f(-x) = (-x)^3 = -x^3$.

Therefore, $f(-x) = x^3 = -f(x)$, so f is odd.

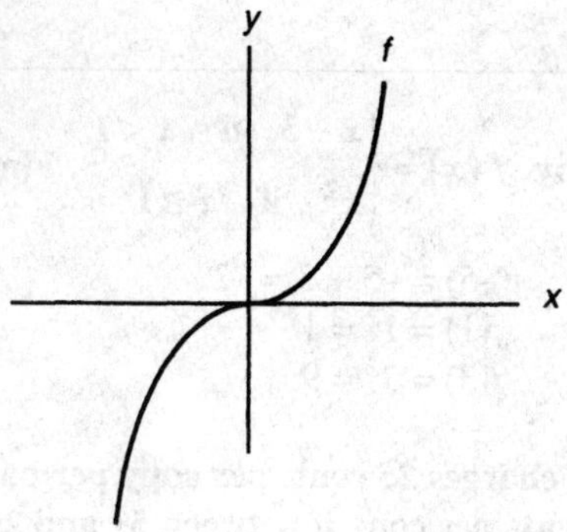

(P) $f(x) = \dfrac{1}{x}$ **and** $f(-x) = \dfrac{1}{-x}$.

Therefore, $f(-x) = -\dfrac{1}{x} = -f(x)$, so f is odd.

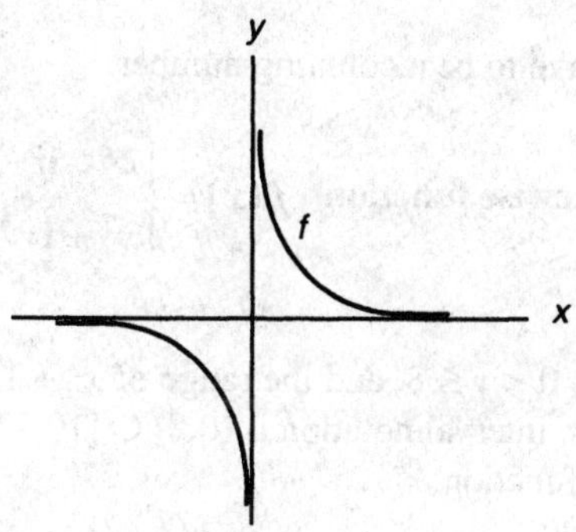

(Q) $f(x) = \sin x$ **is odd because** $\sin(-x) = -\sin x$.

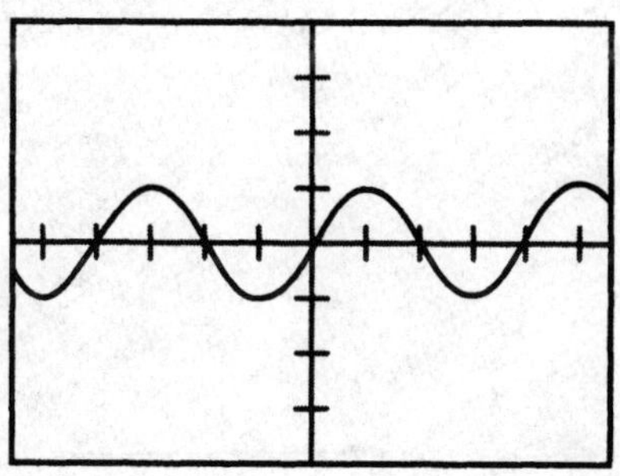

TIP

Relations can be either odd, even, or neither. They can also be both odd and even!

A **piecewise function** is a function that is defined by different equations on different parts of its domain. Piecewise functions provide useful illustrations of calculus concepts, but they also occur in real-life situations.

Examples

(R) The function f is defined by $f(x)=\begin{cases} x+3 & \text{if} \quad x<1 \\ x^2 & \text{if} \quad x\geq 1 \end{cases}$ **. Find $f(-5)$, $f(1)$, and $f(3)$.**

$$f(-5) = -5 + 3 = -2$$
$$f(1) = 1^2 = 1$$
$$f(3) = 3^2 = 9$$

(S) A store that makes copies charges 25 cents per copy per page if 50 or fewer copies of each page are made; 20 cents per copy if between 51 and 200 copies of each page are made; and 15 cents per copy if more than 200 copies of each page are made. How would this be written as a piecewise function?

$$f(x)=\begin{cases} 0.25x & \text{if} \quad x\leq 50 \\ 0.20x & \text{if} \quad 51\leq x\leq 200 \\ 0.15x & \text{if} \quad x>200 \end{cases}$$

In this example, x would have to be a counting number.

(T) Find the range of the piecewise function $f(x)=\begin{cases} 2^x & \text{if} \quad x\leq 3 \\ x^2+1 & \text{if} \quad x>3 \end{cases}$ **and write it in interval notation.**

The range of 2^x for $x \leq 3$ is $0 < y \leq 8$, and the range of $x^2 + 1$ for $x > 3$ is $10 < y < \infty$. The union of these two ranges in interval notation is $(0,8] \cup [10,\infty)$. There is a "gap" between 8 and 10 in the range of this function.

Piecewise functions are discussed at greater length in Chapter 11.

EXERCISES 习题

1. If {(3,2),(4,2),(3,1),(7,1),(2,3)} is to be a function, which one of the following must be removed from the set?

    (A) (3,2)
    (B) (4,2)
    (C) (2,3)
    (D) (7,1)
    (E) none of the above

2. For $f(x) = 3x^2 + 4$, $g(x) = 2$, and $h = \{(1,1), (2,1), (3,2)\}$,

    (A) f is the only function
    (B) h is the only function
    (C) f and g are the only functions
    (D) g and h are the only functions
    (E) f, g, and h are all functions

TIP

Looking for answers? All answers to exercises appear at the end of each chapter. Resist the urge to peek before trying the problems on your own.

3. What value(s) must be excluded from the domain of $f(x) = \dfrac{x+2}{x-2}$?

    (A) −2
    (B) 0
    (C) 2
    (D) 2 and −2
    (E) no value

4. If $f(x) = 3x^2 - 2x + 4$, $f(-2) =$

    (A) −12
    (B) −4
    (C) −2
    (D) 12
    (E) 20

5. If $f(x) = 4x - 5$ and $g(x) = 3^x$, then $f(g(2)) =$

    (A) 3
    (B) 9
    (C) 27
    (D) 31
    (E) none of the above

6. If $f(g(x)) = 4x^2 - 8x$ and $f(x) = x^2 - 4$, then $g(x) =$

    (A) $4 - x$
    (B) x
    (C) $2x - 2$
    (D) $4x$
    (E) x^2

7. What values must be excluded from the domain of $\left(\dfrac{f}{g}\right)(x)$ if $f(x) = 3x^2 - 4x + 1$ and $g(x) = 3x^2 - 3$?

    (A) 0
    (B) 1
    (C) 3
    (D) both ±1
    (E) no values

8. If $g(x) = 3x + 2$ and $g(f(x)) = x$, then $f(2) =$

(A) 0
(B) 1
(C) 2
(D) 6
(E) 8

9. If $p(x) = 4x - 6$ and $p(a) = 0$, then $a =$

(A) -6
(B) $-\frac{3}{2}$
(C) $\frac{3}{2}$
(D) $\frac{2}{3}$
(E) 2

10. If $f(x) = e^x$ and $g(x) = \sin x$, then the value of $(f \circ g)(\sqrt{2})$ is

(A) -0.01
(B) -0.8
(C) 0.34
(D) 1.8
(E) 2.7

11. If $f(x) = 2x - 3$, the inverse of f, f^{-1}, could be represented by

(A) $f^{-1}(x) = 3x - 2$
(B) $f^{-1}(x) = \frac{1}{2x-3}$
(C) $f^{-1}(x) = \frac{x-2}{3}$
(D) $f^{-1}(x) = \frac{x+2}{3}$
(E) $f^{-1}(x) = \frac{x+3}{2}$

12. If $f(x) = x$, the inverse of f, f^{-1}, could be represented by

(A) $f^{-1}(x) = x$
(B) $f^{-1}(x) = 1$
(C) $f^{-1}(x) = \frac{1}{x}$
(D) $f^{-1}(x) = y$
(E) f^{-1} does not exist

13. The inverse of $f = \{(1,2),(2,3),(3,4),(4,1),(5,2)\}$ would be a function if the domain of f is limited to

(A) $\{1,3,5\}$
(B) $\{1,2,3,4\}$
(C) $\{1,5\}$
(D) $\{1,2,4,5\}$
(E) $\{1,2,3,4,5\}$

14. Which of the following could represent the equation of the inverse of the graph in the figure?

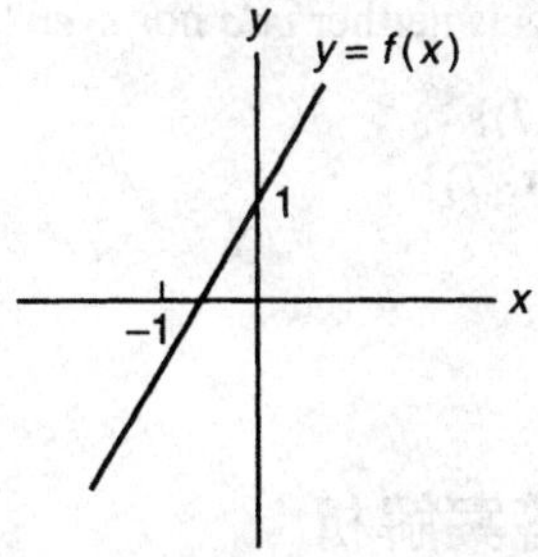

(A) $y = -2x + 1$
(B) $y = 2x + 1$
(C) $y = \frac{1}{2}x + 1$
(D) $y = \frac{1}{2}x - 1$
(E) $y = \frac{1}{2}x - \frac{1}{2}$

15. Which of the following relations are *even*?

I. $y = 2$
II. $f(x) = x$
III. $x^2 + y^2 = 1$

(A) only I
(B) only I and II
(C) only II and III
(D) only I and III
(E) I, II, and III

16. Which of the following relations are *odd*?

I. $y = 2$
II. $y = x$
III. $x^2 + y^2 = 1$

(A) only II
(B) only I and II
(C) only I and III
(D) only II and III
(E) I, II, and III

17. Which of the following relations are both *odd* and *even*?

I. $x^2 + y^2 = 1$
II. $x^2 - y^2 = 0$
III. $x + y = 0$

(A) only III
(B) only I and II
(C) only I and III
(D) only II and III
(E) I, II, and III

18. Which of the following functions is neither *odd* nor *even*?

(A) $\{(1,2),(4,7),(-1,2),(0,4),(-4,7)\}$
(B) $\{(1,2),(4,7),(-1,-2),(0,0),(-4,-7)\}$
(C) $y = x^3 - 1$
(D) $y = x^2 - 1$
(E) $f(x) = -x$

Answers Explained 答案解析

1. **(A)** Either (3,2) or (3,1), which is not an answer choice, must be removed so that 3 will be paired with only one number.

2. **(E)** For each value of x there is only one value for y in each case. Therefore, f, g, and h are all functions.

3. **(C)** Since division by zero is forbidden, x cannot equal 2.

4. **(E)** $f(-2) = 3(-2)^2 - 2(-2) + 4 = 20$.

5. **(D)** $g(2) = 3^2 = 9$. $f(g(2)) = f(9) = 31$.

6. **(C)** To get from $f(x)$ to $f(g(x))$, x^2 must become $4x^2$. Therefore, the answer must contain $2x$ since $(2x)^2 = 4x^2$.

7. **(D)** $g(x)$ cannot equal 0. Therefore, $x \neq \pm 1$.

8. **(A)** Since $f(2)$ implies that $x = 2$, $g(f(2)) = 2$. Therefore, $g(f(2)) = 3(f(2)) + 2 = 2$. Therefore, $f(2) = 0$.

9. **(C)** $p(a) = 0$ implies $4a - 6 = 0$, so $a = \dfrac{3}{2}$.

* 10. **(E)** $(f \circ g)(\sqrt{2}) = f(g(\sqrt{2})) = f(\sin\sqrt{2}) = e^{\sin\sqrt{2}} \approx 2.7$.

11. **(E)** If $y = 2x - 3$, the inverse is $x = 2y - 3$, which is equivalent to $y = \dfrac{x+3}{2}$.

12. **(A)** By definition.

13. **(B)** The inverse is $\{(2,1),(3,2),(4,3),(1,4),(2,5)\}$, which is not a function because of (2,1) and (2,5). Choice B is the only answer choice that does not include both 1 and 5.

14. **(E)** If this line were reflected about the line $y = x$ to get its inverse, the slope would be less than 1 and the y-intercept would be less than zero. The only possibilities are Choices D and E. Choice D can be excluded because since the x-intercept of $f(x)$ is greater than -1, the y-intercept of its inverse must be greater than -1.

15. **(D)** Use the appropriate test for determining whether a relation is even.
    I. The graph of $y = 2$ is a horizontal line, which is symmetric about the y-axis, so $y = 2$ is even.
    II. Since $f(-x) = -x \neq x = f(x)$ unless $x = 0$, this function is not even.
    III. Since $(-x)^2 + y^2 = 1$ whenever $x^2 + y^2 = 1$, this relation is even.

16. **(D)** Use the appropriate test for determining whether a relation is odd.
    I. The graph of $y = 2$ is a horizontal line, which is not symmetric about the origin, so $y = 2$ is not odd.
    II. Since $f(-x) = -x = -f(x)$, this function is odd.
    III. Since $(-x)^2 + (-y)^2 = 1$ whenever $x^2 + y^2 = 1$, this relation is odd.

17. **(B)** The analysis of relation III in the above examples indicates that I and II are both even and odd. Since $-x + y \neq 0$ when $x + y = 0$ unless $x = 0$, III is not even, and is therefore not both even and odd.

18. **(C)** A is even, B is odd, D is even, and E is odd. C is not even because $(-x)^3 - 1 = -x^3 - 1$, which is neither $x^3 - 1$ nor $-x^3 + 1$.

Linear Functions
第2章 线性函数

2

- → DEFINITIONS
- → SLOPE
- → DISTANCE
- → MIDPOINT

The equation of a **linear function** is $L(x) = mx + b$, and its graph is a line. If (x_1, y_1) and (x_2, y_2) are any two points on the line, the slope of the line is $m = \frac{y_2 - y_1}{x_2 - x_1}$, and the y-intercept of the graph is b, the value of y when x is zero. Vertical lines have undefined slopes and are not graphs of functions.

When given the slope m of the line and a point (x_1, y_1) on the line, a point-slope equation of the line can be written readily as $y - y_1 = m(x - x_1)$. The slope-intercept form may then be written, if required, by solving this equation for y.

The general equation of a line is $Ax + By = C$. If $B \neq 0$, this equation can be solved for y: $y = -\frac{A}{B}x + \frac{C}{B}$. Thus, the slope is $m = -\frac{A}{B}$, and the y-intercept is $b = \frac{C}{B}$. If $B = 0$ and $A \neq 0$, the general equation reduces to $x = \frac{C}{A}$, a vertical line.

Other important facts about nonvertical lines:

- Parallel lines have equal slopes.
- The product of the slopes of perpendicular lines is –1, or the slopes of perpendicular lines are opposite reciprocals
- The distance between two points (x_1, y_1) and (x_2, y_2) is $\sqrt{(x_2 - x_1)^2 + (y_2 - y_1)^2}$
- The coordinates of the midpoint of (x_1, y_1) and (x_2, y_2) is $\left(\frac{x_1 + x_2}{2}, \frac{y_1 + y_2}{2}\right)$
- The slope of a horizontal line is 0, and its equation is $y = b$.

TIP

The standard window on most graphing calculators is defined by the intervals [–10, 10] in both directions. Because the screen is not square, perpendicular lines will look distorted. In order to achieve a visual of perpendicular lines on a graphing calculator, key ZOOM/Z-Square.

➡ Examples

(A) Describe the line $3x = 12$.

Divide both sides by 3 to get $x = 4$. This is the vertical line 4 units to the right of the y-axis.

(B) Describe the line $x - 3y = 6$.

Solve for $y = \frac{1}{3}x - 2$. The slope is $-\frac{1}{3}$, and the y-intercept is –2.

(C) Write an equation of the line containing (6,–5) and having slope $\frac{3}{4}$.

In point-slope form, the equation is $y + 5 = \frac{3}{4}(x - 6)$.

(D) Write an equation of the line containing (1,–3) and (–4,–2).

First find the slope $m = \frac{-3+2}{1+4} = -\frac{1}{5}$. Then use the point (1,–3) and this slope to write the point-slope equation $y + 3 = -\frac{1}{5}(x - 1)$.

(E) The equation of line l_1 is $y = 2x + 3$, and the equation of line l_2 is $y = 2x - 5$.

These lines are parallel because the slope of each line is 2, and the *y*-intercepts are different.

(F) The equation of line l_1 is $y = \frac{5}{2}x - 4$, and the equation of line l_2 is $y = -\frac{2}{5}x + 9$.

These lines are perpendicular because the slope of l_2, $-\frac{2}{5}$, is the negative reciprocal of the slope of l_1, $\frac{5}{2}$.

You can use these facts to write an equation of a line that is parallel or perpendicular to a given line and that contains a given point.

(G) Write an equation of the line containing (1,7) and parallel to the line $3x + 5y = 8$.

The slope of the given line is $-\frac{A}{B} = -\frac{3}{5}$. The point-slope equation of the line containing (1,7) is therefore $y - 7 = -\frac{3}{5}(x - 1)$.

(H) Write an equation of the line containing (–3,2) and perpendicular to $y = 4x - 5$.

The slope of the given line is 4, so the slope of a line perpendicular to it is $-\frac{1}{4}$. The desired equation is $y - 2 = -\frac{1}{4}(x + 3)$.

The distance between two points *P* and *Q* whose coordinates are (x_1,y_1) and (x_2,y_2) is given by the formula

$$\text{Distance } = \sqrt{(x_1 - x_2)^2 + (y_1 - y_2)^2}$$

and the midpoint, *M*, of the segment $\overline{PQ}$ has coordinates $\left(\frac{x_1 + x_2}{2}, \frac{y_1 + y_2}{2}\right)$.

(I) Given point (2,–3) and point (–5,4), find the length of $\overline{PQ}$ and the coordinates of the midpoint, *M*.

$$PQ = \sqrt{(2-(-5))^2 + (-3-4)^2} \approx 9.9$$

$$M = \left(\frac{2+(-5)}{2}, \frac{-3+4}{2}\right) = \left(\frac{-3}{2}, \frac{1}{2}\right)$$

EXERCISES 习题

1. The slope of the line through points $A(3,-2)$ and $B(-2,-3)$ is

(A) -5
(B) $-\frac{1}{5}$
(C) $\frac{1}{5}$
(D) 1
(E) 5

2. The slope of line $8x + 12y + 5 = 0$ is

(A) $-\frac{3}{2}$
(B) $-\frac{2}{3}$
(C) $\frac{2}{3}$
(D) 2
(E) 3

3. The slope of the line perpendicular to line $3x - 5y + 8 = 0$ is

(A) $-\frac{5}{3}$
(B) $-\frac{3}{5}$
(C) $\frac{3}{5}$
(D) $\frac{5}{3}$
(E) 3

4. The y-intercept of the line through the two points whose coordinates are $(5,-2)$ and $(1,3)$ is

(A) $-\frac{5}{4}$
(B) $\frac{5}{4}$
(C) $\frac{17}{4}$
(D) 7
(E) 17

5. The equation of the perpendicular bisector of the segment joining the points whose coordinates are (1,4) and (–2,3) is

(A) $3x - 2y + 5 = 0$
(B) $x - 3y + 2 = 0$
(C) $3x + y - 2 = 0$
(D) $x - 3y + 11 = 0$
(E) $x + 3y - 10 = 0$

6. The length of the segment joining the points with coordinates (–2,4) and (3,–5) is

(A) 2.8
(B) 3.7
(C) 10.0
(D) 10.3
(E) none of the above

7. The slope of the line parallel to the line whose equation is $2x + 3y = 8$ is

(A) –2

(B) $-\frac{3}{2}$

(C) $-\frac{2}{3}$

(D) $\frac{2}{3}$

(E) $\frac{3}{2}$

Answers Explained 答案解析

1. **(C)** Slope = $\frac{-3-(-2)}{-2-3}=\frac{1}{5}$.

2. **(B)** $y=-\frac{2}{3}x-\frac{5}{12}$. The slope is $-\frac{2}{3}$.

3. **(A)** $y=\frac{3}{5}x+\frac{8}{5}$. The slope of the given line is $\frac{3}{5}$. The slope of a perpendicular line is $-\frac{5}{3}$.

4. **(C)** The slope of the line is $\frac{-2-3}{5-1}=-\frac{5}{4}$, so the point-slope equation is $y-3=-\frac{5}{4}(x-1)$. Solve for y to get $y=-\frac{5}{4}x+\frac{17}{4}$. The y-intercept of the line is $\frac{17}{4}$.

5. **(C)** The slope of the segment is $\frac{3-4}{-2-1}=\frac{1}{3}$. Therefore, the slope of a perpendicular line is –3. The midpoint of the segment is $\left(\frac{1-2}{2},\frac{4+3}{2}\right)=\left(-\frac{1}{2},\frac{7}{2}\right)$. Therefore, the point-slope equation is $y-\frac{7}{2}=-3(x+\frac{1}{2})$. In general form, this equation is $3x+y-2=0$.

* 6. **(D)** Length = $\sqrt{(3+2)^2+(-5-4)^2}\approx 10.3$

7. **(C)** $y=-\frac{2}{3}x+\frac{8}{3}$. Therefore, the slope of a parallel line = $-\frac{2}{3}$.

Quadratic Functions
第3章 二次函数

3

- → DEFINITIONS
- → PARABOLAS
- → COMPLETING THE SQUARE
- → QUADRATIC FORMULA
- → DISCRIMINANT

Quadratic functions are polynomials in which the largest exponent is $n = 2$. The standard equation of a quadratic function is $P(x) = ax^2 + bx + c$, and its graph is called a parabola. If $a > 0$, the parabola opens up, and the lowest point on the parabola is called the vertex. If $a < 0$, the parabola opens down, and the vertex is the highest point on the parabola. The x-coordinate of the vertex is given by the formula $h = -\frac{b}{2a}$. Substitute h for x in the equation of the parabola to get $k = \frac{4ac - b^2}{4a}$, the y-coordinate of the vertex.

The domain of a quadratic function is all real numbers, unless otherwise specified, and the range is all real numbers greater than the maximum (if $a > 0$) or all real numbers less than the minimum (if $a < 0$).

The following examples demonstrate how to analyze the graph of a parabola.

➥ Examples

(A) Analyze the graph of $y = -x^2 + 4x + 5$.

First observe that $a = 1, b = 4, c = 5$. Since $a < 0$, the parabola opens down, and the vertex is a maximum. Since $h = -\frac{4}{-2} = 2$ and $k = -(2)^2 + 4(2) + 5 = 9$, the vertex is (2,9), the maximum is 9, and the range is $(-\infty,9)$. The axis of symmetry is $x = 2$, and the graph crosses the x-axis twice, at $x = -1$ and at $x = 5$. These are the two zeros of the function and these are also the solutions to the equation $-x^2 + 4x + 5 = 0$. The figure below shows the graph of $y = -x^2 + 4x + 5$.

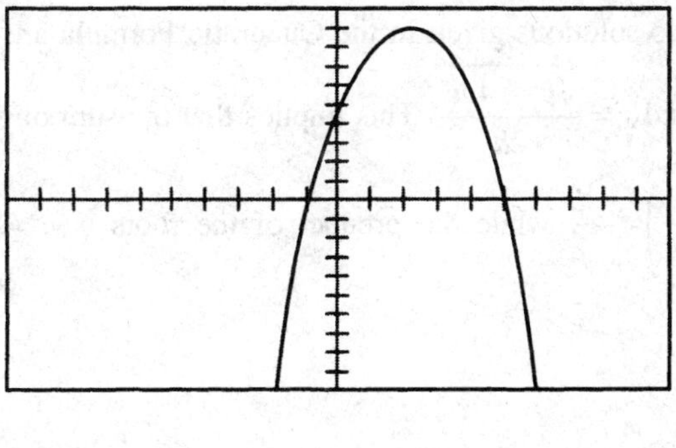

(B) Analyze the graph of $y = 3x^2 + 2x + 5$.

First observe that $a = 3$, $b = 2$, $c = 5$. Since $a > 0$, the graph opens up, and the vertex is a minimum. Since $h = -\frac{2}{6} = -\frac{1}{3}$ and $k = 3\left(-\frac{1}{3}\right)^2 + 2\left(-\frac{1}{3}\right) + 5 = \frac{14}{3}$, the vertex is $\left(-\frac{1}{3}, \frac{14}{3}\right)$, the minimum is $\frac{14}{3}$, and the range is $\left(\frac{14}{3}, \infty\right)$. The axis of symmetry is $x = -\frac{1}{3}$. The figure below shows the graph of $y = 3x^2 + 2x + 5$. The graph does not cross the x-axis. This means that the solutions to the equation $3x^2 + 2x + 5 = 0$ are imaginary numbers.

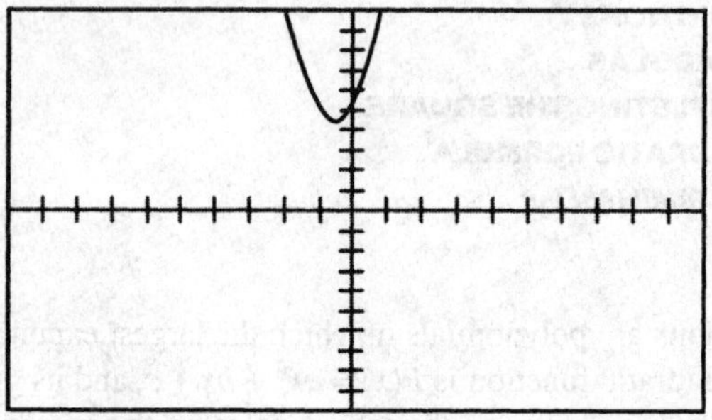

TIP

If the zeros are complex, the parabola does not cross the x-axis.

As seen in Example A, one method of solving certain quadratic equations is to transform the equation so that one side is equal to zero, factor the other side, use the Zero Product Property to equate each linear factor to zero, and then solve each linear equation.

Examples

(C) Solve $x^2 - x - 12 = 0$.

Factor the left side to get $(x - 4)(x - 3) = 0$. Set each factor to zero and solve each linear equation: $x - 4 = 0$ or $x + 3 = 0$, whence $x = 4$ or $x = -3$.

(D) Solve $(x - 6)^2 = 0$.

In this case, $x = 6$ twice, so $x = 6$ is said to have **multiplicity** 2.

The Quadratic Formula $x = \frac{-b \pm \sqrt{b^2 - 4ac}}{2a}$ can be used to obtain the exact solutions of any quadratic equation of the form $ax^2 + bx + c = 0$. This formula is the result of **completing the square** for the general quadratic.

The expression $b^2 - 4ac$ under the radical in the Quadratic Formula is called the **discriminant**. If the discriminant is positive, there are two real roots. If the discriminant is zero, there is one root of multiplicity 2. If the discriminant is negative, there is a conjugate pair of imaginary roots.

Note also that the two solutions given in the Quadratic Formula are conjugates $u + v$ and $u - v$, where $u = -\frac{b}{2a}$ and $v = \frac{\sqrt{b^2 - 4ac}}{2a}$. This implies that the sum of the root of a quadratic equation is $2u = 2\left(-\frac{b}{2a}\right) = -\frac{b}{a}$ while the product of the roots is $u^2 - v^2 = \frac{b^2}{4a^2} - \frac{b^2 - 4ac}{4a^2} = \frac{4ac}{4a^2} = \frac{c}{a}$.

TIP

The sum of the zeros is $-\frac{b}{a}$ and the product of the zeros is $\frac{c}{a}$.

➡ Examples

(E) Solve $2x^2 - 8x + 6 = 0$ by completing the square.

First divide both sides of the equation by 2, to make the coefficient of x^2 equal to 1: $x^2 - 4x + 3 = 0$. Next, isolate the constant term by subtracting 3 from both sides of the equation: $x^2 - 4x = -3$, and add the square of half the linear coefficient (–4) to both sides: $x^2 - 4x + 4 = 1$. The left side of the equation is now a perfect square: $(x - 2)^2 = 1$. Taking the positive and negative square roots, we get $x - 2 = 1$ or $x - 2 = -1$. Therefore, $x = 3$ or $x = 1$.

(F) Use the Quadratic Formula to solve $3x^2 - 4x + 1 = 0$.

$a = 3, b = -4$, and $c = 1$. Substituting these into the Quadratic Formula,

$$x = \frac{4 \pm \sqrt{16-12}}{6} = \frac{4 \pm 2}{6} = 1 \text{ or } \frac{1}{3}.$$

(G) What is the product of the roots of $3x^2 = 6x + 4$? Transform so that one side of the equation is zero: $3x^2 - 6x - 4 = 0$.

The product of the roots is $\frac{c}{a} = -\frac{4}{3}$.

EXERCISES 习题

1. The coordinates of the vertex of the parabola whose equation is $y = 2x^2 + 4x - 5$ are

(A) (2, 11)
(B) (–1, –7)
(C) (1, 1)
(D) (–2, –5)
(E) (–4, 11)

2. The range of the function $f(x) = 5 - 4x - x^2$ is

(A) $\{y{:}y \le 0\}$
(B) $\{y{:}y \ge -9\}$
(C) $\{y{:}y \le 9\}$
(D) $\{y{:}y \ge 0\}$
(E) $\{y{:}y \le 1\}$

3. The equation of the axis of symmetry of the function $y = 2x^2 + 3x - 6$ is

(A) $x = -\frac{3}{2}$
(B) $x = -\frac{3}{4}$
(C) $x = -\frac{1}{3}$
(D) $x = \frac{1}{3}$
(E) $x = \frac{3}{4}$

4. Find the zeros of $y = 2x^2 + x - 6$.

(A) 3 and 2
(B) −3 and 2
(C) $\frac{1}{2}$ and $\frac{3}{2}$
(D) $-\frac{3}{2}$ and 1
(E) $\frac{3}{2}$ and −2

5. The sum of the zeros of $y = 3x^2 - 6x - 4$ is

(A) −2
(B) $-\frac{4}{3}$
(C) $\frac{4}{3}$
(D) 2
(E) 6

6. $x^2 + 2x + 3 = 0$ has

(A) two real rational roots
(B) two real irrational roots
(C) two equal real roots
(D) two equal rational roots
(E) two complex conjugate roots

7. A parabola with a vertical axis has its vertex at the origin and passes through point (7,7). The parabola intersects line $y = 6$ at two points. The length of the segment joining these points is

(A) 14
(B) 13
(C) 12
(D) 8.6
(E) 6.5

Answers Explained 答案解析

1. **(B)** The x-coordinate of the vertex is $x = -\frac{b}{2a} = -\frac{4}{4} = -1$ and the y-coordinate is $y = 2(-1)^2 + 4(-1) - 5 = -7$. Hence the vertex is the point $(-1,-7)$.

2. **(C)** Find the vertex: $x = -\frac{b}{2a} = \frac{4}{-2} = -2$ and $y = 5 - 4(-2) - (-2)^2 = 9$. Since $a = -1 < 0$ the parabola opens down, so the range is $\{y : y \le 9\}$.

3. **(B)** The x coordinate of the vertex is $x = -\frac{b}{2a} = -\frac{3}{4}$. Thus, the equation of the axis of symmetry is $x = -\frac{3}{4}$.

4. **(E)** $2x^2 + x - 6 = (2x - 3)(x + 2) = 0$. The zeros are $\frac{3}{2}$ and -2.

5. **(D)** Sum of zeros $= -\frac{b}{a} = -\frac{-6}{3} = 2$.

6. **(E)** From the discriminant $b^2 - 4ac = 4 - 4 \cdot 1 \cdot 3 = -8 < 0$.

* 7. **(B)** The equation of a vertical parabola with its vertex at the origin has the form $y = ax^2$. Substitute (7,7) for x and y to find $a = \frac{1}{7}$. When $y = 6$, $x^2 = 42$. Therefore, $x = \pm\sqrt{42}$, and the segment $= 2\sqrt{42} \approx 13$.

Higher Degree Polynomials
第4章　高阶多项式

4

- → **ANALYSIS OF GRAPHS**
- → **SUM AND DIFFERENCE OF CUBES**
- → **QUADRATIC FORM**
- → **SYNTHETIC DIVISION**
- → **SOLVING EQUATIONS GRAPHICALLY**

Graphs of polynomials of degree greater than 2 are not as readily analyzed as are linear and quadratic polynomials. All polynomials have graphs that are continuous. Loosely speaking, this means that graphs of polynomials can be drawn without lifting the pencil from the paper. If the degree n is an even number, both ends of the graph leave the coordinate system at either the top or bottom, such as depicted in the figures below.

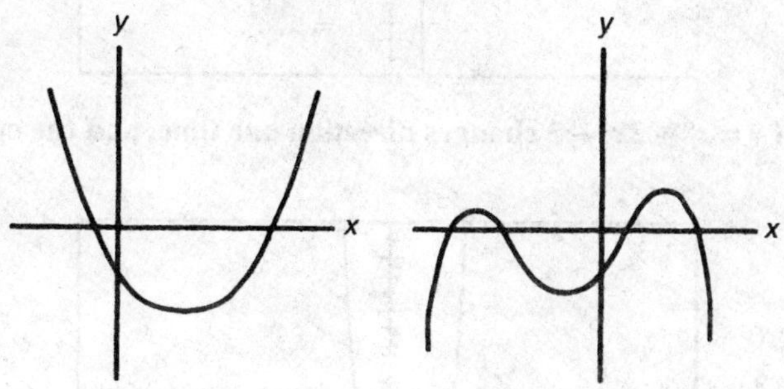

If n is an odd number, then the ends of the graph leave the coordinate system at opposite ends, such as those depicted in the following figures.

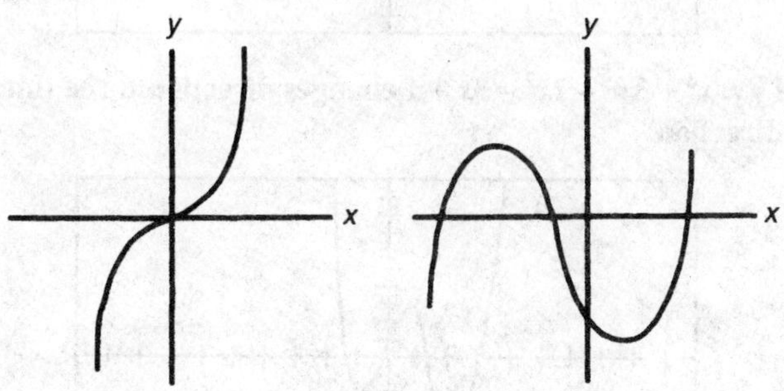

These results depict the **end behavior** of a polynomial. The continuity and end behavior polynomials make their graphs reasonably "safe" to analyze on a graphing calculator: there are no breaks or holes in the graph.

Multiplicity is the number of times a particular value appears as a root of a polynomial. Thus, for example, in the polynomial equation $f(x) = x(x-2)^3(x+1)^2$, $x = 0$ has multiplicity one; $x = 2$ has multiplicity three; and $x = -1$ has multiplicity two. The sum of the multiplicities of a polynomial is equal to the number of roots of a polynomial. These are both equal to the degree of the polynomial. In this example, the degree of f is six, and the sum of the multiplicities is also six. This result is the **Fundamental Theorem of Algebra**.

➥ Examples

(A) The graph of $y = x^3 + 2x - 3$ doesn't change direction at all, and the ends go in opposite directions.

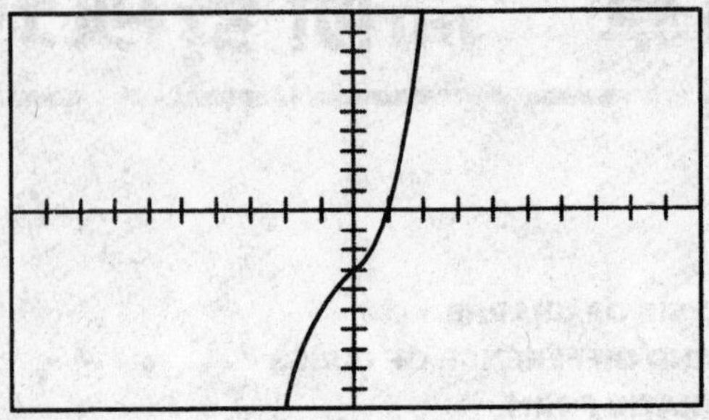

(B) The graph of $y = x^3 - 3x^2 + 1$ changes direction twice, and the ends go in opposite directions.

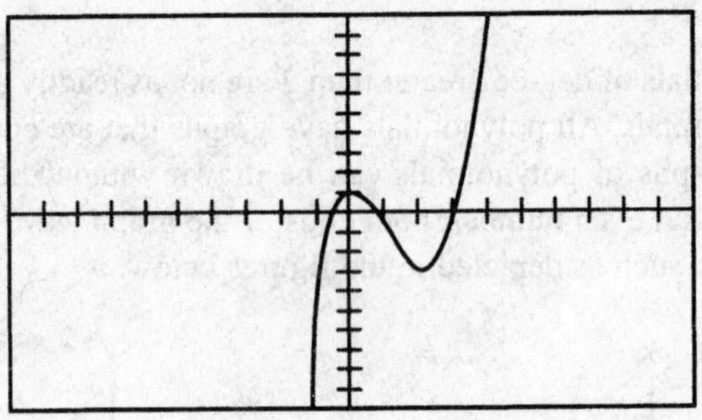

(C) The graph of $y = x^4 + 2x^3 - 3$ changes direction one time, and the ends go in the same direction.

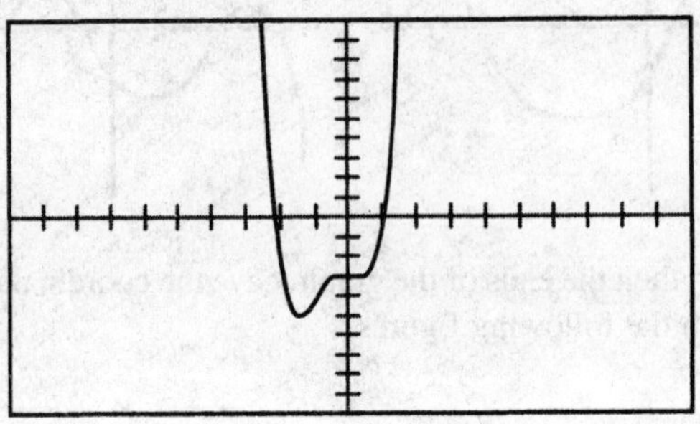

(D) The graph of $y = x^4 + 3x^3 - 2x^2 - 5x + 1$ changes direction three times, and the ends go in the same direction.

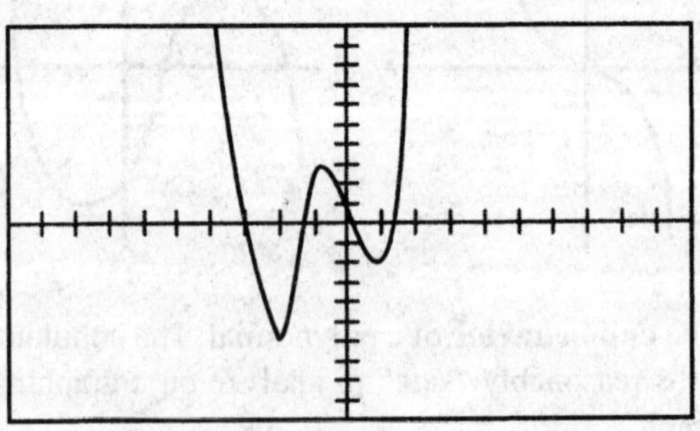

There are no general formulas for solving higher degree polynomial equations, but there are techniques for solving some of them. Sums and differences of cubes can be solved by factoring using the formulas:

$$a^3 + b^3 = (a + b)(a^2 - ab + b^2)$$

$$a^3 - b^3 = (a - b)(a^2 + ab + b^2)$$

Example

(E) Solve $x^3 + 27 = 0$.

Using the formula for the sum of cubes, factor $x^3 + 27 = (x + 3)(x^2 - 3x + 9)$. By the Zero Product Property, $x + 3 = 0$ so $x = -3$, or $x^2 - 3x + 9 = 0$, which can be solved using the Quadratic Formula: $x = \frac{3 \pm \sqrt{9-36}}{2} = \frac{3 \pm 3i\sqrt{3}}{2}$. The three roots are -3, $\frac{3+3i\sqrt{3}}{2}$, and $\frac{3-3i\sqrt{3}}{2}$.

Higher degree polynomials can also take a **quadratic form**.

Example

(F) Solve $x^4 - 3x^2 + 2 = 0$.

To see that this is a quadratic form, substitute $u = x^2$. The equation becomes $u^2 - 3u + 2 = 0$, which can be solved by factoring: $(u - 2)(u - 1) = 0$, so $u = 2$ or $u = 1$. Therefore, $x^2 = 2$ or $x^2 = 1$, from which it follows that $x = \pm\sqrt{2}$ or $x = \pm 1$. These are the four roots of the original equation.

Another strategy for solving higher degree polynomial equations is based on the Rational Root Theorem. This theorem states that if a rational number (the ratio of two integers $\frac{p}{q}$ where $q \neq 0$) is a root of a polynomial equation, then p is a divisor of the constant term and q is a divisor of the leading coefficient. Therefore the ratios of these divisors form a list of possible rational roots of the equation. It is then a matter of substituting each of these ratios into the equation to see if any of them produces 0.

To find out whether a number r is a root, enter the polynomial into Y_1 on the graphing calculator, select "Ask" under 2nd TblSet, and enter the possible roots one at a time until $Y_1 = 0$. If all the roots are rational, they can all be found using this method. Suppose a cubic equation has exactly one rational root r. The Factor Theorem states that if r is a zero of $P(x)$, then $x - r$ is a factor. This means that the quotient $\frac{P(x)}{x-r}$ is a quadratic expression whose zeros are the remaining two roots of the original cubic equation. This quotient can be found by using **synthetic division**.

Example

(G) Solve $x^3 - 8x - 3 = 0$.

The possible rational roots are $\pm 1, \pm 3$. Substitute each of the numbers in turn into the equation and determine whether it is a root. In this case, $(3)^3 - 8(3) - 3 = 0$, 3 is the only rational root. Use synthetic division:

3	1	0	−8	−3
		3	9	3
	1	3	1	0

to determine that $\dfrac{x^3-8x-3}{x-3}=x^2+3x+1$ and then use the Quadratic Formula to conclude that the other two roots are $\dfrac{-3\pm\sqrt{5}}{2}$.

If none of the possible rational roots are actually roots, the equation can only be solved for real (irrational) roots by finding decimal approximations on the graphing calculator. One method is to graph the polynomial, analyze the graph as described above to obtain a calculator window that shows all the roots (x-intercepts), and use calculator commands to obtain approximations of the zeros. The following example illustrates this technique.

➡ Example

(H) Solve $x^3 - 2x^2 + 2x + 4 = 0$.

Enter $x^3 - 2x^2 + 2x + 4$ into Y_1, and enter ZOOM 6. This gives you the graph of the polynomial on the standard [–10,10] screen in both the x and y directions. Since the graph changes direction twice, and the end behavior is up as x gets larger and down as x gets smaller, all the important features of the graph are on the standard screen. The fact that the graph has only one x-intercept indicates that there is one real root and a conjugate pair of imaginary roots. To find the real root, enter 2nd CALC and select "zero." This command returns to the graphing screen where you scroll the cursor to the left, then the right, or the x-intercept to select lower and upper bounds. Then enter a guess (usually the right bound is fine), and the approximate zero is shown. The sequence of screens is shown below.

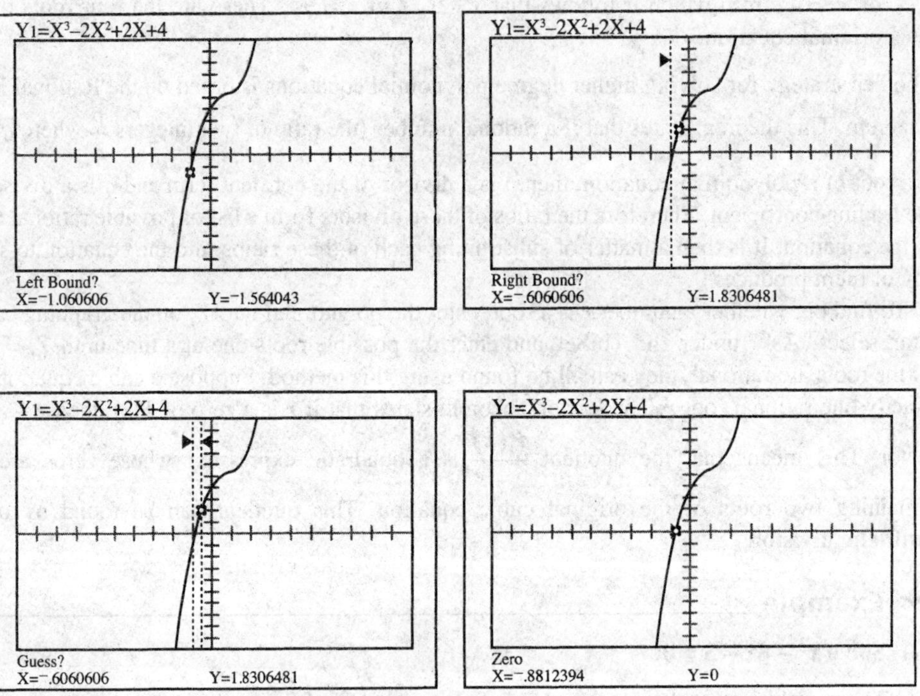

EXERCISES 习题

1. $P(x) = ax^4 + x^3 - bx^2 - 4x + c$. If $P(x)$ increases without bound as x increases without bound, then, as x decreases without bound, $P(x)$

   (A) increases without bound
   (B) decreases without bound
   (C) approaches zero from above the x-axis
   (D) approaches zero from below the x-axis
   (E) cannot be determined

2. Which of the following is an odd function?

   I. $f(x) = 3x^3 + 5$
   II. $g(x) = 4x^6 + 2x^4 - 3x^2$
   III. $h(x) = 7x^5 - 8x^3 + 12x$

   (A) only I
   (B) only II
   (C) only III
   (D) only I and II
   (E) only I and III

3. How many possible rational roots are there for $2x^4 + 4x^3 - 6x^2 + 15x - 12 = 0$?

   (A) 4
   (B) 6
   (C) 8
   (D) 12
   (E) 16

4. If both $x - 1$ and $x - 2$ are factors of $x^3 - 3x^2 + 2x - 4b$, then b must be

   (A) 0
   (B) 1
   (C) 2
   (D) 3
   (E) 4

5. If $3x^3 - 9x^2 + Kx - 12$ is divisible by $x - 3$, then $K =$

   (A) −40
   (B) −3
   (C) 3
   (D) 4
   (E) 22

6. Write the equation of lowest degree with real coefficients if two of its roots are −1 and $1 + i$.

   (A) $x^3 + x^2 + 2 = 0$
   (B) $x^3 - x^2 - 2 = 0$
   (C) $x^3 - x + 2 = 0$
   (D) $x^3 - x^2 + 2 = 0$
   (E) none of the above

Answers Explained 答案解析

1. **(A)** Since the degree of the polynomial is an even number, both ends of the graph go off in the same direction. Since $P(x)$ increases without bound as x increases, $P(x)$ also increases without bound as x decreases.

2. **(C)** Since the exponents are all odd, and there is no constant term, III is the only odd function.

3. **(E)** Rational roots have the form $\frac{p}{q}$, where p is a factor of 12 and q is a factor of 2.

   $\frac{p}{q} \in \left\{\pm 12, \pm 6, \pm 4, \pm 3, \pm 2, \pm 1, \pm \frac{3}{2}, \pm \frac{1}{2}\right\}$. The total is 16.

* 4. **(A)** Since $x - 1$ is a factor, $P(1) = 1^3 - 3 \bullet 1^2 + 2 \bullet 1 - 4b = 0$. Therefore, $b = 0$.

* 5. **(D)** Substitute 3 for x set equal to zero and solve for K.

6. **(D)** $1 - i$ is also a root. To find the equation, multiply $(x + 1)[x - (1 + i)][x - (1 - i)]$, which are the factors that produced the three roots.

Solving Polynomial Inequalities
第5章 多项式不等式的求解 5

→ SOLVE BY FACTORING
→ ANALYSIS OF GRAPHS

To solve polynomial inequalities, transform the inequality so that one side is zero; then solve the corresponding equation. Because of the continuity of polynomials, these solutions are the only points where the sign of the polynomial can change. Graphically, if $P(x)$ is a polynomial, the solutions to $P(x) = 0$ are the x-intercepts of the graph. If the graph actually crosses the x-axis, then the graph either goes from above the x-axis to below it, or vice versa, in which case the sign of $y = P(x)$ changes from positive to negative or negative to positive. It is also possible for the graph to just "kiss" the x-axis from either above or below. These are the cases where the sign of $P(x)$ does not change at a point where $P(x) = 0$.

Examples

(A) Solve the inequality $(x - 1)(x + 4)(x + 2) < 0$.

The polynomial is already in factored form, and the x-intercepts are 1,–4, and –2. By inspection of the graph below, the graph lies below the x-axis when $x < 4$ or when $-2 < x < 1$.

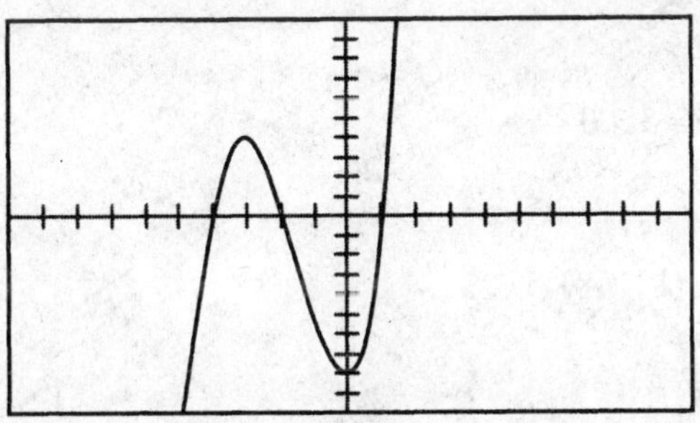

(B) Solve the inequality $P(x) = x^3 - 4x^2 + x + 4 > 0$.

Use a calculator to graph $y = P(x)$ and find its (approximate) zeros: –0.814, 1.471, and 3.343.

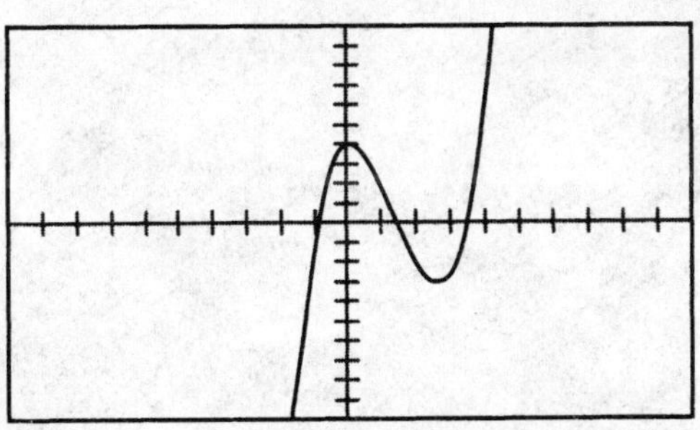

Observe that the graph of $y = P(x)$ is above the x-axis for $-0.814 < x < 1.471$ or $x > 3.343$.

(C) Solve the inequality $Q(x) = x^3 - 4x^2 + 4x > 0$.

Graph $y = Q(x)$ and factor $Q = x(x-2)^2$ to observe that $x = 2$ with multiplicity 2, and $x = 0$.

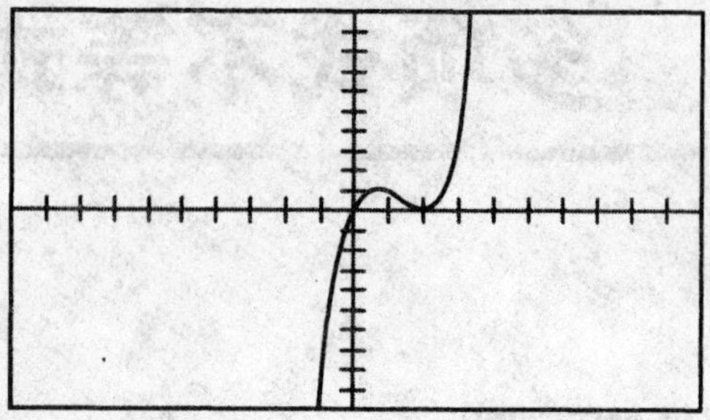

The graph "kisses" the x-axis where a zero has even multiplicity. Therefore, $y = Q(x)$ is above the x-axis if $0 < x < 2$ or $x > 2$.

EXERCISES 习题

1. Which of the following is equivalent to $3x^2 - x < 2$?

(A) $-\frac{3}{2} < x < 1$

(B) $-1 < x < \frac{2}{3}$

(C) $-\frac{2}{3} < x < 1$

(D) $-1 < x < \frac{3}{2}$

(E) $x < -\frac{2}{3}$ or $x > 1$

2. Solve $x^5 - 3x^3 + 2x^2 - 3 > 0$.

(A) $(-\infty,-0.87)$
(B) $(-1.90,-0.87)$
(C) $(-1.90,-0.87) \cup (1.58,\infty)$
(D) $(-0.87,1.58)$
(E) $(1.58,\infty)$

3. The number of integers that satisfy the inequality $x^2 + 48 < 16x$ is

(A) 0
(B) 4
(C) 7
(D) an infinite number
(E) none of the above

Answers Explained 答案解析

1. **(C)** $3x^2 - x - 2 = (3x + 2)(x - 1) = 0$ when $x = -\frac{2}{3}$ or 1. Numbers between these satisfy the original inequality.

* 2. **(C)** Graph the function, and determine that the three zeros are -1.90, -0.87, and 1.58. The parts of the graph that are above the x-axis have x-coordinates between -1.90 and -0.87 and are larger than 1.58.

3. **(C)** $x^2 - 16x + 48 = (x - 4)(x - 12) = 0$, when $x = 4$ or 12. Numbers between these satisfy the original inequality.

Triangle Trigonometry
第6章 三角几何

6

- → SOLVING TRIANGLES
- → LAW OF SINES
- → LAW OF COSINES
- → AMBIGUOUS CASE
- → FINDING AREA
- → SPECIAL ANGLES

Trigonometry is often introduced in geometry courses in terms of the ratio of the sides of a right triangle. The right triangle in the figure below has right angle C and acute angles A and B. The sides opposite these angles are the hypotenuse c and legs b and a.

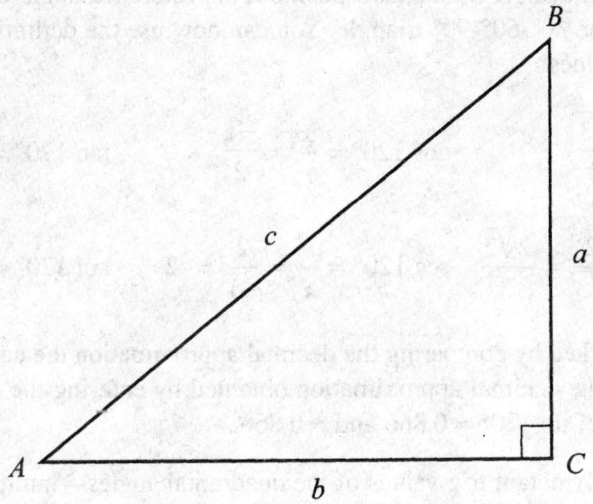

The trigonometric ratios of one of the acute angles (say A) are defined as

$$\sin A = \frac{\textit{opposite side}}{\textit{hypotenuse}} = \frac{a}{c},\ \cos A = \frac{\textit{adjacent side}}{\textit{hypotenuse}} = \frac{b}{c},\ \text{and } \tan A = \frac{\textit{opposite side}}{\textit{adjacent side}} = \frac{a}{b}.$$

The mnemonic SOHCAHTOA helps students remember these ratios. It derives from **S**in is **O**pposite/**H**ypotenuse, **C**osine is **A**djacent/**H**ypotenuse, and **T**angent is **O**pposite/**A**djacent.

When you use a calculator to evaluate most trig values, you will get a decimal approximation. You can use your knowledge of the definitions of the trigonometric functions, reference angles, and the ratios of the sides of the 45°-45°-90° triangle and the 30°-60°-90° triangle ("special" triangles) to get exact trig values for "special" angles: multiples of 30°, 45°, 60°.

The ratios of the sides of the two special triangles are shown in the figures below.

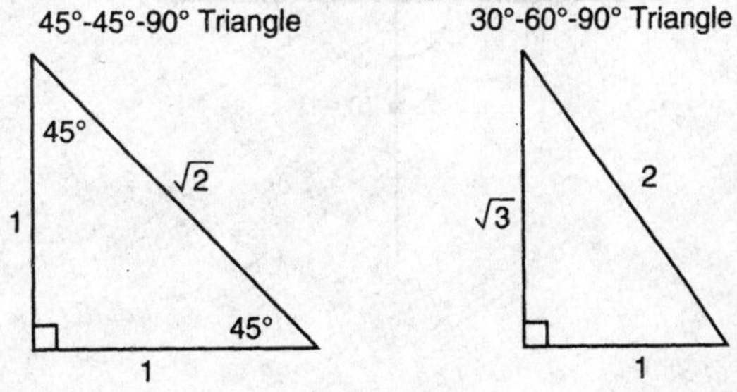

To illustrate how this can be done, suppose you want to find the trig values of 120°. First sketch the following graph.

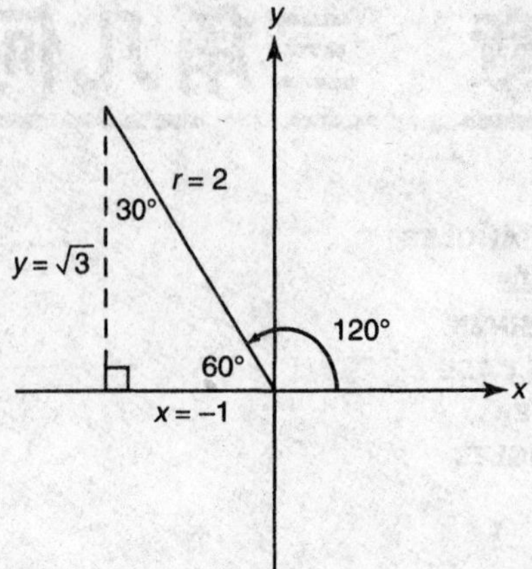

The graph shows the angle in standard position, the reference angle 60°, and the (signed) side length ratios for the 30°-60°-90° triangle. You can now use the definitions of the trig functions to find the trig values:

$\sin 120° = \frac{y}{r} = \frac{\sqrt{3}}{2}$ $\cos 120° = \frac{x}{r} = \frac{-1}{2}$ $\tan 120° = \frac{y}{x} = \frac{\sqrt{3}}{-1} = -\sqrt{3}$

$\csc 120° = \frac{r}{y} = \frac{2}{\sqrt{3}} = \frac{2\sqrt{3}}{3}$ $\sec 120° = \frac{r}{x} = \frac{2}{-1} = -2$ $\cot 120° = \frac{x}{y} = \frac{-1}{\sqrt{3}} = -\frac{\sqrt{3}}{3}$

Values can be checked by comparing the decimal approximation the calculator provides for the trig function with the decimal approximation obtained by entering the exact value in a calculator. In this example, sin 120° ≈ 0.866 and ≈ 0.866.

You can also readily obtain trig values of the quadrantal angles—multiples of 90°. The terminal sides of these angles are the *x*- and *y*-axes. In these cases, you don't have a triangle at all; instead, either *x* or *y* equals 1 or –1, the other coordinate equals zero, and *r* equals 1. To illustrate how to use this method to evaluate the trig values of 270°, first draw the figure below.

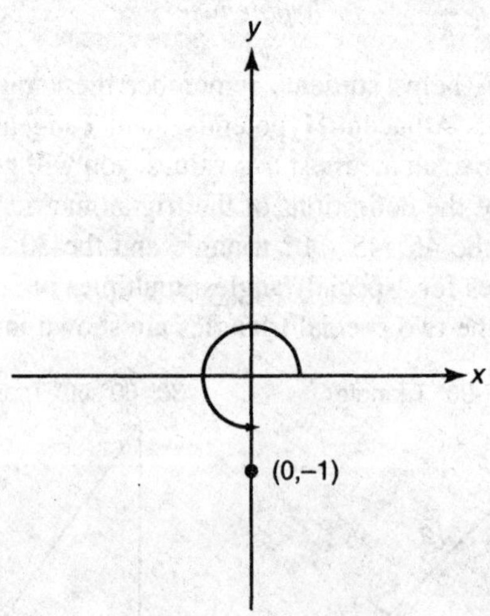

The figure indicates $x = 0$ and $y = -1$ ($r = 1$). Therefore,

$\sin 270° = \frac{-1}{1} = -1$ $\cos 270° = \frac{0}{1} = 0$ $\tan 270° = \frac{-1}{0}$, which is undefined

$\csc 270° = \frac{1}{-1} = -1$ $\sec 270° = \frac{1}{0}$, which is undefined $\cot 270° = \frac{0}{-1} = 0$

An arbitrary triangle has 6 parts (3 angles and 3 sides). The labeling of the angles and sides of an arbitrary triangle is the same as described for a right triangle: angles A,B,C and their opposite sides a,b,c. Typical problems in triangle trig ask you to find 3 of these values given 3 others. There are three important theorems about triangles that are based on the relationships between the trig ratios and the angles and sides of the triangle. Consider the triangle in the diagram below.

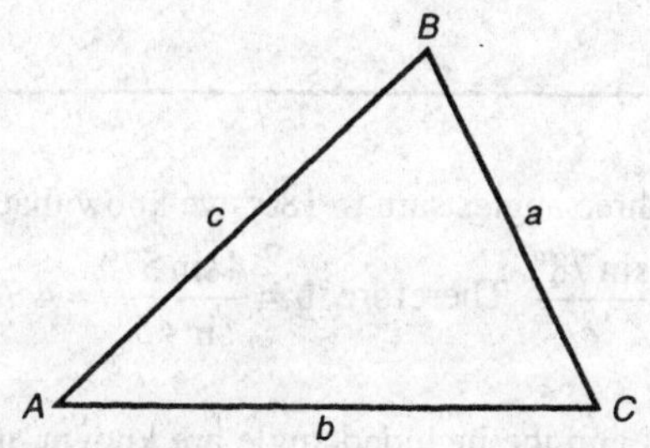

Depending on which sides and angles of the triangle are given, the following formulas can be used to find the missing parts of a triangle.

Recall from geometry that you can prove that two triangles are congruent if the three sides of one triangle are congruent to those of the other (SSS) or if two sides and the included angle of one triangle are congruent to those of the other (SAS) or if two angles and one side of one triangle are congruent to those of the other (ASA or AAS). If you know three of these values for one triangle, then any other triangle that has the same three values must be congruent to the first. In other words, the other three values can be determined uniquely.

The Law of Sines and the Law of Cosines are two theorems that relate the sides and angles of a triangle.

$$\text{Law of Sines: } \frac{\sin A}{a} = \frac{\sin B}{b} = \frac{\sin C}{c}$$

The Law of Sines says that the sine of the angles of a triangle and the lengths of the opposite sides are proportional.

$$\text{Law of Cosines: } a^2 = b^2 + c^2 - 2bc \cos A$$
$$b^2 = a^2 + c^2 - 2ac \cos B$$
$$c^2 = a^2 + b^2 - 2ab \cos C$$

The Law of Cosines is a generalization of the Pythagorean theorem. Since $\cos 90° = 0$, the three forms reduce to the Pythagorean theorem with A, B, or C as the right angle. The last term of each form represents the "correction" for A, B, or C not being a right angle. Since the cosine of an acute angle is positive, this correction is negative if A, B, or C has measure less than 90°, and since the cosine of an obtuse angle is negative, the correction is positive if A, B, or C has measure greater than 90°.

When the measures of two angles and a side are known, the third angle can be found by subtraction, and the Law of Sines can be used to find the other two sides.

➡ Example

(A) Solve $\triangle ABC$ if $m\angle A = 45°$, $m\angle B = 57°$, $a = 4$.

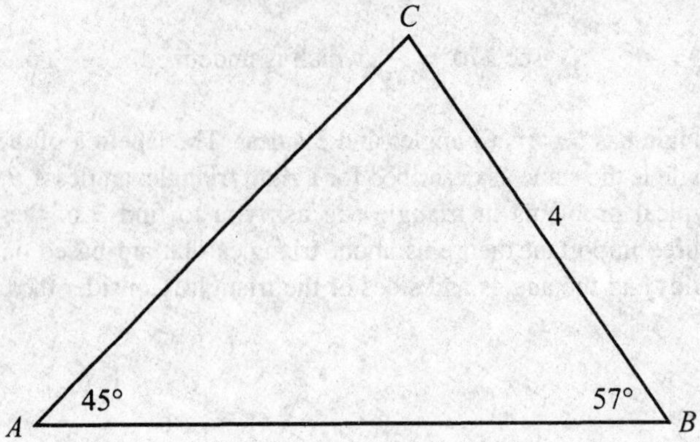

Since the measures of the three angles sum to 180° we know that $m\angle C = 78°$. By the Law of Sines: $\frac{\sin 45°}{4} = \frac{\sin 57°}{b} = \frac{\sin 78°}{c}$. Therefore, $b = \frac{4\sin 57°}{\sin 45°} \approx 4.74$ and $c = \frac{4\sin 78°}{\sin 45°} \approx 5.53$.

If the measures of two sides and the included angle are known, use the Law of Cosines first to find the measure of the third side. Then use the Law of Sines to find the measure of a second angle. Finally, use the fact that the sum of the angles of a triangle is 180° to find the measure of the third angle.

➡ Example

(B) Solve $\triangle ABC$ if $a = 7$, $b = 12$, $m\angle C = 62°$

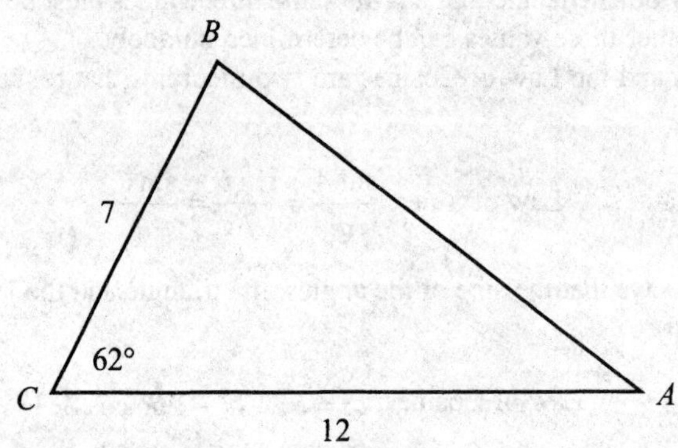

By the Law of Cosines, $c^2 = 7^2 + 12^2 - 2(7)(12)\cos 62° \approx 10.68$. By the Law of Sines, $\frac{\sin A}{7} = \frac{\sin 62°}{10.68}$, so $\sin A \approx 0.5787$ and $m\angle A \approx 35.36°$. Finally, $m\angle C = 180° - m\angle A - m\angle B \approx 82.64$.

If the lengths of three sides of a triangle are known, use the Law of Cosines first to find the measure of one of the angles. Then use the Law of Sines to find a second angle. Finally, use the fact that the angle measures sum to 180° to find the measure of the third angle.

Example

(C) Solve ΔABC if $a = 3, b = 5, c = 7$.

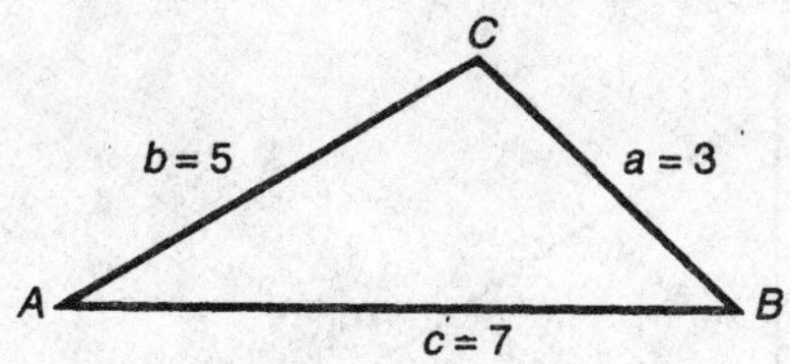

By the Law of Cosines $m\angle A$: $3^2 = 5^2 + 7^2 - 2(5)(7)\cos A$, so $\cos A = \dfrac{3^2 - 5^2 - 7^2}{-2(5)(7)} \approx 0.9285$ and $m\angle A \approx 21.79$.

By the Law of Sines, $\dfrac{\sin B}{5} = \dfrac{21.79}{3}$, so $m\angle B \approx 38.21°$.

Finally, $m\angle C \approx 180° - 21.79° - 38.21 = 120°$.

You also learned in geometry that knowing the measures of two sides and a nonincluded angle of one triangle are congruent to those of another triangle (SSA) does not guarantee congruence of the triangles. This SSA case is called the "ambiguous case" because there are several possible outcomes, depending on the values of the measures.

Case 1: In the diagram below, $\angle A$, the given angle, is obtuse. The side with measure a is the side opposite $\angle A$ and must be one of the given sides. The other given side in the diagram is $\overline{AC}$, and it has measure b. In the diagram, $\angle A$ is obtuse. The diagram shows clearly that there is no triangle unless $a > b$. In this case, the Law of Sines can be used first to find $m\angle B$. Subtract the measures of the two known angles to get $m\angle C$; then use the Law of Sines again to find c.

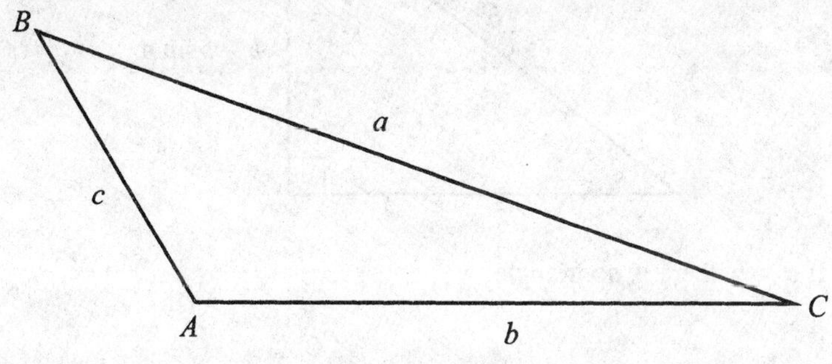

Example

(D) Solve ΔABC if $m\angle A = 125°, a = 10, b = 8$.

By the Law of Sines, $\dfrac{\sin 125°}{10} = \dfrac{\sin B}{8}$. Therefore, $\sin B = \dfrac{5\sin 125°}{10} \approx 0.6553$, and

$m\angle B \approx 40.94°$. $m\angle C \approx 180° - 125° - 40.94° = 14.06°$. By the Law of Sines again,

$\dfrac{\sin 125°}{10} = \dfrac{\sin 14.06°}{c}$, so $c = \dfrac{10 \sin 14.06°}{\sin 125°} \approx 2.96$.

Case 2: In the diagram that follows, $\angle A$ is a right angle, a is the length of the hypotenuse, and $m\angle B = \sin^{-1}\left(\dfrac{b}{a}\right)$. Use the fact that the sum of the angles of a triangle is 180° to find the measure of the third angle, and use the Pythagorean theorem to find c, the length of the third side. This case is not likely to be seen on the Math Level 2 Test, but it is included here for completeness.

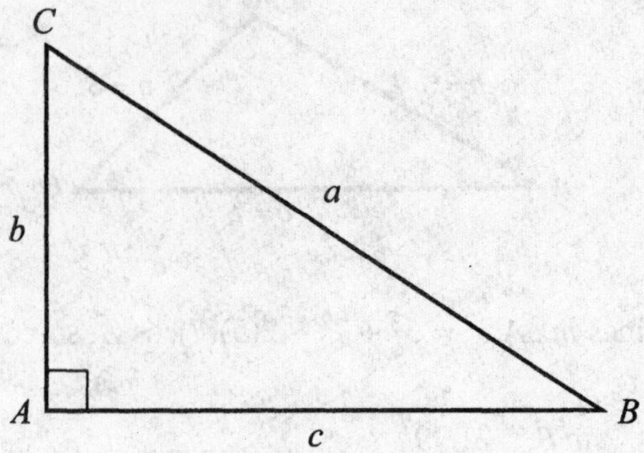

➡ Example

(E) Solve ΔABC if $m\angle A = 90°$, $a = 7$, $b = 5$.

$\sin B = \dfrac{5}{7}$, so $m\angle B \approx 45.58$. $m\angle C \approx 90° - 45.58° = 44.42°$, and $c = \sqrt{7^2 - 5^2} \approx 4.90$.

Case 3: In the diagram below, $\angle A$ is an acute angle at the bottom left, and $h = b \sin A$ is the length of the perpendicular from C to $\overline{AB}$. There are 4 subcases summarized below.

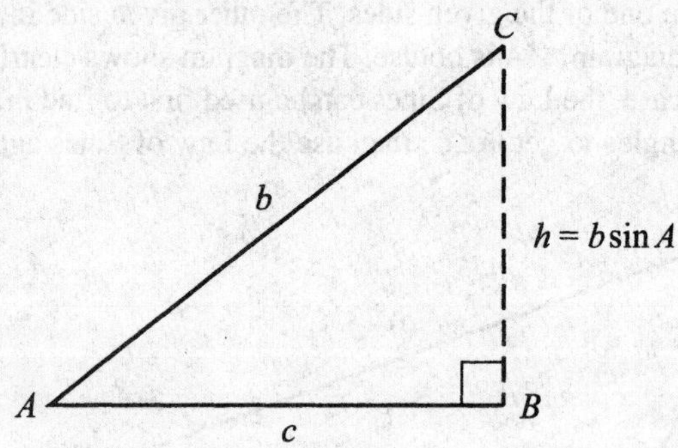

Case 3a: If $a < h$, there is no triangle.

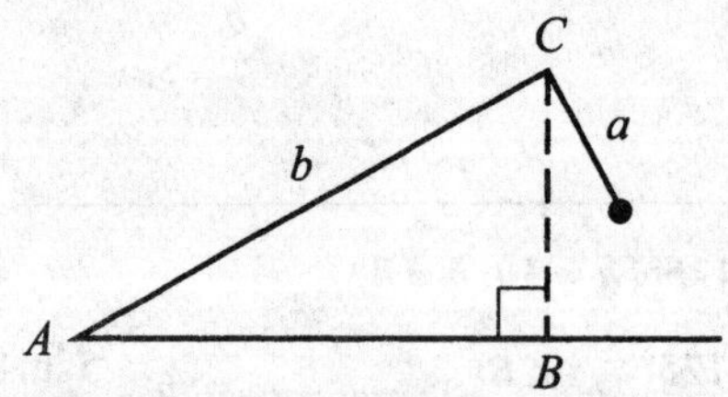

Case 3b: If $a > b$, there is one (obtuse) triangle.

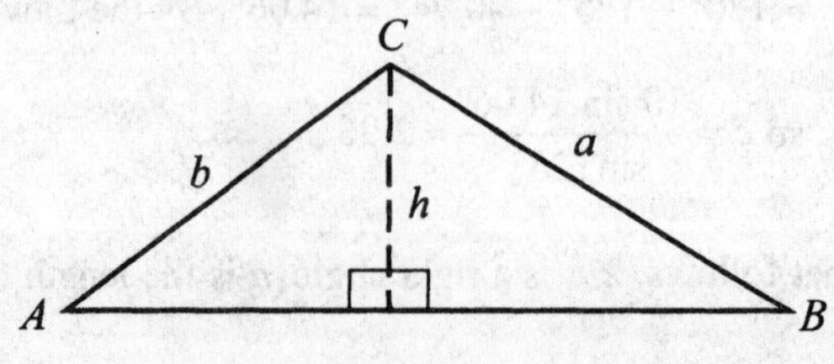

Case 3c: If $a > h$ but $a < b$, there are two possible triangles. These are shown as $\triangle ABC$ and $\triangle AB'C$ in the figure below.

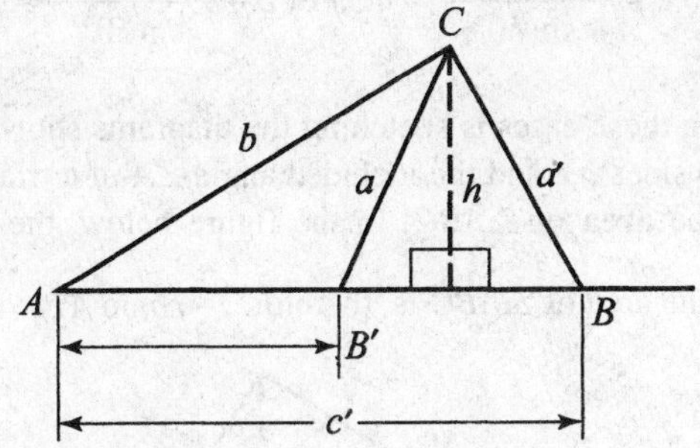

Case 3d: It's not likely but possible that $a = h$ in which case there is one right triangle.

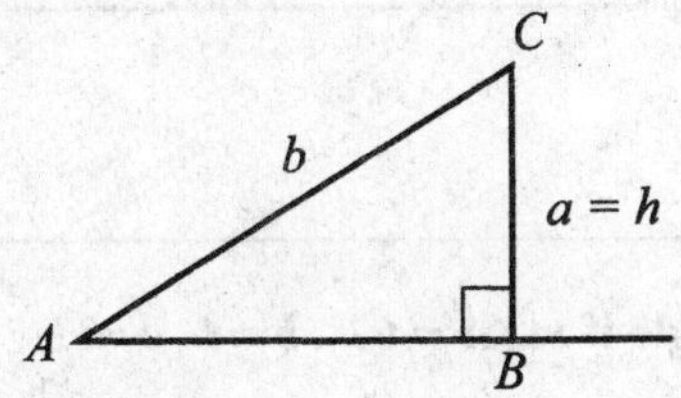

The following examples demonstrate Cases 3a, 3b, and 3c.

Examples

(F) Case 3a. Solve $\triangle ABC$ if $m\angle A = 50°, a = 3, b = 5$.

First calculate $h = 5 \sin 50° \approx 3.83$. Since $3 < 3.83$, there are no triangles.

(G) Case 3b. Solve $\triangle ABC$ if $m\angle A = 50°, a = 7, b = 5$.

Since $7 > 3.83$, there is one triangle, and it is obtuse. Follow the same procedure as in Case 1 to solve this triangle: By the Law of Sines, $\frac{\sin 50°}{7} = \frac{\sin B}{5}$. Therefore,

$\sin B = \frac{5 \sin 50°}{7} \approx 0.5472$, and $m\angle B \approx 33.17$. Calculate the third angle (obtuse $\angle C$)

as $180° - 50° - 33.17° = 96.83°$. By the Law of Sines again, $\frac{\sin 50°}{7} = \frac{\sin 96.83}{c}$,

so $c \approx \frac{7 \sin 96.83°}{\sin 50°} \approx 9.07$.

(H) Case 3c. Solve $\triangle ABC$ if $m\angle A = 50°, a = 4, b = 5$.

Since, $a = 4$, and $3.83 < 4 < 5$, there are two possible sides that have length a, denoted a and a' in the figure under Case 3c, thereby making two noncongruent triangles. In this situation, there are two triangles to be solved because there are two possible values each of $m\angle B$, $m\angle C$, a. The three pairs of values can also be solved by the method shown for Case 1.

By the Law of Sines, $\frac{\sin 50°}{4} = \frac{\sin B}{5}$, so $\sin B = \frac{5 \sin 50°}{4} \approx 0.9576$, and $m\angle B = 73.24$.

But $\sin (90° - 73.24°) = \sin 16.76° \approx 0.9576$ as well. Therefore, $m\angle B = 73.24°$ or $16.76°$. By the fact that the sum of the angle measures in a triangle is $180°$, $m\angle C = 180° - 50° -$

$73.24° = 56.76°$ or $m\angle C = 180° - 50° - 16.76° = 113.24°$. By the Law of Sines again, $\frac{\sin 56.76°}{c} = \frac{\sin 50°}{4}$, so $c \approx \frac{4 \sin 56.76°}{\sin 50°} \approx 4.37$ or $c \approx \frac{\sin 113.24°}{\sin 50°} \approx 3.80$.

The key to remembering these cases is sketching the diagrams shown, especially in Case 3. Given the measures of two sides b,c and the included angle $\angle A$ of a triangle, there is a convenient formula for finding the **area** of $\triangle ABC$. In the figure below, the altitude to the base of measure c is $h = b \sin A$. The area of $\triangle ABC$ is, therefore, $\frac{1}{2} cb \sin A$.

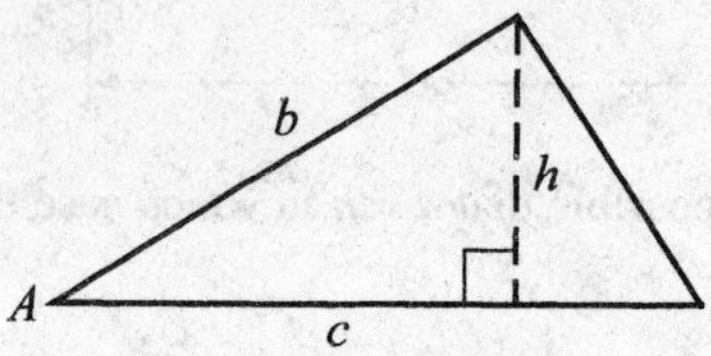

Example

(I) Find the area of the triangle if $m\angle A = 62°, b = 6, c = 12$.

Use the formula directly to find the area of $\triangle ABC$ to be $\frac{1}{2}(12)(6)\sin 62° \approx 31.79$ units^2.

EXERCISES 习题

1. The exact value of $\tan(-60°)$ is

(A) $-\sqrt{3}$

(B) -1

(C) $-\frac{2}{\sqrt{3}}$

(D) $-\frac{\sqrt{3}}{2}$

(E) $-\frac{1}{\sqrt{3}}$

2. The exact value of $\cos \frac{3\pi}{4}$ is

(A) -1

(B) $-\frac{\sqrt{3}}{2}$

(C) $-\frac{\sqrt{2}}{2}$

(D) $-\frac{1}{2}$

(E) 0

3. Csc 540° is

(A) 0

(B) $-\sqrt{3}$

(C) $-\sqrt{2}$

(D) −1

(E) undefined

4. In $\triangle ABC$, $\angle A = 30°$, $b = 8$, and $a = 4\sqrt{2}$. Angle C could equal

(A) 45°
(B) 135°
(C) 60°
(D) 15°
(E) 90°

5. In $\triangle ABC$, $\angle A = 30°$, $a = 6$, and $c = 8$. Which of the following must be true?

(A) $0° < \angle C < 90°$
(B) $90° < \angle C < 180°$
(C) $45° < \angle C < 135°$
(D) $0° < \angle C < 45°$ or $90° < \angle C < 135°$
(E) $0° < \angle C < 45°$ or $135° < \angle C < 180°$

6. The angles of a triangle are in a ratio of 8 : 3 : 1. The ratio of the longest side of the triangle to the next longest side is

(A) $\sqrt{6} : 2$
(B) 8 : 3
(C) $\sqrt{3} : 1$
(D) 8 : 5
(E) $2\sqrt{2} : \sqrt{3}$

7. The sides of a triangle are in a ratio of 4 : 5 : 6. The smallest angle is

(A) 82°
(B) 69°
(C) 56°
(D) 41°
(E) 27°

8. Find the length of the longer diagonal of a parallelogram if the sides are 6 inches and 8 inches and the smaller angle is 60°.

(A) 8
(B) 11
(C) 12
(D) 7
(E) 17

9. What are all values of side a in the figure below such that two triangles can be constructed?

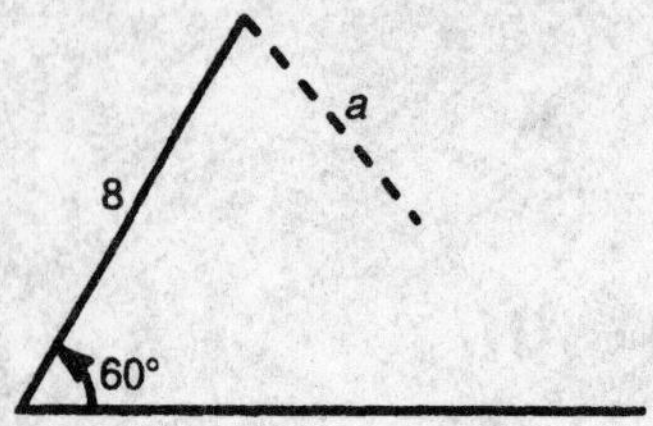

(A) $a > 4\sqrt{3}$

(B) $a > 8$

(C) $a = 4\sqrt{3}$

(D) $4\sqrt{3} < a < 8$

(E) $8 < a < 8\sqrt{3}$

10. In $\triangle ABC$, $\angle B = 30°$, $\angle C = 105°$, and $b = 10$. The length of side a equals

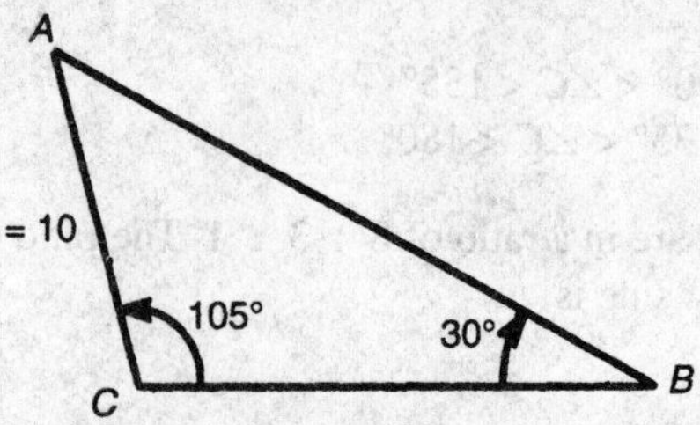

(A) 7
(B) 9
(C) 10
(D) 14
(E) 17

11. The area of $\triangle ABC$, $= 24\sqrt{3}$, side $a = 6$, and side $b = 16$. The value of $\angle C$ is

(A) 30°
(B) 30° or 150°
(C) 60°
(D) 60° or 120°
(E) none of the above

12. The area of $\triangle ABC = 12\sqrt{3}$, side $a = 6$, and side $b = 8$. Side $c =$

(A) $2\sqrt{37}$

(B) $2\sqrt{13}$

(C) $2\sqrt{37}$ or $2\sqrt{13}$

(D) 10

(E) 10 or 12

13. Given the following data, which can form two triangles?

I. $\angle C = 30°, c = 8, b = 12$

II. $\angle B = 45°,\ a = 12\sqrt{2},\ b = 15\sqrt{2}$

III. $\angle C = 60°, b = 12,\ c = 5\sqrt{3}$

(A) only I
(B) only II
(C) only III
(D) only I and II
(E) only I and III

Answers Explained 答案解析

1. **(A)** Sketch a –60° angle in standard position as shown in the figure below.

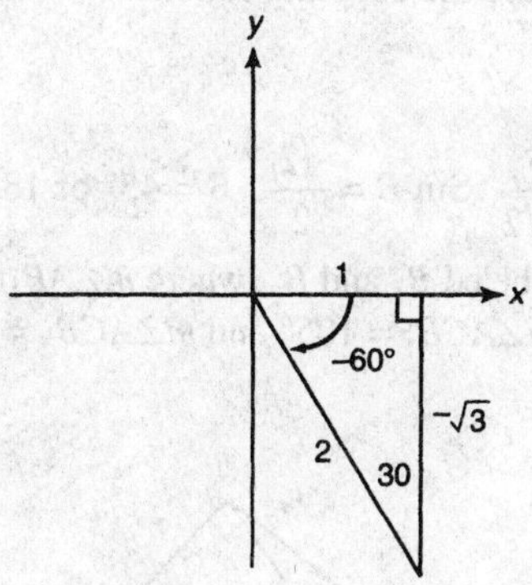

The tangent ratio is $\dfrac{y}{x} = \dfrac{-\sqrt{3}}{1} = -\sqrt{3}$.

2. **(C)** Sketch an angle of $\dfrac{3\pi}{4}$ radians in standard position, as shown in the figure below.

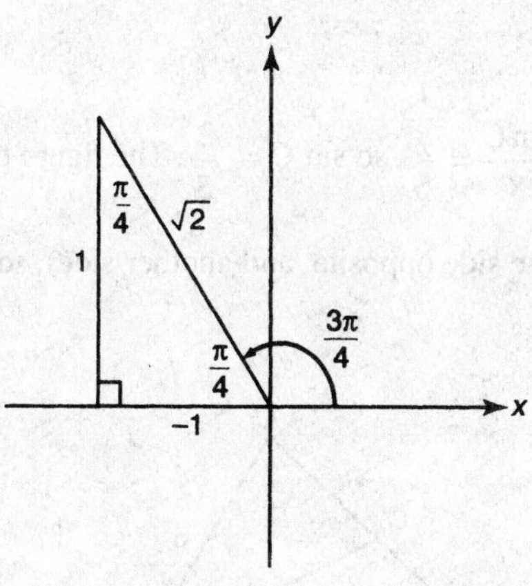

The cosine ratio is $\dfrac{x}{r} = \dfrac{-1}{\sqrt{2}} = \dfrac{-\sqrt{2}}{2}$.

3. **(E)** First, determine an angle between 0° and 360° that is coterminal with 540° by subtracting 360° from 540° repeatedly until the result is in this interval. In this case, one subtraction suffices. Since coterminal angles have the same trig values, csc 540° = csc 180°. Sketch the figure below

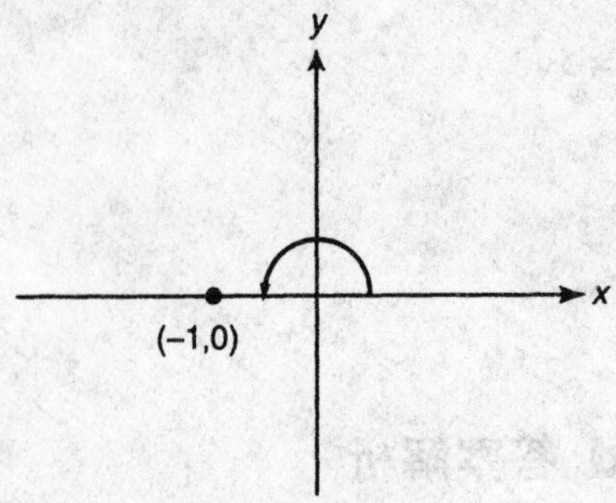

In a quadrantal angle $r = 1$, and the cosecant ratio is $\frac{r}{y}$, which is undefined.

4. **(D)** Law of Sines: $\frac{\sin B}{8} = \frac{\frac{1}{2}}{4\sqrt{2}}$. Sin $B = \frac{\sqrt{2}}{2}$. $B = 45°$ or $135°$. The figure shows two possible locations for B, labeled B_1 and B_2, where $m\angle AB_1C = 45°$ and $m\angle AB_2C = 135°$. Corresponding to these, $m\angle ACB_1 = 105°$ and $m\angle ACB_2 = 15°$. Of these, only 15° is an answer choice.

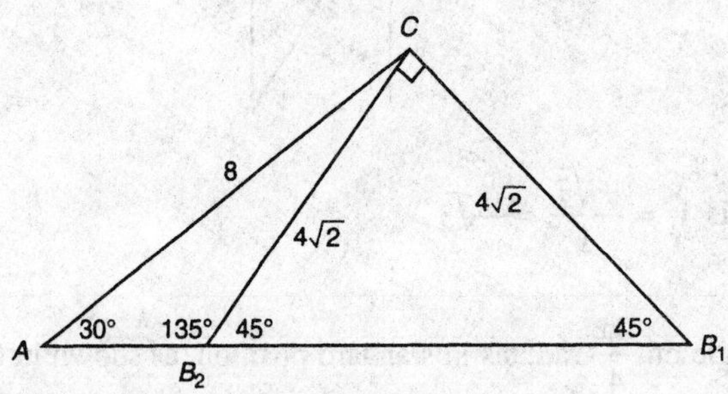

* 5. **(E)** By the Law of Sines: $\frac{\sin C}{8} = \frac{\frac{1}{2}}{6}$, so $\sin C = \frac{2}{3}$. The figure below shows this to be an ambiguous case (an angle, the side opposite, and another side), so $C = \sin^{-1}\frac{2}{3} \approx 41.81°$ or $C = 180° - 41.81° = 138.19°$.

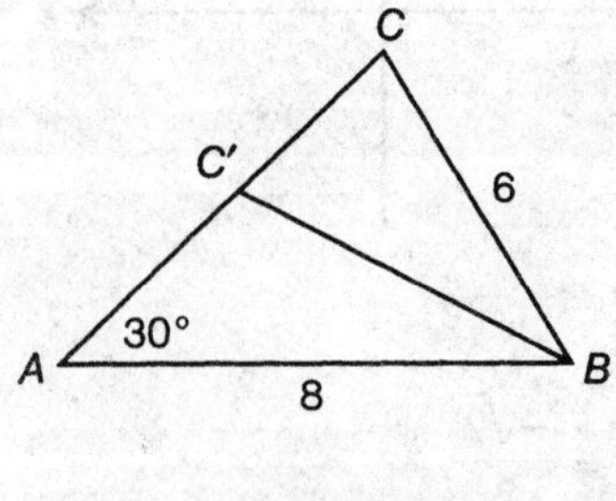

6. **(A)** The angles are 15°, 45°, and 120°. Let c be the longest side and let b be the next longest. $\dfrac{\sin 120°}{c} = \dfrac{\sin 45°}{b}$. $\dfrac{c}{b} = \dfrac{\sin 120°}{\sin 45°} = \dfrac{\frac{\sqrt{3}}{2}}{\frac{\sqrt{2}}{2}} = \dfrac{\sqrt{6}}{2}$.

* 7. **(D)** Use the Law of Cosines. Let the sides be 4, 5, and 6. $16 = 25 + 36 - 60 \cos A$. $\text{Cos } A = \dfrac{45}{60} = \dfrac{3}{4}$, which implies that $A = \cos^{-1}(0.75) \approx 41°$.

* 8. **(C)** Law of Cosines: $d^2 = 36 + 64 - 96 \cos 120°$. $d^2 = 148$. Therefore, $d \approx 12$.

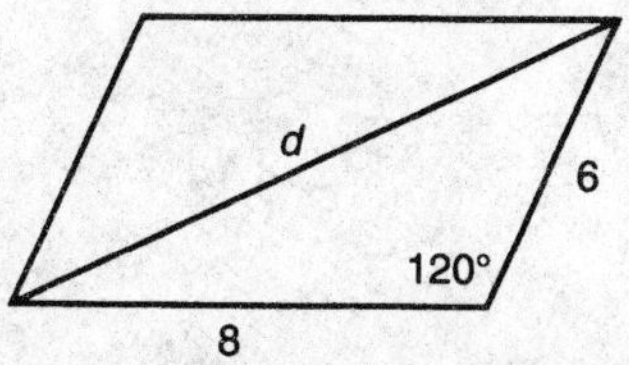

9. **(D)** Altitude to base = $8 \sin 60° = 4\sqrt{3}$. Therefore, $4\sqrt{3} < a < 8$.

* 10. **(D)** $A = 45°$. Law of Sines: $\dfrac{\sin 45°}{a} = \dfrac{\sin 30°}{10}$. Therefore, $a = 10\sqrt{2} \approx 14$.

11. **(D)** Area $= \dfrac{1}{2}ab \sin C$. $24\sqrt{3} = \dfrac{1}{2} \cdot 6 \cdot 16 \sin C$. $\text{Sin } C = \dfrac{\sqrt{3}}{2}$. Therefore, $C = 60°$ or 120°.

12. **(C)** Area $= \dfrac{1}{2}ab \sin C$. $12\sqrt{3} = \dfrac{1}{2} \cdot 6 \cdot 8 \sin C$. $\text{Sin } C = \dfrac{\sqrt{3}}{2}$. $C = 60°$ or 120°.
Use the Law of Cosines with 60° and then with 120°.

Note: At this point in the solution you know there have to be two values for C. Therefore, the answer must be Choice C or Choice E. If $C = 10$ (from Choice E), ABC is a right triangle with area $= \dfrac{1}{2} \cdot 6 \cdot 8 = 24$. Therefore, Choice E is not the answer, and Choice C is the correct answer.

13. **(A)** In I, the altitude $= 12 \cdot \dfrac{1}{2} = 6$, $6 < c < 12$, and so 2 triangles. In II, $b > 12\sqrt{2}$, so only 1 triangle. In III, the altitude $= 12 \cdot \dfrac{\sqrt{3}}{2} > 5\sqrt{3}$, so no triangles.

Trigonometric Functions
第7章 三角函数

7

- → DEFINITIONS
- → SPECIAL ANGLES
- → RADIAN MEASURE
- → GRAPHS/AMPLITUDE/PERIOD/PHASE SHIFT
- → IDENTITIES
- → EQUATIONS
- → INVERSE TRIG FUNCTIONS

The general definitions of the six trigonometric functions are obtained from an angle placed in standard position on a rectangular coordinate system. When an angle θ is placed so that its vertex is at the origin, its initial side is along the positive x-axis, and its terminal side is anywhere on the coordinate system, it is said to be in *standard position*. The angle is given a positive value if it is measured in a counterclockwise direction from the initial side to the terminal side, and a negative value if it is measured in a clockwise direction.

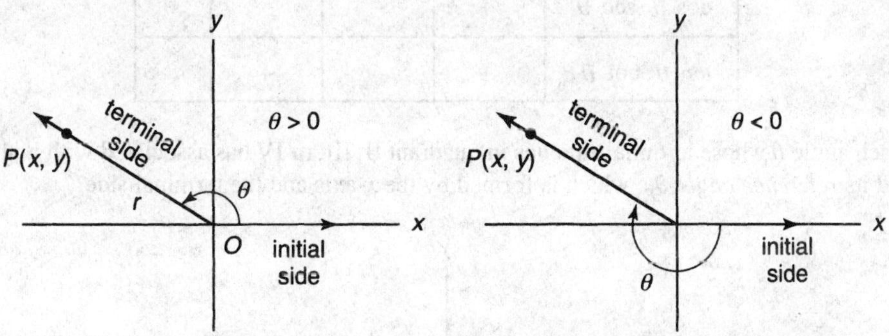

Let $P(x,y)$ be any point on the terminal side of the angle, and let r represent the distance between O and P. The six trigonometric functions are defined to be:

$$\sin\theta = \frac{y}{r}$$

$$\cos\theta = \frac{x}{r}$$

$$\tan\theta = \frac{y}{x}$$

$$\cot\theta = \frac{x}{y}$$

$$\sec\theta = \frac{r}{x}$$

$$\csc\theta = \frac{r}{y}$$

TIP

$\sin\theta$ and $\cos\theta$ are always between -1 and 1.

From these definitions it follows that:

$$\sin\theta \cdot \csc\theta = 1 \qquad \tan\theta = \frac{\sin\theta}{\cos\theta}$$

$$\cos\theta \cdot \sec\theta = 1 \qquad \cot\theta = \frac{\cos\theta}{\sin\theta}$$

$$\tan\theta \cdot \cot\theta = 1$$

If a perpendicular is constructed from P to the x-axis, a right triangle is formed by the perpendicular, the x-axis, and the terminal side. Dividing both sides of the Pythagorean theorem $x^2 + y^2 = r^2$ by r^2 yields the Pythagorean Identity $\cos^2\theta + \sin^2\theta = 1$. The following identities can then be derived from this:

- $\sin^2\theta = 1 - \cos^2\theta$
- $\cos^2\theta = 1 - \sin^2\theta$
- $1 + \tan^2\theta = \sec^2\theta$
- $\cot^2\theta + 1 = \csc^2\theta$

The distance OP is always positive, and the x- and y-coordinates of P are positive or negative depending on which quadrant the terminal side of $\angle\theta$ lies in. The signs of the trigonometric functions are indicated in the following table.

TIP

All trig functions are positive in quadrant I.

Sine and only sine is positive in quadrant II.

Tangent and only tangent is positive in quadrant III.

Cosine and only cosine is positive in quadrant IV.

Just remember: **A**ll **S**tudents **T**ake **C**alculus.

Quadrant	I	II	III	IV
Function: sin θ, csc θ	+	+	–	–
cos θ, sec θ	+	–	–	+
tan θ, cot θ	+	–	+	–

Each angle θ whose terminal side lies in quadrant II, III, or IV has associated with it an angle called its *reference angle* θ_R, which is formed by the x-axis and the terminal side.

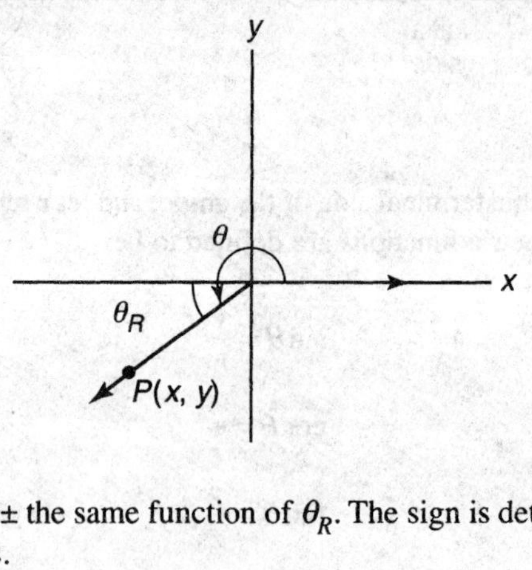

Any trig function of $\theta = \pm$ the same function of θ_R. The sign is determined by the quadrant in which the terminal side lies.

Examples

(A) Express sin 320° in terms of θ_R.

$$\theta_R = 360° - 320° = 40°$$

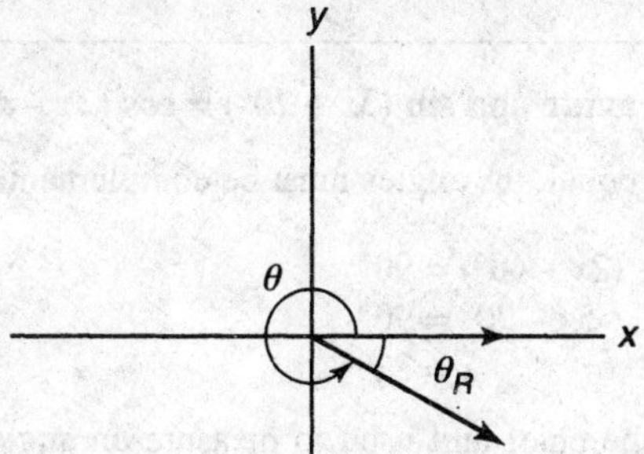

Since the sine is negative in quadrant IV, sin 320° = –sin 40°.

(B) Express cot 200° in terms of θ_R.

$$\theta_R = 200° - 180° = 20°$$

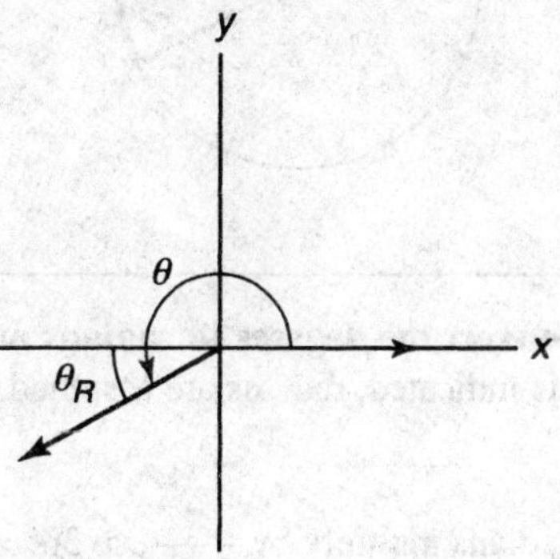

Since the cotangent is positive in quadrant III, cot 200° = cot 20°.

(C) Express cos 130° in terms of θ_R.

$$\theta_R = 180° - 130° = 50°$$

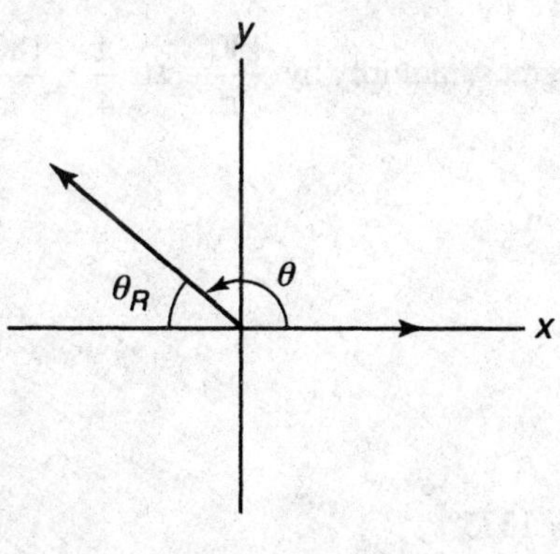

Since the cosine is negative in quadrant II, cos 130° = –cos 50°.

Sine and cosine, tangent and cotangent, and secant and cosecant are *cofunction pairs*. *Cofunctions of complementary angles are equal.* If α and β are complementary, then trig (α) = cotrig (β) and trig (β) = cotrig (α).

Example

(D) If both the angles are acute and sin $(3x + 20°) = \cos(2x - 40°)$, find x.

Since these cofunctions are equal, the angles must be complementary.

$$\begin{aligned}\text{Therefore, } (3x + 20°) + (2x - 40°) &= 90° \\ 5x - 20° &= 90° \\ x &= 22°\end{aligned}$$

Although the degree is the chief unit used to measure an angle in elementary mathematics courses, **radian measure** has several advantages in more advanced mathematics. A radian is one radius length. The circle shown in the figure below has radius r. The circumference of this circle is 360°, or 2π radians, so one radian is $\frac{360°}{2\pi} \approx 57.3°$.

TIP

Although ^{R} can be used to indicate radians, a radian has no units. Radians are pure numbers, so we don't use ^{R} at all.

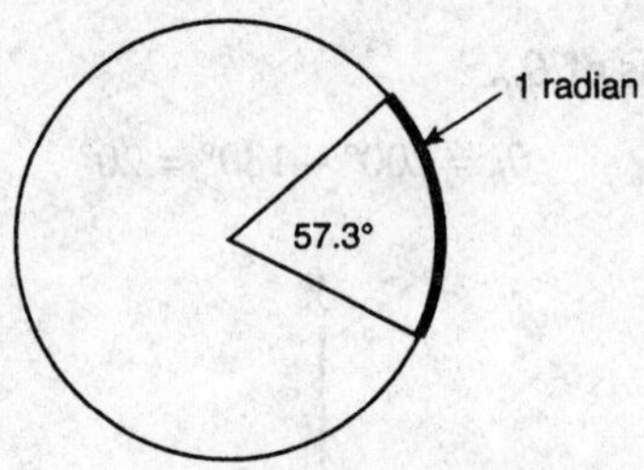

Examples

In each of the following, convert the degrees to radians or the radians to degrees.
(If no unit of measurement is indicated, rac. ..ns are assumed.)

(E) 30°

To change degrees to radians multiply by $\frac{\pi}{180°}$, so $30° = 30°\left(\frac{\pi}{180°}\right) = \frac{\pi}{6}$.

(F) 270°

$$270°\left(\frac{\pi}{180°}\right) = \frac{3\pi}{2}$$

(G) $\frac{\pi}{4}$

To change radians to degrees, multiply by $\frac{180°}{\pi}$, so $\frac{\pi}{4} \bullet \frac{180°}{\pi} = 45°$

(H) $\frac{17\pi}{3}$

$$\frac{17\pi}{3} \bullet \frac{180°}{\pi} = 1020°$$

(I) 24

$$24\left(\frac{180°}{\pi}\right) = \left(\frac{4320}{\pi}\right)^{\circ} \approx 1375°$$

In a circle of radius r inches with an arc subtended by a central angle of θ measured in radians, two important formulas can be derived. The length of the arc, s, is equal to $r\theta$, and the area of the sector, AOB, is equal to $\frac{1}{2}r^2\theta$.

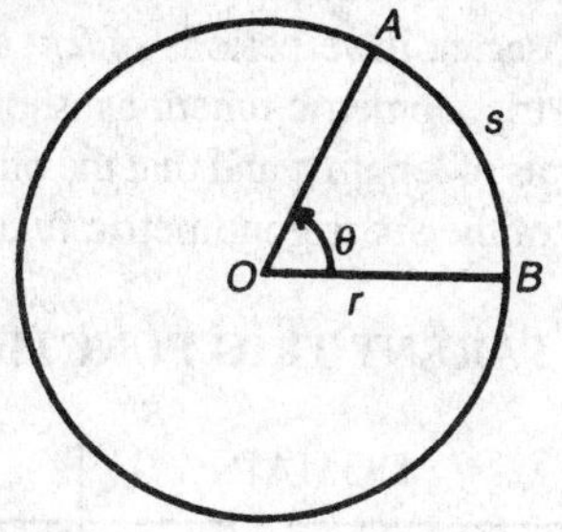

➡ Examples

(J) Find the area of the sector and the length of the arc subtended by a central angle of $\frac{2\pi}{3}$ radians in a circle whose radius is 6 inches.

$s = r\theta$ $\quad\quad A = \frac{1}{2}r^2\theta$

$s = 6 \cdot \frac{2\pi}{3} = 4\pi$ inches $\quad\quad A = \frac{1}{2} \cdot 36 \cdot \frac{2\pi}{3} = 12\pi$ square inches

(K) In a circle of radius 8 inches, find the area of the sector whose arc length is 6π inches.

$s = r\theta$ $\quad\quad A = \frac{1}{2}r^2\theta$

$6\pi = 8\theta$ $\quad\quad A = \frac{1}{2} \cdot 64 \cdot \frac{3\pi}{4} = 24\pi$ square inches

$\theta = \frac{3\pi}{4}$

(L) Find the length of the radius of a circle in which a central angle of 60° subtends an arc of length 8π inches.

The 60° angle must be converted to radians:

$$60° = 60°\left(\frac{\pi}{180°}\right) \text{ radians} = \frac{\pi}{3} \text{ radians}$$

Therefore,

$$s = r\theta$$

$$8\pi = r \cdot \frac{\pi}{3}$$

$$r = 24 \text{ inches}$$

Analyzing the graph of a trigonometric function can be readily accomplished with the aid of a graphing calculator. Such an analysis can determine the amplitude, maximum, minimum, period, or phase shift of a trig function, or solve a trig equation or inequality.

The examples and exercises in this chapter show how a variety of trig problems can be solved without using a graphing calculator. They also explain how to solve trig equations and inequalities and how to analyze inverse trig functions.

Since the values of all the trigonometric functions repeat themselves at regular intervals, and, for some number p, $f(x) = f(x + p)$ for all numbers x, these functions are called *periodic functions*. The smallest positive value of p for which this property holds is called the *period* of the function.

The sine, cosine, secant, and cosecant have periods of 2π, and the tangent and cotangent have periods of π. The graphs of the six trigonometric functions, shown below, demonstrate that the tangent and cotangent repeat on intervals of length π and that the others repeat on intervals of length 2π.

The domain and range of each of the six trigonometric functions are summarized in the table.

PARENT TRIG FUNCTION

	DOMAIN	RANGE
sine	$(-\infty, \infty)$	$-1 \le \sin x \le 1$
cosine	$(-\infty, \infty)$	$-1 \le \cos x \le 1$
tangent	all real numbers except odd multiples of $\frac{\pi}{2}$	all real numbers
cotangent	all real numbers except all multiples of π	all real numbers
secant	all real numbers except odd multiples of $\frac{\pi}{2}$	$(-\infty, -1] \cup [1, \infty)$
cosecant	all real numbers except all multiples of π	$(-\infty, -1] \cup [1, \infty)$

TIP

The **frequency** of a trig function is the reciprocal of its period. Graphs of the parent trig functions follow.

Trig functions can be transformed just like any other function. They can be translated (slid) horizontally or vertically or dilated (stretched or shrunk) horizontally or vertically. The general form of a trigonometric function is $y = A \bullet \text{trig}(Bx + C) + D$, where trig stands for sin, cos, tan, csc, sec, or cot. The parameters A and D accomplish vertical translation and dilation, while B and C accomplish horizontal translation and dilation. When working with trig functions, the vertical dilation results in the **amplitude**, whose value is $|A|$. If B is factored out of $Bx + C$ we get $B\left(x + \frac{C}{B}\right)$. The horizontal translation is $-\frac{C}{B}$ and is called the **phase shift**, and the horizontal dilation of trig functions is measured as the **period**, which is the period of the parent trig function divided by B. Finally, D is the amount of vertical translation.

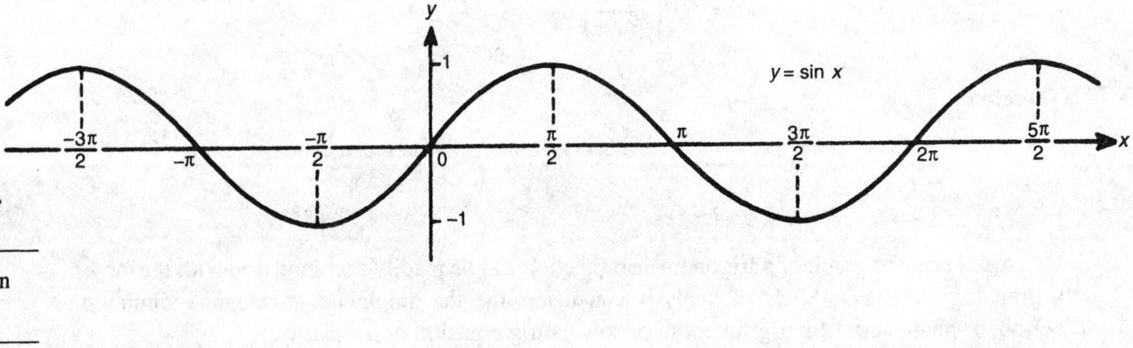

TIP

Note: sin x is an odd function.

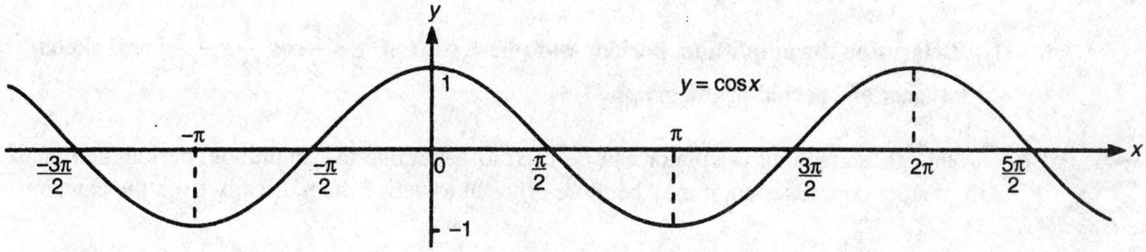

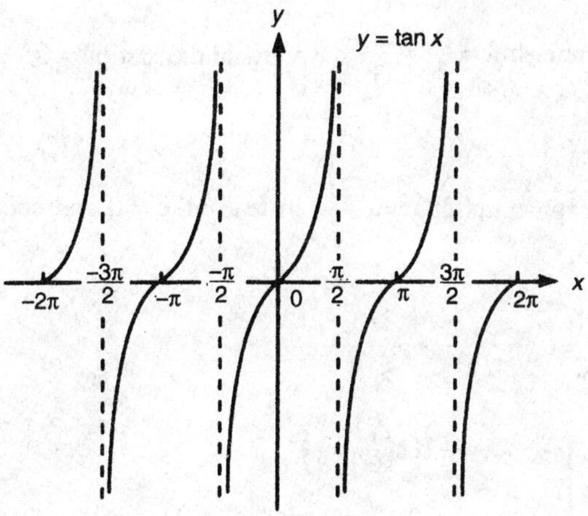

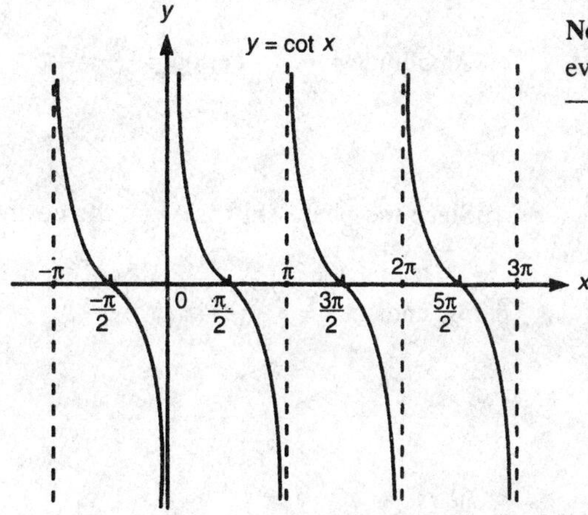

TIP

Note: cos x is an even function.

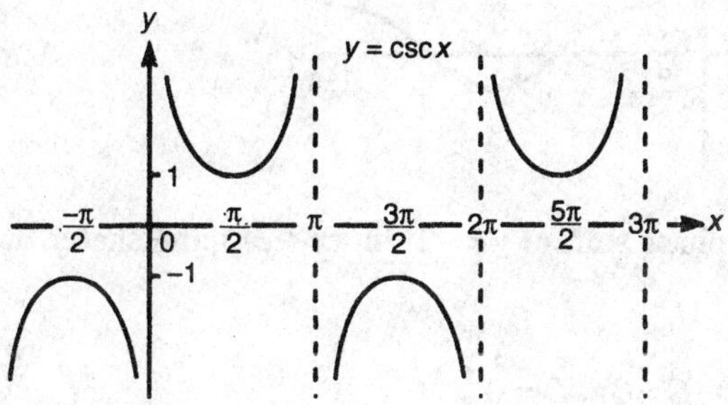

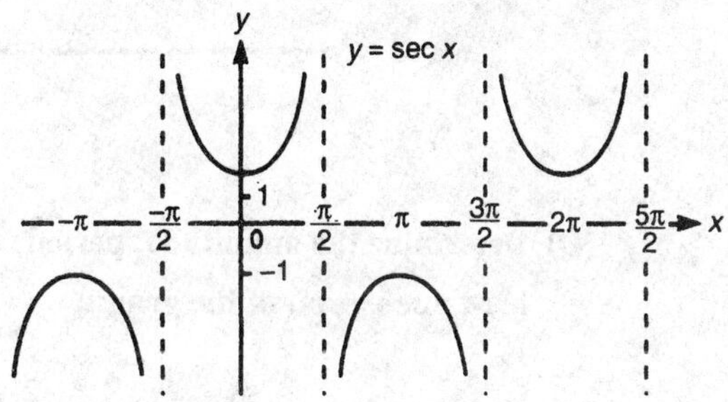

Examples

(M) Determine the amplitude, period, and phase shift of $y = 2\sin 2x$ and sketch at least one period of the graph.

$$A = 2, B = 2, C = 0, D = 0$$

Amplitude = 2 Period = $\frac{2\pi}{2} = \pi$ Phase shift = 0 Vertical translation = 0

Since the phase shift is zero, the sine graph starts at its normal position, (0,0), and is drawn out to the right and to the left.

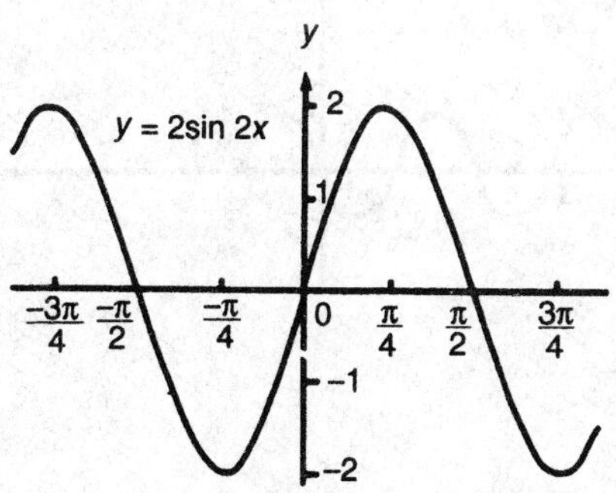

(N) **Determine the amplitude, period, and phase shift of $y = \frac{1}{2}\cos\left(\frac{1}{2}x - \frac{\pi}{3}\right)$ and sketch at least one period of the graph.**

Although a graphing calculator can be used to determine the amplitude, period, and phase shift of a periodic function, it may be more efficient to derive them directly from the equation.

$$A = \frac{1}{2}, B = \frac{1}{2}, C = \frac{-\pi}{3}, D = 0$$

Amplitude $= \frac{1}{2}$ Period $= \frac{2\pi}{\frac{1}{2}} = 4\pi$ Phase shift $= \frac{\frac{\pi}{3}}{\frac{1}{2}} = \frac{2\pi}{3}$ Vertical translation = 0

Since the phase shift is $\frac{2\pi}{3}$, the cosine graph starts at $x = \frac{2\pi}{3}$ instead of $x = 0$ and one period ends at $x = \frac{2\pi}{3} + 4\pi$ or $\frac{14\pi}{3}$.

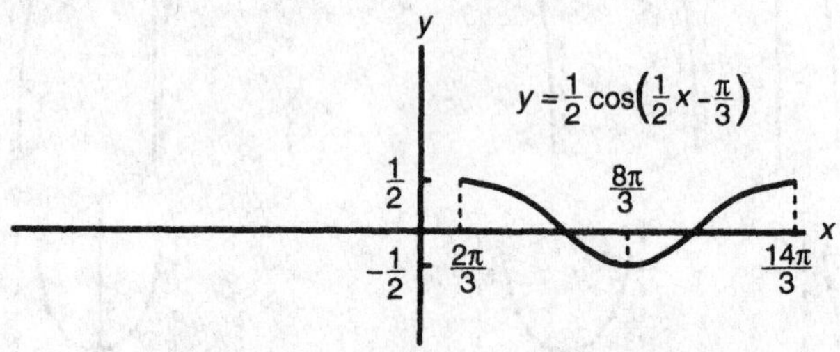

(O) **Determine the amplitude, period, and phase shift of $y = -2\sin(\pi x + 3\pi)$ and sketch at least one period of the graph.**

$$A = -2, B = \pi, C = 3\pi, D = 0$$

Amplitude = 2 Period $= \frac{2\pi}{\pi} = 2$

Phase shift $= -\frac{3\pi}{\pi} = -3$

Since the phase shift is –3, the sine graph starts at $x = -3$ instead of $x = 0$, and one period ends at $-3 + 2$ or $x = -1$. The graph can continue to the right and to the left for as many periods as desired. Since the coefficient of the sine is negative, the graph starts down as x increases from –3, instead of up as a normal sine graph does.

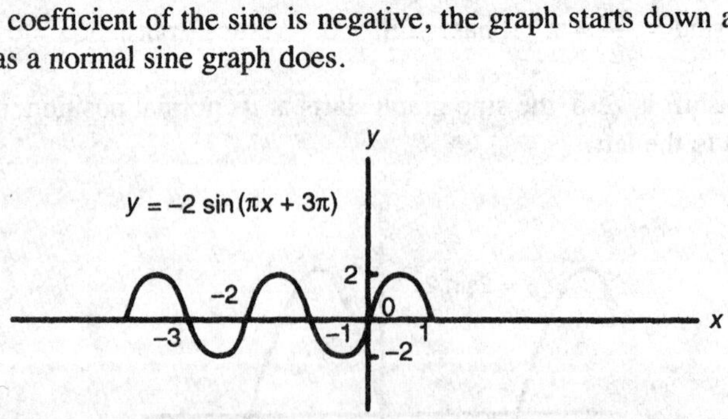

There are a few trigonometric identities you must know for the Mathematics Level 2 Subject Test.

- **Reciprocal Identities** recognize the definitional relationships:

$$\csc x = \frac{1}{\sin x} \qquad \sec x = \frac{1}{\cos x} \qquad \cot x = \frac{1}{\tan x}$$

- **Cofunction Identities** were discussed earlier. Using radian measure:

$$\sin x = \cos\left(\frac{\pi}{2} - x\right) \text{ and } \cos x = \sin\left(\frac{\pi}{2} - x\right)$$

$$\sec x = \csc\left(\frac{\pi}{2} - x\right) \text{ and } \csc x = \sec\left(\frac{\pi}{2} - x\right)$$

$$\tan x = \cot\left(\frac{\pi}{2} - x\right) \text{ and } \cot x = \tan\left(\frac{\pi}{2} - x\right)$$

- **Pythagorean Identities**

$$\sin^2 x + \cos^2 x = 1 \qquad \sec^2 x = 1 + \tan^2 x \qquad \csc^2 x = 1 + \cot^2 x$$

- **Double Angle Formulas**

$$\sin 2x = 2(\sin x)(\cos x) \qquad \cos 2x = \cos^2 x - \sin^2 x$$
$$= 2\cos^2 x - 1$$
$$= 1 - 2\sin^2 x$$

Examples

(P) Given $\cos\theta = -\frac{2}{3}$ and $\frac{\pi}{2} < \theta < \pi$, find $\sin 2\theta$.

Since $\sin 2\theta = 2(\sin\theta)(\cos\theta)$, you need to determine the value of $\sin\theta$. From the figure below, you can see that $\sin\theta = \frac{\sqrt{5}}{3}$. Therefore, $\sin 2\theta = 2\frac{\sqrt{5}}{3}\left(-\frac{2}{3}\right) = -\frac{4}{9}\sqrt{5}$.

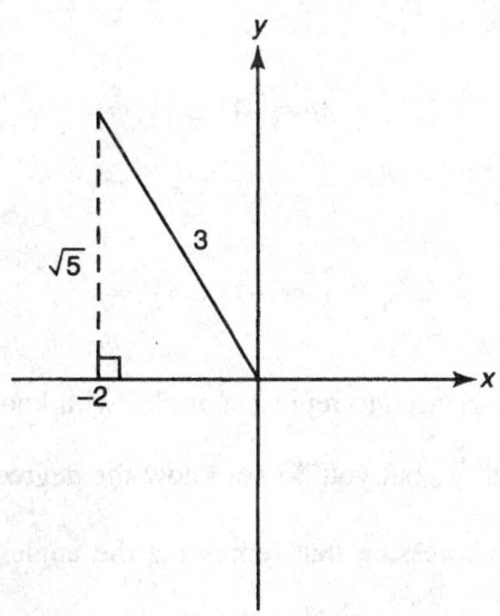

(Q) If $\cos 23° = z$, find the value of $\cos 46°$ in terms of z.

Since 46 = 2(23), a double angle formula can be used: $\cos 2A = 2\cos^2 A - 1$. Substituting 23° for A, $\cos 46° = \cos 2(23°) = 2\cos^2 23° - 1 = 2(\cos 23°)^2 - 1 = 2z^2 - 1$.

(R) If $\sin x = A$, find $\cos 2x$ in terms of A.

Using the identity $\cos 2x = 1 - 2\sin^2 x$, you get $\cos 2x = 1 - 2A^2$.

You may be expected to solve trigonometric equations on the Math Level 2 Subject Test by using your graphing calculator and getting answers that are decimal approximations. To solve any equation, enter each side of the equation into a function (Y_n), graph both functions, and find the point(s) of intersection on the indicated domain by choosing an appropriate window.

(S) Solve $2\sin x + \cos 2x = 2\sin^2 x - 1$ for $0 \le x \le 2\pi$.

Enter $2\sin x + \cos 2x$ into Y_1 and $2\sin^2 x - 1$ into Y_2. Set Xmin = 0, Xmax = 2π, Ymin = –4, and Ymax = 4. Solutions (x-coordinates of intersection points) are 1.57, 3.67, and 5.76.

(T) Find values of x on the interval $[0,\pi]$ for which $\cos x < \sin 2x$.

Enter each side of the inequality into a function, graph both, and find the values of x where the graph of $\cos x$ lies beneath the graph of $\sin 2x$: $0.52 < x < 1.57$ or $2.62 < x < 3.14$.

If the graph of any trig function $f(x)$ is reflected about the line $y = x$, the graph of the inverse (relation) of that trig function is the result. Since all trig functions are periodic, graphs of their inverses are not graphs of functions. The domain of a trig function needs to be limited to one period so that range values are achieved exactly once. The inverse of the restricted sine function is $\sin^{-1}$; the inverse of the restricted cosine function is $\cos^{-1}$, and so forth.

Inverse Trig Function	Domain	Range
$\sin^{-1}$	$[-1, 1]$	$\left[-\frac{\pi}{2}, \frac{\pi}{2}\right]$
$\cos^{-1}$	$[-1, 1]$	$[0, \pi]$
$\tan^{-1}$	$(-\infty, \infty)$	$\left(-\frac{\pi}{2}, \frac{\pi}{2}\right)$
$\cot^{-1}$	$(-\infty, \infty)$	$(0, \pi)$
$\sec^{-1}$	$(-\infty, -1] \cup [1, \infty)$	$\left[0, \frac{\pi}{2}\right) \cup \left(\frac{\pi}{2}, \pi\right]$
$\csc^{-1}$	$(-\infty, -1] \cup [1, \infty)$	$\left[-\frac{\pi}{2}, 0\right) \cup \left(0, \frac{\pi}{2}\right]$

The inverse trig functions are used to represent angles with known trig values. If you know that the tangent of an angle is $\frac{8}{9}$, but you do not know the degree measure or radian measure of the angle, $\tan^{-1}\frac{8}{9}$ is an expression that represents the angle between $\frac{-\pi}{2}$ and $\frac{\pi}{2}$ whose tangent is $\frac{8}{9}$.

You can use your graphing calculator to find the degree or radian measure of an inverse trig value.

➡ Examples

(U) Evaluate the radian measure of $\tan^{-1}\frac{8}{9}$.

Enter 2nd tan $\left(\frac{8}{9}\right)$ with your calculator in radian mode to get 0.73 radian.

(V) Evaluate the degree measure of $\sin^{-1} 0.8759$.

Enter 2nd sin (0.8759) with your calculator in degree mode to get 61.15°.

(W) Evaluate the degree measure of $\sec^{-1} 3.4735$.

First define $x = \sec^{-1} 3.4735$. If $\sec x = 3.4735$, then $\cos x = \frac{1}{3.4735}$. Therefore, enter 2nd

cos $\left(\frac{1}{3.4735}\right)$ with your calculator in degree mode to get 73.27°.

If "trig" is any trigonometric function, $\text{trig}(\text{trig}^{-1}x) = x$. However, because of the range restriction on inverse trig functions, $\text{trig}^{-1}(\text{trig}\ x)$ need *not* equal x.

(X) Evaluate $\cos(\cos^{-1} 0.72)$.

$\cos(\cos^{-1} 0.72) = 0.72$.

(Y) Evaluate $\sin^{-1}(\sin 265°)$.

Enter 2nd $\sin^{-1}(\sin(265))$ with your calculator in degree mode to get –85°. This is because –85° is in the required range [–90°,90°], and –85° has the same reference angle as 265°.

(Z) Evaluate $\sin\left(\cos^{-1}\frac{3}{5}\right)$.

Let $x = \cos^{-1}\frac{3}{5}$. Then $\cos x = \frac{3}{5}$ and x is in the first quadrant. See the figure below.

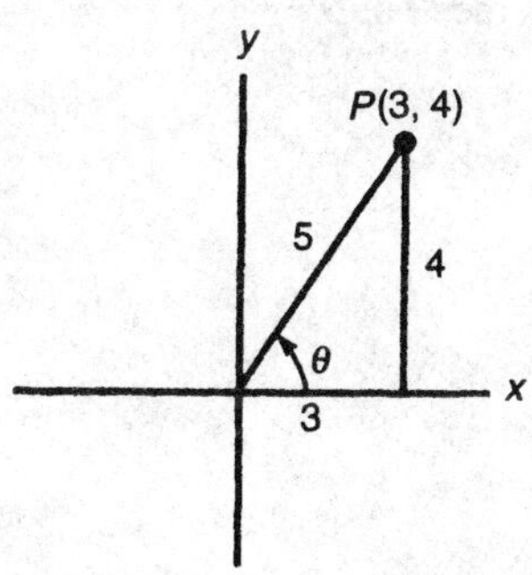

Use the Pythagorean identity $\sin^2 x + \cos^2 x = 1$ and the fact that x is in the first quadrant to

get $\sin x = \sqrt{1-\cos^2 x} = \sqrt{\frac{16}{25}} = \frac{4}{5}$.

(AA) Evaluate $\cot^{-1}(-5.2418)$.

Let $x = \cot^{-1}(-5.2418)$. Then $\cot x = -5.2418$ and $\tan x = -\frac{1}{5.2418}$. Enter $\tan^{-1}\left(-\frac{1}{5.2418}\right)$, and it will return -0.1885. This value is in the range of $\tan^{-1}\left(-\frac{\pi}{2},\frac{\pi}{2}\right)$, but it is not in the range of $\cot^{-1}(0,\pi)$, since $\cot x < 0$, x must be between $\frac{\pi}{2}$ and π and have the same reference angle as -0.1885. Therefore, $x = -0.1885 + \pi \approx 2.953$. This is not an issue with sine and cosecant because they have the same ranges, as do the cosine and secant. Thus, the calculator output for similar problems involving cosecant and secant would be correct.

EXERCISES 习题

1. Express cos 320° as a function of an angle between 0° and 90°.

   I. cos 40°
   II. sin 50°
   III. cos 50°

   (A) I only
   (B) II only
   (C) III only
   (D) I and II
   (E) II and III

2. If point $P(-5,12)$ lies on the terminal side of $\angle\theta$ in standard position, $\sin\theta =$

   (A) $-\frac{12}{13}$
   (B) $\frac{-5}{12}$
   (C) $\frac{-5}{13}$
   (D) $\frac{12}{13}$
   (E) $\frac{12}{5}$

3. If $\sec\theta = -\frac{5}{4}$ and $\sin\theta > 0$, then $\tan\theta =$

   (A) $\frac{4}{3}$
   (B) $\frac{3}{4}$
   (C) $-\frac{3}{4}$
   (D) $-\frac{4}{3}$
   (E) none of the above

4. If x is an angle in quadrant III and $\tan(x - 30°) = \cot x$, find x.

(A) 240°
(B) 225°
(C) 210°
(D) 60°
(E) none of the above

5. If $90° < \alpha < 180°$ and $270° < \beta < 360°$, then which of the following *cannot* be true?

(A) $\sin \alpha = \sin \beta$
(B) $\tan \alpha = \sin \beta$
(C) $\tan \alpha = \tan \beta$
(D) $\sin \alpha = \cos \beta$
(E) $\sec \alpha = \csc \beta$

6. Expressed as a function of an acute angle, $\cos 310° =$

(A) $-\sin 50°$
(B) $-\sin 40°$
(C) $-\cos 50°$
(D) $\cos 40°$
(E) $\cos 50°$

7. An angle of 30 radians is equal to how many degrees?

(A) $\frac{\pi}{30}$
(B) $\frac{\pi}{6}$
(C) $\frac{30}{\pi}$
(D) $\frac{540}{\pi}$
(E) $\frac{5,400}{\pi}$

8. If a sector of a circle has an arc length of 2π inches and an area of 6π square inches, what is the length of the radius of the circle?

(A) 1
(B) 2
(C) 3
(D) 6
(E) 12

9. If a circle has a circumference of 16 inches, the area of a sector with a central angle of 4.7 radians is

(A) 10
(B) 12
(C) 15
(D) 25
(E) 48

10. A central angle of 40° in a circle of radius 1 inch intercepts an arc whose length is s. Find s.

(A) 0.7
(B) 1.4
(C) 2.0
(D) 3.0
(E) 40

11. The pendulum on a clock swings through an angle of 25°, and the tip sweeps out an arc of 12 inches. How long is the pendulum?

(A) 1.67 inches
(B) 13.8 inches
(C) 27.5 inches
(D) 43.2 inches
(E) 86.4 inches

12. In the figure below, part of the graph of $y = \sin 2x$ is shown. What are the coordinates of point P?

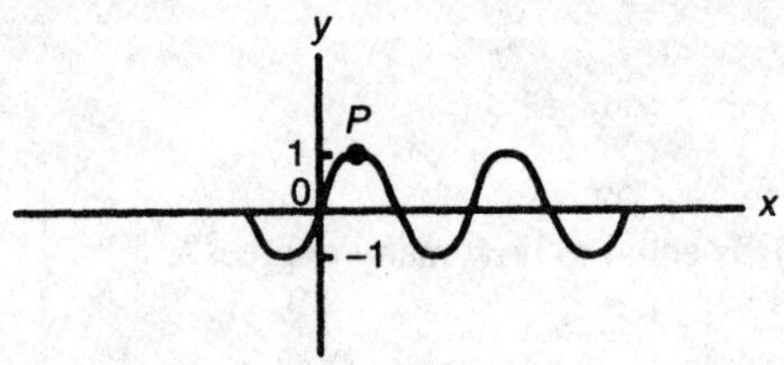

(A) $\left(\frac{\pi}{2}, 1\right)$
(B) $(\pi, 1)$
(C) $\left(\frac{\pi}{4}, 1\right)$
(D) $\left(\frac{\pi}{2}, 2\right)$
(E) $(\pi, 2)$

13. The figure below could be a portion of the graph whose equation is

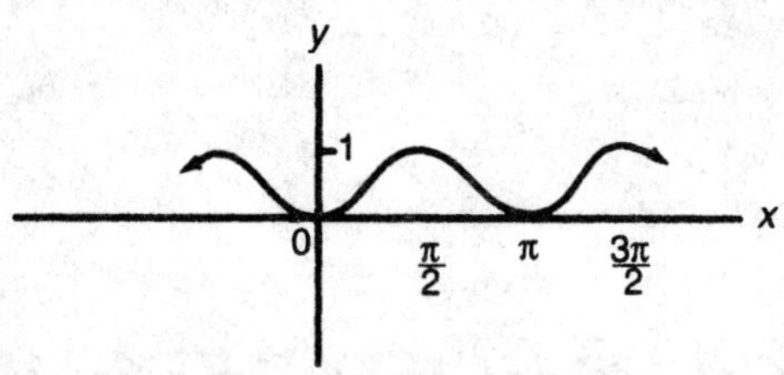

(A) $y - 1 = \sin x \bullet \cos x$
(B) $y \sec x = 1$
(C) $2y + 1 = \sin 2x$
(D) $2y + 1 = \cos 2x$
(E) $1 - 2y = \cos 2x$

14. As θ increases from $\frac{\pi}{4}$ to $\frac{5\pi}{4}$, the value of $4\cos\frac{1}{2}\theta$

(A) increases, and then decreases
(B) decreases, and then increases
(C) decreases throughout
(D) increases throughout
(E) decreases, increases, and then decreases again

15. The function $f(x) = \sqrt{3}\cos x + \sin x$ has an amplitude of

(A) 1.37
(B) 1.73
(C) 2
(D) 2.73
(E) 3.46

16. For what value of P is the period of the function $y = \frac{1}{3}\cos Px$ equal to $\frac{2\pi}{3}$?

(A) $\frac{1}{3}$
(B) $\frac{2}{3}$
(C) 2
(D) 3
(E) 6

17. If $0 \le x \le \frac{\pi}{2}$, what is the maximum value of the function $f(x) = \sin\frac{1}{3}x$?

(A) 0
(B) $\frac{1}{3}$
(C) $\frac{1}{2}$
(D) $\frac{\sqrt{3}}{2}$
(E) 1

18. If the graph in the figure below has an equation of the form $y = \sin(Mx + N)$, what is the value of N?

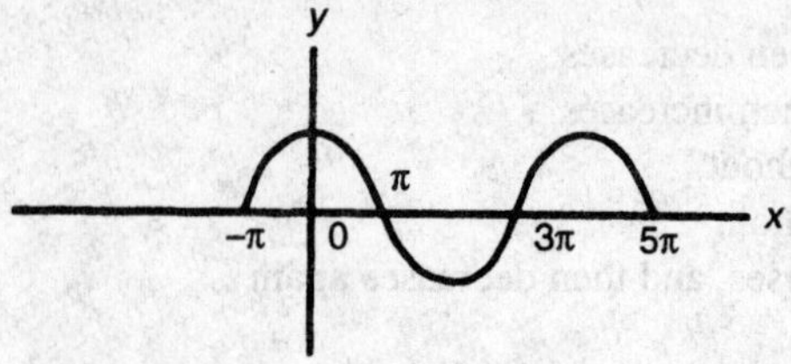

(A) $-\pi$
(B) -1
(C) $-\frac{1}{2}$
(D) $\frac{\pi}{2}$
(E) π

19. If $\sin x = \frac{5}{13}$ and $\cos x = -\frac{12}{13}$, find the value of $\sin 2x$.

(A) $-\frac{120}{169}$
(B) $-\frac{60}{169}$
(C) $\frac{60}{169}$
(D) $\frac{120}{169}$
(E) $\frac{10}{13}$

20. If $\tan A = \cot B$ and angles A and B are acute, then

(A) $A = B$
(B) $A = 90° + B$
(C) $B = 90° + A$
(D) $A + B = 90°$
(E) $A + B = 180°$

21. If $\cos x = \frac{\sqrt{3}}{2}$, find $\cos 2x$.

(A) -0.87
(B) -0.25
(C) 0
(D) 0.5
(E) 0.75

22. If $\sin 37° = z$, express $\sin 74°$ in terms of z.

(A) $2z\sqrt{1-z^2}$
(B) $2z^2 + 1$
(C) $2z$
(D) $2z^2 - 1$
(E) $\dfrac{z}{\sqrt{1-z^2}}$

23. If $\sin x = -0.6427$, what is $\csc x$?

(A) –1.64
(B) –1.56
(C) 0.64
(D) 1.56
(E) 1.70

24. For what value(s) of x, $0 < x < \dfrac{\pi}{2}$, is $\sin x < \cos x$?

(A) $x < 0.79$
(B) $x < 0.52$
(C) $0.52 < x < 0.79$
(D) $x > 0.52$
(E) $x > 0.79$

25. What is the range of the function $f(x) = 5 - 6\sin(\pi x + 1)$?

(A) [–6,6]
(B) [–5,5]
(C) [–1,1]
(D) [–1,11]
(E) [–11,1]

26. Find the number of degrees in $\sin^{-1}\dfrac{\sqrt{2}}{2}$.

(A) –45
(B) –22.5
(C) 0
(D) 22.5
(E) 45

27. Find the number of radians in $\cos^{-1}(-0.5624)$.

(A) –0.97
(B) 0.97
(C) 1.77
(D) 2.17
(E) none of the above

28. Evaluate $\tan^{-1}(\tan 128°)$.

(A) –128°
(B) –52°
(C) 52°
(D) 128°
(E) none of the above

29. Which of the following is (are) true?

I. $\sin^{-1}1 + \sin^{-1}(-1) = 0$
II. $\cos^{-1}1 + \cos^{-1}(-1) = 0$
III. $\cos^{-1}x = \cos^{-1}(-x)$ for all x in the domain of $\cos^{-1}$

(A) only I
(B) only II
(C) only III
(D) only I and II
(E) only II and III

30. Which of the following is a solution of $\cos 3x = \frac{1}{2}$?

(A) 60°

(B) $\frac{5\pi}{3}$

(C) $\cos^{-1}\left(\frac{1}{6}\right)$

(D) $\cos^{-1}\left(\frac{\sqrt{3}}{2}\right)$

(E) $\frac{1}{3}\cos^{-1}\left(\frac{1}{2}\right)$

Answers Explained 答案解析

1. **(D)** Since the reference angle is 40° and cosine in quadrant IV is positive, I is correct. Since $\sin\theta = \cos(90° - \theta)$, II is also correct.

2. **(D)** See corresponding figure. Therefore, $\sin\theta = \frac{12}{13}$.

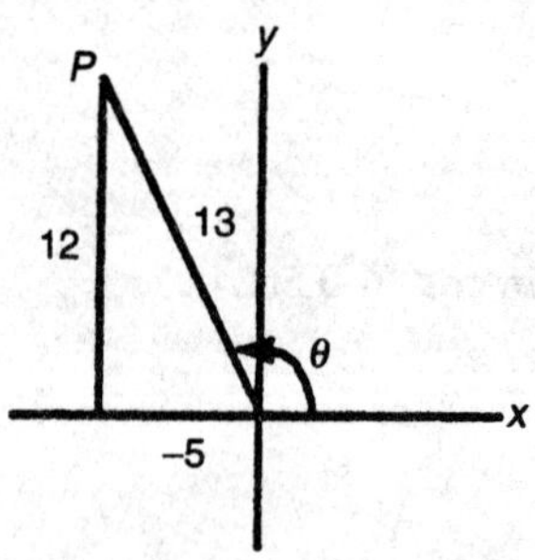

3. **(C)** Angle θ is in quadrant II since sec < 0 and sin > 0. Therefore, $\tan\theta = \frac{3}{-4} = -\frac{3}{4}$.

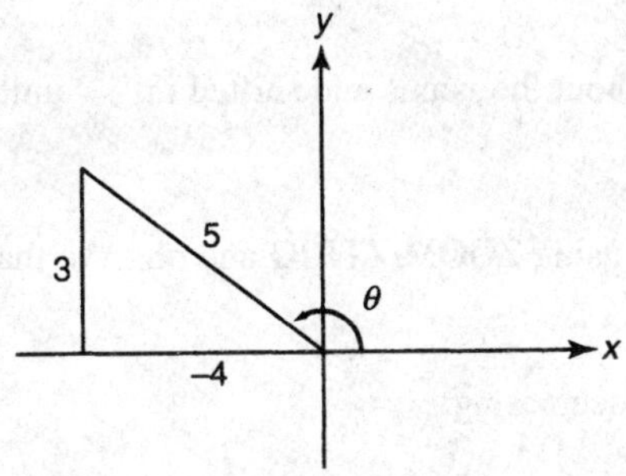

4. **(A)** Cofunctions of complementary angles are equal. $x - 30 + x = 90$ finds a reference angle of 60° for x. The angle in quadrant III that has a reference angle of 60° is 240°.

5. **(A)** Angle α is in quadrant II, and $\sin\alpha$ is positive. Angle β is in quadrant IV, and $\sin\beta$ is negative.

6. **(E)** The reference angle for the fourth quarter angle of 310° is 50°. Since the cosine of a fourth quarter angle is positive, cos 310° = cos 50°.

7. **(E)** $30\left(\frac{180°}{\pi}\right) = \frac{5{,}400°}{\pi}$.

8. **(D)** $s = r\theta$. $2\pi = r\theta$. $A = \frac{1}{2}r^2\theta$.

$6\pi = \frac{1}{2}r^2\theta = \frac{1}{2}r(r\theta) = \frac{1}{2}r(2\pi)$. $r = 6$.

9. **(C)** $C = 2\pi r = 16. r = \frac{8}{\pi} \approx 2.55$.

$A = \frac{1}{2}r^2\theta \approx \frac{1}{2}(2.55)^2(4.7) \approx 15$.

* 10. **(A)** $40° = \frac{2\pi}{9} \approx 0.7$

$s = r\theta \approx 1(0.7) \approx 0.7$.

* 11. **(C)** Change 25° to 0.436 radian $\left(0.436 = 25\left(\frac{\pi}{180}\right)\right)$.

$s = r\theta$, and so $12 = r(0.436)$ and $r = 27.5$ inches.

12. **(C)** Period $= \frac{2\pi}{2} = \pi$. Point P is $\frac{1}{4}$ of the way through the period. Amplitude is 1

because the coefficient of sin is 1. Therefore, point P is at $\left(\frac{\pi}{4}, 1\right)$.

13. **(E)** Amplitude = $\frac{1}{2}$. Period = π. Graph translated $\frac{1}{2}$ unit up. Graph looks like a cosine graph reflected about the x-axis and shifted up $\frac{1}{2}$ unit.

* 14. **(C)** Graph $4\cos\left(\frac{1}{2}x\right)$ using ZOOM/ZTRIG and observe that the portion of the graph between $\frac{\pi}{4}$ and $\frac{5\pi}{4}$ is decreasing.

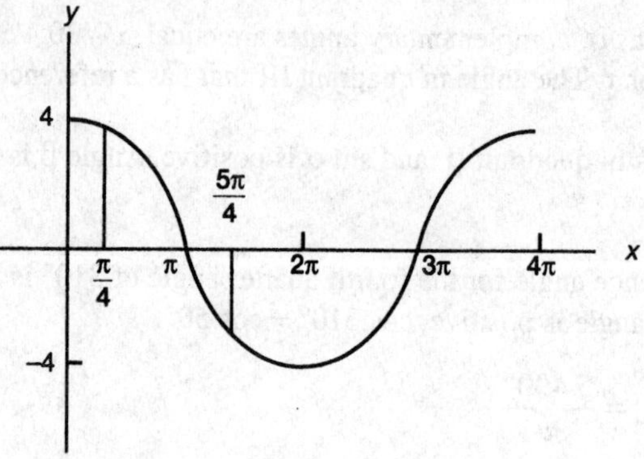

* 15. **(C)** Graph the function and determine its maximum (2) and minimum (–2). Subtract and then divide by 2.

16. **(D)** Period = $\frac{2\pi}{P} = \frac{2\pi}{3}$.

* 17. **(C)** Graph the function using 0 for Xmin and $\frac{\pi}{2}$ for Xmax. Observe that the maximum occurs when $x = \frac{\pi}{2}$. Then $f\left(\frac{\pi}{2}\right) = \sin\frac{\pi}{6} = \frac{1}{2}$.

18. **(D)** Period = $\frac{2\pi}{M} = 4\pi$ (from the figure), so $M = \frac{1}{2}$. Phase shift for a sine curve in the figure is $-\pi$. Therefore, $\frac{1}{2}x + N = 0$ when $x = -\pi$. Therefore, $N = \frac{\pi}{2}$.

* 19. **(A)** $\sin 2x = 2\sin x\cos x = 2\left(\frac{5}{13}\right)\left(-\frac{12}{13}\right) = -\frac{120}{169}$.

20. **(D)** Since tangent and cotangent are cofunctions, $\tan A = \cot(90° - A)$, so $B = 90° - A$, and $A + B = 90°$.

∗ 21. **(D)** $\cos 2x = 2\cos^2 x - 1 = 2\left(\frac{\sqrt{3}}{2}\right)^2 - 1 = \frac{1}{2}$ or 0.5.

22. **(A)** sin 74° = 2 sin 37° cos 37°. Since $\sin^2 z + \cos^2 z = 1$, $\cos z = \pm\sqrt{1-\sin^2 z}$, and 74° is in the first quadrant, the positive square root applies, so $\cos z = \sqrt{1-z^2}$. Therefore, $\sin 74° = 2 \sin 37° \sqrt{1-\sin^2 37°} = 2z\sqrt{1-z^2}$.

∗ 23. **(B)** $\csc x = \frac{1}{\sin x} = \frac{1}{-0.6427} = -1.56$.

∗ 24. **(A)** Graph $y = \sin x$ and $y = \cos x$ in radian mode using the Xmin = 0 and Xmax = $\frac{\pi}{2}$.

Observe that the first graph is beneath the second on [0,0.79].

25. **(D)** Remember that the range of the sine function is [–1,1], so the second term ranges from 6 to –6. This fact results in a range from 5 – 6 = –1 to 5 – (–6) = 11.

∗ 26. **(E)** Set your calculator to degree mode, and enter 2nd $\sin^{-1}\left(\sqrt{2}/2\right)$.

∗ 27. **(D)** Set your calculator to radian mode, and enter 2nd $\cos^{-1}(-0.5624)$.

∗ 28. **(B)** Set your calculator to degree mode, and enter 2nd $\tan^{-1}(\tan 128°)$.

29. **(A)** Since $\sin^{-1} 1 = \frac{\pi}{2}$ and $\sin^{-1}(-1) = -\frac{\pi}{2}$, I is true. Since $\cos^{-1} 1 = 0$ and $\cos^{-1}(-1) = \pi$, II is not true. Since the range of $\cos^{-1}$ is $[0,\pi]$, III is not true because $\cos^{-1}$ can never be negative.

30. **(E)** $3x = \arccos\left(\frac{1}{2}\right)$, and so $x = \frac{1}{3}\arccos\left(\frac{1}{2}\right)$.

Exponential and Logarithmic Functions 8
第8章　指数函数与对数函数

- → **DEFINITIONS**
- → **PROPERTIES**
- → **ANALYSIS OF GRAPHS**

Exponential functions are of the form $y = a^x$, where $a > 0$ and $a \neq 1$. The inverse $x = a^y$ is obtained by interchanging x and y. Begin this statement with y and it reads, "y is the power of a that makes x," or $y = \log_a x$. In other words, $\log_a$ is an abbreviation for the phrase, "the power of a that makes."

The basic exponential properties:

For all positive real numbers x and y, and all real numbers a and b:

$$x^a \cdot x^b = x^{a+b} \qquad x^0 = 1$$

$$\frac{x^a}{x^b} = x^{a-b} \qquad x^{-a} = \frac{1}{x^a}$$

$$(x^a)^b = x^{ab} \qquad x^a \cdot y^a = (xy)^a$$

The basic logarithmic properties:

For all positive real numbers a, b, p, and q, and all real numbers x, where $a \neq 1$ and $b \neq 1$:

$$\log_b(p \cdot q) = \log_b p + \log_b q \qquad \log_b 1 = 0 \qquad b^{\log_b p} = p$$

$$\log_b\left(\frac{p}{q}\right) = \log_b p - \log_b q \qquad \log_b b = 1$$

$$\log_b(p^x) = x \cdot \log_b p \qquad \log_b p = \frac{\log_a p}{\log_a b} \text{ (Change-of-Base Formula)}$$

➡ Examples

(A) Simplify $x^{n-1} \cdot x^{2n} \cdot (x^{2-n})^2$

This is equal to $x^{n-1} \cdot x^{2n} \cdot x^{4-2n} = x^{n-1+2n+4-2n} = x^{n+3}$.

TIP

$\log_b N$ is only defined for positive N.

(B) Simplify $\dfrac{3^{n-2} \cdot 9^{2-n}}{3^{2-n}}$.

In order to combine exponents using the properties above, the base of each factor must be the same.

$$\frac{3^{n-2} \cdot 9^{2-n}}{3^{2-n}} = \frac{3^{n-2} \cdot (3^2)^{2-n}}{3^{2-n}} = \frac{3^{n-2} \cdot 3^{4-2n}}{3^{2-n}}$$

$$= 3^{n-2+4-2n-(2-n)} = 3^0 = 1$$

(C) If $\log 23 = z$, find the value of $\log 2{,}300$ in terms of z.

$\log 2300 = \log(23 \cdot 100) = \log 23 + \log 100 = z + \log 10^2 = z + 2$

(D) If $\ln 2 = x$ and $\ln 3 = y$, find the value of $\ln 18$ in terms of x and y.

$\ln 18 = \ln(3^2 \cdot 2) = \ln 2 + 2\ln 3 = x + 2y$

(E) Solve for x: $\log_b(x + 5) = \log_b x + \log_b 5$.

$\log_b x + \log_b 5 = \log_b (5x)$

Therefore, $\log(x + 5) = \log(5x)$, which is true only when:

$$x+5=5x$$
$$5=4x$$
$$x=\frac{5}{4}$$

(F) Evaluate $\log_{27}\sqrt{54} - \log_{27}\sqrt{6}$.

If you can enter base 27 into your calculator, enter the entire expression to get the answer $0.\bar{3}=\frac{1}{3}$. Otherwise, you can use the change-of-base formula to substitute $\frac{\log 54}{\log 27}$ for $\log_{27}\sqrt{54}$ and $\frac{\log\sqrt{6}}{\log 27}$ for $\log_{27}\sqrt{6}$. If you know your logarithms well, you can use properties to see that

$$\log_{27}\sqrt{54} - \log_{27}\sqrt{6} = \log_{27}\sqrt{\frac{54}{6}}$$
$$= \log_{27}3$$
$$= \frac{1}{3}$$

The graphs of all exponential functions $y = b^x$ have roughly the same shape and pass through point (0,1). If $b > 1$, the graph increases as x increases and approaches the x-axis as an asymptote as x decreases. The amount of curvature becomes greater as the value of b is made greater. If $0 < b < 1$, the graph increases as x decreases and approaches the x-axis as an asymptote as x increases. The amount of curvature becomes greater as the value of b is made closer to zero.

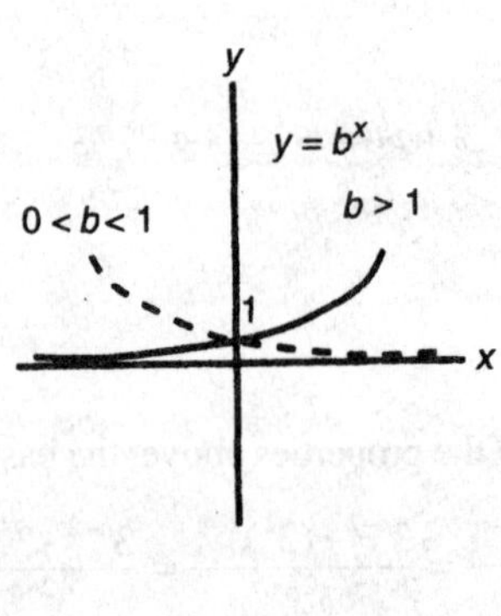

The graphs of all logarithmic functions $y = \log_b x$ have roughly the same shape and pass through point (1,0). If $b > 1$, the graph increases as x increases and approaches the y-axis as an asymptote as x approaches zero. The amount of curvature becomes greater as the value of b is made greater. If $0 < b < 1$, the graph decreases as x increases and approaches the y-axis as an asymptote as x approaches zero. The amount of curvature becomes greater as the value of b is made closer to zero.

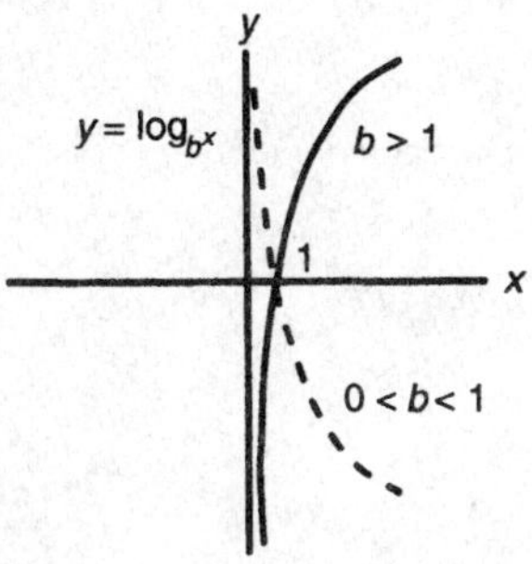

Two numbers serve as special bases of exponential functions. The number 10 is convenient as a base because integer powers of ten determine place values: for instance, $10^2 = 100$ and $10^{-3} = 0.001$. The inverse of 10^x is $\log_{10} x$. By convention, the base is not written when it is 10, so the inverse of 10^x is simply written as log 10. The other special base is the number $e \approx 2.718281828....$ This is a nonterminating and nonrepeating decimal. The inverse of e^x is $\log_e x$, which is further abbreviated $\ln x$, the **natural logarithm** of x. On the TI-84 graphing calculator, the command log will evaluate the logarithm with respect to any base by entering the value whose log is being sought followed by the base. Log base e (ln) can also be entered directly.

Exponential growth is an important application of exponential functions. Exponential growth reflects a constant rate of change from one time period to the next.

Examples

(G) The population of a certain city grows at 7% per year, and the current population is 100,000. What will the population of that city be in 10 years?

Each year, the population will grow by a factor of 1.07. Therefore, after 10 years the population will be $100{,}000(1.07)^{10} \approx 196{,}715$.

(H) A bond pays interest at a rate of 3% compounded annually. How long will it take an initial investment to double?

Each year, the investment grows by a factor of 1.03. Therefore, the growth factor after n years is 1.03^n. Since the investment doubles when its growth factor is 2, we need to solve the equation $1.03^n = 2$. Take the log of both sides to get $n\log 1.03 = \log 2$. It follows that $n = \dfrac{\log 2}{\log 1.03} \approx 23.45$ years.

EXERCISES 习题

1. If $x^a \cdot (x^{a+1})^a \cdot (x^a)^{1-a} = x^k$, then $k =$

   (A) $2a + 1$
   (B) $a + a^2$
   (C) $3a$
   (D) $3a + 1$
   (E) $a^3 + a$

2. If $\log_8 3 = x \cdot \log_2 3$, then $x =$

   (A) $\frac{1}{3}$
   (B) 3
   (C) 4
   (D) $\log_4 3$
   (E) $\log_8 9$

3. If $\log_{10} m = \frac{1}{2}$, then $\log_{10} 10m^2 =$

   (A) 2
   (B) 2.5
   (C) 3
   (D) 10.25
   (E) 100

4. If $\log_b 5 = a$, $\log_b 2.5 = c$, and $5^x = 2.5$, then $x =$

   (A) ac
   (B) $\frac{c}{a}$
   (C) $a + c$
   (D) $c - a$
   (E) The value of x cannot be determined from the information given.

5. If $f(x) = \log_2 x$, then $f\left(\frac{2}{x}\right) + f(x) =$

   (A) $\log_2\left(\frac{2}{x}\right) + \log_2 x$
   (B) 1
   (C) $\log_2\left(\frac{2 + x^2}{x}\right)$
   (D) $\log_2\left(\frac{2}{x}\right) \cdot \log_2 x$
   (E) 0

6. If $\ln(xy) < 0$, which of the following must be true?

(A) $xy < 0$
(B) $xy < 1$
(C) $xy > 1$
(D) $xy > 0$
(E) none of the above

7. If $\log_2 m = \sqrt{7}$ and $\log_7 n = \sqrt{2}$, $mn =$

(A) 1
(B) 2
(C) 96
(D) 98
(E) 103

8. $\text{Log}_7 5 =$

(A) 1.2
(B) 1.1
(C) 0.9
(D) 0.8
(E) – 0.7

9. $\left(\sqrt[3]{2}\right)\left(\sqrt[5]{4}\right)\left(\sqrt[9]{8}\right) =$

(A) 1.9
(B) 2.0
(C) 2.1
(D) 2.3
(E) 2.5

10. If \$300 is invested at 3%, compounded annually, how long (to the nearest year) will it take for the money to increase by 50%?

(A) 11
(B) 12
(C) 13
(D) 14
(E) 15

Answers Explained 答案解析

1. **(C)** $x^a \cdot x^{a^2+a} \cdot x^{a-a^2} = x^{a+a^2+a+a-a^2} = x^{3a}$.

2. **(A)** $x = \dfrac{\log_8 3}{\log_2 3} = \dfrac{\dfrac{\log 3}{\log 8}}{\dfrac{\log 3}{\log 2}} = \dfrac{\log 2}{3\log 2} = \dfrac{1}{3}$.

3. **(A)** $\log(10m^2) = \log 10 + 2\log m = 1 + 2 \cdot \dfrac{1}{2} = 2$.

4. **(B)** $b^a = 5, b^c = 2.5 = 5^x$, using the relationships between logs and exponents: $(b^a)^x = b^{ax} = 5^x = b^c$. Therefore, $ax = c$ and $x = \dfrac{c}{a}$.

5. **(B)** $f\left(\dfrac{2}{x}\right) + f(x) = \log_2\left(\dfrac{2}{x}\right) + \log_2 x$

$= \log_2 2 - \log_2 x + \log_2 x = 1$.

6. **(B)** Since ln stands for $\log_e$, and $e > 1$, $xy < 1$.

* 7. **(D)** Converting the log expressions to exponential expressions gives $m = 2^{\sqrt{7}}$ and $n = 7^{\sqrt{2}}$. Therefore, $mn = 2^{\sqrt{7}} \cdot 7^{\sqrt{2}} \approx 6.2582 \cdot 15.673 \approx 98$.

* 8. **(D)** $\log_7 5 = \dfrac{\log 5}{\log 7} \approx \dfrac{0.699}{0.845} \approx 0.8$.

* 9. **(C)** $\sqrt[3]{2}\sqrt[5]{4}\sqrt[9]{8} = 2^{1/3}4^{1/5}8^{1/9} \approx 2.1$.

* 10. **(D)** Each year, the investment grows by a factor of 1.03. The growth factor after n years is 1.03^n. If the investment grows by 50%, its growth factor must be 1.5. Therefore, $1.03^t = 1.5$. Then take the log of both sides to get $\log 1.5 = t \log 1.03$ so $t = \log 1.5/\log 1.03$. Use your calculator to find that, to the nearest year, $t = 14$.

Rational Functions
第9章 有理函数

9

- → DEFINITION
- → VERTICAL ASYMPTOTES
- → LIMIT/HORIZONTAL ASYMPTOTES

The function f is a rational function if and only if $f(x)=\dfrac{p(x)}{q(x)}$, where $p(x)$ and $q(x)$ are both polynomial functions and $q(x)$ is not zero. As a general rule, the graphs of rational functions are not continuous (i.e., they have holes, or sections of the graphs are separated from other sections by asymptotes). A point of discontinuity occurs at any value of x that would cause $q(x)$ to become zero.

If $p(x)$ and $q(x)$ can be factored so that $f(x)$ can be reduced, removing the factors that caused the discontinuities, the graph will contain only holes. If the factors that caused the discontinuities cannot be removed, asymptotes will occur.

TIP

If p and q are both 0 for some x, there is a hole at that x, but if q is 0 and p is not 0, an asymptote results.

Examples

(A) Sketch the graph of $f(x)=\dfrac{x^2-1}{x+1}$.

There is a discontinuity at $x = -1$ since this value would cause division by zero. The fraction $\dfrac{x^2-1}{x+1}=\dfrac{(x-1)(x+1)}{(x+1)}=(x-1)$, and so the graph of $f(x)$ is the same as the graph of $y = x - 1$ except for a hole at $x = -1$.

TIP

Don't count on seeing holes on a graphing calculator.

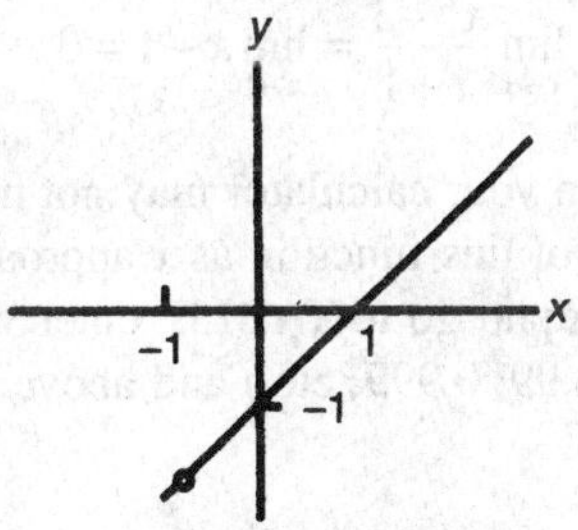

You could also enter this function on the graphing calculator and get the graph shown above, but it is unlikely that you would see the hole at (–1,0).

(B) Sketch the graph of $f(x)=\dfrac{1}{x-2}$.

Since this fraction cannot be reduced, and $x = 2$ would cause division by zero, a vertical asymptote occurs when $x = 2$. This is true because, as x approaches very close to 2, $f(x)$ gets either extremely large or extremely small. As x becomes extremely large or extremely small, $f(x)$ gets closer and closer to zero. This means that a horizontal asymptote occurs when $y = 0$. Plotting a few points indicates that the graph looks like the figure below.

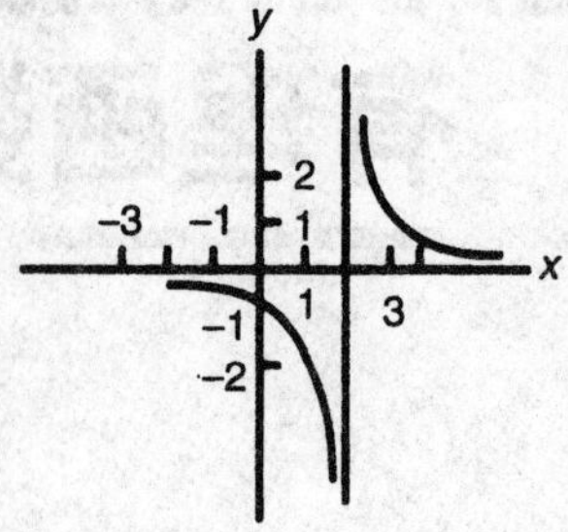

Vertical and horizontal asymptotes can also be described using limit notation. In this example you could write

$\lim_{x \to \pm\infty} f(x) = 0$ to mean $f(x)$ gets closer to 0 as x gets arbitrarily large or small

$\lim_{x \to 2^+} f(x) = \infty$ to mean $f(x)$ gets arbitrarily large as x approaches 2 from the right

$\lim_{x \to 2^-} f(x) = -\infty$ to mean $f(x)$ gets arbitrarily small as x approaches 2 from the left

If you entered this function into a TI-83 calculator, your graph will show what appears to be an asymptote. (Actually, the graphing calculator connects the pixel of the largest x-coordinate for which the y-coordinate is negative to the pixel of the smallest x-coordinate for which the y-pixel is positive.) The TI-84 calculators do not connect these two pixels. In either case, you can "read" the graph to determine the two infinite limits.

(C) What does $\lim_{x \to 1} \frac{x^2 - 1}{x + 1}$ equal?

Since $\frac{x^2 - 1}{x + 1}$ reduces to $x - 1$,

$$\lim_{x \to 1} \frac{x^2 - 1}{x + 1} = \lim_{x \to 1} x - 1 = 0$$

Although the window settings on your calculator may not make it possible to see the hole at $x = 1$, you can determine the limit of this function as x approaches 1 from both sides by using the table feature. Select Ask for Indpnt; go to TABLE; enter values of x that get progressively closer to 1 from below (e.g., 0.9, 0.99, 0.999, etc.) and above (e.g., 1.1, 1.01, 1.001, etc.); and watch y get closer to 1.

(D) What does $\lim_{x \to 2^+} 3x + 5$ equal?

Since "problems" occur only when division by zero appears imminent, this example is extremely easy. As x gets closer and closer to 2, $3x + 5$ seems to be approaching closer and closer to 11. Therefore, $\lim_{x \to 2^+} 3x + 5 = 11$.

(E) What does $\lim_{x\to 2}\left(\frac{3x^2+5}{x-2}\right)$ equal?

The numerator is always positive, so the graph of this rational function has a vertical asymptote. As x approaches 2 from the right (i.e., 2.1, 2.01, 2.001, . . .), the denominator approaches zero from the right so $\frac{3x^2+5}{x-2}$ gets larger and larger and approaches positive infinity. As x approaches 2 from the left (i.e., 1.9, 1.99, 1.999, . . .), the denominator approaches zero from the left so $\frac{3x^2+5}{x-2}$ gets smaller and smaller and approaches negative infinity. Thus, $\lim_{x\to 2^-}\frac{3x^2+5}{x-2}$ does not exist since $\lim_{x\to 2^-}\frac{3x^2+5}{x-2}=-\infty$ and $\lim_{x\to 2^+}\frac{3x^2+5}{x-2}=+\infty$.

As in the previous example, you could enter this function into your graphing calculator. Then, with an appropriate window, you could determine the infinite limits as x approaches 2 from the left and right.

(F) If $f(x)=\begin{cases}3x+2 & \text{when } x\neq 0\\ 0 & \text{when } x=0\end{cases}$, what does $\lim_{x\to 0}f(x)$ equal?

As x approaches zero, $3x+2$ approaches 2, in spite of the fact that $f(x)=0$ when $x=0$. Therefore, $\lim_{x\to 0}f(x)=2$.

(G) What does $\lim_{x\to\infty}\left(\frac{3x^2+4x+2}{2x^2+x-5}\right)$ equal?

As x gets larger and larger, the x^2 terms in the numerator and denominator "dominate" in the sense that the terms of lower degree become negligible. Therefore, the larger x gets, the more the rational function looks like $\frac{3x^2}{2x^2}=\frac{3}{2}$.

You can also see this by dividing each term of the numerator and denominator by x^2, the highest power of x.

$$\lim_{x\to\infty}\left(\frac{3x^2+4x+2}{2x^2+x-5}\right)=\lim_{x\to\infty}\left(\frac{3+\frac{4}{x}+\frac{2}{x^2}}{2+\frac{1}{x}-\frac{5}{x^2}}\right).$$

Now, as $x\to\infty, \frac{4}{x}, \frac{2}{x^2}, \frac{1}{x}$, and $\frac{5}{x^2}$, each approaches zero. Thus, the entire fraction approaches $\frac{3+0+0}{2+0-0}=\frac{3}{2}$. Therefore, $\lim_{x\to\infty}\left(\frac{3x^2+4x+2}{2x^2+x-5}\right)=\frac{3}{2}$.

To use a graphing calculator to find this limit, enter the function, and use the TABLE in Ask mode to enter larger and larger x values. The table will show y values closer and closer to 1.5.

EXERCISES 习题

1. To be continuous at $x = 1$, the value of $\frac{x^4 - 1}{x^3 - 1}$ must be defined to be equal to

   (A) –1
   (B) 0
   (C) 1
   (D) $\frac{4}{3}$
   (E) 4

2. If $f(x) = \begin{cases} \frac{3x^2 + 2x}{x} & \text{when } x \neq 0 \\ k & \text{when } x = 0 \end{cases}$, what must the value of k be equal to in order for $f(x)$ to be a continuous function?

   (A) $-\frac{3}{2}$
   (B) $-\frac{2}{3}$
   (C) 0
   (D) 2
   (E) No value of k can make $f(x)$ a continuous function.

3. $\lim_{x \to 2} \left(\frac{x^3 - 8}{x^4 - 16} \right) =$

   (A) 0
   (B) $\frac{3}{8}$
   (C) $\frac{1}{2}$
   (D) $\frac{4}{7}$
   (E) This expression is undefined.

4. $\lim_{x \to \infty} \left(\frac{5x^2 - 2}{3x^2 + 8} \right) =$

   (A) $-\frac{1}{4}$
   (B) 0
   (C) $\frac{3}{11}$
   (D) $\frac{5}{3}$
   (E) ∞

5. Which of the following is the equation of an asymptote of $y=\dfrac{3x^2-2x-1}{9x^2-1}$?

(A) $x=-\dfrac{1}{3}$

(B) $x=1$

(C) $y=-\dfrac{1}{3}$

(D) $y=\dfrac{1}{3}$

(E) $y=1$

Answers Explained 答案解析

All of these exercises can be completed with the aid of a graphing calculator as described in the example.

1. **(D)** Factor and reduce: $\dfrac{(x-1)(x+1)(x^2+1)}{(x-1)(x^2+x+1)}$. Substitute 1 for x and the fraction equals $\dfrac{4}{3}$.

2. **(D)** Factor and reduce the fraction, which becomes $3x+2$. As x approaches zero, this approaches 2.

3. **(B)** Factor and reduce $\dfrac{(x-2)(x^2+2x+4)}{(x-2)(x+2)(x^2+4)}$. Substitute 2 for x and the fraction equals $\dfrac{3}{8}$.

4. **(D)** Divide the numerator and the denominator through by x^2. As $x\to\infty$, the fraction approaches $\dfrac{5}{3}$.

5. **(D)** Factor and reduce $\dfrac{\cancel{(3x+1)}(x-1)}{\cancel{(3x+1)}(3x-1)}$. Therefore a vertical asymptote occurs when $3x-1=0$ or $x=\dfrac{1}{3}$, but this is not an answer choice. As $x\to\infty$, $y\to\dfrac{1}{3}$. Therefore, $y=\dfrac{1}{3}$ is the correct answer choice.

Parametric Equations
第10章 参数方程

10

- → **DEFINITIONS**
- → **ELIMINATING THE PARAMETER**

At times, it is convenient to express a relationship between x and y in terms of a third variable, usually denoted by a **parameter** t. For example, **parametric equations** $x = x(t)$, $y = y(t)$ can be used to locate a particle on the plane at various times t.

➥ Example

(A) Graph the parametric equations $\begin{cases} x = 3t + 4 \\ y = t - 5 \end{cases}$

Select MODE on your graphing calculator, and select PAR. Enter $3t + 4$ into $X1_T$ and $t - 5$ into $Y1_T$. The standard window uses 0 for Tmin and 6.28… (2π) for Tmax along with the usual ranges for x and y. The choice of 0 for Tmin reflects the interpretation of t as "time." With the standard window, the graph looks like the figure below.

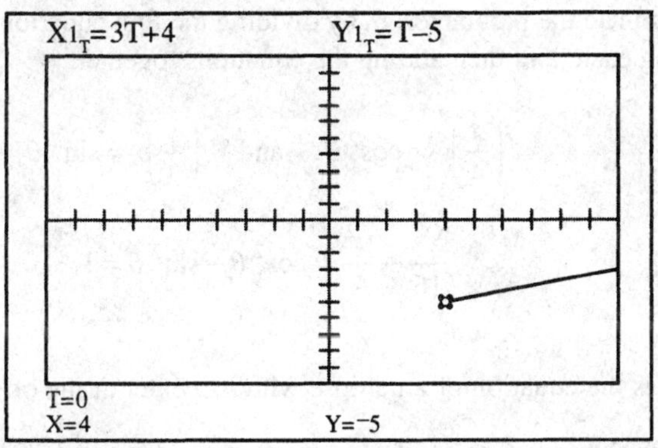

If you use TRACE, the cursor will begin at $t = 0$, where $(x,y) = (4,-5)$. As t increases from 0, the graph traces out a line that ascends as it moves right.

It may be possible to eliminate the parameter and to rewrite the equation in familiar xy-form. Just remember that the resulting equation may consist of points not on the graph of the original set of equations.

➥ Examples

(B) $\begin{cases} x = t^2 \\ y = 3t^2 + 1 \end{cases}$ **Eliminate the parameter and sketch the graph.**

Substituting x for t^2 in the second equation results in $y = 3x + 1$, which is the equation of a line with a slope of 3 and a y-intercept of 1. However, the original parametric equations indicate that $x \ge 0$ and $y \ge 1$ since t^2 cannot be negative. Thus, the proper way to indicate this set of points without the parameter is as follows: $y = 3x + 1$ and $x \geq 0$. The graph is the ray indicated in the figure.

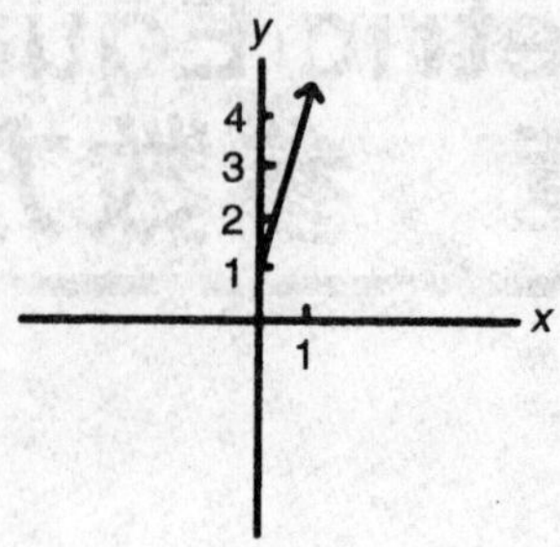

(C) Sketch the graph of the parametric equations $\begin{cases} x = 4\cos\theta \\ y = 3\sin\theta \end{cases}$

Replace the parameter θ with t, and enter the pair of equations. The graph has the shape of an ellipse, elongated horizontally, as shown in this diagram.

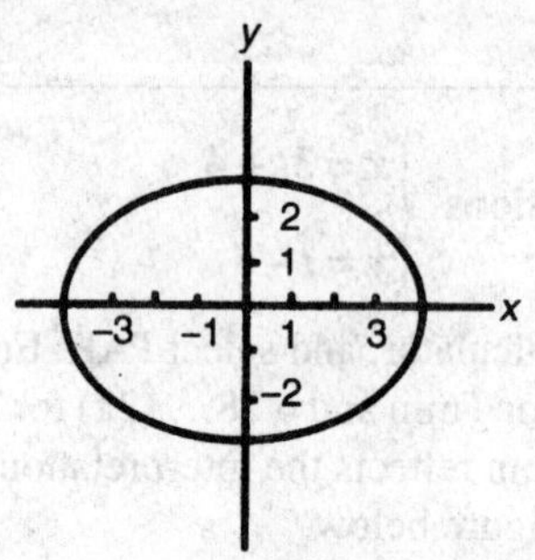

It is possible to eliminate the parameter, θ, by dividing the first equation by 4 and the second equation by 3, squaring each, and then adding the equations together.

$$\left(\frac{x}{4}\right)^2 = \cos^2\theta \quad \text{and} \quad \left(\frac{y}{3}\right)^2 = \sin^2\theta$$

$$\frac{x^2}{16} + \frac{y^2}{9} = \cos^2\theta + \sin^2\theta = 1$$

Here, $\frac{x^2}{16} + \frac{y^2}{9} = 1$ is the equation of an ellipse with its center at the origin, $a = 4$, and $b = 3$ (see Chapter 13). Since $-1 \leq \cos\theta \leq 1$ and $-1 \leq \sin\theta \leq 1$, $-4 \leq x \leq 4$ and $-3 \leq y \leq 3$ from the two parametric equations. In this case the parametric equations do not limit the graph obtained by removing the parameter.

EXERCISES 习题

1. In the graph of the parametric equations $\begin{cases} x = t^2 + t \\ y = t^2 - t \end{cases}$

(A) $x \geq 0$
(B) $x \geq -\dfrac{1}{4}$
(C) x is any real number
(D) $x \geq -1$
(E) $x \leq 1$

2. The graph of $\begin{cases} x = \sin^2 t \\ y = 2\cos t \end{cases}$ is a

(A) straight line
(B) line segment
(C) parabola
(D) portion of a parabola
(E) semicircle

3. Which of the following is (are) a pair of parametric equations that represent a circle?

I. $\begin{cases} x = \sin\theta \\ y = \cos\theta \end{cases}$

II. $\begin{cases} x = t \\ y = \sqrt{1 - t^2} \end{cases}$

III. $\begin{cases} x = \sqrt{s} \\ y = \sqrt{1 - s} \end{cases}$

(A) only I
(B) only II
(C) only III
(D) only II and III
(E) I, II, and III

Answers Explained 答案解析

* 1. **(B)** Graph these parametric equations for values of t between –5 and 5 and for x and y between –2.5 and 2.5.

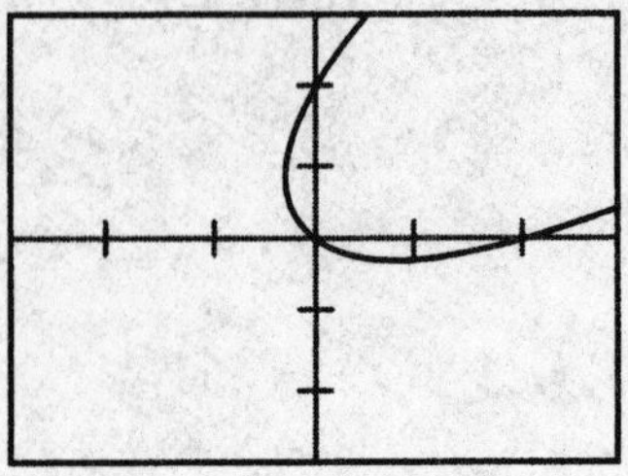

Apparently the x values are always greater than some value. Use the TRACE function to move the cursor as far left on the graph as it will go. This leads to a (correct) guess of $x \ge -\frac{1}{4}$. This can be verified by completing the square on the x equation:

$$x = \left(t^2 + t + \frac{1}{4}\right) - \frac{1}{4} = \left(t + \frac{1}{2}\right)^2 - \frac{1}{4}.$$

This represents a parabola that opens up with vertex at $\left(-\frac{1}{2}, -\frac{1}{4}\right)$. Therefore, $x \ge -\frac{1}{4}$.

* 2. **(D)** Put your calculator in parametric mode, and enter the equations for x and y. Key ZOOM 6 to get the standard window and ZOOM to zoom in. The image is part of a sideways parabola.

* 3. **(A)** You could graph all three parametric pairs to discover that only I gives a circle. (II and III give semicircles). You can also see this by a simple analysis of the equations. Removing the parameter in I by squaring and adding gives $x^2 + y^2 = 1$, which is a circle of radius 1. Substituting x for t in the y equation of II and squaring gives $x^2 + y^2 = 1$, but $y \ge 0$ so this is only a semicircle. Squaring and substituting x^2 for s in the y equation of III gives $x^2 + y^2 = 1$, but $x \ge 0$ and so this is only a semicircle.

Piecewise Functions
第11章 分段函数

11

- → **DEFINITIONS**
- → **ABSOLUTE VALUE FUNCTION**
- → **POSTAGE STAMP FUNCTION**

Piecewise functions are defined by different equations on different parts of their domain. These functions are useful in modeling behavior that exhibits more than one pattern.

➡ Example

(A) Graph the function $f(x) = \begin{cases} 3 - x^2 \text{ if } x < 1 \\ x^3 - 4x \text{ if } x \geq 1 \end{cases}$

You can graph this on your graphing calculator. The 2nd TEST command displays an equal sign and five inequality signs. These return the value 1 if an X pixel satisfies the equality or inequality and 0 if it doesn't. For example, $x < 1$ will take the value 1 for pixel values of x that are less than 1 and the value 0 for pixel values of x that are greater than or equal to 1.

Enter $(3 - x^2)(x < 1) + (x^3 - 4x)(x \geq 1)$ into Y_1. For values of x less than 1, $(x - 1) = 1$ and $(x \geq 1) = 0$, so for these values only $3 - x^2$ will be graphed. The reverse is true for values of x greater than 1, so only $x^3 - 4x$ will be graphed. This graph is shown on the standard grid in the figure below.

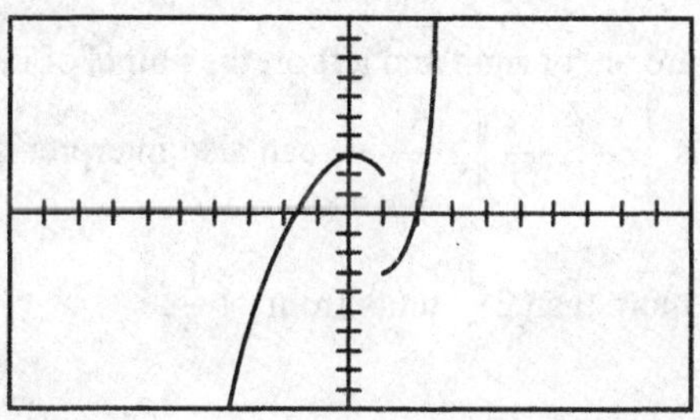

Absolute value functions are a special type of piecewise functions. The absolute value function is defined as $|x| = \begin{cases} x \text{ if } x \geq 0 \\ -x \text{ if } x < 0 \end{cases}$

The general absolute value function has the form $f(x) = a|x - h| + k$, with the vertex at (h,k) and shaped like $\vee$ if $a > 0$ and like $\wedge$ if $a < 0$. The vertex separates the two branches of the graph; h delineates the domain of all real numbers into two parts. The values are the slopes of the sides a.

The absolute value command is in the MATH/NUM menu of your graphing calculator. You can readily solve absolute value equations or inequalities by finding points of intersection.

Examples

(B) If $|x - 3| = 2$, find x.

Enter $|x - 3|$ into Y_1 and 2 into Y_2. As seen in the figure below, the points of intersection are at $x = 5$ and $x = 1$.

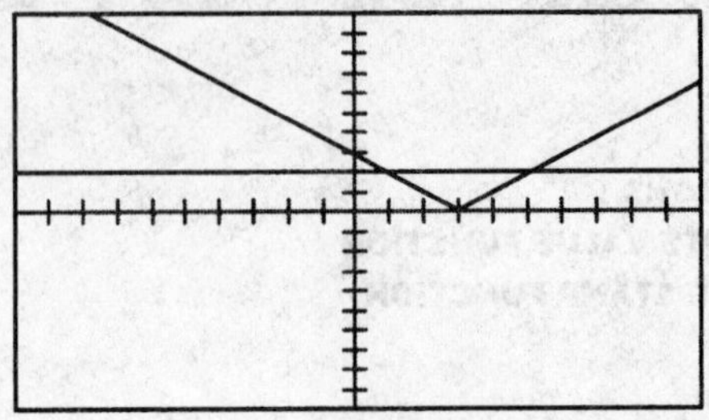

This is also easy to see algebraically. If $|x - 3| = 2$, then $x - 3 = 2$ or $x - 3 = -2$. Solving these equations yields the same solutions: 5 or 1. This equation also has a coordinate geometry solution: $|a - b|$ is the distance between a and b. Thus $|x - 3| = 2$ has the interpretation that x is 2 units from 3. Therefore, x must be 5 or 1.

(C) Find all values of x for which $|2x + 3| \geq 5$.

The graphical solution is shown below.

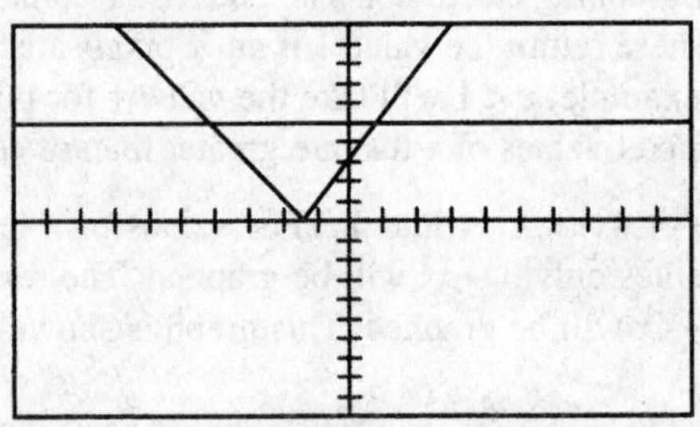

The desired values of x are on, or right and left of, the points of intersection: $x \geq 1$ or $x \leq -4$. By writing the inequality as $\left|x - \left(-\frac{3}{2}\right)\right| \geq \frac{5}{2}$, we can also interpret the solutions to the inequality as those points that are more than $2\frac{1}{2}$ units from $-1\frac{1}{2}$.

Examples

(D) Given the graph of $f(x)$ is shown below.

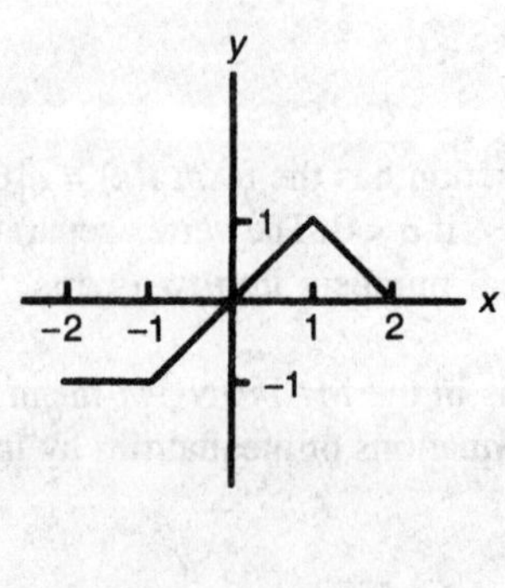

Sketch the graphs of y $|f(x)|$ and $y = f(|x|)$.

Since $|f(x)| \geq 0$, by the definition of absolute value, the graph cannot have any points below the x-axis. If $f(x) < 0$, then $|f(x)| = -f(x)$. Thus, all points below the x-axis are reflected about the x-axis, and all points above the x-axis remain unchanged.

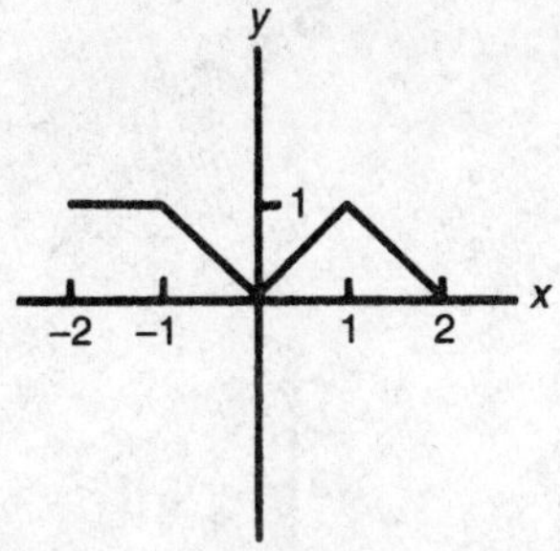

Since the absolute value of x is taken before the function value is found, and since $|x| = -x$ when $x < 0$, any negative value of x will graph the same y-values as the corresponding positive values of x. Thus, the graph to the left of the y-axis will be a reflection of the graph to the right of the y-axis.

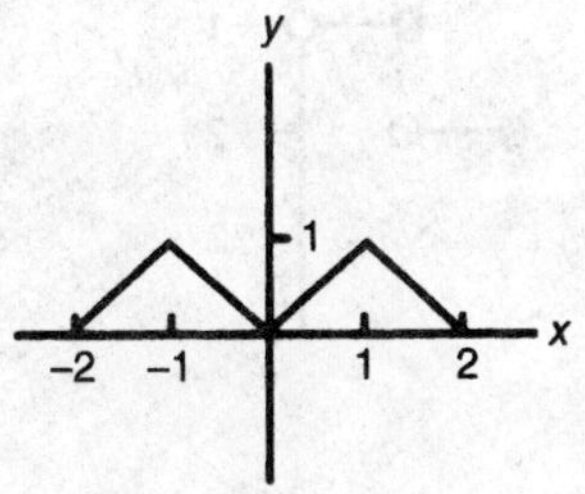

(E) If $f(x) = |x + 1| - 1$, what is the minimum value of $f(x)$?

Since $|x + 1| \geq 0$, its smallest value is 0. Therefore, the smallest value of $f(x)$ is $0 - 1 = -1$. The graph of $f(x)$ is indicated below.

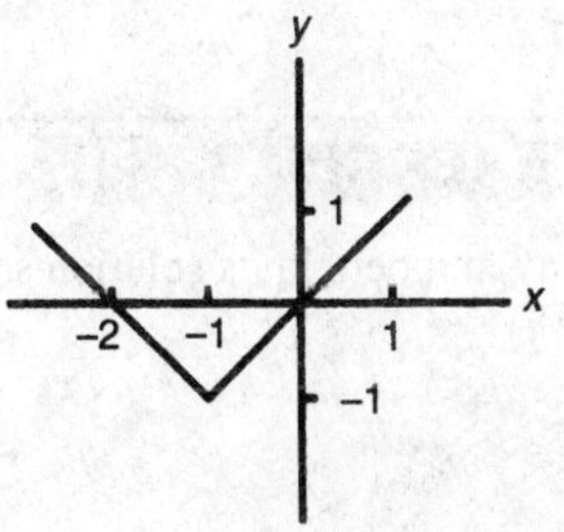

Step functions are another special type of piecewise function. These functions are constant over different parts of their domains so that their graphs consist of horizontal segments. The greatest integer function, denoted by $[x]$, is an example of a step function. If x is an integer, then $[x] = x$. If x is not an integer, then $[x]$ is the largest integer less than x.

The greatest integer function is in the MATH/NUM menu as int on TI-83/84 calculators.

(F) Five examples of the greatest integer function integer notation are:

- [3.2] = 3
- [1.999] = 1
- [5] = 5
- [–3.12] = –4
- [–0.123] = – 1.

(G) Sketch the graph of $f(x) = [x]$.

TIP

On the graphing calculator, you can't tell which side of each horizontal segment has the open and closed point.

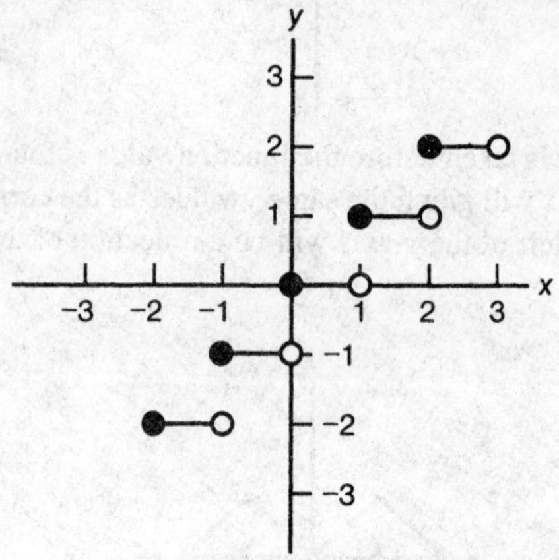

(H) What is the range of $f(x) = \left[\frac{[x]}{x}\right]$.

Enter int(int(x)/x) into Y_1 and choose Auto for both Indpnt and Depend in TBLSET. Set TblStart to 0 and ΔTbl to 0.1. Inspection of TABLE shows only 0s and 1s as Y_1, so the range is the two-point set {0,1}.

EXERCISES 习题

1. $|2x - 1| = 4x + 5$ has how many numbers in its solution set?

   (A) 0
   (B) 1
   (C) 2
   (D) an infinite number
   (E) none of the above

2. Which of the following is equivalent to $1 \le |x - 2| \le 4$?

   (A) $3 \le x \le 6$
   (B) $x \le 1$ or $x \ge 3$
   (C) $1 \le x \le 3$
   (D) $x \le -2$ or $x \ge 6$
   (E) $-2 \le x \le 1$ or $3 \le x \le 6$

3. The area bound by the relation $|x| + |y| = 2$ is

(A) 8
(B) 1
(C) 2
(D) 4
(E) There is no finite area.

4. Given a function, $f(x)$, such that $f(x) = f(|x|)$. Which one of the following could be the graph of $f(x)$?

(A)

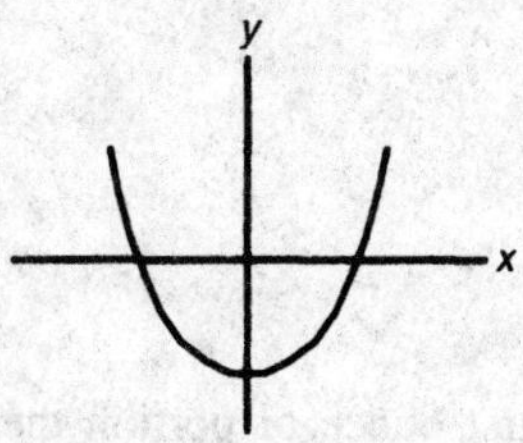

(B)

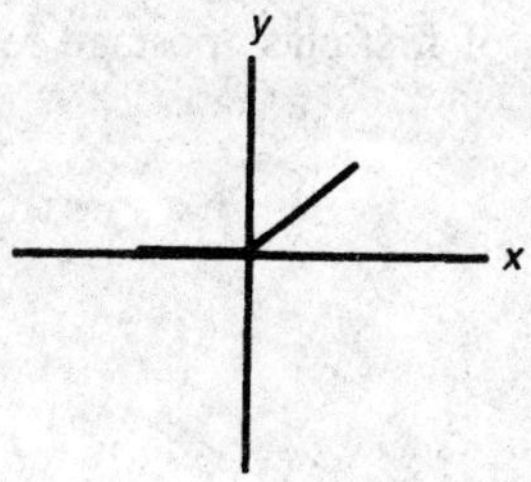

(C)

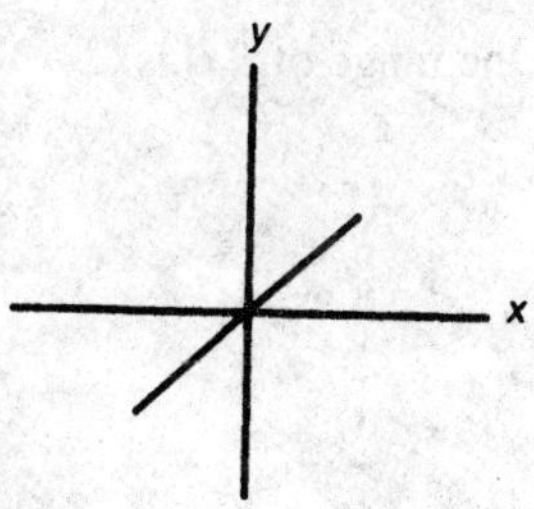

(D)

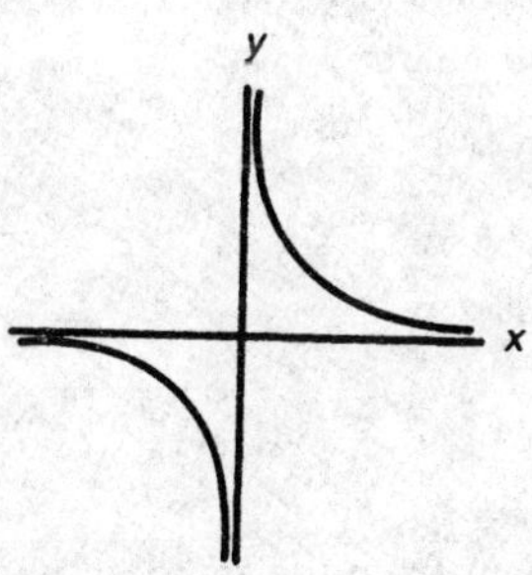

(E)

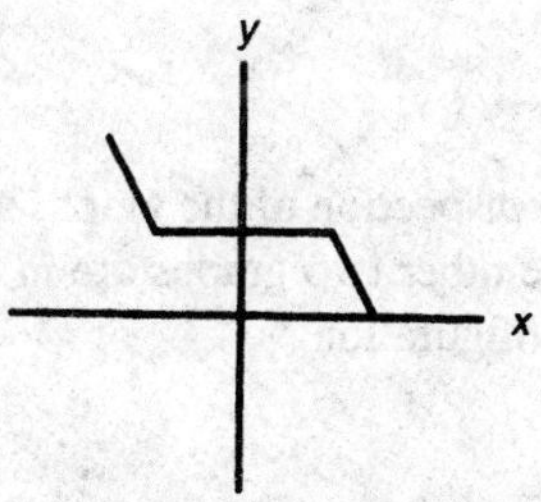

5. The figure shows the graph of which one of the following?

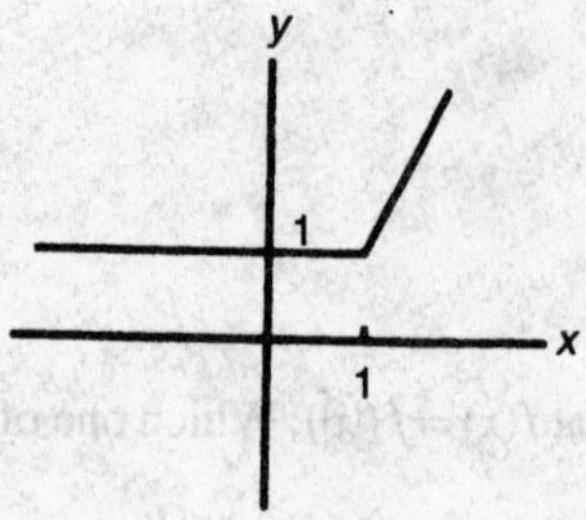

(A) $y = 2x - |x|$
(B) $y = |x - 1| + x$
(C) $y = |2x - 1|$
(D) $y = |x + 1| - x$
(E) $y = 2|x| - |x|$

6. The postal rate for first-class mail is 44 cents for the first ounce or portion thereof and 17 cents for each additional ounce or portion thereof up to 3.5 ounces. The cost of a 3.5-ounce letter is 95¢. A formula for the cost in cents of first-class postage for a letter weighing N ounces ($N \le 3.5$) is

(A) $44 + [N - 1] \cdot 17$
(B) $[N - 44] \cdot 17$
(C) $44 + [N] \cdot 17$
(D) $1 + [N] \cdot 17$
(E) none of the above

7. If $f(x) = n$, where n is an integer such that $n \le x < n + 1$, the range of $f(x)$ is

(A) the set of all real numbers
(B) the set of all positive integers
(C) the set of all integers
(D) the set of all negative integers
(E) the set of all nonnegative real numbers

8. If $f(x) = [4x] - 2x$ with domain $0 \le x \le 2$, then $f(x)$ can also be written as

(A) $2x$
(B) $-x$
(C) $-2x$
(D) $x^2 - 4x$
(E) none of the above

Answers Explained 答案解析

* 1. **(B)** Enter abs$(2x - 1)$ into Y_1 and $4x + 5$ into Y_2. It is clear from the standard window that the two graphs intersect only at one point.

* 2. **(E)** Enter abs$(x - 2)$ into Y_1, 1 into Y_2, and 4 into Y_3. An inspection of the graphs shows that the values of x for which the graph of Y_1 is between the other two graphs are in two intervals. Choice E is the only answer choice having this configuration.

∗ 3. **(A)** Subtract $|x|$ from both sides of the equation. Since $|y|$ cannot be negative, graph the piecewise function

$$Y_1 = (2 - |x|)(x \geq -2 \text{ and } x \leq 2)$$
$$Y_2 = -Y_1$$

In the first command, the word "and" is in TEST/LOGIC. The result is a square that is $2\sqrt{2}$ on a side. Therefore, the area is 8.

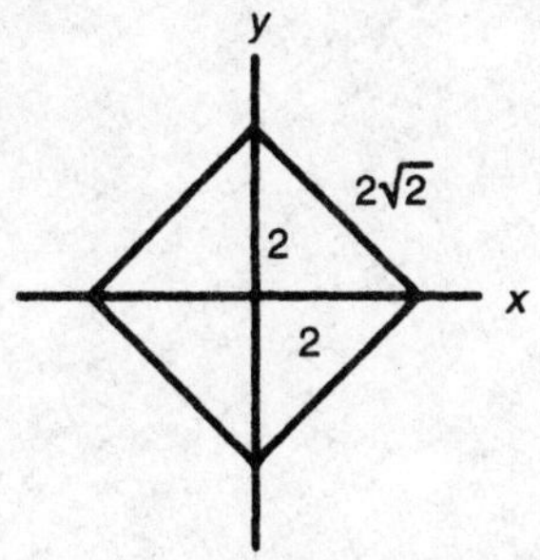

4. **(A)** Since $f(x)$ must $= f(|x|)$, the graph must be symmetric about the y-axis. The only graph meeting this requirement is Choice A.

∗ 5. **(B)** Since the point where a major change takes place is at (1,1), the expression in the absolute value should equal zero when $x = 1$. This occurs only in Choice B. Check your answer by graphing the function in B on your graphing calculator.

6. **(E)** Choice A fails if $N = 0.5$. Choice B subtracts cents from ounces. Choice C fails if $N = 1$. Choice D adds cents to ounces.

7. **(C)** Since $f(x)$ = an integer by definition, the answer is Choice C.

∗ 8. **(E)** Enter int(4x) – 2x into Y_1. The graph is shown in the figure below.

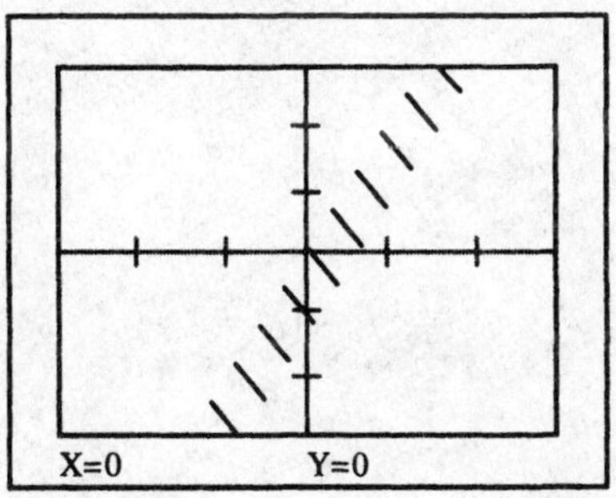

The breaks in the graph indicate that it cannot be the graph of any of the first four answer choices.

Transformations and Symmetry 第12章 变换及对称

12

- → **TRANSLATIONS**
- → **DILATIONS**
- → **REFLECTIONS**

The three types of transformations in the coordinate plane are translations, stretches/shrinks, and reflections. Translation preserves the shape of a graph, only moving it around the coordinate plane. Translation is accomplished by addition. Changing the scale (stretching and shrinking) can change the shape of a graph. This is accomplished by multiplication. Finally, reflection preserves the shape and size of a graph but changes its orientation. Reflection is accomplished by negation.

Suppose $y = f(x)$ defines any function.

- $y = f(x) + k$ translates $y = f(x)$ k units vertically (up if $k > 0$; down if $k < 0$)
- $y = f(x - h)$ translates $y = f(x)$ h units horizontally (right if $h > 0$; left if $h < 0$)

➡ Examples

(A) Suppose $y = f(x) = e^x$. Describe the graph of $y = e^x + 3$.

In this example, $k = 3$, so $e^x + 3 = f(x) + 3$. As shown in the figures below, each point on the graph of $y = e^x + 3$ is 3 units above the corresponding point on the graph of $y = e^x$.

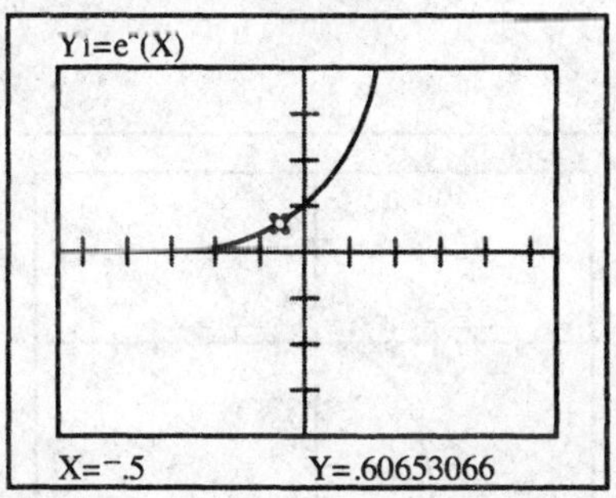

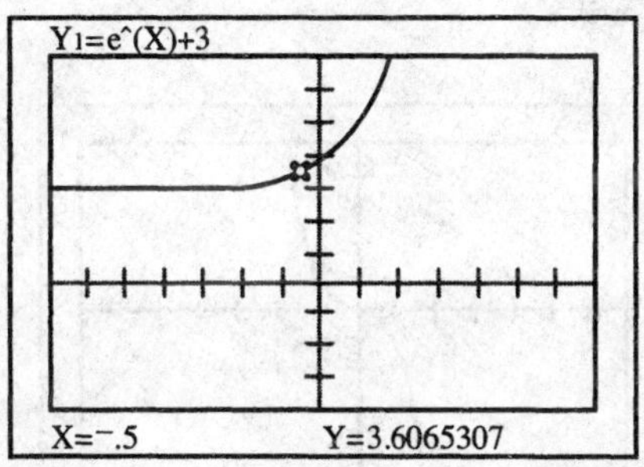

(B) Suppose $y = x^2$. Describe the graph of $y = (x + 2)^2$.

In this example $h = -2$, so $(x + 2)^2 = f(x + 2)$. As shown in the figures below, each point on the graph of $y = (x + 2)^2$ is 2 units to the left of the corresponding point on the graph of $y = x^2$.

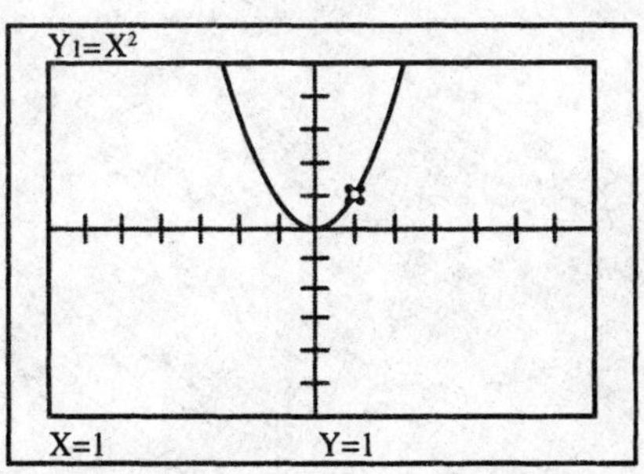

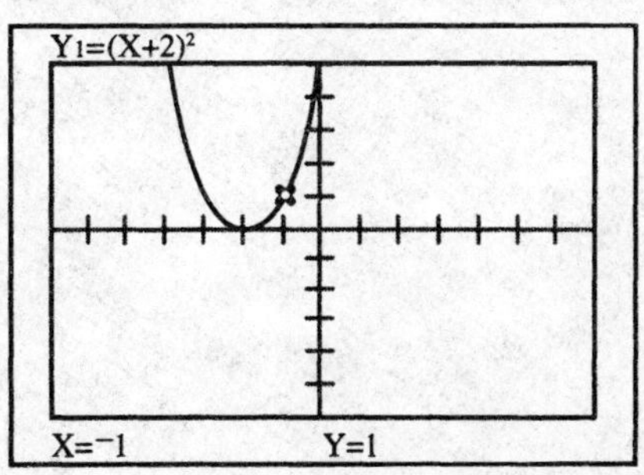

- $y = af(x)$ stretches (shrinks) $f(x)$ vertically by a factor of $|a|$ if $|a| > 1(|a| < 1)$.
- $y = f(ax)$ shrinks (stretches) $f(x)$ horizontally by a factor of $\left|\frac{1}{a}\right|$ if $|a| > 1(|a| < 1)$.

(C) Suppose $y = x - 1$. Describe the graph of $y = 3(x - 1)$.

In this example $|a| = 3$, so $3(x + 1) = 3f(x)$. As shown in the graphs below, for $x = 1.5$ the y-coordinate of each point on the graph of $y = 3(x - 1)$ is 3 times the y-coordinate of the corresponding point on the graph of $y = x - 1$.

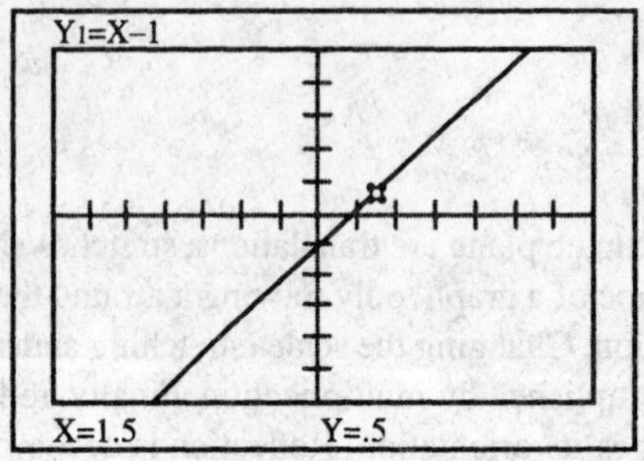

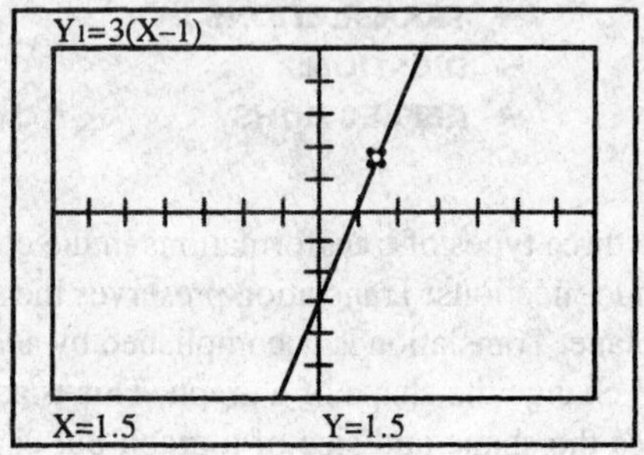

(D) Suppose $y = x^3$. Describe the graph of $y = \left(\frac{1}{2}x\right)^3$.

In this example, $|a| = \frac{1}{2}$. As shown in the graphs below, for $y = 0.729$ the x-coordinate of each point on the graph of $y = \left(\frac{1}{2}x\right)^3$ is 2 times the x-coordinate of the corresponding point on the graph of $y = x^3$.

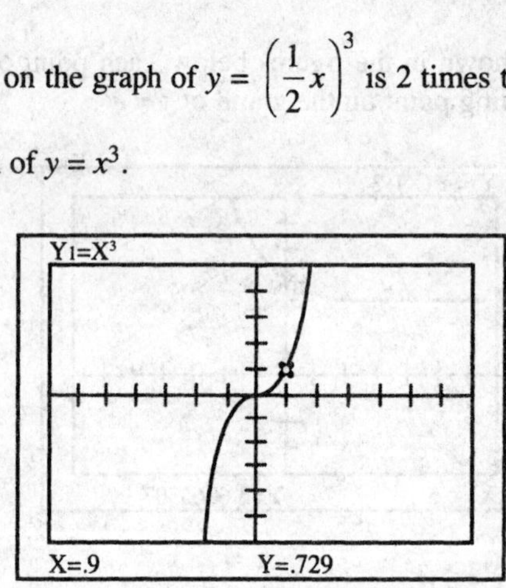

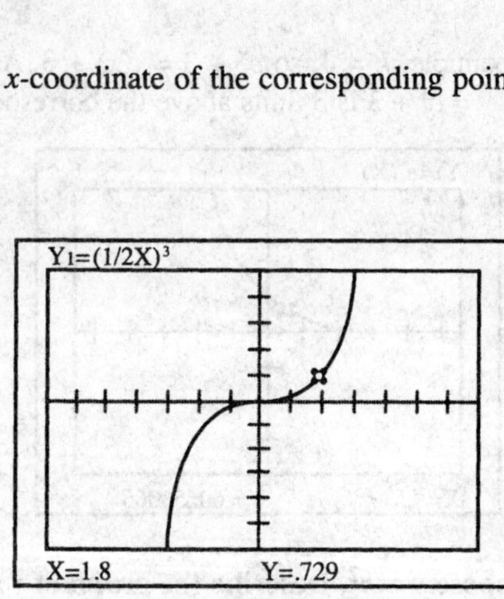

- $y = -f(x)$ reflects $y = f(x)$ about the x-axis. (The reflection is vertical.)
- $y = f(-x)$ reflects $y = f(x)$ about the y-axis. (The reflection is horizontal.)

(E) Suppose $y = \ln x$. Describe the graphs of $y = -\ln x$ and $y = \ln(-x)$.

As shown in the graphs below, the graph of $y = -\ln x$ is the reflection of the graph of $y = \ln x$ about the x-axis, and the graph of $y = \ln(-x)$ is the reflection about the y-axis.

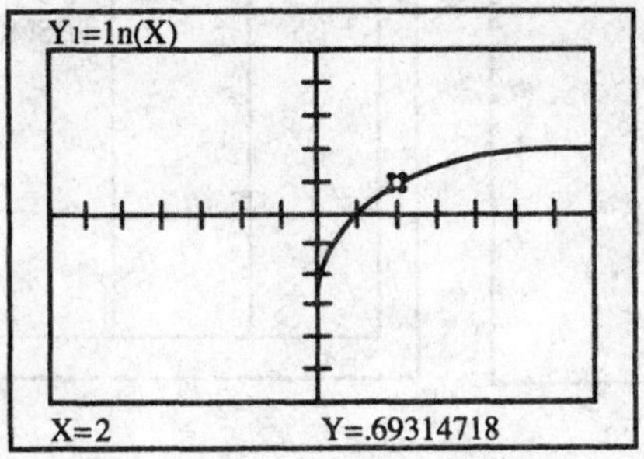

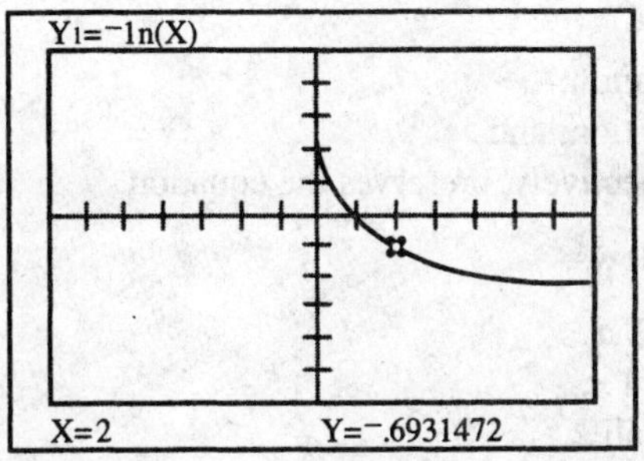

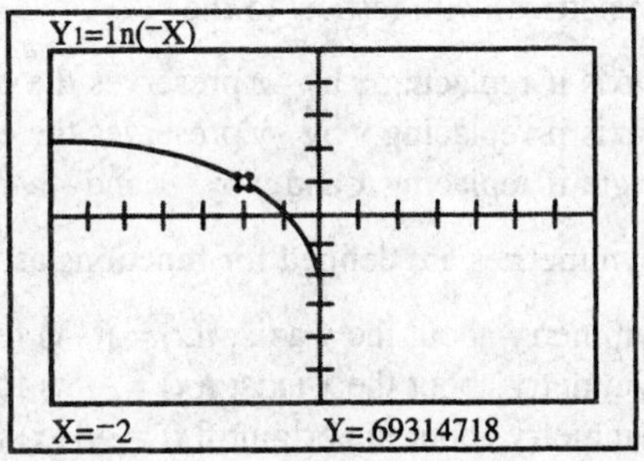

Translations, stretching/shrinking, and reflections can be combined to produce functions. Vertical transformations occur when adding, multiplying, or negating takes place after the function is applied (i.e., to y). The order in which multiple vertical transformations are executed does not matter. Horizontal transformations occur when adding, multiplying, or negating takes place before the function is applied (i.e., to x). Unless an order of doing transformations is specified, these transformations must be taken in the following order: reflect; change the scale; then translate. Moreover, the scale factor $|a|$ must be factored out of a translation.

(F) Suppose $y = f(x)$. Use words to describe the transformation $y = f(-ax + b)$.

Observe that all of these transformations are horizontal. First we have to write $-ax + b$ as $-a\left(x - \frac{b}{a}\right)$. The x-coordinate of a point (x,y) on the graph of $y = f(x)$ goes through the following sequence of transformations: reflected about the y-axis; horizontally shrunk by a factor of $|a|$ $\left(\text{or stretched by a factor of } \left|\frac{1}{a}\right|\right)$ and translated $\frac{b}{a}$ to the right.

(G) Suppose $y = \sin x$. Describe the sequence of transformations to get the graph of $y = \sin(-2x + 1)$.

Observe that all transformations are horizontal. Write the function as $y = \sin\left(-2\left(x - \frac{1}{2}\right)\right)$.

Consider the point $(4,-0.7568\ldots)$ on the graph of $y = \sin x$. First reflect this point about the y-axis to $(-4,-0.7568\ldots)$. Then shrink by a factor of 2 to $(-2,-0.7568\ldots)$. Then translate $\frac{1}{2}$ units right, to (–1.5,–0.7568...). The screens below show $Y_1 = \sin x$ and $Y_2 = \sin(-2x + 1)$ and a table showing the points (4,–0.7568...) for Y_1 and (–1.5,–0.7568...) for Y_2.

```
Plot1   Plot2   Plot3
\Y1■sin(X)
\Y2■sin(-2X+1)■
\Y3=
\Y4=
\Y5=
\Y6=
\Y7=
\Y8=
\Y9=
```

X	Y1	Y2		
4	−.7568	−.657		
−1.5	−.9975	−.7568		

X=4

Reflections about the *x*- and *y*-axes represent two types of symmetry in a graph. Symmetry through the origin is a third type of graphical symmetry. A graph defined by an equation in *x* and *y* is symmetrical with respect to the

- *x*-axis if replacing *x* by $-x$ preserves the equation;
- *y*-axis if replacing *y* by $-y$ preserves the equation; and
- origin if replacing *x* and *y* by $-x$ and $-y$, respectively, preserves the equation.

These symmetries are defined for functions as follows:

- Symmetry about the *y*-axis: $f(x) = f(-x)$ for all *x*.
- Symmetry about the *x*-axis: $f(x) = -f(x)$ for all *x*.
- Symmetry about the origin: $f(x) = -f(-x)$ for all *x*.

As defined previously, functions that are symmetric about the *y*-axis are even functions, and those that are symmetric about the origin are odd functions.

(H) Discuss the symmetry of $f(x) = \cos x$.

Since $\cos x = \cos(-x)$, cosine is symmetric about the *y*-axis (an even function).

However, since $\cos x \neq -\cos x$ and $\cos(-x) \neq -\cos x$, the cosine is not symmetric with respect to the *x*-axis or origin.

(I) Discuss the symmetry of $x^2 + xy + y^2 = 0$.

If you substitute $-x$ for *x* or $-y$ for *y*, but not both, the equation becomes $x^2 - xy + y^2 = 0$, which does not preserve the equation. Therefore, the graph is not symmetrical with respect to either axis. However, if you substitute both $-x$ for *x* and $-y$ for *y*, the equation is preserved, so the equation is symmetric about the origin.

EXERCISES 习题

1. Which of the following functions transforms $y = f(x)$ by moving it 5 units to the right?

   (A) $y = f(x + 5)$
   (B) $y = f(x - 5)$
   (C) $y = f(x) + 5$
   (D) $y = f(x) - 5$
   (E) $y = 5f(x)$

2. Which of the following functions stretches $y = \cos(x)$ vertically by a factor of 3?

(A) $y = \cos(x + 3)$
(B) $y = \cos(3x)$
(C) $y = \cos\left(\frac{1}{3}x\right)$
(D) $y = 3 \cos x$
(E) $y = \frac{1}{3}\cos x$

3. The graph of $y = f(x)$ is shown.

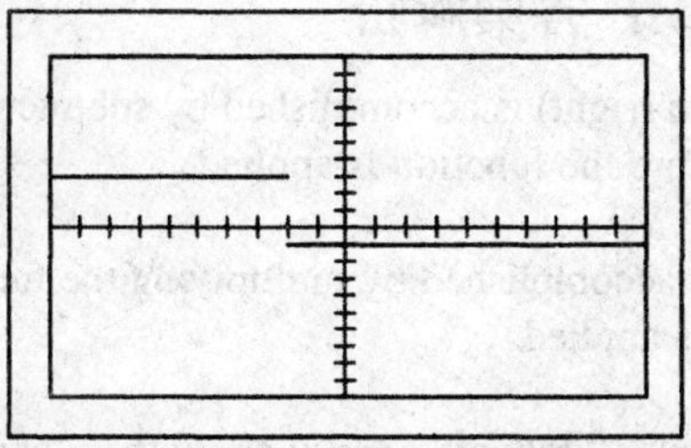

Which of the following is the graph of $y = f(-x) - 2$?

(A)
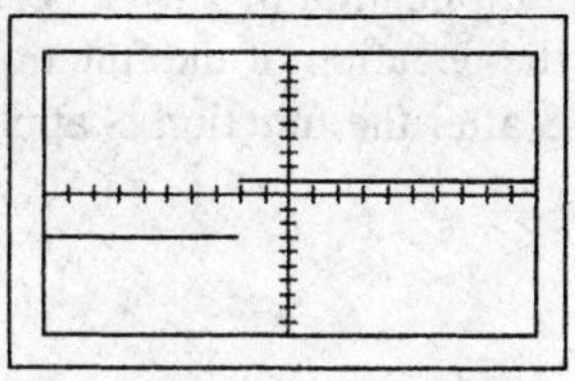

(B)
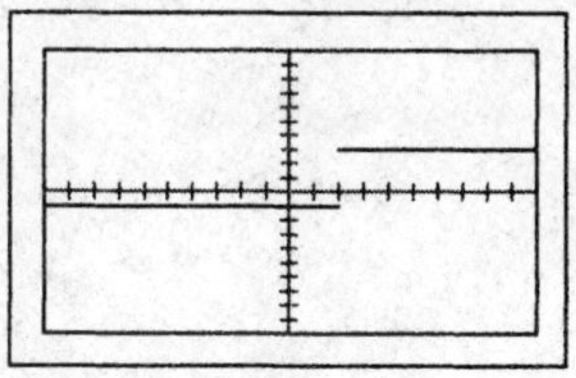

(C)
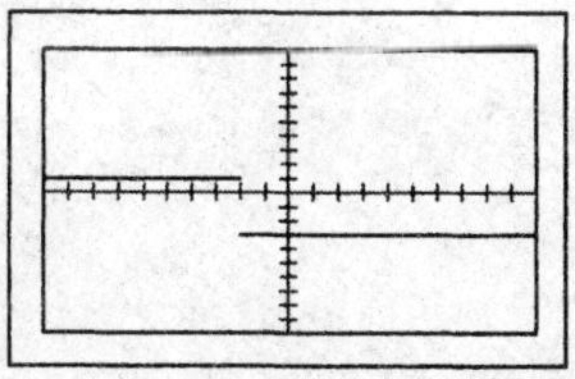

(D)
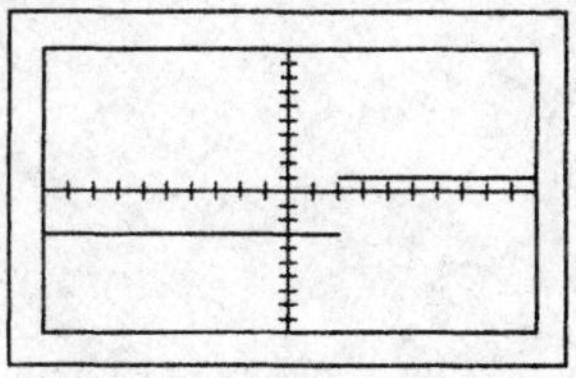

(E)
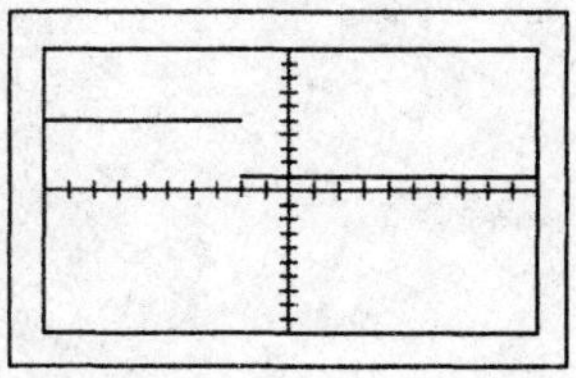

4. Which of the following is a transformation of $y = f(x)$ that translates this function down 3, shrinks it horizontally by a factor of 2, and reflects it about the x-axis?

(A) $y = -2f(x - 3)$
(B) $y = f(-2x) - 3$
(C) $y = -f\left(\frac{1}{2}x\right) - 3$
(D) $y = -f(2x) - 3$
(E) $y = 2f\left(-\frac{1}{2}x\right) - 3$

Answers Explained 答案解析

1. **(B)** Horizontal translation (right) is accomplished by subtracting the amount of the translation (5) from x before the function is applied.

2. **(D)** Vertical stretching is accomplished by multiplying the function by the stretching factor after the function is applied.

3. **(D)** The graph of $y = f(-x) - 2$ reflects $y = f(x)$ about the y-axis and translates it down 2.

4. **(D)** The horizontal shrinking by a factor of 2 is the multiplication of x by 2 before the function is applied. The reflection about the x-axis is the negation of the function after it is applied. The translation down 3 is the addition of -3 after the function is applied.

Conic Sections
第13章 圆锥截面

13

- → PARABOLAS
- → ELLIPSES
- → HYPERBOLAS

Geometrically, the conic sections are formed by the intersection of a plane and the two nappes of a right cone. The plane does not intersect the cone's vertex (see below). In a **parabola**, the plane is parallel to a lateral edge of the cone. In a **hyperbola**, the plane is parallel to the axis of the cone. In an **ellipse**, the plane is not parallel to either a lateral edge or the axis of the cone. Intersections that contain the cone's vertex are called **degenerate conics** and are not covered on the Math Level 2 Test.

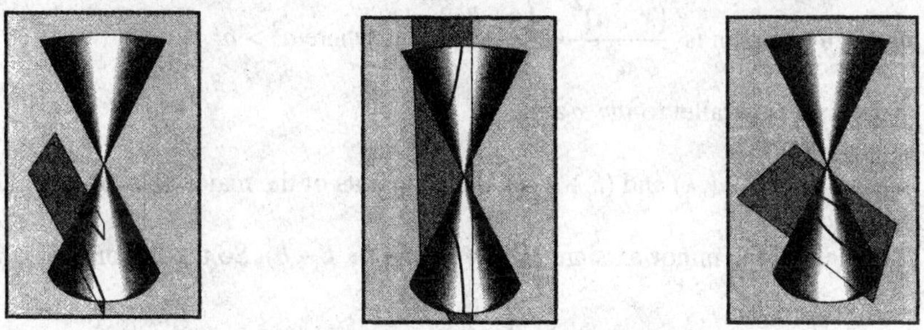

Conics are also defined in terms of points in the coordinate plane. Formulas for the distance between two points and the distance between a point and a line are then used to derive **standard equations** of the conics. Each conic has a pair of standard equations, depending on whether the conic has an orientation to the x- or y-axis. The equations presented below include translation parameters h and k, which allow for horizontal and vertical translations, respectively, of their graphs. The pair $(h, k) = (0,0)$ corresponds to the parent relations that are "centered" at the origin.

A **parabola** is the set of points that are equidistant from a given point (**focus**) and a given line (**directrix**). The "center" of a parabola is its **vertex**.

If a parabola has an x-orientation:

- It opens to the left ($p < 0$) or right ($p > 0$).
- The standard equation is $(y - k)^2 = 4p(x - h)$.
- The focus is $(h + p, k)$, and the directrix is $x = h - p$.
- The vertex is (h, k).
- The common distance from the parabola to the focus and directrix is $|p|$.

If a parabola has a y-orientation:

- It opens up ($p > 0$) or down ($p < 0$).
- The standard equation is $(x - h)^2 = 4p(y - k)$.
- The focus is $(h, k + p)$, and the directrix is $y = k - p$.
- The vertex is (h, k).
- The common distance from the parabola to the focus and directrix is $|p|$.

TIP

When you studied quadratics in Algebra 2, x was the squared variable and the parabolas opened up or down. This should help you determine the correct orientation when you look at the equation.

These points are illustrated in the figures below.

Graph of $(y-k)^2 = 4p(x-h)$ $\quad p > 0$

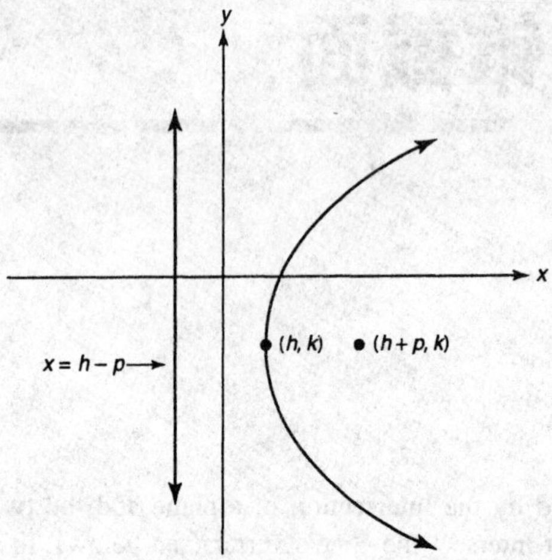

Graph of $(x-h)^2 = 4p(y-k)$ $\quad p < 0$

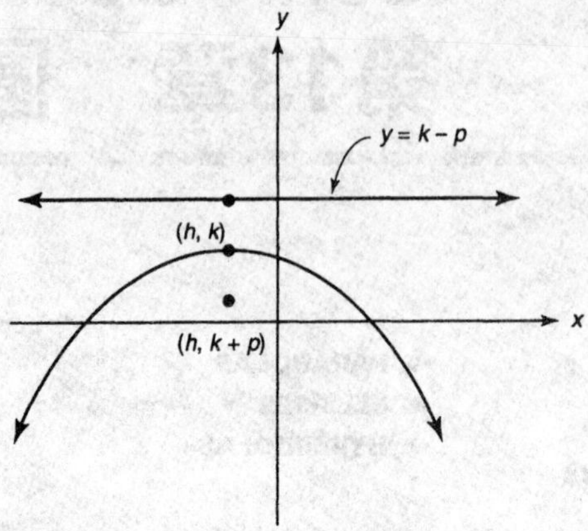

An **ellipse** is the set of points whose distances from two given points (**foci**, plural of **focus**) sum to a constant. The "center" of an ellipse is (h, k), the intersection of its major and minor axes.

If an ellipse has an x-orientation:

- The standard equation is $\dfrac{(x-h)^2}{a^2} + \dfrac{(y-k)^2}{b^2} = 1$, where $a^2 > b^2$.
- The major axis is parallel to the x-axis.
- The center is (h, k).
- The vertices are $(h-a, k)$ and $(h+a, k)$, the endpoints of the major axis. So the major axis is $2a$ units long.
- The endpoints of the minor axis are $(h, k-b)$ and $(h, k+b)$. So the minor axis is $2b$ units long.
- The foci are on the major axis. Each focus is at a distance of $c = \sqrt{a^2 - b^2}$ from the center, so the foci are at $(h-c, k)$ and $(h+c, k)$.

If an ellipse has a y-orientation:

- The standard equation is $\dfrac{(x-h)^2}{b^2} + \dfrac{(y-k)^2}{a^2} = 1$, where $a^2 > b^2$.
- The major axis is parallel to the y-axis.
- The center is (h, k).
- The vertices are $(h, k-a)$ and $(h, k+a)$, the endpoints of the major axis.
- The endpoints of the minor axis are $(h-b, k)$ and $(h+b, k)$.
- The foci are on the major axis. Each focus is at a distance of $c = \sqrt{a^2 - b^2}$ from the center, so the foci are at $(h, k-c)$ and $(h, k+c)$.

If the larger denominator in an equation of an ellipse is under the x-term, the ellipse has an x-orientation. If the larger denominator is under the y-term, the ellipse has a y-orientation.

Note that an ellipse with $a = b$ is a circle whose equation is $(x-h)^2 + (y-k)^2 = r^2$, where r is the common value of a and b.

These points are illustrated in the figures below.

Graph of $\dfrac{(x-h)^2}{a^2}+\dfrac{(y-k)^2}{b^2}=1$

$a^2 > b^2 \quad c^2 = a^2 - b^2$

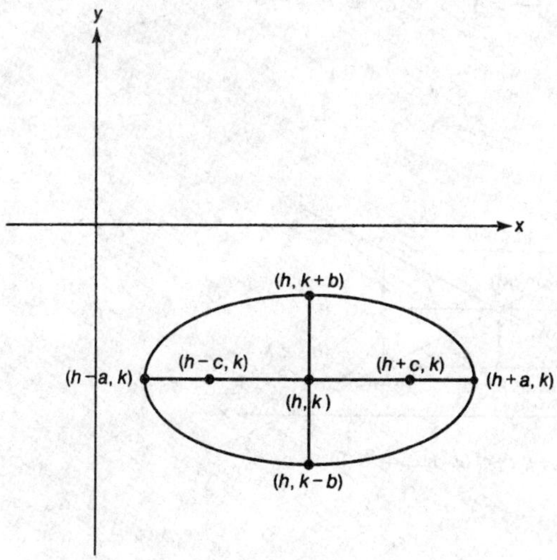

Graph of $\dfrac{(x-h)^2}{b^2}+\dfrac{(y-k)^2}{a^2}=1$

$a^2 > b^2 \quad c^2 = a^2 - b^2$

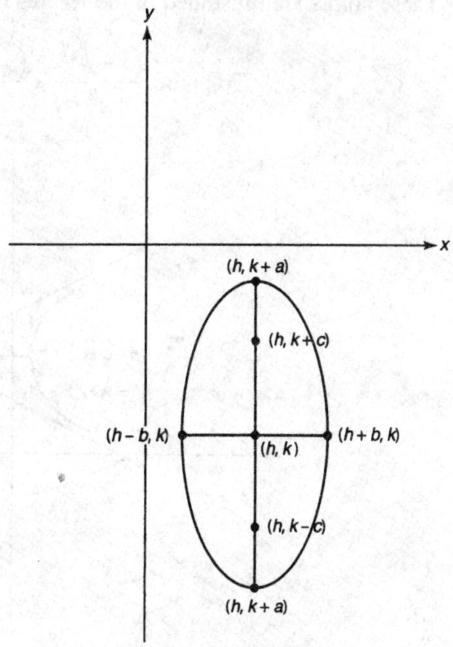

A **hyperbola** is the set of points whose distances from two fixed points (foci) differ by a constant. A hyperbola has two halves, corresponding to the two nappes of the cone. Each half has a vertex and sides that are asymptotic to a pair of intersecting lines. The "center" of a hyperbola is (h, k), the intersection of its transverse and conjugate axes.

If a hyperbola has an x-orientation:

- The hyperbola opens to the sides.
- The standard equation is $\dfrac{(x-h)^2}{a^2}-\dfrac{(y-k)^2}{b^2}=1$.
- The center is (h, k).
- The vertices are $(h-a, k)$ and $(h+a, k)$. The segment joining the two vertices is called the **transverse axis**. This axis is horizontal and has length $2a$.
- The foci are on the transverse axis. The distance between the center and each focus is $c=\sqrt{a^2+b^2}$, so the foci are $(h-c, k)$ and $(h+c, k)$.
- The vertical segment through the center, with endpoints $(h, k-b)$ and $(h, k+b)$, which has length $2b$, is called the **conjugate axis**. The endpoints of this axis are not on the hyperbola.
- The equations of the asymptotes are $y-k=\pm\dfrac{b}{a}(x-h)$.

If a hyperbola has a y-orientation:

- The hyperbola opens up and down.
- The standard equation is $\dfrac{(y-k)^2}{a^2}-\dfrac{(x-h)^2}{b^2}=1$.
- The center is (h, k).
- The vertices are $(h, k-a)$ and $(h, k+a)$. The transverse axis is vertical and has length $2a$.

- The foci are $(h, k - c)$ and $(h, k + c)$.
- The conjugate axis is horizontal, has endpoints $(h - b, k)$ and $(h + b, k)$, and has length $2b$.
- The equations of the asymptotes are $y - k = \pm\frac{a}{b}(x - h)$.

If the x-term of the equation is positive, the hyperbola has an x-orientation. If the y-term is positive, it has a y-orientation.

These points are illustrated in the figures below.

Graph of $\frac{(x-h)^2}{a^2} - \frac{(y-k)^2}{b^2} = 1 \qquad c^2 = a^2 + b^2$

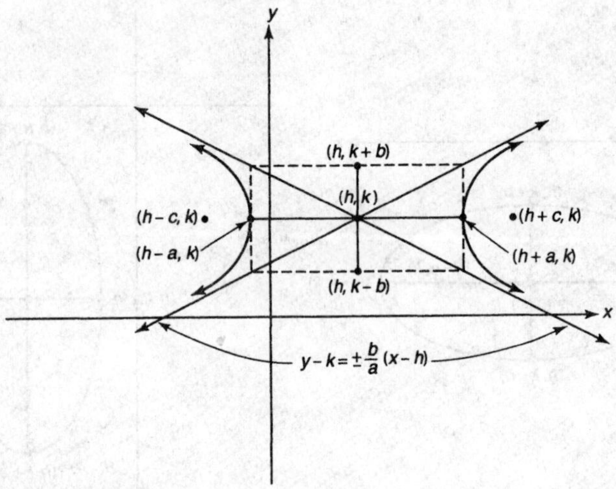

Graph of $\frac{(y-k)^2}{a^2} - \frac{(x-h)^2}{b^2} = 1 \qquad c^2 = a^2 + b^2$

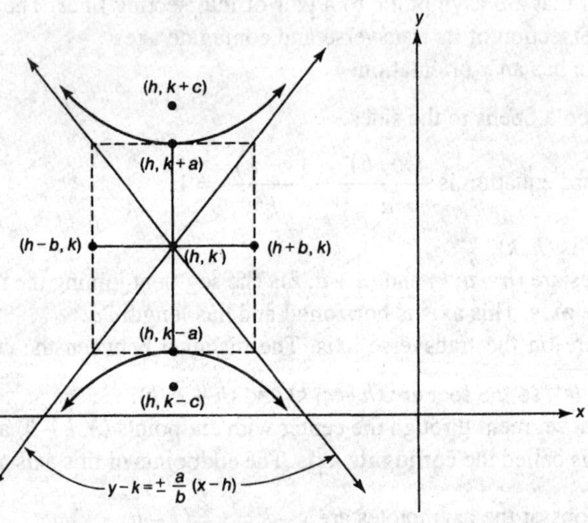

The **eccentricity** of an ellipse or hyperbola is a measure of its degree of elongation. The eccentricity of an ellipse is $\frac{c}{a}$, which is less than 1 since $c < a$. The closer c is to a, the more circular the ellipse. The eccentricity of a hyperbola is also $\frac{c}{a}$. However, it is greater than 1 since $c > a$ in a hyperbola. The farther c is from a, the more elongated the hyperbola.

Examples

(A) $\dfrac{(y-3)^2}{9} - \dfrac{(x-1)^2}{16} = 1$

Which conic section does this equation define? Also find, if they exist,

(i) the center
(ii) the vertex/vertices
(iii) the focus/foci
(iv) the directrix
(v) the asymptotes
(vi) the eccentricity

This is a hyperbola with a *y*-orientation. In this problem, $h = 1$, $k = 3$, $a = 3$, $b = 4$, and $c = \sqrt{3^2 + 4^2} = 5$.

(i) The center is $(1, 3)$.
(ii) The vertices are $(1, 0)$ and $(1, 6)$.
(iii) The foci are $(1, -2)$ and $(1, 8)$.
(iv) A hyperbola does not have a directrix.
(v) The asymptotes are $y - 3 = \pm\frac{3}{4}(x - 1)$.
(vi) The eccentricity is $\frac{5}{3}$.

(B) $(y + 4)^2 = -6(x - 2)$

Which conic section does this equation define? Also find, if they exist,

(i) the center
(ii) the vertex/vertices
(iii) the focus/foci
(iv) the directrix
(v) the asymptotes
(vi) the eccentricity

This is a parabola with an *x*-orientation opening left. In this problem, $h = 2$, $k = -4$, and $p = -\frac{3}{2}$.

(i) A parabola does not have a center.
(ii) The vertex is $(2, -4)$.
(iii) The focus is $\left(\frac{1}{2}, -4\right)$.
(iv) The directrix is $x = \frac{7}{2}$.
(v) A parabola does not have asymptotes.
(vi) The eccentricity of a parabola is 1.

(C) $\dfrac{(x+3)^2}{25}+\dfrac{(y-8)^2}{100}=1$

Which conic section does this equation define? Also find, if they exist,

(i) the center
(ii) the vertex/vertices
(iii) the focus/foci
(iv) the directrix
(v) the asymptotes
(vi) the eccentricity

This is an ellipse with a y-orientation since the larger denominator has y in the numerator. In this problem $h = -3$, $k = 8$, $a = 10$, $b = 5$, and $c = \sqrt{10^2 - 5^2} = \sqrt{75} = 5\sqrt{3}$.

(i) The center is $(-3, 8)$.
(ii) The vertices are $(-3, -2)$ and $(-3, 18)$.
(iii) The foci are $(-3, 8 + 5\sqrt{3})$ and $(-3, 8 - 5\sqrt{3})$.
(iv) An ellipse does not have a directrix.
(v) An ellipse does not have asymptotes.
(vi) The eccentricity is $\dfrac{\sqrt{3}}{2}$.

If an equation of a conic is not in standard form, completing the square will yield a standard-form equation. If the equation has squared terms in both x and y, completing the square in both variables will result in the standard equation of an ellipse or hyperbola. If only one of the variables is squared in the original equation, completing the square in that variable will result in the standard equation of a parabola.

(D) Name the conic by finding its standard-form equation.

$$2x^2 + 3y^2 + 12x - 24y + 60 = 0$$

$$2(x^2 + 6x + 9) + 3(y^2 - 8y + 16) = -60 + 18 + 48$$

$$2(x + 3)^2 + 3(y - 4)^2 = 6$$

$$\frac{(x+3)^2}{3}+\frac{(y-4)^2}{2}=1$$

This conic is an ellipse.

(E) Name the conic by finding its standard-form equation.

$$4x^2 + 4y^2 - 12x - 20y - 2 = 0$$

$$4\left(x^2-3x+\frac{9}{4}\right)+4\left(y^2-5y+\frac{25}{4}\right)=2+9+25$$

$$4\left(x-\frac{3}{2}\right)^2+4\left(y-\frac{5}{2}\right)^2=36$$

$$\left(x-\frac{3}{2}\right)^2+\left(y-\frac{5}{2}\right)^2=9$$

This is a circle with center $\left(\dfrac{3}{2}, \dfrac{5}{2}\right)$ and radius 3.

(F) Find the foci of the conic $y^2 + 2x + 2y = 5$.

Since there is only one squared term, the conic is a parabola. A parabola has only one focus, $(h + p, k)$. Complete the square in y to get the standard equation:

$$(y + 1)^2 = -2(x - 3)$$

Therefore, $h = 3$, $k = -1$, and $p = -\frac{1}{2}$.

The focus is $\left(\frac{5}{2}, -1\right)$.

(G) Find the standard equation of a hyperbola with center (3, –4), vertices (3, 1) and (3, 7), and asymptotes $y + 4 = \pm\frac{3}{4}(x - 3)$.

Since the vertices have the same x-coordinate, the hyperbola has a y-orientation. The length of the transverse axis is 6, implying that $a = 3$. The slope of the asymptote is $\frac{a}{b}$, so $b = 4$. The center is (h, k), so $h = 3$ and $k = -4$.

The standard equation is $\frac{(y+4)^2}{9} - \frac{(x-3)^2}{16} = 1$.

EXERCISES 习题

1. Which of the following is a focus of $\frac{(x-2)^2}{4} + \frac{(y+1)^2}{5} = 1$?

   (A) (1, –1)
   (B) (2, –1)
   (C) (3, –1)
   (D) (2, –2)
   (E) (–2, 1)

2. Which of the following is an asymptote of $3x^2 - 4y^2 - 12 = 0$?

   (A) $y = \frac{4}{3}x$

   (B) $y = -\frac{2}{\sqrt{3}}x$

   (C) $y = -\frac{3}{4}x$

   (D) $y = \frac{\sqrt{3}}{2}x$

   (E) $y = \frac{2}{3}x$

3. The standard equation of a parabola with focus (2, –3) and directrix $x = 6$ is

(A) $(y + 3)^2 = 8(x - 2)$
(B) $(y + 3)^2 = -8(x - 4)$
(C) $(x - 2)^2 = 8(y + 3)$
(D) $(x + 2)^2 = -8(y - 3)$
(E) $(x + 4)^2 = -8(y - 3)$

4. The standard equation of an ellipse with vertices (–5, 2) and (3, 2) and minor axis of length 6 is

(A) $\frac{(x+1)^2}{16}+\frac{(y-2)^2}{9}=1$

(B) $\frac{(x-1)^2}{9}+\frac{(y+2)^2}{16}=1$

(C) $\frac{(x+1)^2}{9}+\frac{(y-2)^2}{16}=1$

(D) $\frac{(x-1)^2}{16}+\frac{(y-2)^2}{9}=1$

(E) $\frac{(x-1)^2}{7}+\frac{(y+2)^2}{16}=1$

5. Which of the following is a vertex of $16x^2 - y^2 - 32x - 6y - 57 = 0$?

(A) (1, –1)
(B) (1, 3)
(C) (1, 5)
(D) (–1, –3)
(E) (–1, 3)

6. The graph of $x^2 = (2y + 3)^2$ is

(A) an ellipse
(B) a parabola
(C) a hyperbola
(D) a circle
(E) intersecting lines

Answers Explained 答案解析

1. **(D)** This is the standard equation of an ellipse with center $(2, -1)$, $a^2 = 5$, $b^2 = 4$, and y-orientation. Since $c^2 = a^2 - b^2 = 1$, the foci are 1 unit above and below the center.

2. **(D)** Complete the square in both x and y to put the equation in standard form:

$$\frac{x^2}{4} - \frac{y^2}{3} = 1$$

This hyperbola has x-orientation, with $a^2 = 4$ and $b^2 = 3$. Its asymptotes are $y = \pm\frac{\sqrt{3}}{2}x$.

3. **(B)** The directrix is a vertical line 4 units to the right of the focus. Therefore, the parabola has an x-orientation (the y-term is square). The vertex is 2 units right of the focus at $(4, -3)$ so $p = -2$.

4. **(A)** Since the vertices have the same y-coordinate, the major axis is horizontal, has length 8, and $a^2 = 16$. Therefore, the center of the ellipse is $(-1, 2)$. Since the minor axis has length 6, $b^2 = 9$.

5. **(D)** Complete the square in both x and y to get the standard equation:

$$\frac{(x-1)^2}{4} - \frac{(y+3)^2}{64} = 1$$

The transverse axis has length 4, so the vertices of the hyperbola are 2 units left and right of the center $(1, -3)$.

6. **(E)** Expand the right side of the equation and bring all but the constant term to the left side. This yields $x^2 - 4(y^2 + 3y) = 9$. Complete the square in y to get

$$x^2 - 4\left(y^2 + 3y + \frac{9}{4}\right) = 9 - 9 = 0$$

Then $x^2 = (2y + 3)^2$ or $x = \pm(2y + 3)$. These are intersecting lines.

Polar Coordinates
第14章　极坐标

14

→ DEFINITIONS
→ RELATIONSHIPS TO RECTANGULAR COORDINATES

Although the most common way to represent a point in a plane is in terms of its distances from two perpendicular axes, there are several other ways. One such way is in terms of the distance of the point from the origin and the angle between the positive x-axis and the ray emanating from the origin going through the point.

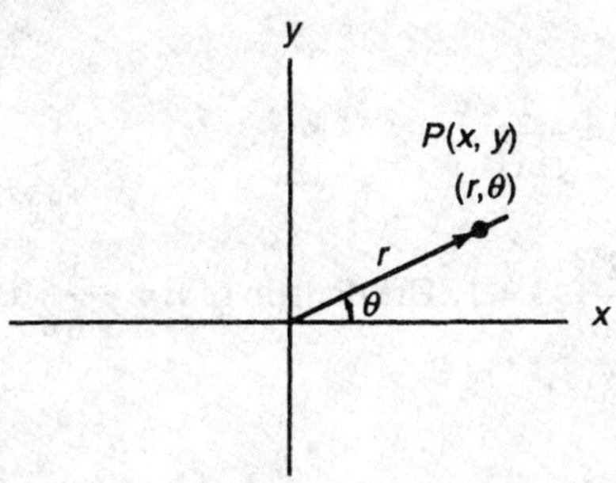

In the figure, the regular rectangular coordinates of P are (x,y) and the *polar coordinates* are (r,θ). If $r > 0$, it is measured along the ray of the terminal side of θ. If $r < 0$, it is measured in the direction of the opposite ray.

Since $\sin\theta = \dfrac{y}{r}$ and $\cos\theta = \dfrac{x}{r}$, there is an easy relationship between rectangular and polar coordinates:

$x = r\cos\theta$
$y = r\sin\theta$
$x^2 + y^2 = r^2$, using the Pythagorean theorem.

Unlike the case involving rectangular coordinates, each point in the plane can be named by an infinite number of polar coordinates.

➥ Examples

(A) $(2,30°)$, $(2,390°)$, $(2,-330°)$, $(-2,210°)$, $(-2,-150°)$ all name the same point.

In general, a point in the plane represented by (r,θ) can also be represented by $(r,\theta + 2\pi n)$ or $(-r,\theta + (2n-1)\pi)$, where n is an integer.

(B) Express point P, whose rectangular coordinates are $(3, 3\sqrt{3})$, in terms of polar coordinates.

$$r^2 = x^2 + y^2 = 9 + 27 = 36$$
$$r = 6$$
$$r\cos\theta = x$$
$$\cos\theta = \frac{3}{6} = \frac{1}{2}$$

Therefore, $\theta = 60°$ and $(6, 60°)$ are the polar coordinates of P.

(C) Describe the graphs of $r = 2$.

$r^2 = x^2 + y^2$
$r = 2$

Therefore, $x^2 + y^2 = 4$, which is the equation of a circle whose center is at the origin and whose radius is 2.

(D) Describe the graph of $r = \frac{1}{\sin\theta}$.

Since $r\sin\theta = y$ and $r = \frac{1}{\sin\theta}$, $y = 1$. The domain of $r = \frac{1}{\sin\theta}$ is all real θ that are not multiples of π.

Thus, $r = \frac{1}{\sin\theta}$ is the equation of a horizontal line with holes in it at multiples of π one unit above the x-axis.

Both $r = 2$ and $r = \frac{1}{\sin\theta}$ are examples of polar functions. Such functions can be graphed on a graphing calculator by using POLAR mode. Enter 2 into r_1 and graph using ZOOM 6, the standard window.

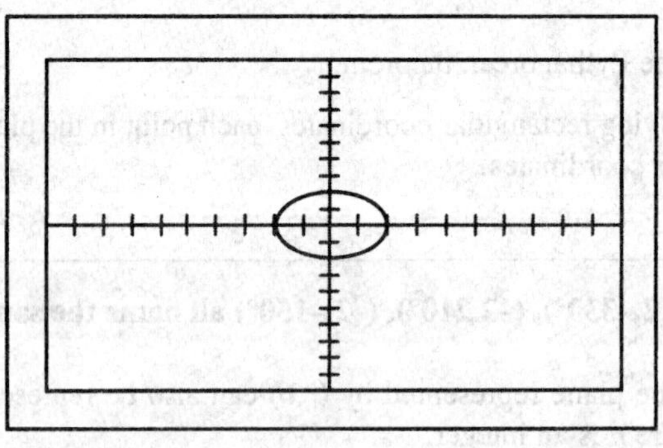

Although the graph is accurate for the scale given, the shape looks like that of an ellipse, not a circle. This is because the standard screen has a scale on the x-axis that is larger than that on the y-axis, resulting in a distorted graph. The graph below is obtained by using the ZOOM ZSquare command.

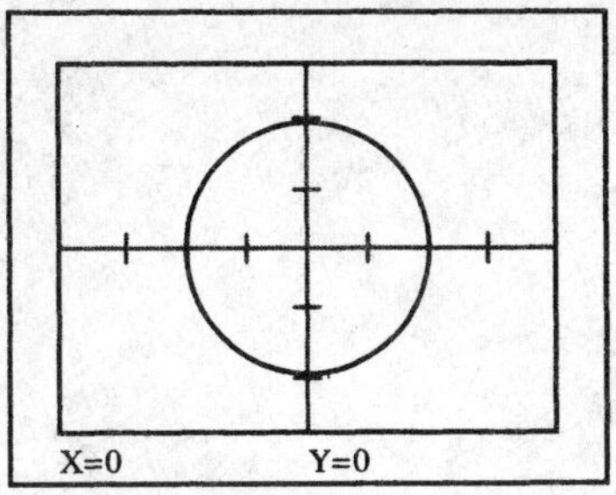

EXERCISES 习题

1. A point has polar coordinate (2,60°). The same point can be represented by

   (A) (–2,240°)
   (B) (2,240°)
   (C) (–2,60°)
   (D) (2,–60°)
   (E) (2,–240°)

2. The polar coordinates of a point P are (2,200°). The rectangular coordinates of P are

   (A) (–1.88,–0.68)
   (B) (–0.68,–1.88)
   (C) (–0.34,–0.94)
   (D) (–0.94,–0.34)
   (E) (–0.47,–0.17)

3. Describe the graph of $r = \dfrac{3}{\cos\theta}$.

   (A) a parabola
   (B) an ellipse
   (C) a circle
   (D) a vertical line
   (E) the x-axis

Answers Explained 答案解析

1. **(A)** The angle must either be coterminal with $(60 \pm 360n)$ with $r = 2$ or $(60 \pm 180)°$ with $r = -2$. Choice A is the only answer choice that meets these criteria.

* 2. **(A)** With your calculator in degree mode, evaluate $x = r\cos\theta = 2\cos 200 \approx -1.88$ and $y = r\sin 200 = 2\sin 200 \approx -0.68$.

* 3. **(D)** With your graphing calculator in POLAR mode, enter $\dfrac{3}{\cos\theta}$ as r_1, and observe that the graph is a vertical line with holes where $\cos\theta = 0$.

Three-Dimensional Geometry 第15章 三维几何 15

→ **FORMULAS FOR VOLUMES AND SURFACE AREAS OF SOLIDS**
→ **RECTANGULAR COORDINATES**
→ **DISTANCE AND MIDPOINT**

The Level 2 test may have problems involving five types of solids: prisms, pyramids, cylinders, cones, and spheres. Rectangular solids and cubes are special types of prisms. In a rectangular solid, the bases are rectangles, so any pair of opposite sides can be bases. In a cube, the bases are squares, and the altitude is equal in length to the sides of the base.

On the Level 2 test, all figures are assumed to be right solids. Formulas for the volumes of regular pyramids, circular cones, and spheres and formulas for the lateral areas of circular cones and spheres are given in the test book. For convenience, formulas for the volumes and lateral areas of all of these figures are summarized below.

Solid	Volume	Surface Area
Prism	$V = Bh$	$SA = Ph + 2B$
Rectangular solid	$V = lwh$	$SA = 2lw + 2lh + 2wh$
Cube	$V = s^3$	$SA = 6s^2$
Pyramid	$V = \frac{1}{3}Bh$	$SA = \frac{1}{2}PL + B$
Cylinder	$V = \pi r^2 h$	$SA = 2\pi rh + 2\pi r^2$
Cone	$V = \frac{1}{3}\pi r^2 h$	$SA = \pi rL + \pi r^2$
Sphere	$V = \frac{4}{3}\pi r^3$	$SA = 4\pi r^2$

The variables in these formulas are defined as follows:

V = volume	h = altitude
SA = surface area	l = length
B = base area	w = width
P = base perimeter	r = radius
L = slant height	s = side length

Using the notation above, the formula for the length of a diagonal of a rectangular solid is $D = \sqrt{l^2 + w^2 + h^2}$, which is derived from two applications of the Pythagorean theorem.

Examples

(A) The length, width, and height of a right prism are 9, 4, and 2, respectively. What is the length of the longest segment whose endpoints are vertices of the prism?

The longest such segment is a diagonal of the prism. The length of this diagonal is

$$l = \sqrt{9^2 + 4^2 + 2^2} = \sqrt{101}$$

One type of problem that might be found on a Math Level 2 test is to find the volume of the space between two solids, one inscribed in the other. This is solved by finding the difference of volumes. In this type of problem, you are given only some of the necessary dimensions. You must use these dimensions to find the others.

(B) A sphere with diameter 10 meters is inscribed in a cube. What is the volume of the space between the sphere and the cube?

You need to subtract the volume of the sphere from the volume of the cube. The radius of the sphere is 5 and the volume is $\frac{4}{3}\pi(5)^3 \approx 523.6\text{ m}^3$. Since the sphere is inscribed in the cube, the side length of the cube is 10 m and its volume is 1,000 m^3. The volume of the space between them is 476.4 m^3.

You might be asked to find a dimension of a figure if its volume and surface area are equal.

(C) A cylinder has a volume of 500 in^3. What is the radius of this cylinder if its altitude equals the diameter of its base?

The formula for the volume of a cylinder is $V = \pi r^2 h$. If $h = 2r$, this formula becomes $V = 2\pi r^3$. Substitute 500 for V and solve for r to get $r = 4.3$ in.

A third type of problem involves percent changes in the dimensions of a figure.

(D) If the volume of a right circular cone is reduced by 15% by reducing its height by 5%, by what percent must the radius of the base be reduced?

If the volume of the cone is reduced by 15%, then 85% of its original volume remains. If its height is reduced by 5%, 95% of its original height remains. Use the formula for the volume of a cone, and let p be the proportion of the radius that remains,

$$0.85\left(\frac{1}{3}\pi r^2 h\right) = \frac{1}{3}\pi(pr)^2(0.95h)$$

This equation simplifies to $0.85 = 0.95p^2$, so $p \approx 0.946$. Therefore, the radius must be reduced by 5.4%.

A solid figure can be obtained by rotating a plane figure about some line in the plane that does not intersect the figure.

The coordinate plane can be extended by adding a third axis, the z-axis, which is perpendicular to the other two. Picture the corner of a room. The corner itself is the origin. The edges between the walls and the floor are the x- and y-axes. The edge between the two walls is the z-axis. The first octant of this three-dimensional coordinate system and the point (1,2,3) are illustrated below.

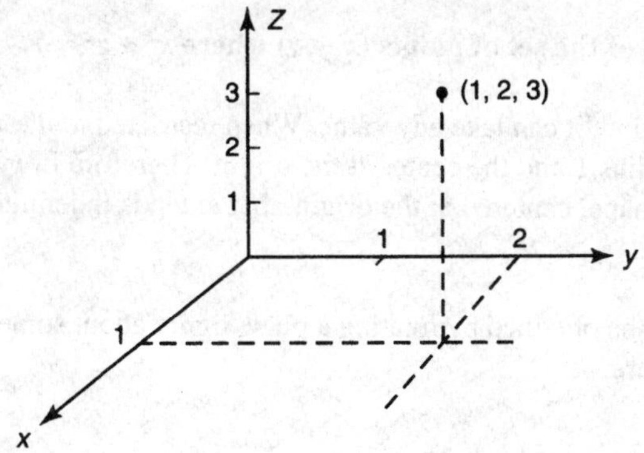

A point that has zero as any coordinate must lie on the plane formed by the other two axes. If two coordinates of a point are zero, then the point lies on the nonzero axis. The three-dimensional Pythagorean theorem yields a formula for the distance between two points (x_1,y_1,z_1) and (x_2,y_2,z_2) in space:

$$d = \sqrt{(x_2 - x_1)^2 + (y_2 - y_1)^2 + (z_2 - z_1)^2}$$

A three-dimensional coordinate system can be used to graph the variable z as a function of the two variables x and y, but such graphs are beyond the scope of the Level 2 Test.

Examples

(E) The distance between two points in space $A(2, y, -3)$ and $B(1, -1, 4)$ is 9. Find the possible values of y.

Use the formula for the distance between two points and set this equal to 9:

$$\sqrt{(2-1)^2 + (y+1)^2 + (-3-4)^2} = 9$$

Square both sides and simplify to get $(y + 1)^2 = 31$. Therefore, $y \approx 4.6$ or $y \approx -6.6$.

A sphere is the set of points in space that are equidistant from a given point. If the given point is (a, b, c) and the given distance is r, an equation of the sphere is $(x - a)^2 + (y - b)^2 + (z - c)^2 = r^2$.

(F) Describe the graph of the set of points (x, y, z) where $(x - 6)^2 + (y + 3)^2 + (z - 2)^2 = 36$.

This equation describes the set of points whose distance from $(6, -3, 2)$ is 6. This is a sphere of radius 6 with the center at $(6, -3, 2)$.

If only two of the variables appear in an equation, the equation describes a planar figure. The third variable spans the entire number line. The resulting three-dimensional figure is a solid that extends indefinitely in both directions parallel to the axis of the variable that is not in the equation, with cross sections congruent to the planar figure.

(G) Describe the graph of the set of points (x, y, z) where $x^2 + z^2 = 1$.

Since y is not in the equation, it can take any value. When restricted to the xz plane, the equation is that of a circle with radius 1 and the center at the origin. Therefore in xyz space, the equation represents a cylindrical shape, centered at the origin, that extends indefinitely in both directions along the y-axis.

A solid figure can also be obtained by rotating a plane figure about some line in the plane that does not intersect the figure.

(H) If the segment of the line $y = -2x + 2$ that lies in quadrant I is rotated about the y-axis, a cone is formed. What is the volume of the cone?

As shown in the figure below on the left, the part of the segment that lies in the first quadrant and the axes form a triangle with vertices at (0,0), (1,0), and (0,2). Rotating this triangle about the y-axis generates the cone shown in the figure below on the right.

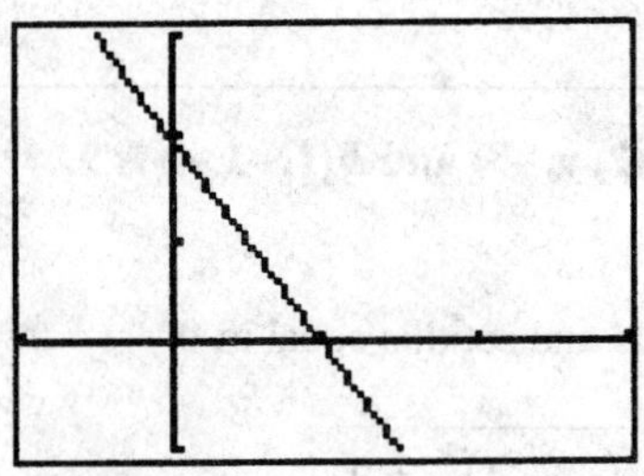

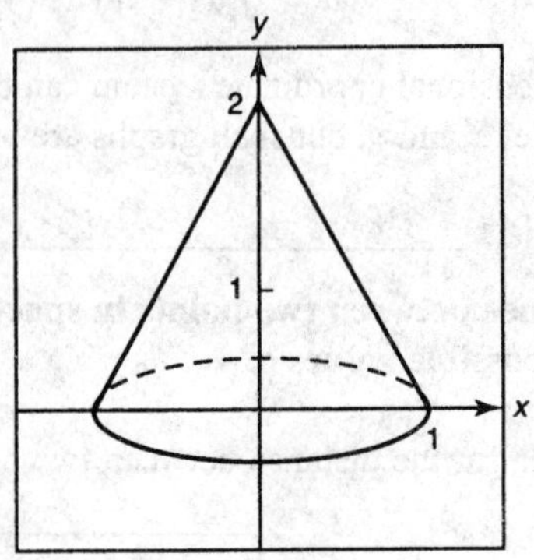

The radius of the base is 1, and the height is 2. Therefore, the volume is

$$V = \frac{1}{3}\pi(1)^2(2) = \frac{2}{3}\pi$$

EXERCISES 习题

1. The figure below shows a right circular cylinder inscribed in a cube with edge of length x. What is the ratio of the volume of the cylinder to the volume of the cube?

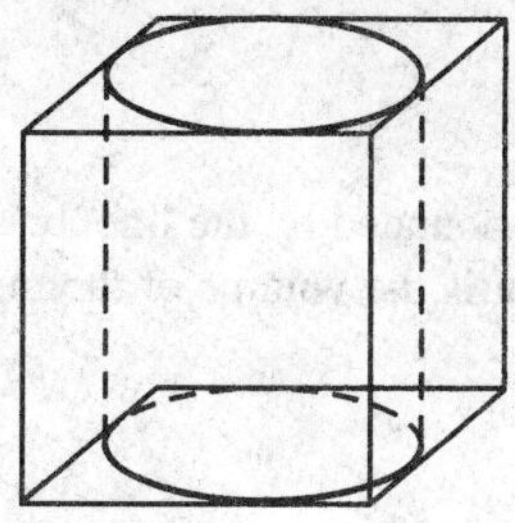

(A) $\frac{2}{3}$

(B) $\frac{3}{4}$

(C) $\frac{\pi}{4}$

(D) $\frac{\pi}{2}$

(E) $\frac{4}{5}$

2. The volume of a right circular cylinder is the same numerical value as its total surface area. Find the smallest integral value for the radius of the cylinder.

(A) 1
(B) 2
(C) 3
(D) 4
(E) This value cannot be determined.

3. The length, width, and height of a rectangular solid are 5 cm, 3 cm, and 7 cm, respectively. What is the length of the longest segment whose endpoints are vertices of the rectangular solid?

(A) 5.8 cm
(B) 7.6 cm
(C) 8.6 cm
(D) 9.1 cm
(E) 15 cm

4. The distance between two points in space, $P(x,-1,-1)$ and $Q(3,-3,1)$, is 3. Find the possible values of x.

(A) 1 or 2
(B) 2 or 3
(C) -2 or -3
(D) 2 or 4
(E) -2 or -4

5. The point (–4,0,7) lies on the

(A) y-axis
(B) xy plane
(C) yz plane
(D) xz plane
(E) z-axis

6. The region in the first quadrant bounded by the line $3x + 2y = 7$ and the coordinate axes is rotated about the x-axis. What is the volume of the resulting solid?

(A) 8 units^3
(B) 20 units^3
(C) 30 units^3
(D) 90 units^3
(E) 120 units^3

Answers Explained 答案解析

1. **(C)** The volume of the cube is x^3. The radius of the cylinder is $\frac{x}{2}$, and its height is x.

Substitute these into the formula for the volume of a cylinder:

$$V = \pi r^2 h$$

$$= \pi\left(\frac{x}{2}\right)^2 x$$

$$= \frac{\pi}{4}x^3$$

2. **(C)** $V = \pi r^2 h$, and total area $= 2\pi r^2 + 2\pi rh$. Setting these two equal yields $rh = 2r + 2h$. Therefore, $h = \frac{2r}{r-2}$. Since h must be positive, the smallest integer value of r is 3.

* 3. **(D)** The length of the longest segment is $\sqrt{5^2 + 3^2 + 7^2} \approx 9.1$.

4. **(D)** The square of the distance between P and Q is 9, so

$$(x-3)^2 + (-1-(-3))^2 + (-1-1)^2 = 9, \text{ or } (x-3)^2 = 1$$

Therefore, $x - 3 = \pm 1$, so $x = 2$ or 4.

5. **(D)** Since the y-coordinate is zero, the point must lie in the xz plane.

* 6. **(C)** The line $3x + 2y = 7$ has x-intercept $\frac{7}{3}$ and y-intercept $\frac{7}{2}$. The part of this line that lies in the first quadrant forms a triangle with the coordinate axes. Rotating this triangle about the x-axis produces a cone with radius $\frac{7}{2}$ and height $\frac{7}{3}$. The volume of this cone is $\frac{1}{3}\pi\left(\frac{7}{2}\right)^2\left(\frac{7}{3}\right) \approx 30$.

Counting
第16章　计算

16

- → **VENN DIAGRAMS**
- → **GENERAL MULTIPLICATION PRINCIPLE**
- → **FACTORIAL**
- → **PERMUTATIONS**
- → **COMBINATIONS**

Counting problems usually begin with the phrase "How many . . ." or the phrase "In how many ways . . ." Illustrating counting techniques by example is best.

Examples

(A) A certain sports club has 50 members. Of these, 35 golf, 30 hunt, and 18 do both. How many club members do neither?

Add 35 and 30, then subtract the 18 that were counted twice. This makes 47 who golf, hunt, or do both. Therefore, only 3 (50 – 47) do neither.

(B) Among the seniors at a small high school, 80 take math, 41 take Spanish, and 54 take physics. Ten seniors take math and Spanish; 19 take math and physics; and 12 take physics and Spanish. Seven seniors take all three. How many seniors take math but not Spanish or physics?

A Venn diagram will help you sort out this complicated-sounding problem.

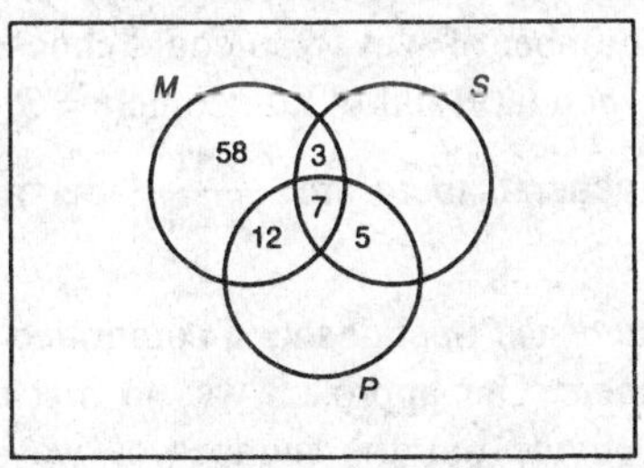

Start with the 7 who take all three courses. Since 10 take math and Spanish, this leaves 3 who take math and Spanish but not physics. Use similar reasoning to see that 5 take physics and Spanish but not math, and 12 take math and physics but not Spanish.

Finally, using the totals for how many students take each course, we can conclude that 58 (80 – 3 – 7 – 12) take math but not physics or Spanish.

Many other counting problems use the multiplication principle.

(C) Suppose you have 5 shirts, 4 pairs of pants, and 9 ties. How many outfits can be made consisting of a shirt, a pair of pants, and a tie?

For each of the 5 shirts, you can wear 4 pairs of pants, so there are $5 \cdot 4 = 20$ shirt-pants combinations. For each of these 20 shirt-pants combinations, there are 9 ties, so there are $20 \cdot 9 = 180$ shirt-pants-tie combinations.

(D) Six very good friends decide they will have lunch together every day. In how many different ways can they line up in the lunch line?

Any one of the 6 could be first in line. For each person who is first, there are 5 who could be second. This means there are 30 ($6 \cdot 5$) ways of choosing the first two people. For each of these 30 ways, there are 4 ways of choosing the third person. This makes 120 ($30 \cdot 4$) ways of choosing the first 3 people. Continuing in this fashion, there are $6 \cdot 5 \cdot 4 \cdot 3 \cdot 2 \cdot 1 = 720$ ways these 6 friends can stand in the cafeteria line. (This means that if they all have perfect attendance for 4 years of high school, they could stand in line in a different order every day, because $720 = 4 \cdot 180$.)

(E) The math team at East High has 20 members. They want to choose a president, vice president, and treasurer. In how many ways can this be done?

Any one of the 20 members could be president. For each choice, there are 19 who could be vice president. For each of these 380 ($20 \cdot 19$) ways of choosing a president and a vice president, there are 18 choices for treasurer. Therefore, there are $20 \cdot 19 \cdot 18 = 6{,}840$ ways of choosing these three club officers.

(F) The student council at West High has 20 members. They want to select a committee of 3 to work with the school administration on policy matters affecting students directly. How many committees of 3 students are possible?

This problem is similar to Example E, so we will start with the fact that if they were electing 3 officers, the student council would be able to do this in 6,840 ways. However, it does not matter whether member A is president, B is vice president, and C is treasurer or some other arrangement, as long as all 3 are on the committee. Therefore, we can divide 6,840 by the number of ways the 3 students selected could be president, vice president, and treasurer. This latter number is $3 \cdot 2 \cdot 1 = 6$, so there are 1,140 ($6{,}840 \div 6$) committees of 3.

Counting problems like the ones in Examples D, E, and F occur frequently enough that they have special designations.

Example D asked for the number of ways 6 friends could stand in line. By using the multiplication principle, we found that there were $6 \cdot 5 \cdot 4 \cdot 3 \cdot 2 \cdot 1$ ways. A special notation for this product is 6! (6 **factorial**). In general, the number of ways "n" objects can be ordered is n!

Example E asked for the number of ways you could choose a first (president), second (vice president), and third person (secretary) out of 20 people($r = 3$, $n = 20$). The answer is $20 \cdot 19 \cdot 18$, or $\frac{20!}{17!} = \frac{20!}{(20-3)!}$. In general, there are $\frac{n!}{(n-r)!}$ **permutations** of r objects of n. This appears as $_nP_r$ in the calculator menu.

In Example F, we were interested in choosing a committee of 3 where there was no distinction among committee members. Our approach was to first compute the number of ways of choosing officers and then divide out the number of ways the three officers could hold the different offices. This led to the computation $\frac{20!}{17!3!} = \frac{20!}{(20-3)!3!}$. In general, the number of ways of choosing r of n objects is $\frac{n!}{(n-r)!r!}$. This quantity appears on the calculator menu as $_nC_r$. However, there is a special notation for **combinations**: $_nC_r = \binom{n}{r}$ = the number of ways r objects can be chosen from n.

Calculator commands for all three of these functions are in the MATH/PRB menu.

```
MATH NUM CMPLX PROB FRAC
1:rand
2:nPr
3:nCr
4:!
5:randInt(
6:randNorm(
7:randBin(
8:randIntNoRep(
```

These 3 commands can also be found on scientific calculators.

EXERCISES 习题

1. There are 50 people in a room. Twenty-eight are male, and 32 are under the age of 30. Twelve are males under the age of 30. How many women over the age of 30 are in the group?

   (A) 2
   (B) 3
   (C) 4
   (D) 5
   (E) 6

2. A student has 8 shirts, 5 pairs of pants, and 3 pairs of shoes. How many outfits consisting of a shirt, pair of pants, and pair of shoes can this student form?

   (A) 16
   (B) 120
   (C) 560
   (D) 4,096
   (E) 2,903,400

3. M & M plain candies come in six colors: brown, green, orange, red, blue, and yellow. Assume there are at least 3 of each color. If you pick three candies from a bag, how many color possibilities are there?

   (A) 18
   (B) 20
   (C) 120
   (D) 216
   (E) 729

4. A code consists of two letters of the alphabet followed by 5 digits. How many such codes are possible?

   (A) 7
   (B) 10
   (C) 128
   (D) 20,000
   (E) 67,600,000

5. A salad bar has 7 ingredients, excluding the dressing. How many different salads are possible where two salads are different if they don't include identical ingredients?

(A) 7
(B) 14
(C) 128
(D) 5,040
(E) 823,543

6. How many 3-person committees can be selected from a fraternity with 25 members?

(A) 15,625
(B) 13,800
(C) 2,300
(D) 75
(E) 8

7. A basketball team has 5 centers, 9 guards, and 13 forwards. Of these, 1 center, 2 guards, and 2 forwards start a game. How many possible starting teams can a coach put on the floor?

(A) 56,160
(B) 14,040
(C) 585
(D) 197
(E) 27

8. Five boys and 6 girls would like to serve on the homecoming court, which will consist of 2 boys and 2 girls. How many different homecoming courts are possible?

(A) 30
(B) 61
(C) 150
(D) 900
(E) 2,048

9. In a plane there are 8 points, no three of which are collinear. How many lines do the points determine?

(A) 7
(B) 16
(C) 28
(D) 36
(E) 64

10. If $\binom{6}{x} = \binom{4}{x}$, then $x =$

(A) 0
(B) 1
(C) 4
(D) 5
(E) 10

Answers Explained 答案解析

1. **(A)** A Venn diagram will help you solve this problem.

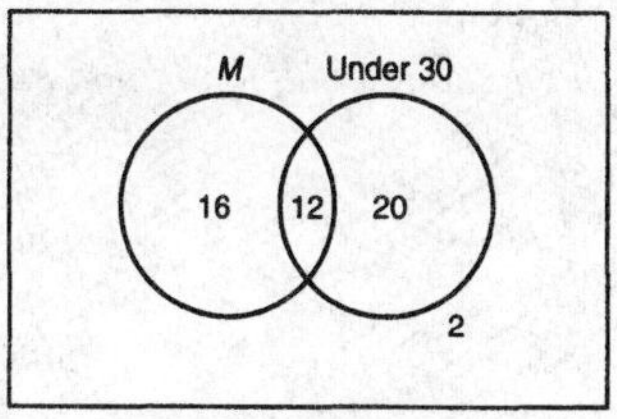

The two circles represent males and people who are at most 30 years of age, respectively. The part of the rectangle outside both circles represents people who are in neither category, i.e., females over the age of 30. First fill in the 12 males who are less than or equal to 30 years of age in the intersection of the circles. Since there are 28 males altogether, 16 are male and over 30. Since there are 32 people age 30 or less, there are 20 women that age. Add these together to get 48 people. Since there are 50 in the group, 2 must be women over 30.

2. **(B)** This is a direct application of the multiplication rule: $8 \times 5 \times 3 = 120$.

* 3. **(D)** There are 6 choices of color for each of the three candies selected. Therefore, there are $6 \times 6 \times 6 = 216$ color possibilities altogether.

* 4. **(E)** The multiplication rule applies. There are $(26)(26)(10)^5 = 67{,}600{,}000$ possible codes.

* 5. **(C)** You can either include or exclude each of the seven ingredients in your salad, which means there are 2 choices for each ingredient. According to the multiplication rule, there are $2^7 = 128$ ways of making these yes-no choices.

* 6. **(C)** This is the number of ways 3 objects can be chosen from 25, or $\binom{25}{3} =$ $25{}_nC_r3 = 2{,}300$.

* 7. **(B)** There are $\binom{5}{1} = 5$ ways of choosing the one center, $\binom{9}{2} = 36$ ways of choosing the two guards, and $\binom{13}{2} = 78$ ways of choosing the two forwards. Therefore, there are $5 \times 36 \times 78 = 14{,}040$ possible starting teams.

* 8. **(C)** There are $\binom{5}{2} = 10$ ways of choosing 2 boys out of 5 and $\binom{6}{2} = 15$ ways of choosing 2 girls out of 6. Therefore, there are $10 \times 15 = 150$ ways of choosing the homecoming court.

* 9. **(C)** Since no three points are collinear, every pair of points determines a distinct line. There are $\binom{8}{2} = 28$ such lines.

10. **(A)** $\binom{n}{0} = 1$ for any n.

Complex Numbers
第17章 复数

17

→ POWERS OF *I*
→ ARITHMETIC OF COMPLEX NUMBERS
→ GRAPHING COMPLEX NUMBERS

The square of a real number is never negative. This means that the square root of a negative number cannot be a real number. The symbol $i = \sqrt{-1}$ is called the **imaginary unit**, $i^2 = -1$. Powers of i follow a pattern:

Power of *i*	Intermediate Steps	Value
i^1	i	i
i^2	$i \cdot i = -1$	-1
i^3	$i^2 \cdot i = (-1) \cdot i = -i$	$-i$
i^4	$i^3 \cdot i = (-i) \cdot i = -i^2 = -(-1) = 1$	1
i^5	$i^4 \cdot i = 1 \cdot i = i$	i

In other words, powers of i follow a cycle of four. This means that $i^n = i^{n \bmod 4}$, where n mod 4 is the remainder when n is divided by 4. For example, $i^{58} = i^2 = -1$.

The imaginary numbers are numbers of the form bi, where b is a real number. The square root of any negative number is i times the square root of the positive of that number. Thus for example, $\sqrt{-9} = i\sqrt{9} = 3i$, $\sqrt{-12} = i\sqrt{12} = 2i\sqrt{3}$, and $\sqrt{-7} = i\sqrt{7}$.

The complex numbers are formed by "attaching" imaginary numbers to real numbers using a plus sign (+). The standard form of a complex number is $a + bi$, where a and b are real. The number a is called the real part of the complex number, and the b number is called the imaginary part. If $b = 0$, then the complex number is just a real number. If $b \neq 0$, the complex number is called imaginary. If $a = 0$, bi is called a pure imaginary number. Examples of imaginary numbers are $2 + 3i, -\frac{3}{5} + 4i, 6i, 0.11 + (-0.45)i$, and $\pi - i\sqrt{5}$.

When the imaginary part of a complex number is a radical, write the i to the left in order to avoid ambiguity about whether i is under the radical.

Finding sums, differences, products, quotients, and reciprocals of complex numbers can be accomplished directly on your calculator. The imaginary unit i is the 2nd decimal point on the graphing calculator. If you enter an expression with i in it, the calculator will do imaginary arithmetic in REAL mode. If the expression entered does not include i but the output is imaginary, the calculator gives you the error message NONREAL ANS. For example, if you tried to calculate $\sqrt{-3}$ in REAL mode, you would get this error message. In $a + bi$ mode, however, $\sqrt{-3}$ would calculate as $1.732\cdots i$. You should use $a + bi$ mode exclusively for the Level 2 test. Although complex number arithmetic per se is not likely to be on a Level 2 test, an understanding of how it is done may be. A review of the main features of complex number arithmetic is provided in the next several paragraphs.

To add or subtract complex numbers, add or subtract their real and imaginary parts.

Examples

(A) Evaluate (5 – 7*i*) + (2 + 4*i*).

$$(5 - 7i) + (2 + 4i) = 7 - 3i$$

To multiply complex numbers, multiply like you would any two binomial expressions, using FOIL. Thus

$$(a + bi)(c + di) = ac + adi + bci + bdi^2 = (ac - bd) + (ad + bc)i$$

(B) Evaluate (4 + 5*i*) (2 – 3*i*).

$$(4 + 5i)(2 - 3i) = 8 + 10i - 12i - 15i^2 = 8 - 2i + 15 = 23 - 2i$$

The difference of the first and last terms makes the real part, and the sum of the outer and inner terms makes the imaginary part.

To find the quotient of two complex numbers, multiply the denominator and numerator by the conjugate of the denominator. Then simplify.

(C) Evaluate $\frac{2-7i}{3+5i}$.

$$\frac{2-7i}{3+5i} = \left(\frac{2-7i}{3+5i}\right)\cdot\left(\frac{3-5i}{3-5i}\right) = \frac{-29-31i}{9+25} = -\frac{29}{34} - \frac{31}{34}i$$

A complex number can be represented graphically as rectangular coordinates, with the *x*-coordinate as the real part and the *y*-coordinate as the imaginary part. The modulus of a complex number is its distance to the origin. The Pythagorean theorem tells us that this distance is $\sqrt{a^2+b^2}$. The conjugate of the imaginary number $a + bi$ is $a - bi$, so the graphs of conjugates are reflections about the *y*-axis. Also, the product of an imaginary number and its conjugate is the square of the modulus because $(a + bi)(a - bi) = a^2 - b^2i^2 = a^2 + b^2$.

EXERCISES 习题

1. $i^{29} =$

   (A) 1
   (B) i
   (C) $-i$
   (D) –1
   (E) none of the above

2. Evaluate $(2 + 3i)(4 - 5i)$.

   (A) $-7 - 23i$
   (B) $-7 + 2i$
   (C) $23 - 7i$
   (D) $23 + 2i$
   (E) $23 - 2i$

3. Evaluate $\frac{i}{2-i}$.

(A) $-1+\frac{1}{2}i$

(B) $\frac{1}{5}-\frac{2}{5}i$

(C) $-\frac{1}{5}+\frac{2}{5}i$

(D) $-1+2i$

(E) $-1-2i$

4. If $z=8-2i$, $z^2=$

(A) $60-32i$
(B) $64+4i$
(C) $64-4i$
(D) 60
(E) 68

5. If z is the complex number shown in the figure, which of the following points could be iz?

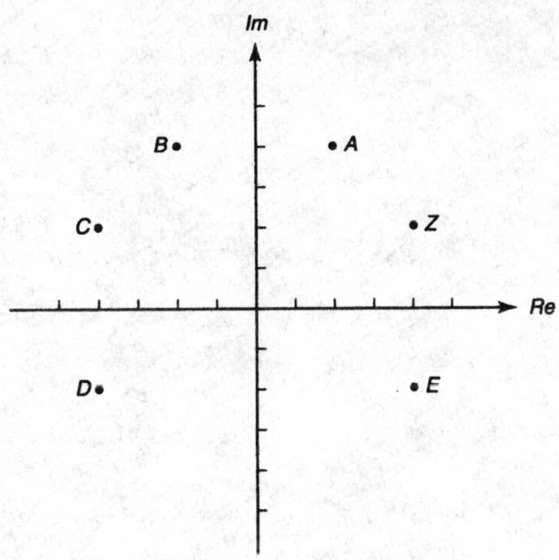

(A) A
(B) B
(C) C
(D) D
(E) E

6. Which of the following is the modulus of $2+i$?

(A) $\sqrt{2}$

(B) 2

(C) $\sqrt{3}$

(D) $\sqrt{5}$

(E) 5

Answers Explained 答案解析

1. **(B)** $i^{29} = i^1 = i$.

2. **(D)** If you enter imaginary numbers into the calculator, it will do imaginary arithmetic without changing mode. The imaginary unit is the 2nd decimal point. Enter the product, and read the solution $23 + 2i$.

* 3. **(C)** Simply enter the expression into the graphing calculator.

* 4. **(A)** Simply enter the expression into the graphing calculator.

5. **(B)** $z = 4 + 2i$, so $iz = -2 + 4i$, which is point B.

6. **(D)** The real and imaginary parts are 2 and 1, respectively, so the modulus is $\sqrt{2^2 + 1^2} = \sqrt{5}$.

Matrices
第18章　矩阵

18

- ➔ ADDITION AND SUBTRACTION
- ➔ SCALAR MULTIPLICATION
- ➔ MATRIX MULTIPLICATION
- ➔ DETERMINANTS
- ➔ SYSTEMS OF EQUATIONS

A matrix is a rectangular array of numbers. The size of a matrix is r by c, where r is the number of rows and c is the number of columns. The numbers in a matrix are called entries, and the entry in the ith row and jth column is named x_{ij}. Two matrices are equal if they are the same size and their corresponding entries are equal.

➥ Examples

(A) Evaluate x and y if $\begin{bmatrix} 5 & -3 \\ x & 4 \end{bmatrix} = \begin{bmatrix} y-3 & -3 \\ 2x+2 & 4 \end{bmatrix}$.

These two matrices are equal if $y - 3 = 5$ and $x = 2x + 2$. Therefore, $y = 8$ and $x = -2$.

If $r = 1$, the matrix is called a row matrix. If $c = 1$, the matrix is called a column matrix. If $r = c$, the matrix is called a square matrix. The numbers from the upper left corner to the bottom right corner of a square matrix form the main diagonal.

Scalar multiplication takes place when each number in a matrix is multiplied by a constant. If two matrices are the same size, they can be added or subtracted by adding or subtracting corresponding entries.

(B) Simplify: $3\begin{bmatrix} -2 & 3 \\ 1 & 5 \\ -4 & 3 \end{bmatrix} - 2\begin{bmatrix} 3 & -1 \\ 2 & 1 \\ -4 & 6 \end{bmatrix}$.

$$3\begin{bmatrix} -2 & 3 \\ 1 & 5 \\ -4 & 3 \end{bmatrix} - 2\begin{bmatrix} 3 & -1 \\ 2 & 1 \\ -4 & 6 \end{bmatrix} = \begin{bmatrix} -6 & 9 \\ 3 & 15 \\ -12 & 9 \end{bmatrix} - \begin{bmatrix} 6 & -2 \\ 4 & 2 \\ -8 & 12 \end{bmatrix} = \begin{bmatrix} -12 & 11 \\ -1 & 13 \\ -4 & -3 \end{bmatrix}$$

(C) **Solve the matrix equation:** $2x + \begin{bmatrix} -3 & 2 & 6 \\ 5 & -1 & 0 \\ 3 & -6 & -2 \end{bmatrix} = \begin{bmatrix} 5 & -8 & -4 \\ 1 & 3 & 10 \\ -5 & 8 & 0 \end{bmatrix}$.

$$2x = \begin{bmatrix} 5 & -8 & -4 \\ 1 & 3 & 10 \\ -5 & 8 & 0 \end{bmatrix} - \begin{bmatrix} -3 & 2 & 6 \\ 5 & -1 & 0 \\ 3 & -6 & -2 \end{bmatrix} = \begin{bmatrix} 8 & -10 & -10 \\ -4 & 4 & 10 \\ -8 & 14 & 2 \end{bmatrix}$$

$$x = \begin{bmatrix} 4 & -5 & -5 \\ -2 & 2 & 5 \\ -4 & 7 & 1 \end{bmatrix}$$

Matrix multiplication takes place when two matrices, A and B, are multiplied to form a new matrix, AB. Matrix multiplication is possible only under certain conditions. Suppose A is r_1 by c_1 and B is r_2 by c_2. If $c_1 = r_2$, then AB is defined and has size r_1 by c_2. The entry x_{ij} of AB is the ith row of A times the jth column of B. If A and B are square matrices, BA is also defined but not generally equal to AB.

➡ Example

(D) **Evaluate** $AB = \begin{bmatrix} 3 & -1 \\ 3 & 5 \\ -2 & 1 \end{bmatrix} \begin{bmatrix} 1 & -2 \\ 5 & -3 \end{bmatrix}$. **$A$ is 3 by 2, and B is 2 by 2.**

The product matrix is 3 by 2, with entries x_{ij} calculated as follows:

$x_{11} = (3)(1) + (-1)(5) = -2$, the "product" of row 1 of A and column 1 of B
$x_{12} = (3)(-2) + (-1)(-3) = -3$, the "product" of row 1 of A and column 2 of B
$x_{21} = (3)(1) + (5)(5) = 28$, the "product" of row 2 of A and column 1 of B
$x_{22} = (3)(-2) + (5)(-3) = -21$, the "product" of row 2 of A and column 2 of B
$x_{31} = (-2)(1) + (1)(5) = 3$, the "product" of row 3 of A and column 1 of B
$x_{32} = (-2)(-2) + (1)(-3) = 1$, the "product" of row 3 of A and column 2 of B

Therefore, $AB = \begin{bmatrix} 3 & -1 \\ 3 & 5 \\ -2 & 1 \end{bmatrix} \begin{bmatrix} 1 & -2 \\ 5 & -3 \end{bmatrix} = \begin{bmatrix} -2 & -3 \\ 28 & -21 \\ 3 & 1 \end{bmatrix}$. Note that BA is not defined.

Matrix calculations can be done on a graphing calculator. To define a matrix, enter 2nd MATRIX, highlight and enter EDIT, enter the number of rows followed by the number of columns, and finally enter the entries. The figures below show the result of these steps for matrices A and B of Example D.

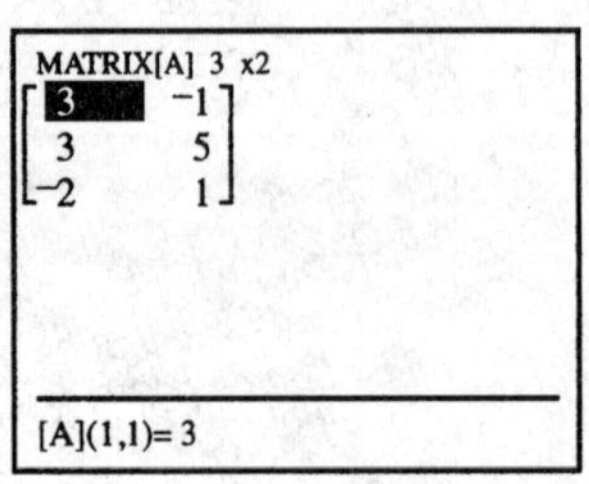

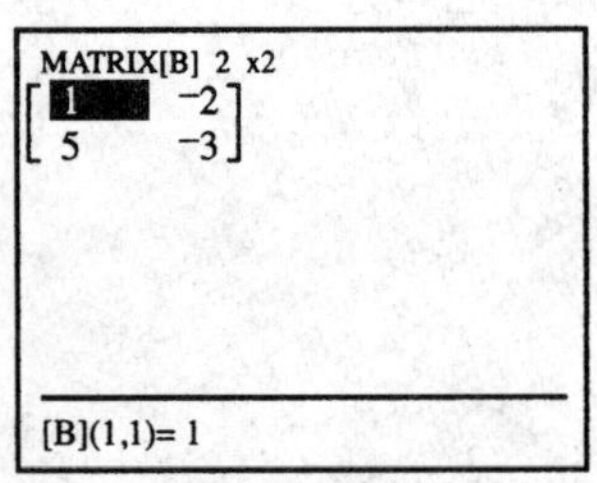

To find the product, enter 2nd MATRIX/NAMES/[*A*], which returns [*A*] to the home screen. Also enter 2nd MATRIX/NAMES/[*B*], which returns [*B*] to the home screen. Hit ENTER again to get the product.

[A][B]

$$\begin{bmatrix} -2 & -3 \\ 28 & -21 \\ 3 & 1 \end{bmatrix}$$

Square matrices of the same size can always be multiplied. The product of square *n* by *n* matrices is a square *n* by *n* matrix. An identity matrix I_n is a square matrix consisting of 1's down the main diagonal and 0's elsewhere. The product of *n* by *n* square matrices *A* and I_n is *A*. In other words, I_n is a multiplicative identity for *n* by *n* square matrices.

➡ Example

(E) The identity matrix $I_2 = \begin{bmatrix} 1 & 0 \\ 0 & 1 \end{bmatrix}$. **If** $A = \begin{bmatrix} 2 & -3 \\ 5 & 1 \end{bmatrix}$, **evaluate** $AI_2 = I_2A = A$.

$$AI_n = \begin{bmatrix} 2 & -3 \\ 5 & 1 \end{bmatrix}\begin{bmatrix} 1 & 0 \\ 0 & 1 \end{bmatrix} = \begin{bmatrix} 2 & -3 \\ 5 & 1 \end{bmatrix} \text{ and } I_nA = \begin{bmatrix} 1 & 0 \\ 0 & 1 \end{bmatrix}\begin{bmatrix} 2 & -3 \\ 5 & 1 \end{bmatrix} = \begin{bmatrix} 2 & -3 \\ 5 & 1 \end{bmatrix}$$

In general, matrix multiplication is *not* commutative.

➡ Example

(F) If $A = \begin{bmatrix} -2 & 5 \\ 1 & 3 \end{bmatrix}$ **and** $B = \begin{bmatrix} 6 & 0 \\ 3 & -5 \end{bmatrix}$, **evaluate *AB* and *BA*.**

$$AB = \begin{bmatrix} -2 & 5 \\ 1 & 3 \end{bmatrix}\begin{bmatrix} 6 & 0 \\ 3 & -5 \end{bmatrix} = \begin{bmatrix} 3 & -25 \\ 15 & -15 \end{bmatrix}, \text{ while } BA = \begin{bmatrix} 6 & 0 \\ 3 & -5 \end{bmatrix}\begin{bmatrix} -2 & 5 \\ 1 & 3 \end{bmatrix} = \begin{bmatrix} -12 & 30 \\ -11 & 0 \end{bmatrix}.$$

The **determinant** of an *n* by *n* square matrix is a number. The determinant of the 2 by 2 matrix $\begin{bmatrix} a & b \\ c & d \end{bmatrix}$ is denoted by $\begin{vmatrix} a & c \\ b & d \end{vmatrix}$, which equals $ad - bc$. Determinants of larger square matrices can be evaluated by keying 2nd/MATRIX/MATH/det on the graphing calculator.

➡ Examples

(G) Write an expression for the determinant of $\begin{bmatrix} 2 & -1 \\ 3 & x \end{bmatrix}$.

By definition, $\begin{vmatrix} 2 & -1 \\ 3 & x \end{vmatrix} = 2x - (-3) = 2x + 3$.

(H) Solve for *x*: $\begin{vmatrix} x & x \\ 8 & x \end{vmatrix} = \begin{vmatrix} 7 & -2 & 1 \\ 0 & 3 & -1 \\ 5 & -4 & 2 \end{vmatrix}$.

The determinant on the left side is $x^2 - 8x$. Use the calculator to evaluate the determinant on the right as 9. This yields the quadratic equation $x^2 - 8x - 9 = 0$. This can be solved by factoring to get $x = 9$ or $x = -1$.

A square matrix is called **singular** if its determinant is zero and **nonsingular** if its determinant is not zero. **Only nonsingular matrices have inverses.** The **inverse of a nonsingular square matrix**, A, is defined as a square matrix A^{-1} of the same size such that $AA^{-1} = A^{-1}A = I$.

The inverse of a nonsingular square n by n matrix A has a multiplicative inverse, A^{-1}, where $A^{-1}A = AA^{-1} = I$. A^{-1} can be found on the graphing calculator by entering MATRIX/NAMES/A, which will return A to the home screen, followed by x^{-1} and ENTER.

(I) If $A = \begin{bmatrix} 7 & -3 \\ 1 & 4 \end{bmatrix}$ **and** $B = \begin{bmatrix} 5 \\ 2 \end{bmatrix}$**, solve for X when $AX = B$.**

Matrix multiply both sides on the left by A^{-1}: $A^{-1}AX = A^{-1}B$. This yields $IX = X = A^{-1}B = \begin{bmatrix} 26/31 \\ 9/31 \end{bmatrix}$.

The fractional form of the answer can be obtained by keying MATH/ENTER/ENTER.

An important application of matrices is writing and solving systems of equations in matrix form.

Example

(J) Solve the system $\begin{aligned} x - y + 2z &= -3 \\ 2x + y - z &= 0 \\ -x + 2y - 3z &= 7 \end{aligned}$

The matrix form of this system is $AX = B$, where $A = \begin{bmatrix} 1 & -1 & 2 \\ 2 & 1 & -1 \\ -1 & 2 & -3 \end{bmatrix}$, $X = \begin{bmatrix} x \\ y \\ z \end{bmatrix}$, and

$B = \begin{bmatrix} -3 \\ 0 \\ 7 \end{bmatrix}$. A is the **coefficient matrix**, X is the **variables matrix**, and B is the **constant matrix**.

This system can be represented by the single 3×4 matrix $\begin{bmatrix} 1 & -1 & 2 & -3 \\ 2 & 1 & -1 & 0 \\ -1 & 2 & -3 & 7 \end{bmatrix}$. In general, if there were n equations and n variables, then matrix A would have n rows and $n + 1$ columns.

You can use the calculator to transform this matrix to **reduced row echelon form**. This transformation involves multiplying a row by a constant, or multiplying a row by a constant and adding the result to another row, and replacing the second row with the sum. (This is the same procedure used to solve a system of two equations in two variables.) These operations are done with the intent of transforming the first three columns into a 3×3 identity matrix. As this is done, the fourth column transforms into the solution. In the example above,

$\begin{bmatrix} 1 & -1 & 2 & -3 \\ 2 & 1 & -1 & 0 \\ -1 & 2 & -3 & 7 \end{bmatrix} \to \begin{bmatrix} 1 & 0 & 0 & -2 \\ 0 & 1 & 0 & 7 \\ 0 & 0 & 1 & 3 \end{bmatrix}$, so $x = -2, y = 7, z = 3$.

EXERCISES 习题

1. $\begin{bmatrix} 1 & 3 \\ -2 & 4 \end{bmatrix} + \begin{bmatrix} 11 & 5 \\ -6 & 12 \end{bmatrix} = K\begin{bmatrix} 3 & 2 \\ J & M \end{bmatrix}$. Find the value of $K+J+M$.

   (A) 2
   (B) 4
   (C) 6
   (D) 7
   (E) 8

2. Evaluate x and y if $\begin{bmatrix} x & 2 \\ -3 & y \end{bmatrix} = 2\begin{bmatrix} x^2 & 1 \\ -\frac{3}{2} & 3y-5 \end{bmatrix}$.

   (A) $x=0;\ y=2$
   (B) $x=1;\ y=2$
   (C) $x=-1, 1;\ y=\frac{5}{3}$
   (D) $x=-\frac{1}{2}, \frac{1}{2};\ y=\frac{5}{6}$
   (E) $x=0, \frac{1}{2};\ y=2$

3. Solve for X: $\begin{bmatrix} 1 & 2 & -3 \\ 2 & 1 & 3 \end{bmatrix} - X = \begin{bmatrix} 5 & 1 & 8 \\ -6 & 0 & 5 \end{bmatrix}$.

   (A) $\begin{bmatrix} 4 & 1 & -11 \\ -8 & 1 & -2 \end{bmatrix}$

   (B) $\begin{bmatrix} -4 & 1 & -11 \\ 8 & 1 & -2 \end{bmatrix}$

   (C) $\begin{bmatrix} -5 & -2 & 24 \\ 12 & 0 & -15 \end{bmatrix}$

   (D) $\begin{bmatrix} 5 & 2 & -24 \\ -12 & 0 & 15 \end{bmatrix}$

   (E) $\begin{bmatrix} 6 & 3 & 5 \\ -4 & 1 & 8 \end{bmatrix}$

Use $A = [-2 \quad -1 \quad 5 \quad 9]$ and $B = \begin{bmatrix} 0 & -5 \\ 3 & -2 \\ 4 & 0 \\ -6 & 1 \end{bmatrix}$ for question 4.

4. The product $AB =$

(A) $\begin{bmatrix} 0 & 10 \\ -3 & 2 \\ 20 & 0 \\ -54 & 9 \end{bmatrix}$

(B) $[-37 \quad 21]$

(C) $\begin{bmatrix} 10 \\ -2 \\ 20 \\ -45 \end{bmatrix}$

(D) $\begin{bmatrix} 0 \\ 6 \\ 0 \\ -54 \end{bmatrix}$

(E) product is not defined

5. The first row, second column of the product $\begin{bmatrix} x & 1 \\ 2 & -3 \end{bmatrix}\begin{bmatrix} 5 & -x \\ 2 & 1 \end{bmatrix}$ is

(A) $-5x - 3$
(B) $-x - 3$
(C) $1 - x^2$
(D) $4x$
(E) $2x + 2$

6. If $A = \begin{bmatrix} -3 & 1 & 6 \\ 2 & -5 & 0 \\ 1 & -3 & 4 \end{bmatrix}$, $B = \begin{bmatrix} 4 & 7 \\ -4 & 2 \\ -1 & -5 \end{bmatrix}$, and $AX = B$, then the size of X is

(A) 3 rows, 3 columns
(B) 3 rows, 2 columns
(C) 2 rows, 2 columns
(D) 2 rows, 3 columns
(E) cannot be determined

7. The chart below shows the number of small and large packages of a certain brand of cereal that were bought over a three-day period. The price of a small box of this brand is \$2.99, and the price of a large box is \$3.99. Which of the following matrix expressions represents the income, in dollars, received from the sale of cereal each of the three days?

	Day 1	**Day 2**	**Day 3**
Large	75	82	57
Small	43	36	50

(A) $\begin{bmatrix} 75 & 82 & 57 \\ 43 & 36 & 50 \end{bmatrix} \begin{bmatrix} 2.99 & 3.99 \end{bmatrix}$

(B) $\begin{bmatrix} 75 & 43 \\ 82 & 36 \\ 57 & 50 \end{bmatrix} \begin{bmatrix} 3.99 \\ 2.99 \end{bmatrix}$

(C) $\begin{bmatrix} 75 & 82 & 57 \\ 43 & 36 & 50 \end{bmatrix} \begin{bmatrix} 2.99 \\ 3.99 \end{bmatrix}$

(D) $\begin{bmatrix} 2.99 \\ 3.99 \end{bmatrix} \begin{bmatrix} 75 & 43 \\ 82 & 36 \\ 57 & 50 \end{bmatrix}$

(E) $2.99 \begin{bmatrix} 75 & 82 & 57 \\ 43 & 36 & 50 \end{bmatrix} + 3.99 \begin{bmatrix} 75 & 82 & 57 \\ 43 & 36 & 50 \end{bmatrix}$

8. The determinant of $\begin{bmatrix} p & 3 \\ -2 & 1 \end{bmatrix}$ is

(A) $p - 6$
(B) $p + 6$
(C) $3p - 2$
(D) $3 - 2p$
(E) $-6 - p$

9. Find all values of x for which $\begin{vmatrix} 2 & -1 & 4 \\ 3 & 0 & 5 \\ 4 & 1 & 6 \end{vmatrix} = \begin{vmatrix} x & 4 \\ 5 & x \end{vmatrix}$.

(A) ±3.78
(B) ±4.47
(C) ±5.12
(D) ±6.19
(E) ±6.97

10. If $X\begin{bmatrix} -7 & 2 \\ 0 & -5 \end{bmatrix} = \begin{bmatrix} 2 & -3 \\ 5 & 4 \end{bmatrix}$, then $X =$

(A) $\begin{bmatrix} -\frac{2}{7} & -\frac{3}{2} \\ 0 & -\frac{5}{4} \end{bmatrix}$

(B) $\begin{bmatrix} -\frac{7}{2} & -\frac{2}{3} \\ 0 & -\frac{4}{5} \end{bmatrix}$

(C) $\begin{bmatrix} -\frac{2}{7} & \frac{17}{35} \\ -\frac{5}{7} & -\frac{38}{351} \end{bmatrix}$

(D) $\begin{bmatrix} -14 & -6 \\ 0 & -20 \end{bmatrix}$

(E) undefined

11. Find the matrix equation that represents the system $\begin{cases} 2x - 3 = 3y \\ y - 5x = 14 \end{cases}$

(A) $\begin{bmatrix} 2 & -3 \\ 1 & 5 \end{bmatrix}\begin{bmatrix} x \\ y \end{bmatrix} = \begin{bmatrix} 3 \\ 14 \end{bmatrix}$

(B) $\begin{bmatrix} 2 & -3 \\ -5 & 1 \end{bmatrix}\begin{bmatrix} x \\ y \end{bmatrix} = \begin{bmatrix} 3 \\ 14 \end{bmatrix}$

(C) $\begin{bmatrix} x \\ y \end{bmatrix}\begin{bmatrix} 2 & -3 \\ -5 & 1 \end{bmatrix} = \begin{bmatrix} 3 \\ 14 \end{bmatrix}$

(D) $\begin{bmatrix} 3 \\ 13 \end{bmatrix}\begin{bmatrix} x & y \end{bmatrix} = \begin{bmatrix} 2 & -3 \\ 5 & 1 \end{bmatrix}$

(E) This system cannot be represented as a matrix equation.

12. Find $\begin{bmatrix} x \\ y \end{bmatrix}$ if $\begin{bmatrix} 3 & 2 \\ -1 & 4 \end{bmatrix}\begin{bmatrix} x \\ y \end{bmatrix}=\begin{bmatrix} -5 \\ 4 \end{bmatrix}$.

(A) $[-2 \quad 0.5]$

(B) $\begin{bmatrix} -5/6 \\ 1 \end{bmatrix}$

(C) $[-1 \quad 3/4]$

(D) $\begin{bmatrix} -2 \\ 1/2 \end{bmatrix}$

(E) $[-5 \quad -4/5]$

Answers Explained 答案解析

1. **(C)** First find the sum of the matrices to the left of the equals sign: $\begin{bmatrix} 12 & 8 \\ -8 & 16 \end{bmatrix}$.

Since the first row of the matrix to the right of the equals sign is $(3 \quad 2)$, K must be 4. Since $(J \quad M)$ is the bottom row, $J = -2$ and $M = 4$. Therefore, $K + J + M = 6$.

2. **(E)** In order for these matrices to be equal, $\begin{bmatrix} x & 2 \\ -3 & y \end{bmatrix}=\begin{bmatrix} 2x^2 & 2 \\ -3 & 6y-10 \end{bmatrix}$.

Therefore, $x = 2x^2$ and $y = 6y - 10$. Solving the first equation yields $x = 0, \frac{1}{2}$ and $y = 2$.

3. **(B)** To solve for X, first subtract $\begin{bmatrix} 1 & 2 & -3 \\ 2 & 1 & 3 \end{bmatrix}$ from both sides of the equation.

Then $-X = \begin{bmatrix} 4 & -1 & 11 \\ -8 & -1 & 2 \end{bmatrix}$, so $X = \begin{bmatrix} -4 & 1 & -11 \\ 8 & 1 & -2 \end{bmatrix}$.

4. **(B)** By definition, $AB = \begin{bmatrix} (-2)(0)+(-1)(3)+(5)(4)+(9)(-6) \\ (-2)(-5)+(-1)(-2)+(5)(0)+(9)(1) \end{bmatrix} = [-37 \quad 21]$.

5. **(C)** By definition, the first row, second column of the product is $(x)(-x) + (1)(1) = -x^2 + 1$.

6. **(B)** X must have as many rows as A has columns, which is 3. X must have as many columns as B does, which is 2.

7. **(B)** Matrix multiplication is row by column. Since the answer must be a 3 by 1 matrix, the only possible answer choice is Choice B.

8. **(B)** By definition, the determinant of $\begin{bmatrix} p & 3 \\ -2 & 1 \end{bmatrix}$ is $(p)(1) - (3)(-2) = p + 6$.

9. **(B)** Enter the 3 by 3 matrix on the left side of the equation into your graphing calculator and evaluate its determinant (zero). The determinant on the right side of the equation is $x^2 - 20$. Therefore $x = \pm\sqrt{20} \approx \pm 4.47$.

∗ 10. **(C)** To find X, multiply both sides of the equation by $\begin{bmatrix} -7 & 2 \\ 0 & -5 \end{bmatrix}^{-1}$ on the right. Enter both matrices in your calculator, key the product $\begin{bmatrix} 2 & -3 \\ 5 & 4 \end{bmatrix}\begin{bmatrix} -7 & 2 \\ 0 & -5 \end{bmatrix}^{-1}$ on your graphing calculator, and key MATH/ENTER/ENTER to convert the decimal answer to a fraction.

11. **(B)** First, write the system in standard form: $\begin{cases} 2x - 3y = 3 \\ -5x + y = 14 \end{cases}$. The matrix form of this equation is $\begin{bmatrix} 2 & -3 \\ -5 & 1 \end{bmatrix}\begin{bmatrix} x \\ y \end{bmatrix} = \begin{bmatrix} 3 \\ 14 \end{bmatrix}$.

12. **(D)** This is the matrix form $AX = B$ of a system of equations. Multiply both sides of the equation by A^{-1} on the left to get the solution $X = \begin{bmatrix} x \\ y \end{bmatrix} = A^{-1}B$. Enter the 2 by 2 matrix, A, and the 2 by 1 matrix, B, into your graphing calculator. Return to the home screen and enter $A^{-1}B = \begin{bmatrix} -2 \\ 0.5 \end{bmatrix}$.

Sequences and Series
第19章　数列与级数

19

- → SIGMA NOTATION
- → ARITHMETIC SEQUENCES
- → GEOMETRIC SEQUENCES
- → INFINITE GEOMETRIC SERIES

A **sequence** is a function with a domain consisting of the natural numbers. A *series* is the sum of the terms of a sequence.

➡ Examples

(A) an infinite sequence

$\frac{1}{2}, \frac{1}{3}, \frac{1}{4}, \frac{1}{5}, \ldots, \frac{1}{n+1}, \ldots$, is an **infinite sequence** with

$t_1 = \frac{1}{2}, t_2 = \frac{1}{3}, t_3 = \frac{1}{4}, t_4 = \frac{1}{5}, \ldots, t_n = \frac{1}{n+1}$.

(B) a finite sequence

$2, 4, 6, \ldots, 20$ is a **finite sequence** with $t_1 = 2, t_2 = 4, t_3 = 6, \ldots, t_{10} = 20$.

(C) an infinite series

$\frac{1}{2}+\frac{1}{4}+\frac{1}{8}+\frac{1}{16}+\cdots+\frac{1}{2^n}+\cdots$ is an **infinite series**.

(D) If $t_n = \frac{2n}{n+1}$, find the first five terms of the sequence.

When 1, 2, 3, 4, and 5 are substituted for n, $t_1 = \frac{2}{2} = 1$, ,$t_2 = \frac{4}{3}$, $t_3 = \frac{6}{4} = \frac{3}{2}$, $t_4 = \frac{8}{5}$, and $t_5 = \frac{10}{6} = \frac{5}{3}$.

The first five terms are 1, $\frac{4}{3}, \frac{3}{2}, \frac{8}{5}, \frac{5}{3}$.

In Examples A through D, formulas are given for finding each term of the sequence. Another way of specifying a sequence provides a formula that gives each term as a function of its predecessor terms. Examples E and F illustrate this method.

(E) If $a_1 = 3$ and $a_n = 2a_{n-1} + 5$, find a_4.

Put (or a_1) into your graphing calculator, and press ENTER. Then multiply by 2 and add 5. Hit ENTER 3 more times to get $a_4 = 59$.

(F) If $a_1 = 1, a_2 = 1$, and $a_n = a_{n-1} + a_{n-2}$ for $n \geq 3$, find the first 7 terms of the sequence.

The recursive formula indicates that each term is the sum of the two terms before it. Therefore, the first seven terms of this sequence are 1, 1, 2, 3, 5, 8, 13. This is called the Fibonacci sequence.

A **series** is the sum of the terms in a sequence. The expression $\sum_{k=1}^{n} t_k$ represents the sum of n terms beginning with t_1. The lower limit of the sum shows the starting point, in this case 1, and the upper limit is the ending point, in this case n. Each t_k represents the kth term of the sequence $(k = 1, 2, \ldots, n)$.

(G) Express the series 2 + 4 + 6 + · · · + 20 in sigma notation.

The series $2+4+6+\cdots+20 = \sum_{i=1}^{10} 2i = 110$.

(H) Evaluate $\sum_{k=0}^{5} k^2$.

$$\sum_{k=0}^{5} k^2 = 0^2 + 1^2 + 2^2 + 3^2 + 4^2 + 5^2 = 0 + 1 + 4 + 9 + 16 + 25 = 55$$

One of the most common sequences studied at this level is an **arithmetic sequence** (or **arithmetic progression**). Each term differs from the preceding term by a common difference. The first n terms of an arithmetic sequence can be denoted by

$$t_1, t_1 + d, t_1 + 2d, t_1 + 3d, \ldots, t_1 + (n-1)d$$

where d is the common difference and $t_n = t_1 + (n-1)d$. The sum of n terms of the series constructed from an arithmetic sequence is given by the formula

$$S_n = \frac{n}{2}(t_1 + t_n) \quad \text{or} \quad S_n = \frac{n}{2}[2t_1 + (n-1)d]$$

➥ Examples

(I) Find the 28th term of the arithmetic sequence 2, 5, 8, ...

$$t_n = t_1 + (n-1)d$$
$$t_1 = 2, d = 3, n = 28$$
$$t_{28} = 2 + 27 \cdot 3 = 83$$

(J) Express the sum of 28 terms of the series of this sequence using sigma notation.

$$\sum_{k=0}^{27}(3k+2) \text{ or } \sum_{j=1}^{28}(3j-1)$$

(K) Find the sum of the first 28 terms of the series.

$$S_n = \frac{n}{2}(t_1 + t_n)$$
$$S_{28} = \frac{28}{2}(2+83) = 14 \cdot 85 = 1{,}190$$

(L) If $t_8 = 4$ and $t_{12} = -2$, find the first three terms of the arithmetic sequence.

$$t_n = t_1 + (n-1)d$$
$$4 = t_1 + 7d$$
$$-2 = t_1 + 11d$$

To solve these two equations for d, subtract the second equation from the third.

$$-6 = 4d$$
$$d = -\frac{3}{2}$$

Substituting in the first equation gives $4 = t_1 + 7\left(-\frac{3}{2}\right)$. Thus,

$$t_1 = 4 + \frac{21}{2} = \frac{29}{2}$$
$$t_2 = \frac{29}{2} + \left(-\frac{3}{2}\right) = \frac{26}{2} = 13$$
$$t_3 = \frac{29}{2} + 2\left(-\frac{3}{2}\right) = \frac{23}{2}$$

The first three terms are $\frac{29}{2}$, 13, $\frac{23}{2}$.

(M) In an arithmetic series, if $S_n = 3n^2 + 2n$, find the first three terms.

When $n = 1, S_1 = t_1$. Therefore, $t_1 = 3(1)^2 + 2 \cdot 1 = 5$.

$$\begin{aligned} S_2 = t_1 + t_2 &= 3(2)^2 + 2 \cdot 2 = 16 \\ 5 + t_2 &= 16 \\ t_2 &= 11 \end{aligned}$$

Therefore, $d = 6$, which leads to a third term of 17. Thus, the first three terms are 5, 11, 17.

Another common type of sequence studied at this level is a **geometric sequence** (or geometric progression). In a geometric sequence the ratio of any two successive terms is a constant r called the constant ratio. The first n terms of a geometric sequence can be denoted by

$$t_1, t_1r, t_1r^2, t_1r^3, \ldots, t_1r^{n-1} = t_n$$

The sum of the first n terms of a geometric series is given by the formula

$$Sn = \frac{t_1(1-r^n)}{1-r}$$

➡ Examples

(N) Find the seventh term of the geometric sequence 1, 2, 4, . . . , and

$$r = \frac{t_2}{t_1} = \frac{2}{1} = 2;\ t_7 = t_1r^{7-1};\ t_7 = 1 \cdot 2^6 = 64$$

(O) the sum of the first seven terms.

$$S_7 = \frac{1(1-2^7)}{1-2} = \frac{1-128}{-1} = 127$$

(P) The first term of a geometric sequence is 64, and the common ratio is $\frac{1}{4}$.

For what value of n is $t_n = \frac{1}{4}$?

$$\frac{1}{4} = 64\left(\frac{1}{4}\right)^{n-1}$$

$$\left(\frac{1}{4}\right)^{2-n} = 64 = 4^3$$

$$4^{n-2} = 4^3$$

$$n = 5$$

In a geometric sequence, if $|r| < 1$, the sum of the series approaches a limit as n approaches infinity. In the formula $S_n = \frac{t_1(1-r^n)}{1-r}$, if $|r| < 1$, the term $r^n \to 0$ as $n \to \infty$. Therefore, as long as $|r| < 1$, $\lim_{n\to\infty} S_n = \frac{t_1}{1-r}$, or $S = \frac{t_1}{1-r}$.

Examples

(Q) Evaluate $\lim_{n\to\infty} \sum_{k=1}^{n} \frac{1}{2^k}$ and

When the first few terms, $\frac{1}{2}+\frac{1}{4}+\frac{1}{8}+\cdots$, are listed, it can be seen that $t_1 = \frac{1}{2}$ and the common ratio $r = \frac{1}{2}$. Therefore,

$$S = \frac{\frac{1}{2}}{1-\frac{1}{2}} = 1$$

(R) $\sum_{j=0}^{\infty} (-3)^{-j}$

When the first few terms, $\frac{1}{1}-\frac{1}{3}+\frac{1}{9}-\cdots$, are listed, it can be seen that $t_1 = 1$ and the common ratio $r = -\frac{1}{3}$. Therefore,

$$S = \frac{1}{1-\left(-\frac{1}{3}\right)} = \frac{1}{\frac{4}{3}} = \frac{3}{4}$$

(S) Find the exact value of the repeating decimal 0.4545 . . . .

This can be represented by a geometric series, $0.45 + 0.0045 + 0.000045 + \cdots$, with $t_1 = 0.45$ and $r = 0.01$.
Since $|r| < 1$,

$$S = \frac{0.45}{1-0.01} = \frac{0.45}{0.99} = \frac{45}{99} = \frac{5}{11}$$

EXERCISES 习题

1. If $a_1 = 3$ and $a_n = n + a_{n-1}$, the sum of the first five terms is

(A) 17
(B) 30
(C) 42
(D) 45
(E) 68

2. If $a_1 = 5$ and $a_n = 1 + \sqrt{a_{n-1}}$, find a_3.

(A) 2.623
(B) 2.635
(C) 2.673
(D) 2.799
(E) 3.323

3. If the repeating decimal $0.237\overline{37}\ldots$ is written as a fraction in lowest terms, the sum of the numerator and denominator is

(A) 16
(B) 47
(C) 245
(D) 334
(E) 1,237

4. The first three terms of a geometric sequence are $\sqrt[4]{3}$, $\sqrt[8]{3}$, 1. The fourth term is

(A) $\sqrt[32]{3}$
(B) $\sqrt[16]{3}$
(C) $\dfrac{1}{\sqrt[16]{3}}$
(D) $\dfrac{1}{\sqrt[8]{3}}$
(E) $\dfrac{1}{\sqrt[4]{3}}$

5. In an infinite geometric series $S = \dfrac{2}{3}$ and $t_1 = \dfrac{2}{7}$. What is r?

(A) $\dfrac{2}{3}$
(B) $-\dfrac{4}{7}$
(C) $\dfrac{2}{7}$
(D) $\dfrac{4}{7}$
(E) $-\dfrac{2}{7}$

Answers Explained 答案解析

1. **(D)** $a_2 = 5, a_3 = 8, a_4 = 12, a_5 = 17$. Therefore, $S_5 = 45$.

2. **(D)** Press 5 ENTER into your graphing calculator. Then enter $1 + \sqrt{\text{Ans}}$ and press ENTER twice more to get a_3.

3. **(C)** The decimal $0.23\overline{737} = 0.2 + (0.037 + 0.00037 + 0.0000037 + \cdots)$, which is 0.2 + an infinite geometric series with a common ratio of 0.01.

   $$S_n = 0.2 + \frac{0.037}{0.99} = \frac{2}{10} + \frac{37}{990} = \frac{235}{990} = \frac{47}{198}$$

   The sum of the numerator and the denominator is 245.

4. **(D)** Terms are $3^{1/4}, 3^{1/8}, 1$. Common ratio $= 3^{-1/8}$. Therefore, the fourth term is $1 \cdot 3^{-1/8} = 3^{-1/8}$ or $\frac{1}{\sqrt[8]{3}}$.

5. **(D)** $\frac{2}{3} = \frac{\frac{2}{7}}{1-r}$. $2 - 2r = \frac{6}{7}$. $14 - 14r = 6$. Therefore, $r = \frac{4}{7}$.

Vectors
第20章 向量

20

- → DEFINITION
- → RESULTANT
- → NORM OF A VECTOR
- → DOT PRODUCT

A vector in a plane is defined to be an ordered pair of real numbers. A vector in space is defined as an ordered triple of real numbers. On a coordinate system, a vector is usually represented by an arrow whose initial point is the origin and whose terminal point is at the ordered pair (or triple) that named the vector. Vector quantities always have a magnitude or **norm** (the length of the arrow) and direction (the angle the arrow makes with the x-axis). Vectors are often used to represent motion or force.

Properties of two-dimensional vectors can be extended to three-dimensional vectors. We will express the properties in terms of two-dimensional vectors for convenience. If vector $\vec{V}$ is designated by (v_1, v_2) and vector $\vec{U}$ is designated by (u_1, u_2), vector $\overrightarrow{U+V}$ is designated by $(u_1 + v_1, u_2 + v_2)$ and called the **resultant** of $\vec{U}$ and $\vec{V}$. Vector $-\vec{V}$ has the same magnitude as $\vec{V}$ but has a direction opposite that of $\vec{V}$.

On the plane, every vector $\vec{V}$ can be expressed in terms of any other two unit (magnitude 1) vectors parallel to the x- and y-axes. If vector $\vec{i} = (1, 0)$ and vector $\vec{j} = (0, 1)$, any vector $\vec{V} = ai + bj$, where a and b are real numbers. A unit vector parallel to $\vec{V}$ can be determined by dividing $\vec{V}$ by its norm, denoted by $\| \vec{V} \|$ and equal to $\sqrt{a^2 + b^2}$.

It is possible to determine algebraically whether two vectors are perpendicular by defining the **dot product** or **inner product** of two vectors, $\vec{V}(v_1, v_2)$ and $\vec{U}(u_1, u_2)$.

$$\vec{V} \cdot \vec{U} = v_1 u_1 + v_2 u_2$$

Notice that the dot product of two vectors is a *real number*, not a vector. Two vectors, $\vec{V}$ and $\vec{U}$, are perpendicular if and only if $\vec{V} \cdot \vec{U} = 0$.

➡ Examples

(A) Let vector $\vec{V} = (2, 3)$ and vector $\vec{U} = (6, -4)$.

(i) What is the resultant of $\vec{U}$ and $\vec{V}$?

The resultant, $\overrightarrow{U+V}$, equals $(6 + 2, -4 + 3) = (8, -1)$.

(ii) What is the norm of $\vec{U}$?

The norm of $\vec{U}$, $||\vec{U}|| = \sqrt{36+16} = \sqrt{52} = 2\sqrt{13}$.

(iii) Express $\vec{V}$ in terms of $\vec{i}$ and $\vec{j}$.

$\vec{V} = 2\vec{i} + 3\vec{j}$. To verify this, use the definitions of $\vec{i}$ and $\vec{j} \cdot \vec{V} = 2(1, 0) + 3(0, 1) =$

$(2, 0) + (0, 3) = (2, 3) = \vec{V}$.

(iv) Are $\vec{U}$ and $\vec{V}$ perpendicular?

$\vec{U} \cdot \vec{V} = 6 \cdot 2 + (-4) \cdot 3 = 12 - 12 = 0$. Therefore, $\vec{U}$ and $\vec{V}$ are perpendicular because the dot product is equal to zero.

(B) If $\vec{U} = (-1, 4)$ and the resultant of $\vec{U}$ and $\vec{V}$ is (4, 5), find $\vec{V}$.

Let $\vec{V} = (v_1, v_2)$. The resultant $\overrightarrow{U+V} = (-1, 4) + (v_1, v_2) = (4, 5)$. Therefore, $(-1 + v_1, 4 + v_2) =$

$(4, 5)$, which implies that $-1 + v_1 = 4$ and $4 + v_2 = 5$. Thus, $v_1 = 5$ and $v_2 = 1$. $\vec{V} = (5, 1)$.

EXERCISES 习题

1. Suppose $\vec{x} = (-3, -1)$, $\vec{y} = (-1, 4)$. Find the magnitude of $\vec{x} + \vec{y}$.

(A) 2
(B) 3
(C) 4
(D) 5
(E) 6

2. If $\vec{V} = 2\vec{i} + 3\vec{j}$ and $\vec{U} = \vec{i} - 5\vec{j}$, the resultant vector of $2\vec{U} + 3\vec{V}$ equals

(A) $3\vec{i} - 2\vec{j}$

(B) $5\vec{i} + \vec{j}$

(C) $7\vec{i} - 9\vec{j}$

(D) $8\vec{i} - \vec{j}$

(E) $2\vec{i} + 3\vec{j}$

3. A unit vector perpendicular to vector $\vec{V} = (3, -4)$ is

(A) $(4, 3)$

(B) $\left(\frac{3}{5}, \frac{4}{5}\right)$

(C) $\left(-\frac{3}{5}, -\frac{4}{5}\right)$

(D) $\left(-\frac{4}{5}, -\frac{3}{5}\right)$

(E) $\left(-\frac{4}{5}, \frac{3}{5}\right)$

Answers Explained 答案解析

1. **(D)** Add the components to get $\vec{x} + \vec{y} = (-4,3)$. The magnitude is $\sqrt{(-4)^2 + 3^2} = 5$.

2. **(D)** $2\vec{U} = 2\vec{i} - 10\vec{j}$ and $3\vec{V} = 6\vec{i} + 9\vec{j}$, so $2\vec{U} + 3\vec{V} = 8\vec{i} - \vec{j}$.

3. **(D)** All answer choices except Choice A are unit vectors. Backsolve to find that the only one having a zero dot product with $(3, -4)$ is $\left(-\frac{4}{5}, -\frac{3}{5}\right)$.

Statistics
第21章 统计

21

→ MEAN, MEDIAN, MODE
→ RANGE AND STANDARD DEVIATION
→ *z*-SCORE
→ LINEAR, QUADRATIC, AND EXPONENTIAL MODELS

Quantitative data are number sets such as heights, weights, test scores, tensile strength, and so forth. By contrast, **categorical** data consist of descriptive labels, such as hair color, city of residence, socioeconomic status, and the like. Since the Math Level 2 test is unlikely to include questions about categorical data, the concepts described below pertain to quantitative data only.

Measures of center summarize a data set using a single "typical" value. Three measures of center might be encountered on the Math Level 2 test: mean, median, and mode.

The **mean** is the sum of all the data values divided by the number of values. The formula for the mean $\bar{x}$ of a data set is $\bar{x} = \frac{\sum x_i}{n}$, where Σ indicates the sum of the data values x_i and n is the number of data values.

To determine the **median**, the data must first be ordered. If the number of values is odd, the median is the single middle value. If the number of values is even, the median is the mean of the two middle values. There is no formula for the median of a data set.

The **mode** is the value that appears most often. There is no formula for the mode of a data set.

Examples

(A) The heights of the starting basketball team for South High School are 69″, 72″, 75″, 78″, and 78″. Find the mean, median, and mode of this data set.

The mean is $\frac{69+72+75+78+78}{5} = 74.4''$. The median is 75″. The mode is 78″.

(B) The mean of 24 test scores is 77.5. When the 25th class member takes the test, the mean goes down by 1.1 points. What was that 25th score?

The total of the 24 test scores is $24 \times 77.5 = 1{,}860$, and the total of the 25 test scores is $25 \times 76.4 = 1{,}910$. Therefore, the 25th score is $1{,}910 - 1{,}860 = 50$.

(C) What is the median of the frequency distribution shown in the table?

Data Value	Frequency
24	3
25	7
26	5
27	1

There are 16 data values altogether, so the median is the mean of the 8th and 9th largest values. Both of these values are 25, so the median is also 25.

A **weighted average** is another way of measuring the middle of a data set. The data consist of numbers (often averages themselves) for various categories that are to be combined to form an overall average. Higher weights are given to categories that are considered more important. To get the weighted overall average, the number in each category is then multiplied by the category's weight, and these products are summed across the categories.

➡ Example

(D) In some schools, AP courses, honors courses, and college prep courses carry different weights in the computation of grade point averages. A given grade may carry a weight of 2 in an AP course, a weight of 1.5 in an honors course, and a weight of 1 in a college prep course. Suppose letter grades of A, B, C, D, and F are assigned values of 4, 3, 2, 1, and 0.

A student completes 6 courses with grades of a B and a C in 2 AP courses, an A and a C in 2 honors courses, and 2 As in college prep courses. What would that student's grade point average be?

The student's grade point average is calculated as the weighted average.

$$[2(3 + 2) + 1.5(4 + 2) + 1(4 + 4)] \div 6 = 4.5$$

The Math Level 2 test might ask questions about **measures of spread.** These questions ask about how spread out a set of data values is.

The **range** is a measure of spread. It is the difference between the largest and smallest data values.

➡ Example

(E) Find the range of the data values 85, 96, 72, 89, 66, and 78.

The largest value is 96 and the smallest is 66. The range is 96 – 66 = 30.

Loosely speaking, the **standard deviation** is the "average" difference between individual data values and their mean. The formula for the standard deviation s of a data set is $s = \sqrt{\frac{1}{n-1}\sum(x_i - \bar{x})^2}$. The larger the standard deviation, the more spread out a data set is. Standard deviation is a unit-free measure of the "distance" between a specific data value and the mean. Thus the standard deviation can be used to compare single data values from different data sets. A z-score, where $z = \frac{x - \bar{x}}{s}$, is the number of standard deviations s that a data value x is from the mean $\bar{x}$. The greater the value of $|z|$, the less common the data value x is. In other words, fewer data values have a high z-score.

➡ Examples

(F) Which data set has the smaller standard deviation: {5, 7, 9} or {4, 7, 10}?

Both data sets have a mean of 7. However, the first set is less spread out than the second, so the first has the smaller standard deviation. According to the formula, the standard deviation of the first data set is 2 while that of the second data set is 3.

(G) **A chart showing sports statistics for a particular school is shown below. Which is statistically a better score: 50.30 seconds in the backstroke or 74 inches in the high jump?**

Stroke	**Mean**	**Standard Deviation**
Backstroke	**50.72 sec.**	**0.24 sec.**
High Jump	**72.9 in.**	**0.54 in.**

A time of 50.30 seconds in the backstroke is $z = \dfrac{50.30 - 50.72}{0.24} = -1.75$ standard deviations better (less) than the backstroke mean. A height of 74 inches in the high jump is $z = \dfrac{74 - 72.9}{0.54} = 2.04$ standard deviations better (more) than the high jump mean. Therefore, the high jump performance is better.

Measures of center and spread apply to a single variable. **Regression** is a technique for analyzing the relationship between two variables. This technique summarizes relationships such as mathematical equations in which the two variables are denoted by x (the independent variable) and y (the dependent variable). The Math Level 2 test may ask about any one of three models to capture the relationship between x and y:

- Linear model $y = a_0 + a_1x$
- Quadratic model $y = a_0 + a_1x + a_2x^2$
- Exponential model $y = a_0e^{a_1x}$

The first step when deciding which model should be used in a particular situation is to examine a scatterplot of the data. Enter the data into two lists (STAT/Edit). Clear the Y= screen, key 2nd Y= and select a plot. This takes you to the Statplot screen. Turn the plot on, select the scatterplot image, enter the list names, and key ZOOM/Statplot.

If the points in the scatterplot fall roughly in a straight line, enter STAT/CALC/LinReg (either version). The calculator will return a linear equation. Linear models are appropriate when the dependent variable changes at a constant rate relative to the independent variable.

If the points seem to change direction once, a quadratic model is probably appropriate. Enter STAT/CALC/QuadReg, and the calculator will return a quadratic equation in standard form. Quadratic models apply when the dependent variable varies with the square of the independent variable. Examples are (a) the area of a figure varies with the square of the length of its boundary, and (b) the intensity of light varies with the square of its distance from the light source.

If the scatterplot is curved but does not change direction, an exponential model is probably the best choice. The command on the graphing calculator is STAT/CALC/ExpReg. Exponential models apply when the rate of change in the dependent variable is proportional to the independent variable. Examples are population growth, the spread of disease, and nuclear decay.

The figures below show scatterplots having these shapes. Regression techniques use paired values (x, y) to estimate **parameter** values a_0, a_1, a_2, depending on the model selected. Once this is done, the equation for that model can be used to predict y for a given value of x.

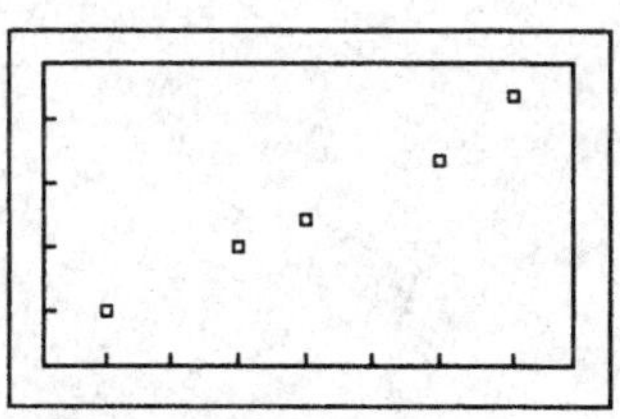

Linear Scatterplot

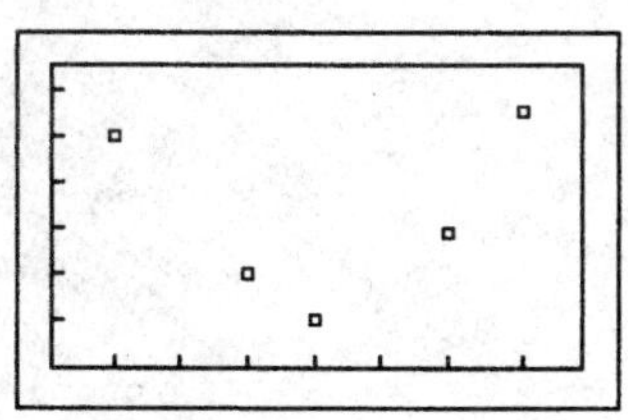

Quadratic Scatterplot

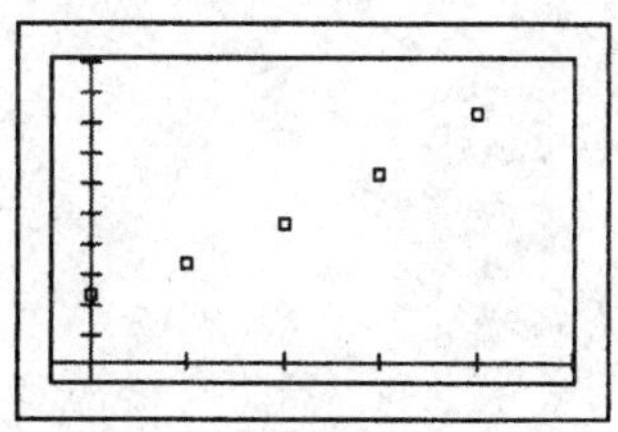

Exponential Scatterplot

The Level 2 test does not require students to know the mathematics of regression techniques. Students should know how to use their calculators to get parameter estimates for a particular model and to use the equation as a prediction tool.

➥ Example

(H) The decennial population of Center City for the past five decades is shown in the table below. Use exponential regression to estimate the 1965 population.

Population of Center City

Year	***Population***
1950	**48,000**
1960	**72,000**
1970	**95,000**
1980	**123,000**
1990	**165,000**

Transform the years to "number of years after 1950" and enter these values into L4. Then enter the populations in thousands. Set up the scatterplot by pressing 2ndY= and selecting a plot (Plot 1). Turn the plot on, select the scatterplot logo, and enter the list names. Then press STAT/CALC/ExpReg L1,L2,blank,Y1,Calculate. This will store the regression equation in Y1. The resulting command is shown in the left screen below. Press ENTER to display the values for the equation. These are shown in the right screen below.

ExpReg
Xlist:L_1
Ylist:L_2
FreqList:
Store RegEQ:Y_1
Calculate

ExpReg
y=a*b^x
a=50.55052533
b=1.030506132
r^2=.9923981043
r=.9961918009

Press ZOOM/9 to view the scatterplot and exponential curve. Press 2nd/CALC/value and enter 15, representing 1965. The cursor moves to the point on the regression curve where $x = 15$ and displays both x and y at the bottom of the screen, as shown below.

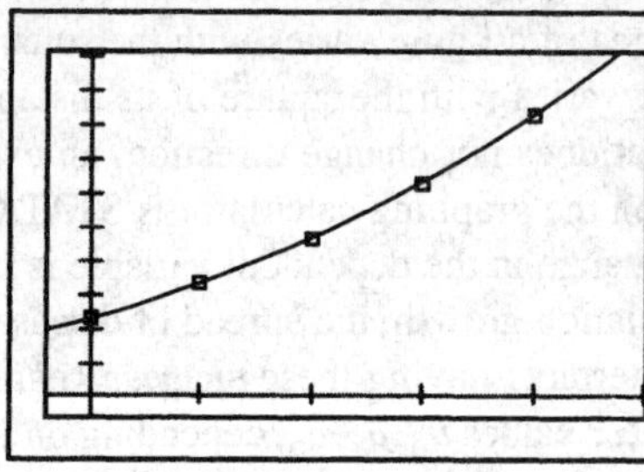

The 1965 population was about 79,300.

EXERCISES 习题

1. Last week, police ticketed 13 men traveling 18 miles per hour over the speed limit and 8 women traveling 14 miles per hour over the speed limit. What was the mean speed over the limit of all 21 drivers?

(A) 16 miles per hour
(B) 16.5 miles per hour
(C) 17 miles per hour
(D) none of the above
(E) cannot be determined

2. Wanda wants to choose her "best-fit" college in a systematic way. Academic reputation (AR), sports reputation (SR), social life (SL), and cost (C) are the four factors that Wanda considers for all her colleges. She plans to score the colleges on these factors using a scale of 1 to 5, with 5 being the highest, and she attaches the following weights: AR (40%), SR (10%), SL (15%), and C (35%). Her scores for these categories at one school are AR, 4; SR, 3; SL, 5; C, 2. What is the weighted overall average score for this school?

(A) 3.35
(B) 3.5
(C) 3.85
(D) 4.25
(E) 4.5

3. If the range of a set of integers is 2 and the mean is 50, which of the following statements must be true?

I. The mode is 50.
II. The median is 50.
III. There are exactly three data values.

(A) only I
(B) only II
(C) only III
(D) I and II
(E) I, II, and III

4. What is the median of the frequency distribution shown below?

Data Value	Frequency
0	1
1	3
2	7
3	15
4	10
5	7
6	3
7	3

(A) 2
(B) 3
(C) 4
(D) 5
(E) cannot be determined

5. Which of the following statements must be true?

I. The range of a data set must be smaller than its standard deviation.
II. The standard deviation of a data set must be smaller than its mean.
III. The median of a data set must be smaller than its mode.

(A) I only
(B) I and II
(C) II only
(D) I, II, and III
(E) none are true

6. The mean and standard deviation for SAT math scores are shown in the table below for five high schools in a large city. A particular score for each school is also shown (in the right column).

School	Mean	Standard Deviation	Single Score
A	532	24	600
B	485	30	560
C	515	22	561
D	396	26	474
E	479	35	552

Which single score has the highest z-score?

(A) 474 in school D
(B) 552 in school E
(C) 560 in school B
(D) 561 in school C
(E) 600 in school A

7. Jack recorded the amount of time he studied the night before each of 4 history quizzes and the score he got on each quiz. The data are in the table below.

Score	Time (min.)
86	45
70	15
90	40
78	35

Use linear regression to estimate the score Jack would get if he studied for 20 minutes.

(A) 71
(B) 72
(C) 73
(D) 74
(E) 75

8. The scatterplot shows gas mileage (miles per gallon) at various speeds (miles per hour) when a car was driven 100 miles at various speeds on a test track.

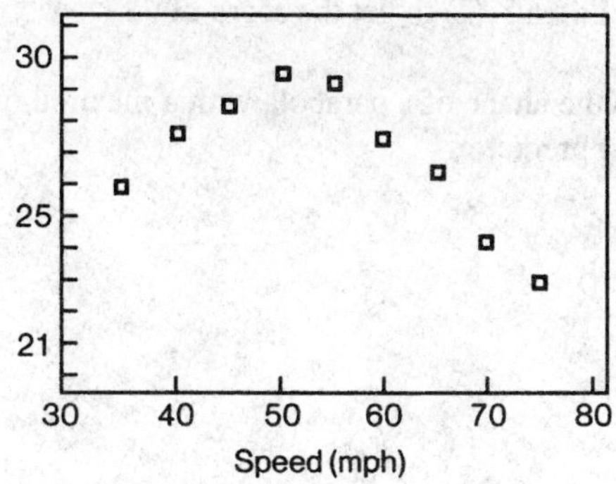

Which regression model is probably the best predictor of gas mileage as a function of speed?

(A) constant
(B) linear
(C) quadratic
(D) cubic
(E) exponential

Answers Explained 答案解析

* 1. **(B)** There are 13 eighteens and 8 fourteens, so the total over the speed limit is 346. Divide this by the 21 people to get 16.5.

* 2. **(A)** The score in each category is multiplied by that category's weight, and these products are added to get $0.4(4) + 0.1(3) + 0.15(5) + 0.35(2) = 3.35$ as the weighted overall average score for that school.

3. **(B)** Since the data values are integers, the range is 2, and the mean is 50, the possible data values are 49, 50, and 51.

   I. The set could consist of equal numbers of 49s and 51s and have a mean of 50 without 50 even being a data value. So I need not be true.
   II. Since the mean is 50, there must be equal numbers of 49s and 51s, so 50 is also the median. II must be true.
   III. Explanations in I and II imply that III need not be true.

4. **(B)** There are 49 data values altogether, so the median is the 25th largest. Adding the frequencies up to 25 puts the 25th number at 3.

5. **(E)** None are true. The range of any data set must be larger than its standard deviation because the range measures total spread while the standard deviation measures average spread. So Choice I is false. Either the mean or standard deviation of a data set can be larger. For example, the mean of the data {1, 5, 10} is 5.3, while its standard deviation is 4.51. The mean of the data set {1, 5, 20} is 8.7, while its standard deviation is 10.0. So Choice II is false. Either the median or mode of a data set can be larger. For example, the median of the data set {1, 2, 3, 4, 4} is 3, while its mode is 4. The median of the data set {1, 1, 2, 3, 4} is 2 while its mode is 1. So Choice III is false.

* 6. **(A)** The z-scores for the five schools are 2.8 for A, 2.5 for B, 2.1 for C, 3 for D, and 2.1 for E.

* 7. **(B)** Enter the data in two lists (study times in L1 and test scores in L2). Enter STAT/CALC/8, and enter VARS/YVARS/Function/Y_1, followed by ENTER. This produces estimates of the slope (b) and y-intercept (a) of the regression line $a + bx$. Enter this expression into Y_1. Enter $Y_1(2)$ to get the score of 72.

* 8. **(C)** The scatterplot has the shape of a parabola with a maximum. Therefore, the quadratic model would be the best predictor.

Probability
第22章 概率

22

→ SAMPLE SPACE
→ MUTUALLY EXCLUSIVE EVENTS
→ CONDITIONAL PROBABILITY AND INDEPENDENT EVENTS

When an "experiment" has an uncertain outcome, probability provides a measure of how likely an outcome or collection of outcomes is. Tossing a coin, rolling dice, drawing cards from a standard deck, and picking marbles out of bowls are simple examples of experiments that illustrate important aspects of probability.

The results of an experiment are called its outcomes. A coin toss has two outcomes: heads (H) and tails (T). Tossing two coins has four (2×2) outcomes: (HH), (HT), (TH), and (TT). Rolling a single die has six possible outcomes, while rolling a pair of dice has thirty-six (6×6) possible outcomes. Drawing a single card from a standard deck has 52 possible outcomes. Drawing five cards from a standard deck has $\binom{52}{5} = 2{,}598{,}960$ possible outcomes (five-card poker hands).

The set of all possible outcomes of some experiment is called its **sample space**.

An **event** is a subset of the sample space (a collection of possible outcomes). The **probability of an event** is the number of outcomes in the event (**favorable outcomes**) divided by the number of outcomes in the sample space.

Let E be an event, $\tilde{E}$ be the set of outcomes that are not in E (the **complement** of E), and $P(E)$ represent the probability of E.

- $0 \le P(E) \le 1$
- $P(\tilde{E}) = 1 - P(E)$

If $P(E) = 0$, E is called the **impossible event**. If $P(E) = 1$, E is called the **certain event**.

Examples

(A) If a card is drawn from a standard deck of 52 cards, what is the probability of the event that the card is a picture card? What is the probability of the event that the card is a spade?

There are 12 picture cards in a standard deck, so if one card is drawn, the probability that it is a picture card is $\frac{12}{52}$. The probability that it is a spade is $\frac{13}{52}$ because a deck has 13 spades.

(B) If a coin is flipped twice, what is the probability of the event 1 head and 1 tail?

Since two of the four possible outcomes have one head and one tail, the probability of this event is $\frac{2}{4}$.

(C) What is the probability of getting a sum of 7 when two dice are thrown?

The outcomes of the rolling of a pair of dice can be more readily understood by assigning colors to the dice (e.g., one red, one green). An outcome of throwing a pair of dice can be represented by an ordered pair, where the first element is the side of the red die facing up, and the second is the side of the green die facing up. Thus, (32) signifies a 3 on the red die and a 2 on the green, while (23) signifies 2 on the red and 3 on the green. Since there are six faces on each die, there are $6 \times 6 = 36$ possible outcomes in the sample space. The outcomes that have a sum of 7 are (61), (16), (52), (25), (43), and (34). Therefore, the probability of getting a sum of 7 is $\frac{6}{36} = \frac{1}{6}$.

Probability questions can also be asked about two events A and B. Questions on the Math Level 2 Test cover the following three ways of combining two events.

- $P(A \cup B)$, the probability of either A *or* B occurring, where $A \cup B$ is called the **disjunction** of A and B.
- $P(A|B)$, the probability of A occurring, *given* that B has occurred. This is called **conditional probability**.
- $P(A \cap B)$, the probability of both A *and* B occurring, where $A \cap B$ is called the **conjunction** of A and B.

If two events have no outcomes in common, they are called **mutually exclusive**, and $P(A \cup B) = P(A) + P(B)$. If two events have outcomes in common, these outcomes would be double counted, resulting in the more general formula $P(A \cup B) = P(A) + P(B) - P(A \cap B)$. Note that A and B are mutually exclusive if and only if $P(A \cap B) = 0$.

Examples

(D) In a group of 40 students, 23 take the AP Psychology class, 18 take the AP Calculus class, and 8 take both classes. What is the probability that a student takes AP Psychology or AP Calculus?

Let A be the event that a student takes AP Psychology and B be the event that a student takes AP Calculus. Then $A \cap B$ represents the event that a student takes both courses. In the formula above, $P(A) = \frac{23}{40}$, $P(B) = \frac{18}{40}$, and $P(A \cap B) = \frac{8}{40}$. Therefore,

$P(A \cup B) = \frac{23}{40} + \frac{18}{40} - \frac{8}{40} = \frac{33}{40}$. Taking both AP Psychology and AP Calculus are *not* mutually exclusive because the probability of taking both courses is not zero.

(E) In a throw of two dice, what is the probability of getting a 7 or 11?

Let A be the event of throwing a 7 and B be the event of throwing (65) or (56) for a total of 11. Since these events are mutually exclusive $P(A \cup B) = P(A) + P(B) = \frac{6}{36} + \frac{2}{36} = \frac{8}{36}$.

In **conditional probability**, the sample space is reduced to the set B rather than the set of all outcomes, and the favorable outcomes are those in both A and B ($A \cap B$). $P(A|B)$ is the probability that A occurs given that B occurred. This results in the formula $P(A|B) = \frac{P(A \cap B)}{P(B)}$. Multiplying both sides of this equation by $P(B)$ produces the equivalent formula $P(A \cap B) = P(B)\,P(A|B)$. If the probability of event A occurring does not depend on whether event B occurs, then A and B are said to be **independent** and $P(A|B) = P(A)$. Thus, if A and B are independent events, $P(A \cap B) = P(B) \cdot P(A)$.

Examples

(F) If you draw two marbles in sequence from a bowl with 10 black and 4 yellow marbles and replace the first marble before picking the second, what is the probability that both marbles are yellow?

Since there are 14 marbles altogether, and 4 are yellow, the probabilities for the first marble are $\frac{4}{14}$ for Y and $\frac{10}{14}$ for B. The return of the first marble makes the first and second picks independent, so the second pick has the same probabilities.

Use the formula $P(A \cap B) = P(A) \cdot P(B)$, where A and B are both Y (yellow), to find $P(Y \cap Y) = \frac{4}{14} \cdot \frac{4}{14} = \frac{16}{196}$.

(G) The scenario is the same as in example F, but this time, the first marble picked is not replaced. What is the probability that both marbles are yellow?

If the first marble is not returned, the first and second picks are not independent, so we must use the formula $P(A \cap B) = P(A|B) \cdot P(B)$. In this case, $P(Y) = \frac{4}{14}$ as before, but $P(Y|Y) = \frac{3}{13}$ because there are only 13 marbles left, of which only 3 are yellow. Therefore, $P(Y \cap Y) = P(Y)P(Y|Y) = \left(\frac{4}{14}\right)\left(\frac{3}{13}\right) = \frac{12}{182} = \frac{6}{91}$.

(H) If the probability that John will buy a certain product is $\frac{3}{5}$, that Bill will buy that product is $\frac{2}{3}$, and that Sue will buy that product is $\frac{1}{4}$, and if their decisions to buy are independent, what is the probability that at least one of them will buy the product?

This is a good example of using complements. Since the question asks for the probability of "at least one," find the probability of "none" and subtract that from 1. The probabilities that John, Bill, and Sue don't buy the product are $\frac{2}{5}$, $\frac{1}{3}$, and $\frac{3}{4}$, respectively. Since their decisions to buy (or equivalently, not to buy) are independent, the probability that none of them buys the product is $\left(\frac{2}{5}\right)\left(\frac{1}{3}\right)\left(\frac{3}{4}\right) = \frac{1}{10}$. Therefore, the probability that at least one of them buys the product is $1 - \frac{1}{10} = \frac{9}{10}$.

(I) Two dice are thrown. Event *A* is "the sum of the two dice is 7" and Event *B* is "at least one die is a 6." Are *A* and *B* independent?

From Example C, $P(A) = \frac{6}{36}$. Event B includes (1 and 6), (2 and 6), . . . , (6 and 6), (6 and 1), (6 and 2), . . . , (6 and 5), so $P(B) = \frac{11}{36}$. Only the two throws (6 and 1) and (1 and 6) are in the event $A|B$, so $P(A|B) = \frac{2}{36}$. $P(B)P(A) = \left(\frac{11}{36}\right)\left(\frac{6}{36}\right) = \frac{11}{216} \neq \frac{2}{36}$, so A and B are *not* independent.

EXERCISES 习题

1. With the throw of two dice, what is the probability that the sum will be a prime number?

   (A) $\frac{4}{11}$

   (B) $\frac{7}{18}$

   (C) $\frac{5}{12}$

   (D) $\frac{5}{11}$

   (E) $\frac{1}{2}$

2. If a coin is flipped and one die is thrown, what is the probability of getting a head or a 4?

   (A) $\frac{1}{12}$

   (B) $\frac{1}{3}$

   (C) $\frac{5}{12}$

   (D) $\frac{7}{12}$

   (E) $\frac{2}{3}$

3. Three cards are drawn from an ordinary deck of 52 cards. Each card is replaced in the deck before the next card is drawn. What is the probability that at least one of the cards will be a spade?

   (A) $\frac{3}{52}$

   (B) $\frac{9}{64}$

   (C) $\frac{3}{8}$

   (D) $\frac{37}{64}$

   (E) $\frac{3}{4}$

4. A coin is tossed three times. Let A = {three heads occur} and B = {at least one head occurs}. What is $P(A \cup B)$?

(A) $\frac{1}{8}$

(B) $\frac{1}{4}$

(C) $\frac{1}{2}$

(D) $\frac{3}{4}$

(E) $\frac{7}{8}$

5. A class has 12 boys and 4 girls. If three students are selected at random from the class, what is the probability that all will be boys?

(A) $\frac{1}{55}$

(B) $\frac{1}{4}$

(C) $\frac{1}{3}$

(D) $\frac{11}{28}$

(E) $\frac{11}{15}$

6. A red box contains eight items, of which three are defective, and a blue box contains five items, of which two are defective. An item is drawn at random from each box. What is the probability that both items will be nondefective?

(A) $\frac{3}{20}$

(B) $\frac{3}{8}$

(C) $\frac{5}{13}$

(D) $\frac{8}{13}$

(E) $\frac{17}{20}$

7. A hotel has five single rooms available, for which six men and three women apply. What is the probability that the rooms will be rented to three men and two women?

(A) $\frac{23}{112}$
(B) $\frac{97}{251}$
(C) $\frac{10}{21}$
(D) $\frac{5}{9}$
(E) $\frac{5}{8}$

8. Of all the articles in a box, 80% are satisfactory, while 20% are not. The probability of obtaining exactly five good items out of eight randomly selected articles is

(A) 0.003
(B) 0.013
(C) 0.132
(D) 0.147
(E) 0.800

Answers Explained 答案解析

1. **(C)** There is 1 way to get a 2, and there are 2 ways to get a 3, 4 ways to get a 5, 6 ways to get a 7, and 2 ways to get an 11. Out of 36 elements in the sample space, 15 successes are possible.

$$P(\text{prime}) = \frac{15}{36} = \frac{5}{12}$$

2. **(D)** The probability of getting neither a head nor a 4 is $\frac{1}{2} \cdot \frac{5}{6} = \frac{5}{12}$. Therefore, the probability of getting either is $1 - \frac{5}{12} = \frac{7}{12}$.

* 3. **(D)** Since the drawn cards are replaced, the draws are independent. The probability that none of the cards was a spade $= \frac{39}{52} \cdot \frac{39}{52} \cdot \frac{39}{52} = \frac{3}{4} \cdot \frac{3}{4} \cdot \frac{3}{4} = \frac{27}{64}$.

Probability that 1 was a spade $= 1 - \frac{27}{64} = \frac{37}{64}$.

4. **(E)** The only situation when neither of these sets is satisfied occurs when three tails appear. $P(A \cup B) = \frac{7}{8}$.

* 5. **(D)** There are 16 students altogether. The probability that the first person chosen is a boy is $\frac{12}{16}$. Now there are only 15 students left, of which 11 are boys, so the probability that the second student chosen is also a boy is $\frac{11}{15}$. By the same reasoning, the probability that the third is a boy is $\frac{10}{14}$. Therefore, the probability that the first and the second and the third students chosen are all boys is $\frac{12}{16} \times \frac{11}{15} \times \frac{10}{14} = \frac{11}{28}$.

6. **(B)** The probability of both items being nondefective = $\frac{5}{8} \cdot \frac{3}{5} = \frac{3}{8}$.

* 7. **(C)** $\binom{6}{3}$ is the number of ways 3 men can be selected. $\binom{3}{2}$ is the number of ways 2 women can be selected. $\binom{9}{5}$ is the total number of ways people can be selected to fill 5 rooms.

$$P(3 \text{ men, } 2 \text{ women}) = \frac{\binom{6}{3}\binom{3}{2}}{\binom{9}{5}} = \frac{10}{21}.$$

* 8. **(D)** Since the problem doesn't say how many articles are in the box, we must assume that it is an unlimited number. The probability of picking 5 satisfactory items (and therefore 3 unsatisfactory ones) is $(0.8)^5(0.2)^3$, and there are $\binom{8}{5}$ ways of doing this. Therefore, the desired probability is $\binom{8}{5}(0.8)^5(0.2)^3 \approx 0.147$.

PART 3
第三部分
Model Tests
测试题

ANSWER SHEET

答题卡

Model Test 1

测试题1

1. Ⓐ Ⓑ Ⓒ Ⓓ Ⓔ	14. Ⓐ Ⓑ Ⓒ Ⓓ Ⓔ	27. Ⓐ Ⓑ Ⓒ Ⓓ Ⓔ	40. Ⓐ Ⓑ Ⓒ Ⓓ Ⓔ
2. Ⓐ Ⓑ Ⓒ Ⓓ Ⓔ	15. Ⓐ Ⓑ Ⓒ Ⓓ Ⓔ	28. Ⓐ Ⓑ Ⓒ Ⓓ Ⓔ	41. Ⓐ Ⓑ Ⓒ Ⓓ Ⓔ
3. Ⓐ Ⓑ Ⓒ Ⓓ Ⓔ	16. Ⓐ Ⓑ Ⓒ Ⓓ Ⓔ	29. Ⓐ Ⓑ Ⓒ Ⓓ Ⓔ	42. Ⓐ Ⓑ Ⓒ Ⓓ Ⓔ
4. Ⓐ Ⓑ Ⓒ Ⓓ Ⓔ	17. Ⓐ Ⓑ Ⓒ Ⓓ Ⓔ	30. Ⓐ Ⓑ Ⓒ Ⓓ Ⓔ	43. Ⓐ Ⓑ Ⓒ Ⓓ Ⓔ
5. Ⓐ Ⓑ Ⓒ Ⓓ Ⓔ	18. Ⓐ Ⓑ Ⓒ Ⓓ Ⓔ	31. Ⓐ Ⓑ Ⓒ Ⓓ Ⓔ	44. Ⓐ Ⓑ Ⓒ Ⓓ Ⓔ
6. Ⓐ Ⓑ Ⓒ Ⓓ Ⓔ	19. Ⓐ Ⓑ Ⓒ Ⓓ Ⓔ	32. Ⓐ Ⓑ Ⓒ Ⓓ Ⓔ	45. Ⓐ Ⓑ Ⓒ Ⓓ Ⓔ
7. Ⓐ Ⓑ Ⓒ Ⓓ Ⓔ	20. Ⓐ Ⓑ Ⓒ Ⓓ Ⓔ	33. Ⓐ Ⓑ Ⓒ Ⓓ Ⓔ	46. Ⓐ Ⓑ Ⓒ Ⓓ Ⓔ
8. Ⓐ Ⓑ Ⓒ Ⓓ Ⓔ	21. Ⓐ Ⓑ Ⓒ Ⓓ Ⓔ	34. Ⓐ Ⓑ Ⓒ Ⓓ Ⓔ	47. Ⓐ Ⓑ Ⓒ Ⓓ Ⓔ
9. Ⓐ Ⓑ Ⓒ Ⓓ Ⓔ	22. Ⓐ Ⓑ Ⓒ Ⓓ Ⓔ	35. Ⓐ Ⓑ Ⓒ Ⓓ Ⓔ	48. Ⓐ Ⓑ Ⓒ Ⓓ Ⓔ
10. Ⓐ Ⓑ Ⓒ Ⓓ Ⓔ	23. Ⓐ Ⓑ Ⓒ Ⓓ Ⓔ	36. Ⓐ Ⓑ Ⓒ Ⓓ Ⓔ	49. Ⓐ Ⓑ Ⓒ Ⓓ Ⓔ
11. Ⓐ Ⓑ Ⓒ Ⓓ Ⓔ	24. Ⓐ Ⓑ Ⓒ Ⓓ Ⓔ	37. Ⓐ Ⓑ Ⓒ Ⓓ Ⓔ	50. Ⓐ Ⓑ Ⓒ Ⓓ Ⓔ
12. Ⓐ Ⓑ Ⓒ Ⓓ Ⓔ	25. Ⓐ Ⓑ Ⓒ Ⓓ Ⓔ	38. Ⓐ Ⓑ Ⓒ Ⓓ Ⓔ	
13. Ⓐ Ⓑ Ⓒ Ⓓ Ⓔ	26. Ⓐ Ⓑ Ⓒ Ⓓ Ⓔ	39. Ⓐ Ⓑ Ⓒ Ⓓ Ⓔ	

Model Test 1 测试题1

Tear out the preceding answer sheet. Decide which is the best choice by rounding your answer when appropriate. Blacken the corresponding space on the answer sheet. When finished, check your answers with those at the end of the test. For questions that you got wrong, note the chapters containing the material that you must review. Also, if you do not fully understand how you arrived at some of the correct answers, you should review the appropriate chapters. Finally, fill out the Self-Evaluation Chart on page 226 in order to pinpoint the topics that give you the most difficulty.

50 questions: 1 hour

Directions: Decide which answer choice is best. If the exact numerical value is not one of the answer choices, select the closest approximation. Fill in the circle on the answer sheet that corresponds to your choice.

Notes:

(1) You will need to use a scientific or graphing calculator to answer some of the questions.
(2) You will have to decide whether to put your calculator in degree or radian mode for some problems.
(3) All figures that accompany problems are plane figures unless otherwise stated. Figures are drawn as accurately as possible to provide useful information for solving the problem, except when it is stated in a particular problem that the figure is not drawn to scale.
(4) Unless otherwise indicated, the domain of a function is the set of all real numbers for which the functional value is also a real number.

Reference Information. The following formulas are provided for your information.

Volume of a right circular cone with radius r and height h: $V = \frac{1}{3}\pi r^2 h$

Lateral area of a right circular cone if the base has circumference C and slant height is l: $S = \frac{1}{2}Cl$

Volume of a sphere of radius r: $V = \frac{4}{3}\pi r^3$

Surface area of a sphere of radius r: $S = 4\pi r^2$

Volume of a pyramid of base area B and height h: $V = \frac{1}{3}Bh$

USE THIS SPACE FOR SCRATCH WORK

1. The slope of a line perpendicular to the line whose equation is $\frac{x}{3} - \frac{y}{4} = 1$ is

(A) −3

(B) $-\frac{4}{3}$

(C) $-\frac{3}{4}$

(D) $\frac{1}{4}$

(E) $\frac{4}{3}$

2. What is the range of the data set 8, 12, 12, 15, 18?

(A) 10
(B) 12
(C) 13
(D) 15
(E) 18

3. If $f(x) = \frac{x-7}{x^2-49}$, for what value(s) of x does the graph of $y = f(x)$ have a vertical asymptote?

(A) −7
(B) 0
(C) −7,0,7
(D) −7,7
(E) 7

4. If $f(x) = \sqrt{2x+3}$ and $g(x) = x^2 + 1$, then $f(g(2)) =$

(A) 2.24
(B) 3.00
(C) 3.61
(D) 6.00
(E) 6.16

5. What is the value of x if $4^{x+1} = 8^x$?

(A) −1
(B) 0
(C) 1
(D) 2
(E) 3

6. The circumference of circle $x^2 + y^2 - 10y - 36 = 0$ is

(A) 38
(B) 49
(C) 54
(D) 125
(E) 192

7. Twenty-five percent of a group of unrelated students are only children. The students are asked one at a time whether they are only children. What is the probability that the 5th student asked is the first only child?

(A) 0.00098
(B) 0.08
(C) 0.24
(D) 0.25
(E) 0.50

8. If $f(x) = 2$ for all real numbers x, then $f(x + 2) =$

(A) 0
(B) 2
(C) 4
(D) x
(E) The value cannot be determined.

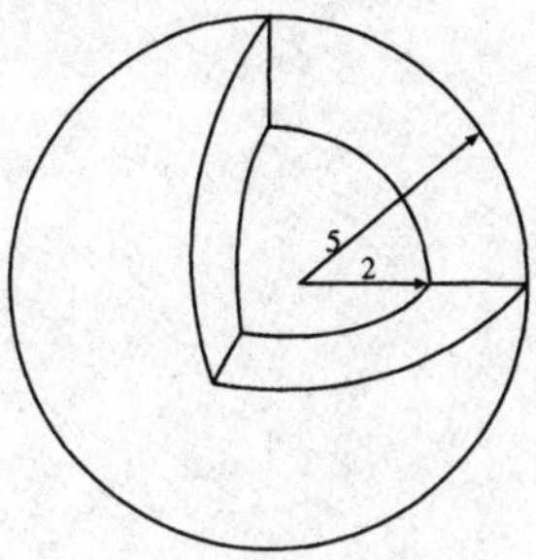

Figure not drawn to scale

9. The volume of the region between two concentric spheres of radii 2 and 5 is

(A) 28
(B) 66
(C) 113
(D) 368
(E) 490

10. If a, b, and c are real numbers and if $a^5b^3c^8 = \frac{9a^3c^8}{b^{-3}}$, then a could equal

(A) $\frac{1}{9}$

(B) $\frac{1}{3}$

(C) 9

(D) 3

(E) $9b^6$

USE THIS SPACE FOR SCRATCH WORK

MODEL TEST 1

MODEL TEST 1

11. In right triangle ABC, $AB = 10$, $BC = 8$, $AC = 6$. The sine of $\angle A$ is

(A) $\frac{3}{5}$

(B) $\frac{3}{4}$

(C) $\frac{4}{5}$

(D) $\frac{5}{4}$

(E) $\frac{4}{3}$

12. If $16^x = 4$ and $5^{x+y} = 625$, then $y =$

(A) 1
(B) 2
(C) $\frac{7}{2}$
(D) 5
(E) $\frac{25}{2}$

13. If the parameter is eliminated from the equations $x = t^2 + 1$ and $y = 2t$, then the relation between x and y is

(A) $y = x - 1$
(B) $y = 1 - x$
(C) $y^2 = x - 1$
(D) $y^2 = (x - 1)^2$
(E) $y^2 = 4x - 4$

14. Let $f(x)$ be a polynomial function: $f(x) = x^5 + \cdots$. If $f(1) = 0$ and $f(2) = 0$, then $f(x)$ is divisible by

(A) $x - 3$
(B) $x^2 - 2$
(C) $x^2 + 2$
(D) $x^2 - 3x + 2$
(E) $x^2 + 3x + 2$

15. If $x - y = 2$, $y - z = 4$, and $x - y - z = -3$, then $y =$

(A) 1
(B) 5
(C) 9
(D) 11
(E) 13

USE THIS SPACE FOR SCRATCH WORK

USE THIS SPACE FOR SCRATCH WORK

16. If $z > 0$, $a = z\cos\theta$, and $b = z\sin\theta$, then $\sqrt{a^2 + b^2} =$

(A) 1
(B) z
(C) $2z$
(D) $z\cos\theta\sin\theta$
(E) $z(\cos\theta + \sin\theta)$

17. If the vertices of a triangle are $(u,0)$, $(v,8)$, and $(0,0)$, then the area of the triangle is

(A) $4|u|$
(B) $2|v|$
(C) $|uv|$
(D) $2|uv|$
(E) $\frac{1}{2}|uv|$

18. What is the difference between the min and max values of the function f defined by $f(x) = 2x^2 + 3x - 8$ on the interval $[-2,5]$?

(A) 7
(B) 57.75
(C) 63.0
(D) 66.13
(E) 71.25

19. What is the probability that a prime number is less than 7, given that it is less than 13?

(A) $\frac{1}{3}$
(B) $\frac{2}{5}$
(C) $\frac{1}{2}$
(D) $\frac{3}{5}$
(E) $\frac{3}{4}$

MODEL TEST 1

20. The ellipse $4x^2 + 8y^2 = 64$ and the circle $x^2 + y^2 = 9$ intersect at points where the y-coordinate is

(A) $\pm\sqrt{2}$
(B) $\pm\sqrt{5}$
(C) $\pm\sqrt{6}$
(D) $\pm\sqrt{7}$
(E) $\pm$ 10.00

21. Each term of a sequence, after the first, is inversely proportional to the term preceding it. If the first two terms are 2 and 6, what is the twelfth term?

(A) 2
(B) 6
(C) 46
(D) $2 \cdot 3^{11}$
(E) The twelfth term cannot be determined.

22. A company offers you the use of its computer for a fee. Plan A costs \$6 to join and then \$9 per hour to use the computer. Plan B costs \$25 to join and then \$2.25 per hour to use the computer. After how many minutes of use would the cost of plan A be the same as the cost of plan B?

(A) 18,052
(B) 173
(C) 169
(D) 165
(E) 157

23. If the probability that the Giants will win the NFC championship is p and if the probability that the Raiders will win the AFC championship is q, what is the probability that only one of these teams will win its respective championship?

(A) pq
(B) $p + q - 2pq$
(C) $|p - q|$
(D) $1 - pq$
(E) $2pq - p - q$

24. What is the sum of the infinite geometric series whose first two terms are 3 and 1?

(A) 1.5
(B) 4.5
(C) 9
(D) 12
(E) infinite

USE THIS SPACE FOR SCRATCH WORK

USE THIS SPACE FOR SCRATCH WORK

25. The value of $\frac{453!}{450!3!}$ is

(A) greater than 10^{100}
(B) between 10^{10} and 10^{100}
(C) between 10^5 and 10^{10}
(D) between 10 and 10^5
(E) less than 10

26. If A is the angle formed by the line $2y = 3x + 7$ and the x-axis, then $\angle A$ equals

(A) $-45°$
(B) $0°$
(C) $56°$
(D) $72°$
(E) $215°$

27. A U.S. dollar equals 0.716 European euros, and a Japanese yen equals 0.00776 European euros. How many U.S. dollars equal a Japanese yen?

(A) 0.0056
(B) 0.011
(C) 0.71
(D) 94.2
(E) 179.98

28. If $(x - 4)^2 + 4(y - 3)^2 = 16$ is graphed, the sum of the distances from any fixed point on the curve to the two foci is

(A) 4
(B) 8
(C) 12
(D) 16
(E) 32

29. In the equation $x^2 + kx + 54 = 0$, one root is twice the other root. The value(s) of k is (are)

(A) -5.2
(B) 15.6
(C) 22.0
(D) ± 5.2
(E) ± 15.6

30. The remainder obtained when $3x^4 + 7x^3 + 8x^2 - 2x - 3$ is divided by $x + 1$ is

(A) -3
(B) 0
(C) 3
(D) 5
(E) 13

MODEL TEST 1

31. If $f(x) = e^x$ and $g(x) = f(x) + f^{-1}(x)$, what does $g(2)$ equal?

(A) 5.1
(B) 7.4
(C) 7.5
(D) 8.1
(E) 8.3

32. If $x_0 = 3$ and $x_{n+1} = \sqrt{4 + x_n}$, then $x_3 =$

(A) 2.65
(B) 2.58
(C) 2.56
(D) 2.55
(E) 2.54

33. For what values of k does the graph of $\frac{(x-2k)^2}{1} - \frac{(y-3k)^2}{3} = 1$ pass through the origin?

(A) only 0
(B) only 1
(C) ± 1
(D) $\pm\sqrt{5}$
(E) no value

34. If $\frac{1-\cos\theta}{\sin\theta} = \frac{\sqrt{3}}{3}$, then $\theta =$

(A) 15°
(B) 30°
(C) 45°
(D) 60°
(E) 75°

35. If $x^2 + 3x + 2 < 0$ and $f(x) = x^2 - 3x + 2$, then

(A) $0 < f(x) < 6$
(B) $f(x) \geq \frac{3}{2}$
(C) $f(x) > 12$
(D) $f(x) > 0$
(E) $6 < f(x) < 12$

36. If $f(x) = \lfloor x \rfloor + [x]$, where $[x]$ is the greatest integer less than or equal to x, the value of $f(-2.5) + f(1.5)$ is

(A) -2
(B) 1
(C) 1.5
(D) 2
(E) 3

USE THIS SPACE FOR SCRATCH WORK

USE THIS SPACE FOR SCRATCH WORK

37. If $(\sec x)(\tan x) < 0$, which of the following must be true?

I. $\tan x < 0$
II. $\csc x \cot x < 0$
III. x is in the third or fourth quadrant

(A) I only
(B) II only
(C) III only
(D) II and III
(E) I and II

38. At the end of a meeting all participants shook hands with each other. Twenty-eight handshakes were exchanged. How many people were at the meeting?

(A) 7
(B) 8
(C) 14
(D) 28
(E) 56

39. Suppose the graph of $f(x) = 2x^2$ is translated 3 units down and 2 units right. If the resulting graph represents the graph of $g(x)$, what is the value of $g(-1.2)$?

(A) −1.72
(B) −0.12
(C) 2.88
(D) 17.48
(E) 37.28

x	−5	−3	−1	1
y	0	4	−3	0

40. Four points on the graph of a polynomial P are shown in the table above. If P is a polynomial of degree 3, then $P(x)$ could equal

(A) $a(x - 5)(x - 2)(x + 1)$
(B) $a(x - 5)(x + 2)(x + 1)$
(C) $a(x + 5)(x - 2)(x - 1)$
(D) $a(x + 5)(x + 2)(x - 1)$
(E) $a(x + 5)(x + 2)(x + 1)$

USE THIS SPACE FOR SCRATCH WORK

41. If $f(x) = ax + b$, which of the following make(s) $f(x) = f^{-1}(x)$?

I. $a = -1, b =$ any real number
II. $a = 1, b = 0$
III. $a =$ any real number, $b = 0$

(A) only I
(B) only II
(C) only III
(D) only I and II
(E) only I and III

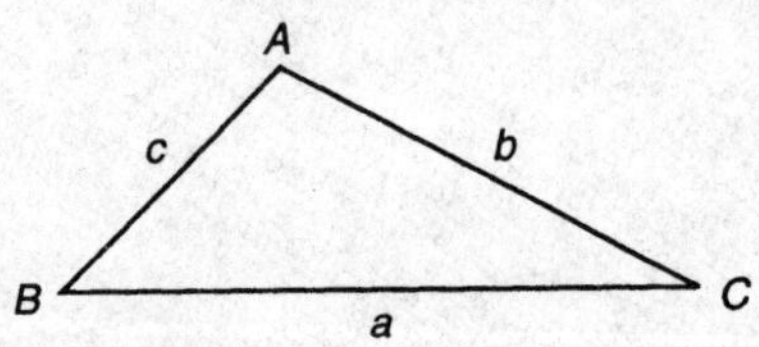

42. In the figure above, $\angle A = 110°$, $a = \sqrt{6}$, and $b = 2$. What is the value of $\angle C$?

(A) 50°
(B) 25°
(C) 20°
(D) 15°
(E) 10°

43. If vector $\vec{v} = (1, \sqrt{3})$ and vector $\vec{u} = (3, -2)$, find the value of $|3\vec{v} - \vec{u}|$.

(A) 5.4
(B) 6
(C) 7
(D) 7.2
(E) 52

44. If $f(x) = \sqrt{x^2 - 1}$ and $g(x) = \dfrac{10}{x+2}$, then $g(f(3)) =$

(A) 0.2
(B) 1.7
(C) 2.1
(D) 3.5
(E) 8.7

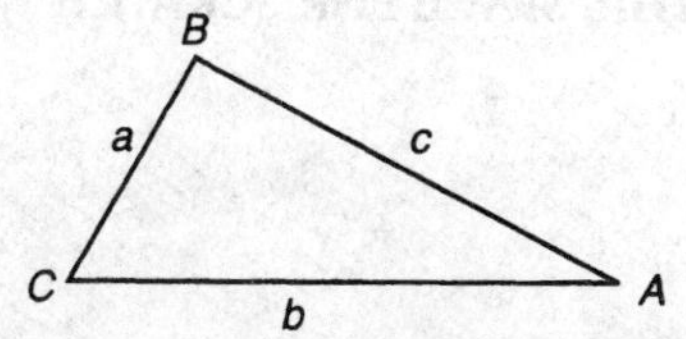

USE THIS SPACE FOR SCRATCH WORK

45. In $\triangle ABC$ above, $a = 2x$, $b = 3x + 2$, $c = \sqrt{12}$, and $\angle C = 60°$. Find x.

(A) 0.50
(B) 0.64
(C) 0.77
(D) 1.64
(E) 1.78

46. If $\log_a 5 = x$ and $\log_a 7 = y$, then $\log_a \sqrt{1.4} =$

(A) $\frac{1}{2}xy$

(B) $\frac{1}{2}x - y$

(C) $\frac{1}{2}(x + y)$

(D) $\frac{1}{2}(y - x)$

(E) $\frac{y}{2x}$

47. If $f(x) = 3x^2 + 4x + 5$, what must the value of k equal so that the graph of $f(x - k)$ will be symmetric to the y-axis?

(A) -4

(B) $-\frac{4}{3}$

(C) $-\frac{2}{3}$

(D) $\frac{2}{3}$

(E) $\frac{4}{3}$

USE THIS SPACE FOR SCRATCH WORK

48. If $f(x) = \cos x$ and $g(x) = 2x + 1$, which of the following are even functions?

I. $f(x) \cdot g(x)$
II. $f(g(x))$
III. $g(f(x))$

(A) only I
(B) only II
(C) only III
(D) only I and II
(E) only II and III

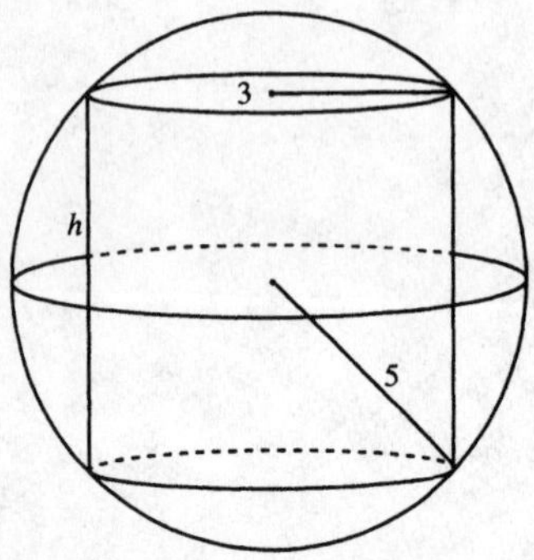

49. A cylinder whose base radius is 3 is inscribed in a sphere of radius 5. What is the difference between the volume of the sphere and the volume of the cylinder?

(A) 88
(B) 297
(C) 354
(D) 448
(E) 1,345

50. Under which conditions is $\frac{xy}{x-y}$ negative?

(A) $0 < y < x$
(B) $x < y < 0$
(C) $x < 0 < y$
(D) $y < x < 0$
(E) none of the above

STOP

If there is still time remaining, you may review your answers.

ANSWER KEY
答案
Model Test 1
测试题1

1. **C**	14. **D**	27. **B**	40. **D**
2. **A**	15. **C**	28. **B**	41. **D**
3. **A**	16. **B**	29. **E**	42. **C**
4. **C**	17. **A**	30. **C**	43. **D**
5. **D**	18. **D**	31. **D**	44. **C**
6. **B**	19. **D**	32. **C**	45. **B**
7. **B**	20. **D**	33. **C**	46. **D**
8. **B**	21. **B**	34. **D**	47. **D**
9. **E**	22. **C**	35. **E**	48. **C**
10. **D**	23. **B**	36. **D**	49. **B**
11. **C**	24. **B**	37. **C**	50. **B**
12. **C**	25. **C**	38. **B**	
13. **E**	26. **C**	39. **D**	

ANSWERS EXPLAINED 答案解析

The following explanations are keyed to the review portions of this book. The number in brackets after each explanation indicates the appropriate chapter in the Review of Major Topics (Part 2). If a problem can be solved using algebraic techniques alone, [algebra] appears after the explanation, and no reference is given for that problem in the Self-Evaluation Chart at the end of the test.

An asterisk appears next to those solutions in which a graphing calculator is necessary or helpful.

1. **(C)** Solve for *y*. $y = \frac{4}{3}x - 4$. Slope $= \frac{4}{3}$. Slope of perpendicular is the opposite reciprocal, $-\frac{3}{4}$. [2]

2. **(A)** Range = largest value – smallest value = 18 – 8 = 10. [21]

3. **(A)** Vertical asymptotes occur where the denominator is zero but the numerator is not. The denominator, $x^2 - 49$, factors into $(x + 7)(x - 7)$. Since both the numerator and the denominator are zero when $x = 7$, a vertical asymptote occurs only at $x = -7$. [9]

* **4.** **(C)** Enter the function *f* into Y_1 and the function *g* into Y_2. Evaluate $Y_1(Y_2(2))$ to get the correct answer, Choice C.
An alternative solution is to evaluate $g(2) = 5$ and $f(5) = \sqrt{13}$, and either use your calculator to evaluate $\sqrt{13}$ or observe that $3 < \sqrt{13} < 4$, indicating 3.61 as the only feasible answer choice. [1]

* **5.** **(D)** $4^{x+1} = (2^2)^{x+1} = 2^{2x+2}$ and $8^x = (2^3)^x = 2^{3x}$. Therefore, $2^{2x+2} = 2^{3x}$. It follows that $2x + 2 = 3x$, and $x = 2$. [8]

* **6.** **(B)** Complete the square to get $x^2 + (y - 5)^2 = 61$.
Radius $= \sqrt{61}$. $C = 2\pi r = 2\pi\sqrt{61} \approx 49$. [15]

* **7.** **(B)** Whether or not students in the group have siblings are independent events. The probability that each of the first four is not an only child is $(0.75)^4$. The probability that the fifth student is an only child is 0.25, so the probability of seeing the first four children with siblings and the fifth an only child is $(0.75)^4(0.25) \approx 0.08$ [22]

8. **(B)** Regardless of what is substituted for *x*, *f*(*x*) still equals 2.

Alternative Solution: $f(x + 2)$ causes the graph of $f(x)$ to be shifted 2 units to the left. Since $f(x) = 2$ for all *x*, $f(x + 2)$ will also equal 2 for all *x*. [1]

* **9.** **(E)** Enter the formula for the volume of a sphere $(4/3)\pi x^3$ (in the reference list of formulas) into Y_1. Return to the Home Screen, and enter $Y_1(5) - Y_1(2)$ to get the correct answer, Choice E.

An alternative solution is to evaluate $V = \frac{4}{3}\pi\ (5^3 - 2^3) = \frac{4}{3}\pi(117)$ directly. [15]

* **10.** **(D)** Since $b^3 = \dfrac{1}{b^{-3}}$, divide out b^3c^8, leaving $a^5 = 9a^3$. Therefore $a = \pm 3$. [8]

11. **(C)** $\sin A = \dfrac{8}{10} = \dfrac{4}{5}$. [6]

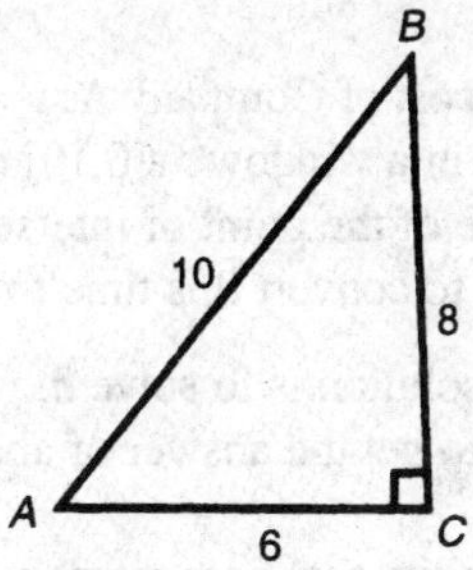

12. **(C)** Since the $\frac{1}{2}$ power is the square root, $x = \frac{1}{2}$ because the square root of 16 is 4.

Since $5^4 = 625$, $x + y = 4$, so that $y = 4 - \frac{1}{2} = \frac{7}{2}$. [8]

13. **(E)** $t = \frac{y}{2}$. Eliminate the parameter and get $x = \frac{y^2}{4} + 1 = x$ or $y^2 = 4x - 4$. [10]

14. **(D)** $f(1) = 0$ and $f(2) = 0$ imply that $x - 1$ and $x - 2$ are factors of $f(x)$. Their product, $x^2 - 3x + 2$, is also a factor. [4]

15. **(C)** Add the first two equations to get $x - z = 6$. Substitute this in the third equation to get $6 - y = -3$, and solve for y. [algebra]

16. **(B)** $a^2 = z^2 \cos^2 \theta$ and $b^2 = z^2 \sin^2 \theta$, so $a^2 + b^2 = z^2(\cos^2 \theta + \sin^2 \theta) = z^2$ because $\cos^2 \theta + \sin^2 \theta = 1$. Since $\sqrt{z^2} = z$ when $z > 0$, the correct answer choice is Choice B. [7]

17. **(A)** Sketch a graph of the three vertices. The base is $|u|$ and the altitude is 8. Therefore, the area is $4|u|$. [15]

* **18.** **(D)** Enter the function into Y_1 in the graphing calculator, with XMIN = –2 and XMAX = 5. In order to see the entire graph, you will have to set YMIN = –10, and YMAX = 60. Use CALC (2nd TRACE) to find the min value –9.13 and the max value 57. The difference is 57 – (–9.13) = 66.13. [4]

19. **(D)** There are 5 prime numbers less than 13: 2, 3, 5, 7, 11. Three of these are less than 7, so the correct probability is $\frac{3}{5}$. [22]

∗ **20.** **(D)** Substituting for x^2 and solving for y gives $4(9 - y^2) + 8y^2 = 64$. $4y^2 = 28$, and so $y^2 = 7$ and $y = \pm\sqrt{7}$. [13]

21. **(B)** $t_n \cdot t_{n+1} = K$. $2 \cdot 6 = K = 12$. Therefore, $6 \cdot t_3 = 12$, and so $t_3 = 2$. Continuing this process gives all odd terms to be 2 and all even terms to be 6. [19]

∗ **22.** **(C)** Graph the cost of Company A, $y = 6 + 9x$, and the cost of Company B, $y = 25 + 2.25x$, in a window $x\varepsilon[0,10]$ and $y\varepsilon[0,50]$. Use CALC/intersect to find the x-coordinate of the point of intersection at 2.8148 hours, the "break-even" point. Multiply by 60 to convert this time to the correct answer choice.

An alternative solution is to solve the equation $6 + 9x = 25 + 2.25x$ and multiply the solution by 60 to get the answer of about 169 minutes. [2]

23. **(B)** The probability that both teams will win is pq. The probability that both will lose is $(1 - p)(1 - q)$. The probability that only one will win is $1 - [pq + (1 - p)(1 - q)] = 1 - (pq + 1 - p - q + pq) = p + q - 2pq$.

Alternative Solution: The probability that the Giants will win and the Raiders will lose is $p(1 - q)$. The probability that the Raiders will win and the Giants will lose is $q(1 - p)$. Therefore, the probability that either one of these results will occur is $p(1 - q) + q(1 - p) = p + q - 2pq$. [22]

24. **(B)** The common ratio r of this geometric sequence is $\frac{1}{3}$, and the first term is 3.

The formula for the sum of an infinite series is $S = \frac{a}{1-r}$, where a is the first term and r is the common ratio. Therefore, $S = \frac{3}{1-\frac{1}{3}} = \frac{3}{\frac{2}{3}} = 4.5$. [19]

∗ **25.** **(C)** No calculator currently on the market can compute 453!, so doing this problem requires some knowledge of factorial arithmetic. The easiest solution to the problem is to observe that $\frac{453!}{450!3!}$ is the number of combinations of 453 taken 3 at a time $({}_{453}C_3)$.

Enter 453MATH/PRB/nCr3 into your calculator to find that the correct answer choice is Choice C.

An alternative solution is to simplify $\frac{453!}{450!3!}$ to $\frac{453 \cdot 452 \cdot 451}{3 \cdot 2 \cdot 1} = 1.5 \cdots \times 10^7$. [16]

∗ **26.** **(C)** Solve for y: $y = \frac{3}{2}x + \frac{7}{2}$. Slope $= \frac{\Delta y}{\Delta x} = \frac{3}{2}$. Tan A also equals $\frac{\Delta y}{\Delta x}$. Therefore,

$\tan A = \frac{3}{2}$. $\text{Tan}^{-1}\left(\frac{3}{2}\right) = \angle A \approx 56°$. [6]

∗ **27.** **(B)** 1 yen equals 0.0076 euros, and 1 euro equals $\frac{1}{0.716} = 1.40$ dollars. Therefore, 1 yen equals $0.0076 \times 1.40 = 0.011$ dollars. [algebra]

28. **(B)** Divide the equation through by 16 to get $\frac{(x-4)^2}{16}+\frac{(y-3)^2}{4}=1$. This is the equation of an ellipse with $a^2 = 16$. The sum of the distances to the foci $= 2a = 8$. [13]

* 29. **(E)** If the roots are r and $2r$, their sum $= -\frac{b}{a} = 3r = -\frac{k}{1}$ and their product $= \frac{c}{a} =$ $2r^2 = \frac{54}{1}$. Therefore, $r = \pm\sqrt{27}$ and $k = \pm 3\sqrt{27} \approx \pm 15.6$.

Alternative Solution: If the roots are r and $2r$, $(x-r)(x-2r) = 0$. Multiply to obtain $x^2 - 3r + 2r^2 = 0$, which represents $x^2 + kx + 54 = 0$. Thus, $-3r = k$ and $2r^2 = 54$. Since $r = -\frac{k}{3}$, then $2\left(-\frac{k}{3}\right) = 54$ and $k = \pm 3\sqrt{27} \approx \pm 15.6$. [3]

30. **(C)** Substituting -1 for x gives 3.

Alternative Solution: Use synthetic division to get

-1	3	7	8	-2	-3
		-3	-4	-4	6
	3	4	4	-6	3 = remainder [4]

* 31. **(D)** The inverse of $f(x) = e^x$ is $f^{-1}(x) = \ln x$. $g(2) = e^2 + \ln 2 \approx 8.1$. [8]

* 32. **(C)** This is a recursively defined sequence. Press 3 ENTER on your calculator. Then enter $\sqrt{4+\text{Ans}}$ and press ENTER 3 times to get $x_3 \approx 2.56$. [19]

33. **(C)** If the graph passes through the origin, $x = 0$ and $y = 0$, then $\frac{4k^2}{1}-\frac{9k^2}{3}=1$. $k^2 = 1$, and so $k = \pm 1$. [13]

* 34. **(D)** Graph $y=\frac{1-\cos x}{\sin x}$ and $y=\frac{\sqrt{3}}{3}$ using Ztrig in degree mode. Find the point of intersection with CALC/intersect to arrive at the correct answer, Choice D.

An alternative solution uses the identities $\tan\frac{\theta}{2}=\frac{1-\cos x}{\sin x}$ and $\tan 30°=\frac{\sqrt{3}}{3}$ to deduce $\frac{\theta}{2}=30°$, so $\theta = 60°$. [7]

* 35. **(E)** The problem is asking for the range of $f(x)$ values for values of x that satisfy the inequality. First graph the inequality in Y_1, starting with the standard window and zooming in until the x values for the portion of the graph that falls below the x-axis can be identified as the interval $(-2,-1)$. Then enter the formula for $f(x)$ in Y_2. Although it can be done graphically, the simplest way to find the range of values of $f(x)$ that correspond to $x\varepsilon(-2,-1)$ is to use the TABLE function. Deselect Y_1 and enter TBLSET and set TblStart to -2, $\Delta Tbl = 0.1$, and Indpnt and Depend to Auto. Then enter TABLE and observe that the Y_2 values range from 12 to 6 as x ranges from -2 to -1, yielding the correct answer, Choice E.

An alternative solution is to solve the inequality algebraically by solving the associated equation $x^2 + 3x + 2 = 0$ and testing points. The left side of the equation factors as $(x + 2)(x + 1)$, and the Zero Product Property implies that $x = -2$ or $x = -1$. Points inside the interval (–2,–1) satisfy the inequality, while those outside it do not. Since the graph of $f(x)$ is a parabola and $f(-2) = 12$ and $f(-1) = 6$, $f(x)$ takes the range of values between 12 and 6. [5]

∗ 36. **(D)** The greatest integer less than or equal to x is int(x) on the graphing calculator. Enter abs(x) + int(x) into Y_1. Return to the Home Screen, and enter $Y_1(-2.5) + Y_1(1.5)$ to get the correct answer, Choice D.

An alternative solution evaluates $|-2.5| + [-2.5] + |1.5| + [1.5]$ without the aid of a calculator. Of these 4 values, only $[-2.5]$ is tricky since $[-2.5] = -3$, not -2. Thus, $|-2.5| + [-2.5] + |1.5| + [1.5] = 2.5 - 3 + 1.5 + 1 = 2$. [11]

37. **(C)** Set up the following table.

	Q1	Q2	Q3	Q4
$\sec x$	+	–	–	+
$\tan x$	+	–	+	–
$\cot x$	+	–	+	–
$\csc x$	+	+	–	–

The product $\sec x \tan x$ is negative only when its factors have different signs, so III is the only true statement. [7]

38. **(B)** $\begin{pmatrix} x \text{ people} \\ 2 \end{pmatrix} = 28$. $\dfrac{x(x-1)}{2\cdot 1} = 28$. $x^2 - x = 56$. $x = 8$. [16]

∗ 39. **(D)** Since the function g is f translated 3 down and 2 right, $g(x) = f(x - 2) - 3$. Therefore, $g(-1.2) = f(-3.2) - 3 = 2(-3.2)^2 - 3 = 17.48$. [12]

40. **(D)** Since –5 and 1 are both zeros, $(x + 5)$ and $(x - 1)$ are factors of $P(x)$. Since $P(x)$ changes sign between $x = -3$ and $x = -1$, there is a zero between these two values. Choice D is the only one that meets all three criteria. [4]

∗ 41. **(D)** The graph of f must be symmetric about the line $y = x$. In other words, interchanging x and y must leave the graph unchanged. In I, $x = -y + b$, which is equivalent to $y = -x + b$, which is symmetric about $y = x$. In II, $x = y$. In III, $x = ay$, or $y = \dfrac{x}{a}$. [2]

∗ 42. **(C)** Law of sines:

$\dfrac{\sin 110°}{\sqrt{6}} = \dfrac{\sin B}{2}$; $\sin B = \dfrac{2\sin 110°}{\sqrt{6}} \approx 0.7673$. $\text{Sin}^{-1}(0.7673) = \angle B = 50°$. Therefore,

$\angle C = 180° - 110° - 50° = 20°$. [6]

∗ 43. **(D)** $\left|3\vec{v} - \vec{u}\right| = \left|(3, 3\sqrt{3}) - (3, -2)\right| = \left|(0, 3\sqrt{3} + 2)\right| = \sqrt{0^2 + \left(3\sqrt{3} + 2\right)^2} = 3\sqrt{3} + 2 \approx 7.2$. [20]

∗ 44. **(C)** $f(3) = \sqrt{8}$ and $g(\sqrt{8}) = \dfrac{10}{\sqrt{8} + 2} \approx 2.1$. [1]

∗ **45.** **(B)** Law of Cosines:

$12=(2x)^2+(3x+2)^2-2\cdot 2x\cdot(3x+2)\cos 60°.$

$12=4x^2+9x^2+12x+4-(12x^2+8x)\cdot\frac{1}{2}.$

$7x^2+8x-8=0.$

Use the quadratic formula to get $x = \pm 0.64$.

Since a side of a triangle must be positive, x can equal only 0.64. [6]

46. **(D)** $\log_a\sqrt{1.4}=\log_a\left(\frac{7}{5}\right)^{1/2}=\frac{1}{2}(\log_a 7-\log_a 5)=\frac{1}{2}(y-x)$. [8]

∗ **47.** **(D)** Graph $y = 3x^2 + 4x + 5$ in the standard window, and observe that the graph must be moved slightly to the right to be symmetric to the y-axis. Therefore, k must be positive. Use CALC/minimum to find the vertex of the parabola and observe that its x-coordinate is –0.66666. . . . If the function entered into Y_1, set $Y_2 = Y_1\left(x-\frac{2}{3}\right)$ and graph Y_2 to verify this answer. [12]

∗ **48.** **(C)** Use ZTrig to plot the graphs of $y = (\cos x)\cdot(2x + 1)$, $y = \cos(2x + 1)$, and $y = 2(\cos x) + 1$ to see that only the third graph is symmetric about the y-axis and thus represents an even function.

An alternative solution is to use your knowledge of transformations. Although f is an even function, g is not; therefore, (I) $f\cdot g$ is not even. Also, $f(g(x)) = \cos(2x + 1)$, which is a cosine curve shifted less than π to the left. Thus, $f(g(x))$ (II) is not even. However, $g(f(x)) = 2\cos x + 1$ is a cosine curve with period 2π, amplitude 2, shifted 1 unit up. Thus, $g(f(x))$ (III) is even. [1]

∗ **49.** **(B)** The height of the cylinder is 8.

The volume of the sphere $=\frac{4}{3}\pi r^3=\frac{4}{3}\pi(125)=\frac{500\pi}{3}$.

The volume of the cylinder $=\pi r^2h=\pi(9)8$.

The difference $=\frac{500}{3}\pi-72\pi\approx 523.6-226.7$

≈ 297 [15]

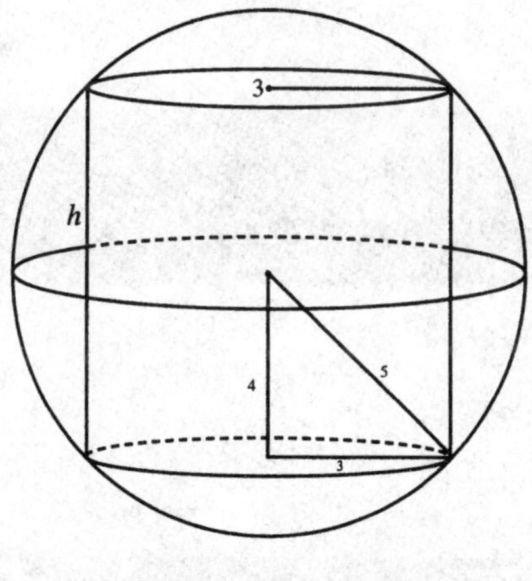

∗ **50.** **(B)** In Choice B, x and y have the same sign, and x is less than y. Therefore, xy is positive, $x - y$ is negative, and the quotient is negative. The numerators and denominators in answer choices A, C, and D both have the same sign, so the quotients are positive. [algebra]

Self-Evaluation Chart for Model Test 1 自评表

Subject Area	Questions and Review Section						Number Right	Number Wrong	Number Omitted
Algebra and Functions	1	3	4	5	8	10			
(24 questions)	2	9	1	8	1	8	____	____	____
	12	13	14	15	18	22			
	8	10	4	—	4	2	____	____	____
	27	29	30	31	35	36			
	—	3	4	8	5	11	____	____	____
	40	41	44	46	48	50			
	4	2	1	8	1	—	____	____	____
Trigonometry	11	16	26	34	37	42			
(7 questions)	6	7	6	7	7	6	____	____	____
	45								
	6						____	____	____
Coordinate and Three-	6	9	17	20	28	33			
Dimensional Geometry	15	15	15	13	13	13	____	____	____
(9 questions)									
	39	47	49						
	12	12	15				____	____	____
Numbers and Operations	21	24	25	32	38	43			
(6 questions)	19	19	16	19	16	20	____	____	____
Data Analysis, Statistics,	2	7	19	23					
and Probability	21	22	22	22			____	____	____
(4 questions)									
TOTALS							____	____	____

Evaluate Your Performance on Model Test 1 自评	
Rating	**Number Right**
Excellent	41–50
Very good	33–40
Above average	25–32
Average	15–24
Below average	Below 15

CALCULATING YOUR SCORE 估分

Raw score R = number right – $\frac{1}{4}$(number wrong), rounded = ______________

Approximate scaled score $S = 800 - 10(44 - R)$ = ______________

If $R \geq 44$, $S = 800$.

ANSWER SHEET
答题卡
Model Test 2
测试题2

1. Ⓐ Ⓑ Ⓒ Ⓓ Ⓔ	14. Ⓐ Ⓑ Ⓒ Ⓓ Ⓔ	27. Ⓐ Ⓑ Ⓒ Ⓓ Ⓔ	40. Ⓐ Ⓑ Ⓒ Ⓓ Ⓔ
2. Ⓐ Ⓑ Ⓒ Ⓓ Ⓔ	15. Ⓐ Ⓑ Ⓒ Ⓓ Ⓔ	28. Ⓐ Ⓑ Ⓒ Ⓓ Ⓔ	41. Ⓐ Ⓑ Ⓒ Ⓓ Ⓔ
3. Ⓐ Ⓑ Ⓒ Ⓓ Ⓔ	16. Ⓐ Ⓑ Ⓒ Ⓓ Ⓔ	29. Ⓐ Ⓑ Ⓒ Ⓓ Ⓔ	42. Ⓐ Ⓑ Ⓒ Ⓓ Ⓔ
4. Ⓐ Ⓑ Ⓒ Ⓓ Ⓔ	17. Ⓐ Ⓑ Ⓒ Ⓓ Ⓔ	30. Ⓐ Ⓑ Ⓒ Ⓓ Ⓔ	43. Ⓐ Ⓑ Ⓒ Ⓓ Ⓔ
5. Ⓐ Ⓑ Ⓒ Ⓓ Ⓔ	18. Ⓐ Ⓑ Ⓒ Ⓓ Ⓔ	31. Ⓐ Ⓑ Ⓒ Ⓓ Ⓔ	44. Ⓐ Ⓑ Ⓒ Ⓓ Ⓔ
6. Ⓐ Ⓑ Ⓒ Ⓓ Ⓔ	19. Ⓐ Ⓑ Ⓒ Ⓓ Ⓔ	32. Ⓐ Ⓑ Ⓒ Ⓓ Ⓔ	45. Ⓐ Ⓑ Ⓒ Ⓓ Ⓔ
7. Ⓐ Ⓑ Ⓒ Ⓓ Ⓔ	20. Ⓐ Ⓑ Ⓒ Ⓓ Ⓔ	33. Ⓐ Ⓑ Ⓒ Ⓓ Ⓔ	46. Ⓐ Ⓑ Ⓒ Ⓓ Ⓔ
8. Ⓐ Ⓑ Ⓒ Ⓓ Ⓔ	21. Ⓐ Ⓑ Ⓒ Ⓓ Ⓔ	34. Ⓐ Ⓑ Ⓒ Ⓓ Ⓔ	47. Ⓐ Ⓑ Ⓒ Ⓓ Ⓔ
9. Ⓐ Ⓑ Ⓒ Ⓓ Ⓔ	22. Ⓐ Ⓑ Ⓒ Ⓓ Ⓔ	35. Ⓐ Ⓑ Ⓒ Ⓓ Ⓔ	48. Ⓐ Ⓑ Ⓒ Ⓓ Ⓔ
10. Ⓐ Ⓑ Ⓒ Ⓓ Ⓔ	23. Ⓐ Ⓑ Ⓒ Ⓓ Ⓔ	36. Ⓐ Ⓑ Ⓒ Ⓓ Ⓔ	49. Ⓐ Ⓑ Ⓒ Ⓓ Ⓔ
11. Ⓐ Ⓑ Ⓒ Ⓓ Ⓔ	24. Ⓐ Ⓑ Ⓒ Ⓓ Ⓔ	37. Ⓐ Ⓑ Ⓒ Ⓓ Ⓔ	50. Ⓐ Ⓑ Ⓒ Ⓓ Ⓔ
12. Ⓐ Ⓑ Ⓒ Ⓓ Ⓔ	25. Ⓐ Ⓑ Ⓒ Ⓓ Ⓔ	38. Ⓐ Ⓑ Ⓒ Ⓓ Ⓔ	
13. Ⓐ Ⓑ Ⓒ Ⓓ Ⓔ	26. Ⓐ Ⓑ Ⓒ Ⓓ Ⓔ	39. Ⓐ Ⓑ Ⓒ Ⓓ Ⓔ	

Model Test 2 测试题2

Tear out the preceding answer sheet. Decide which is the best choice by rounding your answer when appropriate. Blacken the corresponding space on the answer sheet. When finished, check your answers with those at the end of the test. For questions that you got wrong, note the chapters containing the material that you must review. Also, if you do not fully understand how you arrived at some of the correct answers, you should review the appropriate chapters. Finally, fill out the Self-Evaluation Chart on page 252 in order to pinpoint the topics that give you the most difficulty.

50 questions: 1 hour

Directions: Decide which answer choice is best. If the exact numerical value is not one of the answer choices, select the closest approximation. Fill in the circle on the answer sheet that corresponds to your choice.

Notes:

(1) You will need to use a scientific or graphing calculator to answer some of the questions.

(2) You will have to decide whether to put your calculator in degree or radian mode for some problems.

(3) All figures that accompany problems are plane figures unless otherwise stated. Figures are drawn as accurately as possible to provide useful information for solving the problem, except when it is stated in a particular problem that the figure is not drawn to scale.

(4) Unless otherwise indicated, the domain of a function is the set of all real numbers for which the functional value is also a real number.

Reference Information. The following formulas are provided for your information.

Volume of a right circular cone with radius r and height h: $V = \frac{1}{3}\pi r^2 h$

Lateral area of a right circular cone if the base has circumference C and slant height is l: $S = \frac{1}{2}Cl$

Volume of a sphere of radius r: $V = \frac{4}{3}\pi r^3$

Surface area of a sphere of radius r: $S = 4\pi r^2$

Volume of a pyramid of base area B and height h: $V = \frac{1}{3}Bh$

MODEL TEST 2

USE THIS SPACE FOR SCRATCH WORK

1. If $f(x)=\dfrac{x-2}{x^2-4}$, for what value(s) of x does the graph of $f(x)$ have a vertical asymptote?

(A) −2, 0, and 2
(B) −2 and 2
(C) 2
(D) 0
(E) −2

2. What is the distance between the points with coordinates (−3,4,1) and (2,7,−4)?

(A) 5.24
(B) 7.68
(C) 11.45
(D) 13.00
(E) 19.26

3. Log $(a^2 - b^2)$ =

(A) $\log a^2 - \log b^2$

(B) $\log \dfrac{a^2}{b^2}$

(C) $\log \dfrac{a+b}{a-b}$

(D) $2\cdot\log a - 2\cdot\log b$

(E) $\log(a+b)+\log(a-b)$

4. The domain of the function $f(x) = 4 - \sqrt{x^2-9}$ is

(A) $x < -3$
(B) $x > 0$
(C) $x > 3$
(D) $x \le -3$ or $x \ge 3$
(E) all real numbers

5. If the graph of $x + 2y + 3 = 0$ is perpendicular to the graph of $ax + 3y + 2 = 0$, then a equals

(A) −6

(B) $-\dfrac{3}{2}$

(C) $\dfrac{2}{3}$

(D) $\dfrac{3}{2}$

(E) 6

MODEL TEST 2

6. The maximum value of 6 sin x cos x is

(A) $\frac{1}{3}$
(B) 1
(C) 2.6
(D) 3
(E) 6

7. If $f(r,\theta) = r\cos\theta$, then $f(2,3) =$

(A) –3.00
(B) –1.98
(C) 0.10
(D) 1.25
(E) 2.00

8. If 5 and –1 are both zeros of the polynomial $P(x)$, then a factor of $P(x)$ is

(A) $x^2 - 5$
(B) $x^2 - 4x + 5$
(C) $x^2 + 4x - 5$
(D) $x^2 + 5$
(E) $x^2 - 4x - 5$

9. $i^{14} + i^{15} + i^{16} + i^{17} =$

(A) 0
(B) 1
(C) $2i$
(D) $1 - i$
(E) $2 + 2i$

10. The graph of $y = \sin 2x$ for x between 10° and 350° crosses the x-axis

(A) zero times
(B) one time
(C) two times
(D) three times
(E) six times

11. The third term of an arithmetic sequence is 15, and the seventh term is 23. What is the first term?

(A) 1
(B) 6
(C) 9
(D) 11
(E) 13

USE THIS SPACE FOR SCRATCH WORK

12. A particular sphere has the property that its surface area has the same numerical value as its volume. What is the length of the radius of this sphere?

(A) 1
(B) 2
(C) 3
(D) 4
(E) 6

13. $\frac{1}{a}+\frac{1}{b}=$

(A) $\frac{1}{ab}$

(B) $\frac{1}{a+b}$

(C) $\frac{2}{a+b}$

(D) $\frac{a+b}{ab}$

(E) $\frac{ab}{a+b}$

14. The pendulum on a clock swings through an angle of 1 radian, and the tip sweeps out an arc of 12 inches. How long is the pendulum?

(A) 3.8 inches
(B) 6 inches
(C) 7.6 inches
(D) 12 inches
(E) 35 inches

15. What is the domain of the function $f(x) = 4-\sqrt{3x^3-7}$?

(A) $x \geq 1.33$
(B) $x \geq 1.53$
(C) $x \geq 2.33$
(D) $x \leq -1.33$ or $x \geq 1.33$
(E) $x \leq -2.33$ or $x \geq 2.33$

16. If $x + y = 90°$, which of the following must be true?

(A) $\cos x = \cos y$
(B) $\sin x = -\sin y$
(C) $\tan x = \cot y$
(D) $\sin x + \cos y = 1$
(E) $\tan x + \cot y = 1$

USE THIS SPACE FOR SCRATCH WORK

17. The graph of the equation $y = x^3 + 5x + 1$

(A) does not intersect the x-axis
(B) intersects the x-axis at one and only one point
(C) intersects the x-axis at exactly three points
(D) intersects the x-axis at more than three points
(E) intersects the x-axis at exactly two points

18. The length of the radius of the sphere $x^2 + y^2 + z^2 + 2x - 4y = 10$ is

(A) 3.16
(B) 3.38
(C) 3.46
(D) 3.74
(E) 3.87

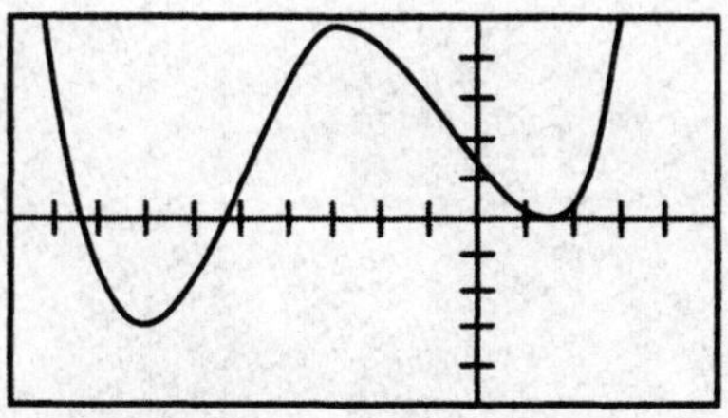

WINDOW
Xmin=⁻10
Xmax=5
Xscl=1
Ymin=⁻250
Ymax=250
Yscl=50
Xres=1
ΔX=.05681818181818
TraceStep=.11363636363636

19. The graph of $y = x^4 + 11x^3 + 9x^2 - 97x + c$ is shown above with the window shown below it. Which of the following values could be c?

(A) –2,820
(B) –80
(C) 80
(D) 250
(E) 2,820

20. Which of the following is the solution set for $x(x - 3)(x + 2) > 0$?

(A) $x < -2$
(B) $-2 < x < 3$
(C) $-2 < x < 3$ or $x > 3$
(D) $x < -2$ or $0 < x < 3$
(E) $-2 < x < 0$ or $x > 3$

USE THIS SPACE FOR SCRATCH WORK

21. Which of the following is the equation of the circle that has its center at the origin and is tangent to the line with equation $3x - 4y = 10$?

(A) $x^2 + y^2 = 2$
(B) $x^2 + y^2 = 3$
(C) $x^2 + y^2 = 4$
(D) $x^2 + y^2 = 5$
(E) $x^2 + y^2 = 10$

22. If $f(x) = 3 - 2x + x^2$, then $\dfrac{f(x+t)-f(x)}{t} =$

(A) $t^2 + 2xt - 2t$
(B) $x^2t^2 - 2xt + 3$
(C) $t + 2x - 2$
(D) $2x - 2$
(E) none of the above

23. If $f(x) = x^3$ and $g(x) = x^2 + 1$, which of the following is an odd function (are odd functions)?

I. $f(x) \bullet g(x)$
II. $f(g(x))$
III. $g(f(x))$

(A) only I
(B) only II
(C) only III
(D) only II and III
(E) I, II, and III

24. In how many ways can a committee of four be selected from nine men so as to always include a particular man?

(A) 48
(B) 56
(C) 70
(D) 84
(E) 126

USE THIS SPACE FOR SCRATCH WORK

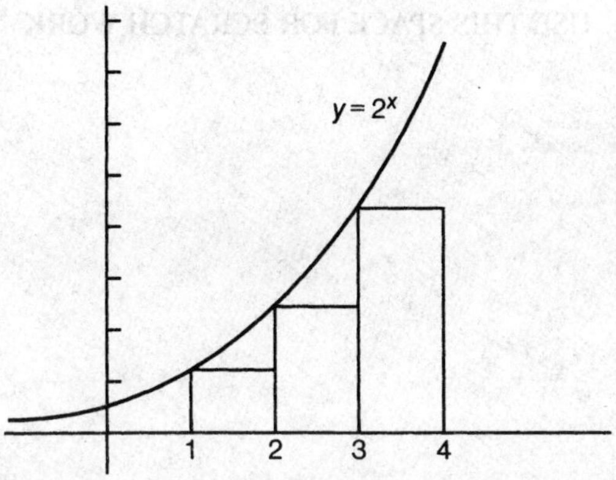

25. The figure above shows a portion of the graph of $y = 2^x$. What is the sum of the areas of the three inscribed rectangles shown?

(A) 14
(B) 28
(C) 128
(D) 256
(E) 384

26. If the mean of the set of data 1, 2, 3, 1, 2, 5, x is $3.\overline{27}$, what is the value of x?

(A) −10.7
(B) 2.5
(C) 5.6
(D) 7.4
(E) 8.9

27. In $\triangle JKL, \sin L = \frac{1}{3}, \sin J = \frac{3}{5}$, and $JK = \sqrt{5}$ inches. The length of KL, in inches, is

(A) 1.7
(B) 3.0
(C) 3.5
(D) 3.9
(E) 4.0

USE THIS SPACE FOR SCRATCH WORK

28. Matrix X has r rows and c columns, and matrix Y has c rows and d columns, where r, c, and d are different. Which of the following statements must be false?

I. The product YX exists.
II. The product of XY exists and has r rows and d columns.
III. The product XY exists and has c rows and c columns.

(A) I only
(B) II only
(C) III only
(D) I and II
(E) I and III

29. Which of the following statements is logically equivalent to: "If he studies, he will pass the course."?

(A) He passed the course; therefore, he studied.
(B) He did not study; therefore, he will not pass the course.
(C) He did not pass the course; therefore he did not study.
(D) He will pass the course only if he studies.
(E) none of the above

30. If $f(x) = x - 7$ and $g(x) = \sqrt{x}$, what is the domain of $g \circ f$?

(A) $x \leq 0$
(B) $x \geq -7$
(C) $x \geq 0$
(D) $x \geq 7$
(E) all real numbers

31. In $\triangle ABC$, $a = 1$, $b = 4$, and $\angle C = 30°$. The length of c is

(A) 4.6
(B) 3.6
(C) 3.2
(D) 2.9
(E) 2.3

32. The solution set of $3x + 4y < 0$ lies in which quadrants?

(A) I only
(B) I and II
(C) I, II, and III
(D) II, III, and IV
(E) I, II, III, and IV

USE THIS SPACE FOR SCRATCH WORK

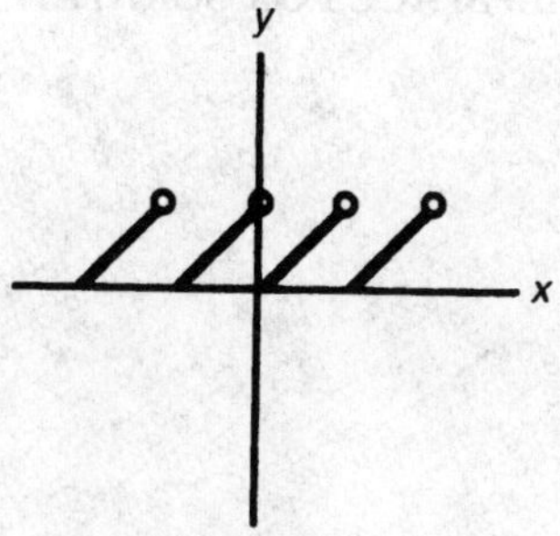

33. Which of the following could represent the inverse of the function graphed above?

(A)

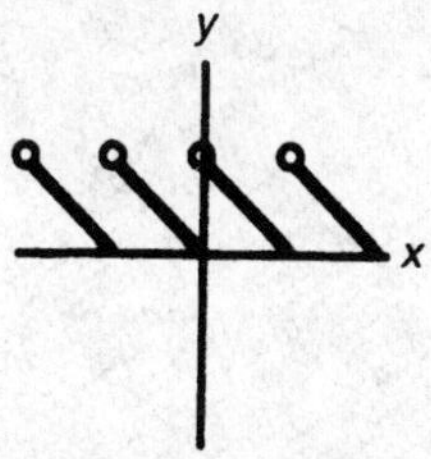

(B)

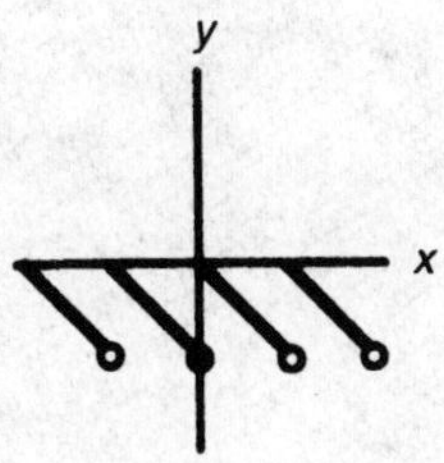

(C)

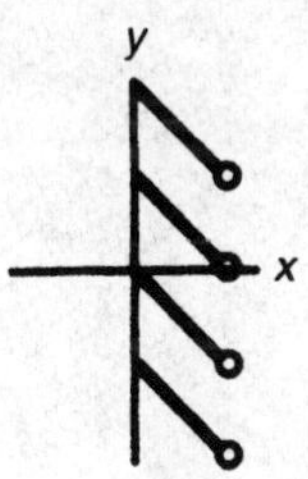

(D)

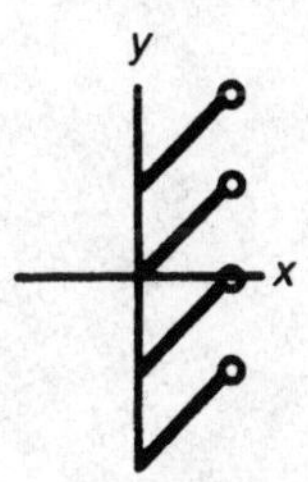

(E)

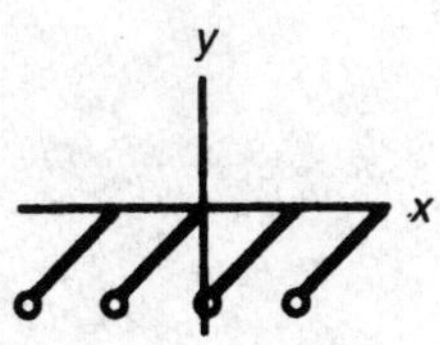

34. If f is a linear function and $f(-2) = 11$, $f(5) = -2$, and $f(x) = 4.3$, what is the value of x?

(A) −3.1
(B) −1.9
(C) 1.6
(D) 2.9
(E) 3.2

35. A taxicab company wanted to determine the fuel cost of its fleet. A sample of 30 vehicles was selected, and the fuel cost for the last month was tabulated for each vehicle. Later it was discovered that the highest amount was mistakenly recorded with an extra zero, so it was 10 times the actual amount. When the correction was made, this was still the highest amount. Which of the following must have remained the same after the correction was made?

(A) mean
(B) median
(C) mode
(D) range
(E) standard deviation

36. The range of the function $y = x^{-2/3}$ is

(A) $y < 0$
(B) $y > 0$
(C) $y \geq 0$
(D) $y \leq 0$
(E) all real numbers

37. The formula $A = Pe^{0.04t}$ gives the amount A that a savings account will be worth if an initial investment P is compounded continuously at an annual rate of 4 percent for t years. Under these conditions, how many years will it take an initial investment of \$10,000 to be worth approximately \$25,000?

(A) 1.9
(B) 2.5
(C) 9.9
(D) 22.9
(E) 25.2

USE THIS SPACE FOR SCRATCH WORK

38. A coin is tossed three times. Given that at least one head appears, what is the probability that exactly two heads will appear?

(A) $\frac{3}{8}$

(B) $\frac{3}{7}$

(C) $\frac{5}{8}$

(D) $\frac{3}{4}$

(E) $\frac{7}{8}$

39. A unit vector parallel to vector $\vec{V} = (2,-3,6)$ is vector

(A) (−2, 3, −6)
(B) (6, −3, 2)
(C) (−0.29, 0.43, −0.86)
(D) (0.29, 0.43, −0.86)
(E) (−0.36, −0.54, 1.08)

40. What is the equation of the horizontal asymptote of the function $f(x) = \dfrac{(2x-1)(x+3)}{(x+3)^2}$?

(A) $y = -9$
(B) $y = -3$
(C) $y = 0$
(D) $y = \frac{1}{2}$
(E) $y = 2$

41. The points in the rectangular coordinate plane are transformed in such a way that each point $A(x,y)$ is moved to a point $A'(kx,ky)$. If the distance between a point A and the origin is d, then the distance between the origin and the point A' is

(A) $\frac{k}{d}$

(B) $\frac{d}{k}$

(C) d
(D) kd
(E) d^2

USE THIS SPACE FOR SCRATCH WORK

42. A committee of 5 people is to be selected from 6 men and 9 women. If the selection is made randomly, what is the probability that the committee consists of 3 men and 2 women?

(A) $\frac{1}{9}$

(B) $\frac{240}{1,001}$

(C) $\frac{1}{3}$

(D) $\frac{1,260}{3,003}$

(E) $\frac{13}{18}$

43. Three consecutive terms, in order, of an arithmetic sequence are $x+\sqrt{2}, 2x+\sqrt{3}$, and $5x-\sqrt{5}$. Then x equals

(A) 2.14
(B) 2.45
(C) 2.46
(D) 3.24
(E) 3.56

44. The graph of $xy - 4x - 2y - 4 = 0$ can be expressed as a set of parametric equations. If $y=\frac{4t}{t-3}$ and $x = f(t)$, then $f(t) =$

(A) $t+1$

(B) $t-1$

(C) $3t-3$

(D) $\frac{t-3}{4t}$

(E) $\frac{t-3}{2}$

45. If $f(x) = ax^2 + bx + c$, how must a and b be related so that the graph of $f(x-3)$ will be symmetric about the y-axis?

(A) $a=b$
(B) $b=0$, a is any real number
(C) $b=3a$
(D) $b=6a$
(E) $a=\frac{1}{9}b$

USE THIS SPACE FOR SCRATCH WORK

46. The graph of $y = \log_5 x$ and $y = \ln 0.5x$ intersect at a point where x equals

(A) 6.24
(B) 5.44
(C) 1.69
(D) 1.14
(E) 1.05

USE THIS SPACE FOR SCRATCH WORK

47. What is the value of x if $\pi \le x \le \frac{3\pi}{2}$ and $\sin x = 5 \cos x$?

(A) 3.399
(B) 3.625
(C) 4.515
(D) 4.623
(E) 4.663

48. The area of the region enclosed by the graph of the polar curve $r = \frac{1}{\sin\theta + \cos\theta}$ and the x- and y-axes is

(A) 0.48
(B) 0.50
(C) 0.52
(D) 0.98
(E) 1.00

49. A rectangular box has dimensions of length = 6, width = 4, and height = 5. The measure of the angle formed by a diagonal of the box with the base of the box is

(A) 27°
(B) 35°
(C) 40°
(D) 44°
(E) 55°

50. If (x,y) represents a point on the graph of $y = 2x + 1$, which of the following could be a portion of the graph of the set of points (x,y^2)?

(A)

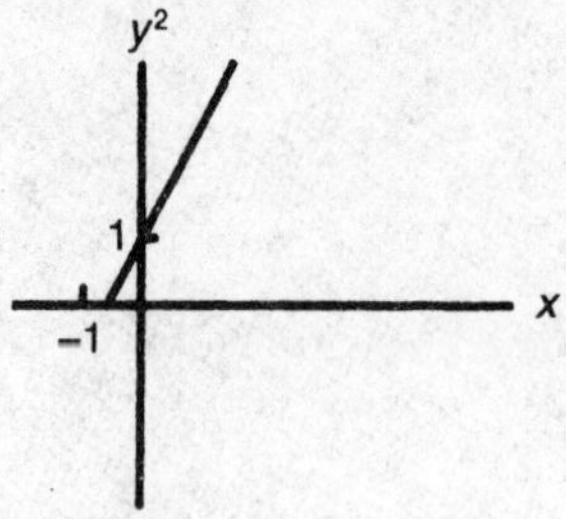

(B)

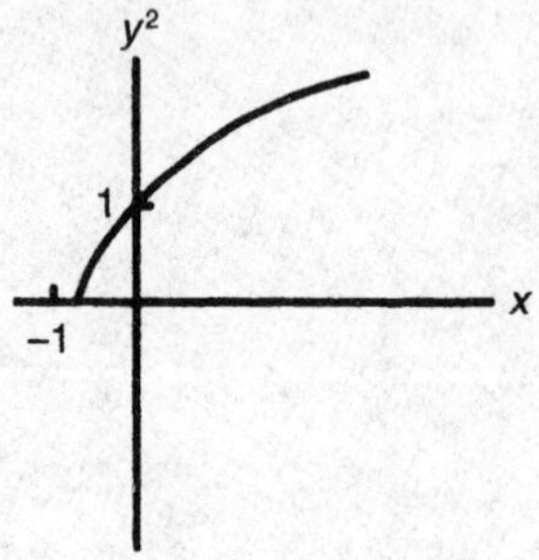

(C)

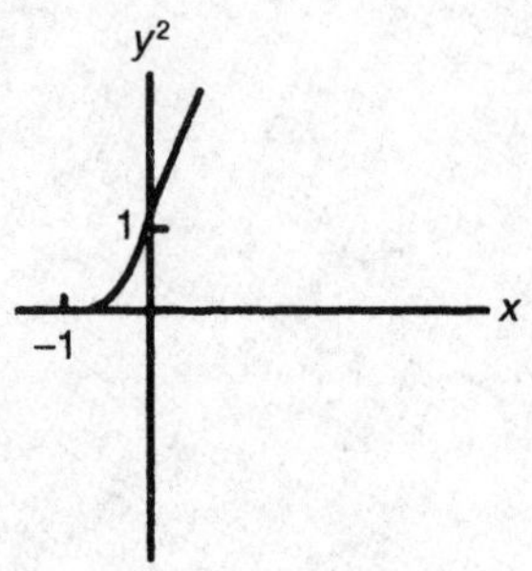

(D)

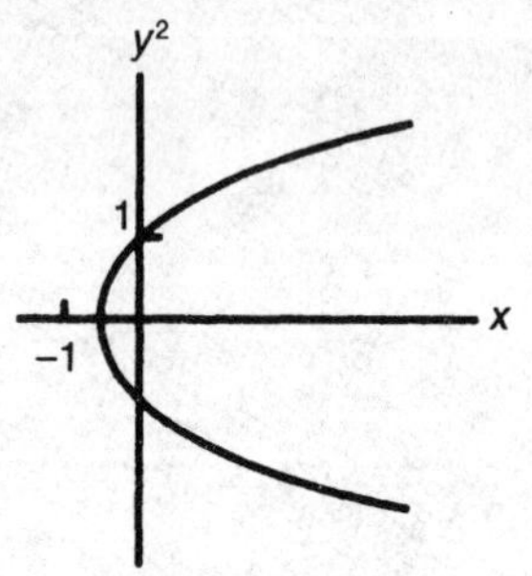

(E)

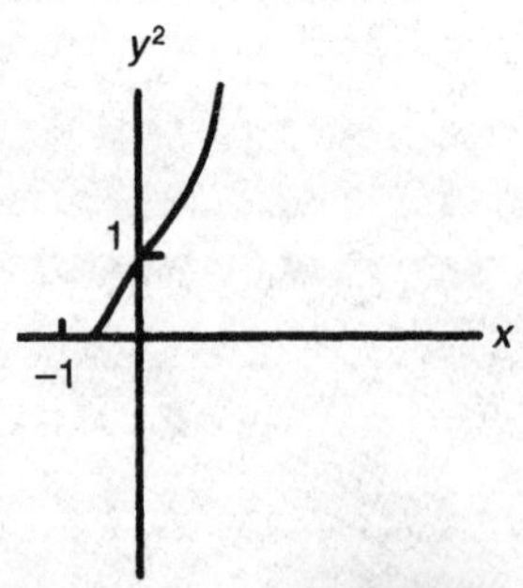

USE THIS SPACE FOR SCRATCH WORK

STOP

If there is still time remaining, you may review your answers.

ANSWER KEY
答案
Model Test 2
测试题2

1. **E**	14. **D**	27. **E**	40. **E**
2. **B**	15. **A**	28. **B**	41. **D**
3. **E**	16. **C**	29. **C**	42. **B**
4. **D**	17. **B**	30. **D**	43. **A**
5. **A**	18. **E**	31. **C**	44. **B**
6. **D**	19. **C**	32. **D**	45. **D**
7. **B**	20. **E**	33. **D**	46. **A**
8. **E**	21. **C**	34. **C**	47. **C**
9. **A**	22. **C**	35. **B**	48. **B**
10. **D**	23. **A**	36. **B**	49. **B**
11. **D**	24. **B**	37. **D**	50. **C**
12. **C**	25. **A**	38. **B**	
13. **D**	26. **E**	39. **C**	

ANSWERS EXPLAINED 答案解析

The following explanations are keyed to the review portions of this book. The number in brackets after each explanation indicates the appropriate chapter in the Review of Major Topics (Part 2). If a problem can be solved using algebraic techniques alone, [algebra] appears after the explanation, and no reference is given for that problem in the Self-Evaluation Chart at the end of the test.

An asterisk appears next to those solutions in which a graphing calculator is necessary or helpful.

* **1.** **(E)** Graph the function f in the standard window and observe the vertical asymptote at $x = -2$.

An alternative solution is to factor the denominator of f as $(x + 2)(x - 2)$; cancel the factor $x - 2$ in the numerator and denominator so that $f(x) = \frac{1}{x+2}$; and recall that a function has a vertical asymptote when the denominator is zero and the numerator isn't. There is a hole in the graph of f at $x = 2$. [9]

* **2.** **(B)** Use the distance formula for three-dimensional space:
$d = \sqrt{(x_2 - x_1)^2 + (y_2 - y_1)^2 + (z_2 - z_1)^2} = \sqrt{(2+3)^2 + (7-4)^2 + (-4-1)^2} \approx 7.68$ [15]

3. **(E)** $\text{Log}(a^2 - b^2) = \log(a + b)(a - b) = \log(a + b) + \log(a - b)$. [8]

4. **(D)** In order that $\sqrt{x^2 - 9}$ be a real number, $x^2 - 9 \geq 0$. Solve this inequality to find that $x \leq -3$ or $x \geq 3$. [1]

5. **(A)** The slope of the first line is $-\frac{1}{2}$, and the slope of the second is $-\frac{a}{3}$. To be perpendicular, $-\frac{1}{2} = \frac{3}{a}$, or $a = -6$. [2]

* **6.** **(D)** Plot the graph of $6 \sin x \cos x$ using ZTrig and observe that the max of this function is 3. (None of the other answer choices are close. If one were, you could use CALC/max to find the maximum value of the function.)

An alternative solution is to recall that $\sin(2x) = 2 \sin x \cos x$, so that $6 \sin x \cos x = 3 \sin 2x$. Since the amplitude of $\sin 2x$ is 1, the amplitude of $3 \sin 2x$ is 3. [7]

* **7.** **(B)** Put your calculator in radian mode. $f(2,3) = 2 \cdot \cos 3 \approx 2(-0.98999) \approx -1.98$. [14]

8. **(E)** Since 5 and -1 are zeros, $x - 5$ and $x + 1$ are factors of $P(x)$, so their product $x^2 - 4x - 5$ is too. [3]

* **9.** **(A)** Enter the expression into your graphing calculator. [17]

* **10.** **(D)** Set the calculator to degree mode and plot the graph of $y = \sin 2x$ in a $[10°, 350°]$ by $[-2,2]$ window. Observe that the graph crosses the axis 3 times.

An alternative explanation uses the fact that the function $\sin 2x$ has period $\frac{2\pi}{2} = \pi$ and the fact that $\sin 2x = 0$ when $2x = 0°, 180°, 360°, 540°, 720°, \ldots$, or when $x = 0°, 90°, 180°, 270°, 360°, \ldots$ Three values of x lie between 10° and 350°. [7]

MODEL TEST 2

11. **(D)** The third and seventh terms are 4 terms apart, and the difference between them is 8. Therefore, the common difference is $8 \div 4 = 2$. Since the first term is two terms prior to the third term, its value is $15 - 2(2) = 11$. [19]

12. **(C)** Surface area = $4\pi r^2$. Volume = $\frac{4}{3}\pi r^3$. Solve $4\pi r^2 = \frac{4}{3}\pi r^3$ to get $r = 3$. [15]

13. **(D)** To add, form the common denominator ab: $\frac{1}{a}+\frac{1}{b}=\frac{b}{ab}+\frac{a}{ab}=\frac{a+b}{ab}$. [algebra]

14. **(D)** $s = r\theta$. $12 = r$. [7]

∗ 15. **(A)** The domain consists of all numbers that make $3x^3 - 7 \geq 0$. Therefore, $x^3 \geq \frac{7}{3}$ and $x \geq 1.33$. [1]

16. **(C)** Cofunctions of complementary angles are equal. Since x and y are complementary, tan and cot are cofunctions.

An alternative solution is to choose any values of x and y such that their sum is 90°. (For example, $x = 40°$ and $y = 50°$.) Test the answer choices with your calculator in degree mode to see that only Choice C is true. [7]

∗ 17. **(B)** Plot the graph of $y = x^3 + 5x + 1$ in the standard window and zoom in a couple of times to see that it crosses the x-axis only once. To make sure you are not missing anything, you should also plot the equation in a $[-1, 1]$ by $[-1, 1]$ window and a $[-100, 100]$, by $[-100, 100]$ window.

An alternative solution is to use Descartes' Rule of Signs, which indicates that the graph does not intersect the positive x-axis, but it does intersect the negative x-axis once. [4]

∗ 18. **(E)** Complete the square in x and y: $(x^2 + 2x + 1) + (y^2 - 4y + 4) + z^2 = 10 + 1 + 4$, so $(x + 1)^2 + (y - 2)^2 + z^2 = 15$. Therefore, $r = \sqrt{15} \approx 3.87$. [15]

19. **(C)** If you substitute 0 for x you get c, so c is the y-intercept of the graph. The graph and window indicate that this value is about 80. [4]

∗ 20. **(E)** Plot the graph of $y = x(x - 3)(x + 2)$ in the standard window, and observe that the graph is above the x-axis when $-2 < x < 0$ or when $x > 3$.

An alternative solution is to find the zeros of the function $x(x - 3)(x + 2)$ as $x = 0,3,-2$ and test points in the intervals established by these zeros. Points between -2 and 0 and greater than 3 satisfy the inequality. [5]

∗ 21. **(C)** Use the formula on page 347 to calculate the distance between the point (0, 0) and the line $3x - 4y = 10$ as 2. Therefore, the radius of the circle is 2, and its equation is $x^2 + y^2 = 4$. [13]

MODEL TEST 2

22. **(C)**

$$\frac{f(x+t)-f(x)}{t}=\frac{3-2(x+t)+(x+t)^2-(3-2x+x^2)}{t}$$

$$=\frac{3-2x-2t+x^2+2xt+t^2-3+2x-x^2}{t}$$

$$=2x-2+t.\ [1]$$

CAUTION: For calculus students only: This difference quotient looks like the definition of the derivative. However, no limit is taken, so don't jump at $f'(x)$, which is Choice D.

* 23. **(A)** Enter x^3 into Y_1 and x^2+1 into Y_2. Then enter Y_1Y_2 into Y_3; $Y_1(Y_2)$ into Y_4; and $Y_2(Y_1)$ into Y_5. De-select Y_1 and Y_2. Inspection of Y_3, Y_4, and Y_5 shows that only Y_3 is symmetric about the origin.

An alternative solution is to define each of the three functions as $h(x)$ and check each against the definition of an odd function, $h(-x)=-h(x)$:

$$h(-x)=(-x)^3((-x)^2+1)=-x^5-x^3=-(x^5+x^3)$$
$$=-h(x)$$
$$h(-x)=f((-x)^2+1)=(x^2+1)^3\neq -h(x)$$
$$h(-x)=g((-x)^3)=((-x)^3)^2+1=x^6+1\neq -h(x)$$

[1]

* 24. **(B)** Since one particular man must be on the committee, the problem becomes: "Form a committee of 3 from 8 men." Calculate $8{}_nC_r3=56$. [16]

25. **(A)** Each rectangle has width 1. The heights of these rectangles are $2^1=2$, $2^2=4$, and $2^3=8$. The sum of these areas is 14. [8]

* 26. **(E)** Mean $=\frac{1+2+3+1+2+5+x}{7}=\frac{14+x}{7}=3.\overline{27}$. Therefore, $x=8.9$. [21]

* 27. **(E)** Law of sines: $\frac{\frac{1}{3}}{\sqrt{5}}=\frac{\frac{3}{5}}{KL};\ \frac{1}{3}KL=\frac{3\sqrt{5}}{5}$.

Therefore, $KL=\frac{9\sqrt{5}}{5}\approx 4.0$. [6]

28. **(B)** Multiplication of matrices is possible only when the number of columns in the matrix on the left equals the number of rows in the matrix on the right. In that case, the product is a matrix with the number of rows in the left-hand matrix and the number of columns of the right-hand matrix. [18]

29. **(C)** Relative to the statement, Choice A is the converse, Choice B is the inverse, Choice C is the contrapositive, and Choice D is another form of the inverse. Of these, the contrapositive is the logical equivalent of the original statement. [logic]

30. **(D)** $(g \circ f)(x) = g(f(x)) = \sqrt{x-7}$. Therefore, $x \geq 7$. [1]

* 31. **(C)** Law of cosines: $c^2 = 16 + 1 - 8 \cdot \frac{\sqrt{3}}{2} = 17 - 4\sqrt{3} \approx 10.07$. Therefore, $c \approx 3.2$. [6]

* 32. **(D)** Use the standard window to graph $y < -\frac{3}{4}x$, by moving the cursor all the way left (past Y =) and keying Enter until a "lower triangle" is observed. The shaded portion of the graph will lie in all but Quadrant I.

An alternative solution is to graph the related equation $y = -\frac{3}{4}x$ and test points to determine which side of the line contains solutions to the inequality. This will indicate the quadrant that the graph does not enter. [2]

33. **(D)** Fold the graph about the line $y = x$, and the resulting graph will be Choice D. [1]

* 34. **(C)** Since these points are on a line, all slopes must be equal.

Slope $= \frac{-2-11}{5-(-2)} = \frac{-13}{7} = \frac{4.3-11}{x-(-2)}$. Cross-multiplying the far right equation gives $-13(x + 2) = 7(-6.7)$, and solving for x yields $x \approx 1.6$. [2]

35. **(B)** Since the median is the middle value, it does not change if the number (quantity) of values above and below it remain the same. [21]

* 36. **(B)** Plot the graph of $y = x^{-2/3}$ in the standard window and observe that the entire graph lies above the x-axis.

An alternative solution uses the fact that $x^{-2/3} = \frac{1}{x^{2/3}}$, and $x^{2/3} = (x^{1/3})^2$, so that for all values of x (except zero) y is positive. Therefore, the range of $y = x^{-2/3}$ is $y > 0$. [8]

* 37. **(D)** Substitute the given values into the formula to get $25{,}000 = 10{,}000e^{0.04t}$. To solve for t, first divide both sides by 10,000. Then take the ln of both sides to get

$\ln 2.5 = 0.04t$. Therefore $t = \frac{\ln 2.5}{0.04} = 22.9$. [8]

38. **(B)** There are 8 elements in the sample space of a coin being flipped 3 times. Of these elements, 7 contain at least 1 head and 3 (HHT, HTH, THH) contain 2 heads.

Probability $= \frac{3}{7}$. [22]

* 39. **(C)** To find a unit vector parallel to (2,–3,6), divide each component by $\sqrt{2^2 + (-3)^2 + 6^2} = \pm 7$. There are two unit vectors, pointing in opposite directions, that meet this requirement: (0.29, –0.43, 0.86) and (–0.29, 0.43, –0.86). Only the second one is an answer choice. [20]

MODEL TEST 2

40. **(E)** To find the horizontal asymptote, you need to see what happens when x gets much larger ($\to\infty$) or much smaller ($\to-\infty$). With the numerator and denominator expanded, $f(x)=\dfrac{2x^2+5x-3}{x^2+6x+9}$. Divide both by x^2 to see that y approaches 2 as x gets much bigger or smaller. [9]

41. **(D)** The distance between the origin and A is $d=\sqrt{x^2+y^2}$. The distance between the origin and A' is $\sqrt{(kx)^2+(ky)^2}=\sqrt{k^2\left(x^2+y^2\right)}=k\sqrt{x^2+y^2}=kd$. [12]

* 42. **(B)** There are $\binom{15}{5}$ ways of selecting a committee of 5 out of 15 people (men and women). There are $\binom{6}{3}$ ways of selecting 3 men of 6, and for each of these, there are $\binom{9}{2}$ ways of selecting 2 women of 9. Therefore, there are $\binom{6}{3}\binom{9}{2}$ ways of selecting 3 men and 2 women. The probability of selecting 3 men and 2 women is $\dfrac{\binom{6}{3}\binom{9}{2}}{\binom{15}{5}}=\dfrac{240}{1{,}001}$. Using the calculator command ${}_{n}C_{r}=\binom{n}{r}$, enter this expression and change to a fraction. [22]

* 43. **(A)** $2x+\sqrt{3}=(x+\sqrt{2})+d$, and $5x-\sqrt{5}=(2x+\sqrt{3})+d$. Eliminate d, and $x+\sqrt{3}-\sqrt{2}=3x-\sqrt{5}-\sqrt{3}$. Thus, $x=\dfrac{2\sqrt{3}-\sqrt{2}+\sqrt{5}}{2}\approx 2.14$. [19]

44. **(B)** Substituting for y gives $x\left(\dfrac{4t}{t-3}\right)-4x-2\left(\dfrac{4t}{t-3}\right)-4=0$, which simplifies to $12x-12t+12=0$. Then $x=t-1$. [10]

45. **(D)** The graph of the function is a parabola, and the equation of its axis of symmetry is $x=-\dfrac{b}{2a}$. Since the graph of $y=f(x-3)$ is the translation of $y=f(x)$ 3 units to the right, $f(x-3)$ will be symmetric about the y-axis when $f(x)$ is symmetric about -3. Therefore, $-\dfrac{b}{2a}=-3$, or $b=6a$. [3]

∗ 46. **(A)** Use the change of base formula and graph $y=\frac{\log x}{\log 5}$ as Y_1. Graph $y = \ln(0.5x)$ as Y_2. The answer choices suggest a [0,10] by [0,2] window. Use the CALC/intersect to find the correct answer, Choice A.

An alternative solution converts the equations to exponential form: $x = 5^y$ and $\frac{1}{2}x = e^y$, or $5^y = 2e^y$. Taking the natural log of both sides gives $y\ln 5 = \ln 2 + y$, and solving for y yields $y=\frac{\ln 2}{\ln 5-1}\approx 1.14$. Finally substituting back to find x, $5^{1.14} \approx 6.24$. [8]

∗ 47. **(C)** With your calculator in radian mode, plot the graphs of $Y_1 = \sin x$ and $Y_2 = 5\cos x$ in a $\left[\pi, \frac{3\pi}{2}\right]$ by [–5,5] window. The solution is the x-coordinate of the point of intersection.
An alternative solution is to divide both sides of the equation by $\cos x$ to get $\tan x = 5$. Use your calculator to get $\tan^{-1} 5 = 1.373$. This is the first-quadrant solution, so add π. [7]

∗ 48. **(B)** With your calculator in polar mode, graph $r=\frac{1}{\sin\theta+\cos\theta}$ in a [–3,3] by [–3,3] window. Let θ run from 0 to 2π in increments of 0.1. The graph of the function and the two axes form an isosceles right triangle of side length 1, so its area is 0.5.

An alternative solution is to multiply both sides of the equation by $\sin\theta + \cos\theta$ to get $r\sin\theta + r\cos\theta = 1$. Since $x = r\cos\theta$ and $y = r\sin\theta$, the rectangular form of the equation is $x + y = 1$. This line makes an isosceles right triangle of unit leg lengths with the axes, the area of which is $\frac{1}{2}(1)(1) = 0.5$. [14]

∗ 49. **(B)** The diagonal of the base is $\sqrt{6^2+4^2} = \sqrt{52}$. The diagonal of the box is the hypotenuse of a right triangle with one leg $\sqrt{52}$ and the other leg 5. Let θ be the angle formed by the diagonal of the base and the diagonal of the box. Tan $\theta = \frac{5}{\sqrt{52}} \approx$ 0.69337, and so $\theta = \tan^{-1} 0.69337 \approx 35°$. [6]

∗ 50. **(C)** Plot $y = (2x + 1)^2$ in a window with a [–2,2] by [–1,5] window, and observe that Choice C is the only possible choice.

An alternative solution is to note that the graph of $y=(2x+1)^2=4\left(x+\frac{1}{2}\right)^2$ is a parabola with vertex at $\left(-\frac{1}{2},0\right)$ that opens up. The only answer choice with these properties is Choice C. [2]

Self-Evaluation Chart for Model Test 2 自评表

Subject Area	Questions and Review Section							Number Right	Number Wrong	Number Omitted
Algebra and Functions	1	3	4	5	8	13				
(25 questions)	9	8	1	2	3	—		____	____	____
	15	17	19	20	22	23				
	1	4	4	5	1	1		____	____	____
	25	29	30	32	33	34	36			
	8	—	1	2	1	2	8	____	____	____
	37	40	44	45	46	50				
	8	9	10	3	8	2		____	____	____
Trigonometry	6	10	14	16	27	31				
(8 questions)	7	7	7	7	6	6		____	____	____
	47	49								
	7	6						____	____	____
Coordinate and Three-	2	7	12	18	21	41	48			
Dimensional Geometry	15	14	15	15	13	12	14	____	____	____
(7 questions)										
Numbers and Operations	9	11	24	28	39					
(6 questions)	17	19	16	18	20			____	____	____
	43									
	19							____	____	____
Data Analysis, Statistics,	26	35	38	42						
and Probability	21	21	22	22				____	____	____
(4 questions)										
TOTALS								____	____	____

Evaluate Your Performance on Model Test 2 自评	
Rating	**Number Right**
Excellent	41–50
Very good	33–40
Above average	25–32
Average	15–24
Below average	Below 15

CALCULATING YOUR SCORE 估分

Raw score R = number right $-\frac{1}{4}$(number wrong), rounded = ______________

Approximate scaled score $S = 800 - 10(44 - R)$ = ______________

If $R \geq 44$, $S = 800$.

MODEL TEST 2

ANSWER SHEET

答题卡

Model Test 3

测试题3

1. Ⓐ Ⓑ Ⓒ Ⓓ Ⓔ	14. Ⓐ Ⓑ Ⓒ Ⓓ Ⓔ	27. Ⓐ Ⓑ Ⓒ Ⓓ Ⓔ	40. Ⓐ Ⓑ Ⓒ Ⓓ Ⓔ
2. Ⓐ Ⓑ Ⓒ Ⓓ Ⓔ	15. Ⓐ Ⓑ Ⓒ Ⓓ Ⓔ	28. Ⓐ Ⓑ Ⓒ Ⓓ Ⓔ	41. Ⓐ Ⓑ Ⓒ Ⓓ Ⓔ
3. Ⓐ Ⓑ Ⓒ Ⓓ Ⓔ	16. Ⓐ Ⓑ Ⓒ Ⓓ Ⓔ	29. Ⓐ Ⓑ Ⓒ Ⓓ Ⓔ	42. Ⓐ Ⓑ Ⓒ Ⓓ Ⓔ
4. Ⓐ Ⓑ Ⓒ Ⓓ Ⓔ	17. Ⓐ Ⓑ Ⓒ Ⓓ Ⓔ	30. Ⓐ Ⓑ Ⓒ Ⓓ Ⓔ	43. Ⓐ Ⓑ Ⓒ Ⓓ Ⓔ
5. Ⓐ Ⓑ Ⓒ Ⓓ Ⓔ	18. Ⓐ Ⓑ Ⓒ Ⓓ Ⓔ	31. Ⓐ Ⓑ Ⓒ Ⓓ Ⓔ	44. Ⓐ Ⓑ Ⓒ Ⓓ Ⓔ
6. Ⓐ Ⓑ Ⓒ Ⓓ Ⓔ	19. Ⓐ Ⓑ Ⓒ Ⓓ Ⓔ	32. Ⓐ Ⓑ Ⓒ Ⓓ Ⓔ	45. Ⓐ Ⓑ Ⓒ Ⓓ Ⓔ
7. Ⓐ Ⓑ Ⓒ Ⓓ Ⓔ	20. Ⓐ Ⓑ Ⓒ Ⓓ Ⓔ	33. Ⓐ Ⓑ Ⓒ Ⓓ Ⓔ	46. Ⓐ Ⓑ Ⓒ Ⓓ Ⓔ
8. Ⓐ Ⓑ Ⓒ Ⓓ Ⓔ	21. Ⓐ Ⓑ Ⓒ Ⓓ Ⓔ	34. Ⓐ Ⓑ Ⓒ Ⓓ Ⓔ	47. Ⓐ Ⓑ Ⓒ Ⓓ Ⓔ
9. Ⓐ Ⓑ Ⓒ Ⓓ Ⓔ	22. Ⓐ Ⓑ Ⓒ Ⓓ Ⓔ	35. Ⓐ Ⓑ Ⓒ Ⓓ Ⓔ	48. Ⓐ Ⓑ Ⓒ Ⓓ Ⓔ
10. Ⓐ Ⓑ Ⓒ Ⓓ Ⓔ	23. Ⓐ Ⓑ Ⓒ Ⓓ Ⓔ	36. Ⓐ Ⓑ Ⓒ Ⓓ Ⓔ	49. Ⓐ Ⓑ Ⓒ Ⓓ Ⓔ
11. Ⓐ Ⓑ Ⓒ Ⓓ Ⓔ	24. Ⓐ Ⓑ Ⓒ Ⓓ Ⓔ	37. Ⓐ Ⓑ Ⓒ Ⓓ Ⓔ	50. Ⓐ Ⓑ Ⓒ Ⓓ Ⓔ
12. Ⓐ Ⓑ Ⓒ Ⓓ Ⓔ	25. Ⓐ Ⓑ Ⓒ Ⓓ Ⓔ	38. Ⓐ Ⓑ Ⓒ Ⓓ Ⓔ	
13. Ⓐ Ⓑ Ⓒ Ⓓ Ⓔ	26. Ⓐ Ⓑ Ⓒ Ⓓ Ⓔ	39. Ⓐ Ⓑ Ⓒ Ⓓ Ⓔ	

Model Test 3 测试题3

Tear out the preceding answer sheet. Decide which is the best choice by rounding your answer when appropriate. Blacken the corresponding space on the answer sheet. When finished, check your answers with those at the end of the test. For questions that you got wrong, note the chapters containing the material that you must review. Also, if you do not fully understand how you arrived at some of the correct answers, you should review the appropriate chapters. Finally, fill out the Self-Evaluation Chart on page 277 in order to pinpoint the topics that give you the most difficulty.

50 questions: 1 hour

Directions: Decide which answer choice is best. If the exact numerical value is not one of the answer choices, select the closest approximation. Fill in the circle on the answer sheet that corresponds to your choice.

Notes:
(1) You will need to use a scientific or graphing calculator to answer some of the questions.
(2) You will have to decide whether to put your calculator in degree or radian mode for some problems.
(3) All figures that accompany problems are plane figures unless otherwise stated. Figures are drawn as accurately as possible to provide useful information for solving the problem, except when it is stated in a particular problem that the figure is not drawn to scale.
(4) Unless otherwise indicated, the domain of a function is the set of all real numbers for which the functional value is also a real number.

Reference Information. The following formulas are provided for your information.

Volume of a right circular cone with radius r and height h: $V = \frac{1}{3}\pi r^2 h$

Lateral area of a right circular cone if the base has circumference C and slant height is l: $S = \frac{1}{2}Cl$

Volume of a sphere of radius r: $V = \frac{4}{3}\pi r^3$

Surface area of a sphere of radius r: $S = 4\pi r^2$

Volume of a pyramid of base area B and height h: $V = \frac{1}{3}Bh$

USE THIS SPACE FOR SCRATCH WORK

1. The slope of a line that is perpendicular to $3x + 2y = 7$ is

(A) -2

(B) $-\frac{3}{2}$

(C) $\frac{2}{3}$

(D) $\frac{3}{2}$

(E) 2

2. What is the remainder when $3x^4 - 2x^3 - 20x^2 - 12$ is divided by $x + 2$?

(A) -60
(B) -36
(C) -28
(D) -6
(E) -4

3. If $1-\frac{1}{x}=2-\frac{2}{x}$, then $3-\frac{3}{x}=$

(A) -3

(B) $-\frac{1}{3}$

(C) 0

(D) $\frac{1}{3}$

(E) 3

4. If $f(x) = 2 \ln x + 3$ and $g(x) = e^x$, then $f(g(3)) =$

(A) 9
(B) 11
(C) 43.17
(D) 47.13
(E) 180.77

5. The domain of $f(x) = \log_{10} (\sin x)$ contains which of the following intervals?

(A) $0 \le x \le \pi$

(B) $-\frac{\pi}{2} \le x \le \frac{\pi}{2}$

(C) $0 < x < \pi$

(D) $-\frac{\pi}{2} < x < \frac{\pi}{2}$

(E) $\frac{\pi}{2} < x < \frac{3\pi}{2}$

6. Which of the following is the ratio of the surface area of the sphere with radius r to its volume?

(A) $\frac{4}{r}$
(B) $\frac{3}{r}$
(C) $\frac{r}{4}$
(D) $\frac{r}{\pi}$
(E) $\frac{4}{\pi}$

7. If the two solutions of $x^2 - 9x + c = 0$ are complex conjugates, which of the following describes all possible values of c?

(A) $c = 0$
(B) $c \neq 0$
(C) $c < 9$
(D) $c > \frac{81}{4}$
(E) $c > 81$

8. If $\tan x = 3$, the numerical value of $\sqrt{\csc x}$ is

(A) 0.32
(B) 0.97
(C) 1.03
(D) 1.78
(E) 3.16

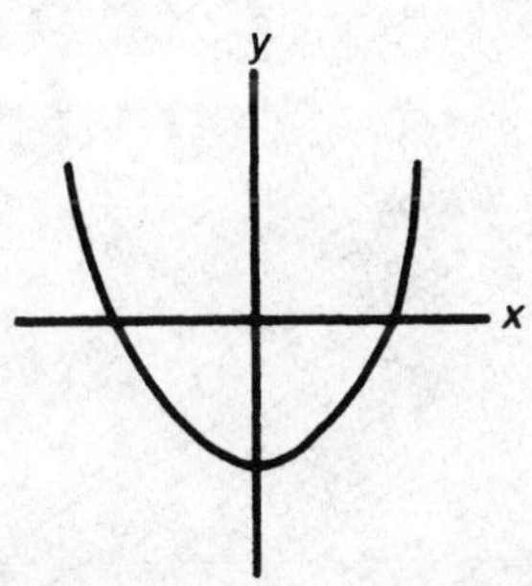

9. In the figure above, the graph of $y = f(x)$ has two transformations performed on it. First it is rotated 180° about the origin, and then it is reflected about the x-axis. Which of the following is the equation of the resulting curve?

(A) $y = -f(x)$
(B) $y = f(x + 2)$
(C) $x = f(y)$
(D) $y = f(x)$
(E) none of the above

USE THIS SPACE FOR SCRATCH WORK

MODEL TEST 3

USE THIS SPACE FOR SCRATCH WORK

10. If $f(x) = \dfrac{3x^3 - 7x^2 + 2}{4x^2 - 3x - 1}$, what does $f(x)$ approach as x gets infinitely larger?

(A) 0
(B) $\dfrac{3}{4}$
(C) 1
(D) 3
(E) ∞

11. The set of points (x, y, z) such that $x = 5$ is

(A) a point
(B) a line
(C) a plane
(D) a circle
(E) a cube

12. The vertical distance between the minimum and maximum values of the function $y = \left|-\sqrt{2}\sin\sqrt{3}x\right|$ is

(A) 1.414
(B) 1.732
(C) 2.094
(D) 2.828
(E) 3.464

13. If the domain of $f(x) = -|x| + 2$ is $-1 \le x \le 3$, $f(x)$ has a minimum value when x equals

(A) –1
(B) 0
(C) 1
(D) 3
(E) There is no minimum value.

14. What is the range of the function $f(x) = x^2 - 14x + 43$?

(A) $x \le 7$
(B) $x \ge 0$
(C) $y \le -6$
(D) $y \ge -6$
(E) all real numbers

USE THIS SPACE FOR SCRATCH WORK

15. A positive rational root of the equation $4x^3 - x^2 + 16x - 4 = 0$ is

(A) $\frac{1}{4}$
(B) $\frac{1}{2}$
(C) $\frac{3}{4}$
(D) 1
(E) 2

16. The norm of vector $\vec{V} = 3\vec{i} - \sqrt{2}\,\vec{j}$ is

(A) 4.24
(B) 3.61
(C) 3.32
(D) 2.45
(E) 1.59

17. If five coins are flipped and all the different ways they could fall are listed, how many elements of this list will contain more than 3 heads?

(A) 5
(B) 6
(C) 10
(D) 16
(E) 32

18. The seventh term of an arithmetic sequence is 5 and the twelfth term is –15. The first term of this sequence is

(A) 28
(B) 29
(C) 30
(D) 31
(E) 32

19. The graph of the curve represented by $\begin{Bmatrix} x = \sec\theta \\ y = \cos\theta \end{Bmatrix}$ is

(A) a line
(B) a hyperbola
(C) an ellipse
(D) a line segment
(E) a portion of a hyperbola

20. Point (3,2) lies on the graph of the inverse of $f(x) = 2x^3 + x + A$. The value of A is

(A) –54
(B) –15
(C) 15
(D) 18
(E) 54

USE THIS SPACE FOR SCRATCH WORK

21. If $f(x) = ax^2 + bx + c$ and $f(1) = 3$ and $f(-1) = 3$, then $a + c$ equals

(A) –3
(B) 0
(C) 2
(D) 3
(E) 6

22. In $\triangle ABC$, $\angle B = 42°$, $\angle C = 30°$, and $AB = 100$. The length of $\overline{BC}$ is

(A) 47.6
(B) 66.9
(C) 133.8
(D) 190.2
(E) 193.7

23. If $4\sin x + 3 = 0$ on $0 \le x < 2\pi$, then $x =$

(A) –0.848
(B) 0.848
(C) 5.435
(D) 0.848 or 5.435
(E) 3.990 or 5.435

24. What is the sum of the infinite geometric series

$$6 + 4 + \frac{8}{3} + \frac{16}{9} + \ldots ?$$

(A) 18
(B) 36
(C) 45
(D) 60
(E) There is no sum.

25. In $a + bi$ form, the reciprocal of $2 + 6i$ is

(A) $\frac{1}{2} + \frac{1}{6}i$
(B) $-\frac{1}{16} + \frac{3}{16}i$
(C) $\frac{1}{16} + \frac{3}{16}i$
(D) $\frac{1}{20} - \frac{3}{20}i$
(E) $\frac{1}{20} + \frac{3}{20}i$

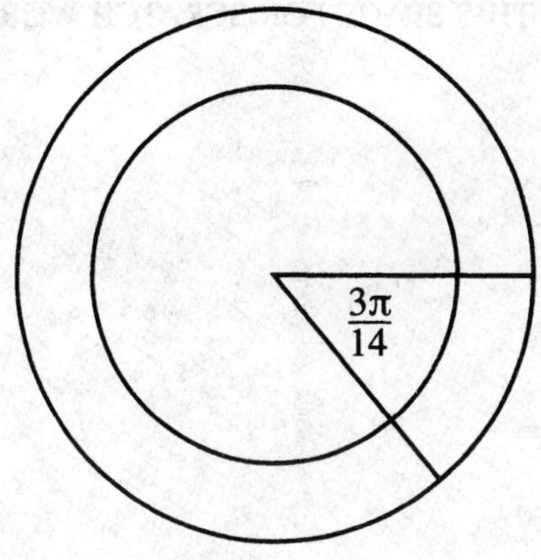

USE THIS SPACE FOR SCRATCH WORK

26. A central angle of two concentric circles is $\frac{3\pi}{14}$.
The area of the large sector is twice the area of the small sector. What is the ratio of the lengths of the radii of the two circles?

(A) 0.25:1
(B) 0.50:1
(C) 0.67:1
(D) 0.71:1
(E) 1:1

27. If the region bounded by the lines $y = -\frac{4}{3}x + 4$, $x = 0$, and $y = 0$ is rotated about the y-axis, the volume of the figure formed is

(A) 18.8
(B) 37.7
(C) 56.5
(D) 84.8
(E) 113.1

28. If there are known to be 4 broken transistors in a box of 12, and 3 transistors are drawn at random, what is the probability that none of the 3 is broken?

(A) 0.250
(B) 0.255
(C) 0.375
(D) 0.556
(E) 0.750

29. What is the domain of $f(x) = \sqrt[3]{15 - x^2}$?

(A) $x > 0$
(B) $x > 2.47$
(C) $-2.47 < x < 2.47$
(D) $-3.87 < x < 3.87$
(E) all real numbers

30. Which of the following is a horizontal asymptote to the function $f(x) = \dfrac{3x^4 - 7x^3 + 2x^2 + 1}{2x^4 - 4}$?

(A) $y = -3.5$
(B) $y = 0$
(C) $y = 0.25$
(D) $y = 0.75$
(E) $y = 1.5$

USE THIS SPACE FOR SCRATCH WORK

31. When a certain radioactive element decays, the amount at any time t can be calculated using the function $E(t) = ae^{\frac{-t}{500}}$, where a is the original amount and t is the elapsed time in years. How many years would it take for an initial amount of 250 milligrams of this element to decay to 100 milligrams?

(A) 125 years
(B) 200 years
(C) 458 years
(D) 496 years
(E) 552 years

32. If n is an integer, what is the remainder when $3x^{(2n+3)} - 4x^{(2n+2)} + 5x^{(2n+1)} - 8$ is divided by $x + 1$?

(A) −20
(B) −10
(C) −4
(D) 0
(E) The remainder cannot be determined.

33. Four men, A, B, C, and D, line up in a row. What is the probability that man A is at either end of the row?

(A) $\frac{1}{2}$
(B) $\frac{1}{3}$
(C) $\frac{1}{4}$
(D) $\frac{1}{6}$
(E) $\frac{1}{12}$

34. $\sum_{i=3}^{10} 5 =$

(A) 260
(B) 50
(C) 40
(D) 5
(E) none of the above

35. The graph of $y^4 - 3x^2 + 7 = 0$ is symmetric with respect to which of the following?

I. the x-axis
II. the y-axis
III. the origin

(A) only I
(B) only II
(C) only III
(D) only I and II
(E) I, II, and III

36. In a group of 30 students, 20 take French, 15 take Spanish, and 5 take neither language. How many students take both French and Spanish?

(A) 0
(B) 5
(C) 10
(D) 15
(E) 20

37. If $f(x) = x^2$, then $\dfrac{f(x+h)-f(x)}{h} =$

(A) 0
(B) h
(C) $2x$
(D) $2x + h$
(E) $\dfrac{x^2}{h}$

38. The plane whose equation is $5x + 6y + 10z = 30$ forms a pyramid in the first octant with the coordinate planes. Its volume is

(A) 15
(B) 21
(C) 30
(D) 36
(E) 45

USE THIS SPACE FOR SCRATCH WORK

USE THIS SPACE FOR SCRATCH WORK

39. What is the range of the function $f(x) = \dfrac{3}{x-5} - 1$?

(A) All real numbers
(B) All real numbers except 5
(C) All real numbers except 0
(D) All real numbers except –1
(E) All real numbers greater than 5

40. Given the set of data 1, 1, 2, 2, 2, 3, 3, x, y, where x and y represent two different integers. If the mode is 2, which of the following statements must be true?

(A) If $x = 1$ or 3, then y must = 2.
(B) Both x and y must be > 3.
(C) Either x or y must = 2.
(D) It does not matter what values x and y have.
(E) Either x or y must = 3, and the other must = 1.

41. If $f(x) = \sqrt{2x+3}$ and $g(x) = x^2$, for what value(s) of x does $f(g(x)) = g(f(x))$?

(A) –0.55
(B) 0.46
(C) 5.45
(D) –0.55 and 5.45
(E) 0.46 and 6.46

42. If $3x - x^2 \ge 2$ and $y^2 + y \le 2$, then

(A) $-1 \le xy \le 2$
(B) $-2 \le xy \le 2$
(C) $-4 \le xy \le 4$
(D) $-4 \le xy \le 2$
(E) $xy = 1, 2$, or 4 only

43. In $\triangle ABC$, if $\sin A = \dfrac{1}{3}$ and $\sin B = \dfrac{1}{4}$, $\sin C =$

(A) 0.14
(B) 0.54
(C) 0.56
(D) 3.15
(E) 2.51

44. The solution set of $\frac{|x-1|}{x} > 2$ is

(A) $0 < x < \frac{1}{3}$
(B) $x < \frac{1}{3}$
(C) $x > \frac{1}{3}$
(D) $\frac{1}{3} < x < 1$
(E) $x > 0$

45. Suppose the graph of $f(x) = -x^3 + 2$ is translated 2 units right and 3 units down. If the result is the graph of $y = g(x)$, what is the value of $g(-1.2)$?

(A) –33.77
(B) –1.51
(C) –0.49
(D) 31.77
(E) 37.77

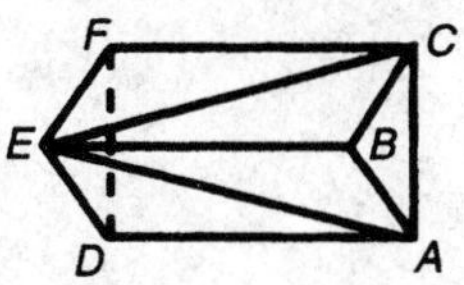

46. In the figure above, the bases, *ABC* and *DEF*, of the right prism are equilateral triangles. The altitude of the prism is *BE*. If a plane cuts the figure through points *A*, *C*, and *E*, two solids, *EABC*, and *EACFD*, are formed. What is the ratio of the volume of *EABC* to the volume of *EACFD*?

(A) $\frac{1}{4}$
(B) $\frac{1}{3}$
(C) $\frac{\sqrt{3}}{4}$
(D) $\frac{1}{2}$
(E) $\frac{\sqrt{3}}{3}$

USE THIS SPACE FOR SCRATCH WORK

USE THIS SPACE FOR SCRATCH WORK

47. The range of the piecewise function

$$f(x)=\begin{cases}3(x-1)^2-2 & \text{if } x<6\\ -2x+5 & \text{if } x\geq 6\end{cases}$$

in interval notation is

(A) $(-\infty,\infty)$
(B) $(-\infty,-7]$
(C) $[-2,\infty)$
(D) $(-7,-2)$
(E) $(-\infty,-7]\cup[-2,\infty)$

48. The length of the major axis of the ellipse $3x^2+2y^2-6x+8y-1=0$ is

(A) $\sqrt{3}$
(B) $\sqrt{6}$
(C) $2\sqrt{3}$
(D) 4
(E) $2\sqrt{6}$

49. A recent survey reported that 60 percent of the students at a high school are girls and 65 percent of girls at this high school play a sport. If a student at this high school were selected at random, what is the probability that the student is a girl who plays a sport?

(A) 0.10
(B) 0.21
(C) 0.32
(D) 0.39
(E) 0.42

50. If $x-7$ divides $x^3-3k^3x^2-13x-7$, then $k=$

(A) 1.19
(B) 1.34
(C) 1.72
(D) 4.63
(E) 5.04

STOP

If there is still time remaining, you may review your answers.

ANSWER KEY

答案

Model Test 3

测试题3

1. **C**
2. **C**
3. **C**
4. **A**
5. **C**
6. **B**
7. **D**
8. **C**
9. **D**
10. **E**
11. **C**
12. **A**
13. **D**
14. **D**
15. **A**
16. **C**
17. **B**
18. **B**
19. **E**
20. **B**
21. **D**
22. **D**
23. **E**
24. **A**
25. **D**
26. **D**
27. **B**
28. **B**
29. **E**
30. **E**
31. **C**
32. **A**
33. **A**
34. **C**
35. **E**
36. **C**
37. **D**
38. **A**
39. **D**
40. **A**
41. **A**
42. **D**
43. **C**
44. **A**
45. **D**
46. **D**
47. **E**
48. **E**
49. **D**
50. **A**

ANSWERS EXPLAINED 答案解析

The following explanations are keyed to the review portions of this book. The number in brackets after each explanation indicates the appropriate chapter in the Review of Major Topics (Part 2). If a problem can be solved using algebraic techniques alone, [algebra] appears after the explanation, and no reference is given for that problem in the Self-Evaluation Chart at the end of the test.

An asterisk appears next to those solutions in which a graphing calculator is necessary or helpful.

1. (C) Transform the given equation into slope-intercept form: $y = -\frac{3}{2}x + \frac{7}{2}$ to see that the slope is $-\frac{3}{2}$. The slope of a perpendicular line is the negative reciprocal, or $\frac{2}{3}$. [2]

* 2. (C) Let $f(x) = 3x^4 - 2x^3 - 20x^2 - 12$ and recall that $f(-2)$ is equal to the remainder upon division of $f(x)$ by $x + 2$. Enter $f(x)$ into Y_1, return to the Home Screen, and enter $Y_1(-2)$ to get the correct answer choice.

An alternative solution is to use synthetic division to find the remainder.

$$\begin{array}{r|rrrrrl} -2 & 3 & -2 & -20 & 0 & -12 & \\ & & -6 & 16 & 8 & -16 & \\ \hline & 3 & -8 & -4 & 8 & -28 & = \text{remainder} \quad [4] \end{array}$$

3. (C) Solve the equation by adding $\frac{2}{x} - 1$ to both sides and getting $\frac{2}{x} - \frac{1}{x} = 2 - 1$ or $\frac{1}{x} = 1$, so $x = 1$. Therefore, $3 - \frac{3}{x} = 3 - 3 = 0$. [algebra]

4. (A) Since $g(3) = e^3$, $f(g(3)) = 2\ln e^3 + 3$. $\ln e^3 = 3$. So $f(g(3)) = 6 + 3 = 9$. [1]

5. (C) Since the domain of $\log_{10}$ is positive numbers, then the domain of f consists of values of x for which $\sin x$ is positive. This is only true for $0 < x < \pi$. [7]

6. (B) $\dfrac{\text{Surface area of sphere}}{\text{Volume of sphere}} = \dfrac{4\pi r^2}{\frac{4}{3}\pi r^3} = \dfrac{12}{4r} = \dfrac{3}{r}$. [15]

* 7. (D) Plot the graph of $y = x^2 - 9x$ in the standard window and observe that you must extend the window in the negative y direction to capture the vertex of the parabola. Since this vertex must lie above the x-axis for the solutions to be complex conjugates, c must be bigger than $|\text{minimum}| = 20.25 = \frac{81}{4}$. (The minimum is found using CALC/minimum.)

An alternative solution is to use the fact that for the solutions to be complex conjugates, the discriminant $b^2 - 4ac = 81 - 4c < 0$, or $c > \frac{81}{4}$. [3]

∗ 8. **(C)** Since $\tan x = 3$, x could be in the first or third quadrants. Since, however, $\sqrt{\csc x}$ is only defined when $\csc x \geq 0$, we need only consider x in the first quadrant. Thus, we can enter $\sqrt{\left(\frac{1}{(\sin(\tan^{-1} 3))}\right)}$ to get the correct answer, Choice C. [7]

9. **(D)** The two transformations put the graph right back where it started. [12]

∗ 10. **(E)** Enter $(3x^3 - 7x^2 + 2)/(4x^2 - 3x - 1)$ into Y_1. Enter TBLSET and set TblStart = 110 and ΔTbl = 10. Then enter TABLE and scroll down to larger and larger x values until you are convinced that Y_1 grows without bound.

An alternative solution is to divide the numerator and denominator by x^3 and then let $x \to \infty$. The numerator approaches 3 while the denominator approaches 0, so the whole fraction grows without bound. [9]

11. **(C)** Since the y- and z-coordinates can have any values, the equation $x = 5$ is a plane where all points have an x-coordinate of 5. [15]

∗ 12. **(A)** Plot the graph of $y = \left|-\sqrt{2}\sin\sqrt{3x}\right|$ using Ztrig. The minimum value of the function is clearly zero, and you can use CALC/maximum to establish 1.414 as the maximum value.

This function inside the absolute value is sinusoidal with amplitude $\sqrt{2} \approx 1.414$. The absolute value eliminates the bottom portion of the sinusoid, so this is the vertical distance between the maximum and the minimum as well. [7]

∗ 13. **(D)** Plot the graph of $y = -|x| + 2$ in a $[-1,3]$ by $[-3,3]$ window. Examine the graph to see that its minimum value is achieved when $x = 3$.

An alternative solution is to realize that y is smallest when x is largest because of the negative absolute value. [11]

∗ 14. **(D)** Plot the graph of $y = x^2 - 14x + 43$, and find its minimum value of -6. All values of y greater than or equal to -6 are in the range of f. [1]

∗ 15. **(A)** Plot the graph of $y = 4x^3 - x^2 + 16x - 4$ in the standard window and zoom in once to get a clearer picture of the location of the zero. Use CALC/zero to determine that the zero is at $x = 0.25$.

An alternative solution is to use the Rational Roots Theorem to determine that the only possible rational roots are $\pm 1, \pm 2, \pm 4, \pm\frac{1}{2}, \frac{1}{4}$. Synthetic division with these values in turn will eventually yield the correct answer choice.

Another alternative solution is to observe that the left side of the equation can be factored: $4x^3 - x^2 + 16x - 4 = x^2(4x - 1) + 4(4x - 1) = (4x - 1)(x^2 + 1) = 0$. Since $x^2 + 1$ can never equal zero, the only solution is $x = \frac{1}{4}$. [4]

∗ 16. **(C)** $\left|\vec{V}\right| = \sqrt{3^2 + \left(-\sqrt{2}\right)^2} = \sqrt{9+2} = \sqrt{11} \approx 3.32$. [20]

∗ 17. (B) "More than 3" implies 4 or 5, and so the number of elements is $\binom{5}{4}+\binom{5}{5}=6$. [16]

18. (B) There are 5 common differences, d, between the seventh and twelfth terms, so $5d = -15 - 5 = -20$, and $d = -4$. The seventh term is the first term plus $6d$, so $5 = t_1 - 24$, and $t_1 = 29$. [19]

∗ 19. (E) In parametric mode, plot the graph of $x = \sec t$ and $y = \cos t$ in the standard window to see that it looks like a portion of a hyperbola. You should verify that it is a portion of a hyperbola rather than the whole hyperbola by noting that $y = \cos t$ implies $-1 \le y \le 1$.

An alternative solution is to use the fact that secant and cosine are reciprocals so that elimination of the parameter t yields the equation $xy = 1$. This is the equation of a hyperbola and again, since $y = \cos t$ implies $-1 \le y \le 1$, the correct answer is Choice E. [10]

20. (B) If (3,2) lies on the inverse of f, (2,3) lies on f. Substituting in f gives $2 \cdot 2^3 + 2 + A = 3$. Therefore, $A = -15$. [1]

21. (D) Substitute 1 for x to get $a + b + c = 3$. Substitute -1 for x to get $a - b + c = 3$. Add these two equations to get $a + c = 3$. [1]

∗ 22. (D) $\angle A = 108°$. Law of sines: $\frac{BC}{\sin 108°} = \frac{100}{\sin 30°}$. Therefore, $BC = \frac{100 \sin 108°}{\sin 30°} = 190.2$. [6]

∗ 23. (E) Plot the graph of $4\sin x + 3$ in radian mode in a $[0,2\pi]$ by $[-2,8]$ window. Use CALC/zero twice to find the correct answer choice.

An alternative solution is to solve the equation for $\sin x$ and use your calculator, in radian mode: $\sin^{-1}\left(-\frac{3}{4}\right) = -0.848$.

Since this value is not between 0 and 2π, you must find the value of x in the required interval that has the same terminal side ($2\pi - 0.848 = 5.435$) as well as the third quadrant angle that has the same reference angle ($\pi + 0.848 = 3.990$). [7]

24. (A) The formula for the sum of a geometric series is $S = \frac{a_1}{1-r}$, where a_1 is the first term and r is the common ratio. In this problem $a_1 = 6$ and $r = \frac{4}{6} = \frac{2}{3}$. [19]

∗ 25. (D) Enter $\frac{1}{2+6i}$ into your calculator and press MATH/ENTER/ENTER/ to get FRACTIONAL real and imaginary parts. An alternative solution is to multiply the numerator and denominator of $\frac{1}{2+6i}$ by the complex conjugate $2 - 6i$:

$$\frac{1}{2+6i} \cdot \frac{2-6i}{2-6i} = \frac{2-6i}{4-(-36)} = \frac{1}{20} - \frac{3}{20}i. \text{ [17]}$$

* 26. (D) The measure $\frac{3\pi}{14}$ of the central angle is superfluous. Areas of similar figures are proportional to the squares of linear measures associated with those figures. Since the ratio of the areas is $1:2$, the ratio of the radii is $1:\sqrt{2}$, or approximately $0.71:1$. [7]

* 27. (B) The line cuts the x-axis at 3 and the y-axis at 4 to form a right triangle that, when rotated about the y-axis, forms a cone with radius 3 and altitude 4.

Volume $= \frac{1}{3}\pi r^2 h = \frac{1}{3}\pi(9)(4) = 12\pi \approx 37.7$. [15]

* 28. (B) Since there are 4 broken transistors, there must be 8 good ones. P(first pick is good) $= \frac{8}{12}$. Of the remaining 11 transistors, 7 are good, and so P(second pick is good) $= \frac{7}{11}$. Finally, P(third pick is good) $= \frac{6}{10}$. Therefore, P(all three are good) $=$

$\frac{8}{12}\cdot\frac{7}{11}\cdot\frac{6}{10} = \frac{14}{55} \approx 0.255$.

Alternative Solution: Note that there are $\binom{8}{3} = 56$ ways to select 3 good transistors.

There are $\binom{12}{3} = 220$ ways to select any 3 transistors.

$P(3 \text{ good ones}) = \frac{56}{220} = \frac{14}{55} \approx 0.255$. [22]

29. (E) The domain of the cube root function is all real numbers, so x can be any real number. [1]

30. (E) Divide each term in the numerator and denominator by x^4. As x increases or decreases, all but the first terms in the numerator and denominator approach zero, leaving a ratio of $\frac{3}{2}$. [9]

* 31. (C) Plot the graphs of $Y_1 = 250e^{-t/500}$ and $Y_2 = 100$. Using the answer choices and information in the problem, choose a [100,600] by [50,300] window, and find the point when Y_1 and Y_2 intersect. The solution is the x-coordinate of this point.

An alternative method is to substitute 250 for a and 100 for E to get $100 = 250e^{\frac{-t}{500}}$. Divide both sides by 250. Take the ln of both sides of the equation. Finally, multiply both sides by -500 to get $t = -500 \ln \frac{2}{5} \approx 458$. [8]

32. (A) According to the Remainder Theorem, simply substitute -1 for x. Since $2n + 3$ and $2n + 1$ are odd, and $2n + 2$ is even, this substitution yields $3(-1) - 4(1) + 5(-1) - 8 = -20$. [4]

33. (A) There are $4! = 24$ arrangements of all 4 men. If man A is on the one end of the line, there are $(2)3! = 12$ arrangements of the other 3 men. Therefore, the probability that man A is at an end seat is $\frac{12}{24} = \frac{1}{2}$. [22]

34. (C) The summation indicates that 5 be summed 8 times (when $i = 3, 4, \ldots, 11$), so the sum is $8 \times 5 = 40$. [19]

* 35. (E) Graph $y = \sqrt[4]{3x^2 + 7}$ and $y = -\sqrt[4]{3x^2 + 7}$ in a standard window. Observe that the graph is symmetrical with respect to the x-axis, the y-axis, and the origin.

An alternative solution is to observe that if x is replaced by $-x$, if y is replaced by $-y$, or if both replacements take place, the equation is unaffected. Therefore, all three symmetries are present. [1]

36. (C) From the Venn diagram below you get the following equations:

$$\begin{aligned} a + b + c + d &= 30 \quad (1) \\ b + c &= 20 \quad (2) \\ c + d &= 15 \quad (3) \\ a &= 5 \end{aligned}$$

Subtract equation (2) from equation (1): $a + d = 10$. Since $a = 5$, $d = 5$. Substituting 5 for d in equation (3) leaves $c = 10$. [16]

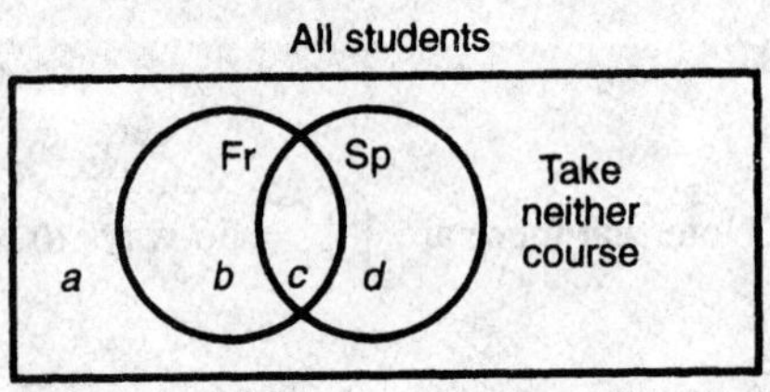

37. (D) First note that $f(x + h) = (x + h)^2 = x^2 + 2xh + h^2$. So $f(x + h) - f(x) = 2xh + h^2$. Divide this expression by h to get the correct answer choice. [1]

38. (A) If $y = z = 0$, $x = 6$, so the plane intersects the x-axis at 6. By similar reasoning, the plane intersects the y-axis at 5 and the z-axis at 3. The figure shows a pyramid with vertex (0,0,3). The base is a right triangle with area $\frac{1}{2}(6)(5) = 15$. Therefore, the volume of the pyramid is $V = \frac{1}{3}(15)(3) = 15$. [15]

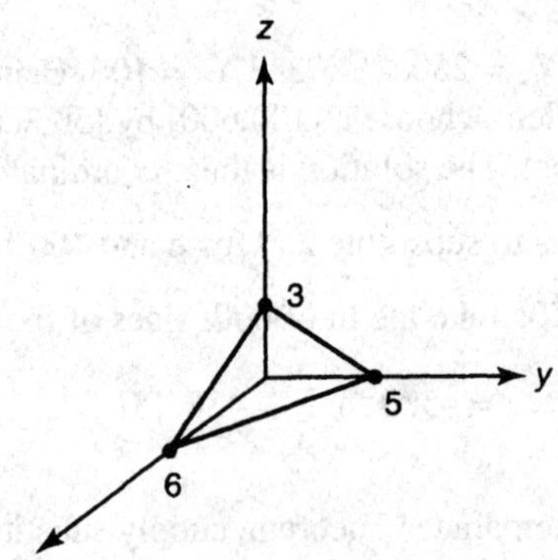

39. **(D)** Replace $f(x)$ with y, interchange x and y, and solve for y. This will give a formula for the inverse of f.

$$x = \frac{1}{y-5} - 1$$

$$x + 1 = \frac{1}{y-5}$$

$$y - 5 = \frac{1}{x+1}$$

$$y = \frac{1}{x+1} + 5$$

The domain of f^{-1} is the range of f, and f^{-1} is defined for all real numbers except $x = -1$. [1]

40. **(A)** The number of 2s must exceed the number of other values. Some of the choices can be eliminated. Choice B: one integer could be 2. Choice C: x or y could be 2, but not necessarily. Choices D and E: if $x = 3$ and $y = 1$, there will be no mode. Therefore, Choice A is the answer. [22]

*** 41.** **(A)** Enter $\sqrt{2x+3}$ into Y_1, x^2 into Y_2, $Y_1(Y_2(X))$ into Y_3, and $Y_2(Y_1(X))$ into Y_4. De-select Y_1 and Y_2, and graph Y_3 and Y_4 in a $[-1.5,2]$ by $[0,5]$ window (because $2x + 3 \geq 0$). Use CALC/intersect to find the correct answer, Choice A.

An alternative solution is to evaluate $f(g(x)) = \sqrt{2x^3+3}$ and $g(f(x)) = 2x + 3$, set the two equal, square both sides, and solve the resulting quadratic: $2x^2 + 3 = (2x + 3)^2 = 4x^2 + 12x + 9$ or $x^2 + 6x + 3 = 0$. The Quadratic Formula yields

$x = \dfrac{-6+\sqrt{24}}{2}$ or $x = \dfrac{-6-\sqrt{24}}{2}$. However, the second is not in the domain of g, so

$x = \dfrac{-6+\sqrt{24}}{2} \approx -0.55$ is the only solution. [1]

42. **(D)** Solve the first inequality to get $1 \leq x \leq 2$. Solve the second inequality to get $-2 \leq y \leq 1$. The smallest product xy possible is -4, and the largest product xy possible is $+2$. [4]

*** 43.** **(C)** Use your calculator to evaluate $\sin\left(180° - \sin^{-1}\frac{1}{3} - \sin^{-1}\frac{1}{4}\right) \approx 0.56$. [6]

*** 44.** **(A)** Graph $y = \dfrac{|x-1|}{x}$ and $y = 2$ in the standard window. There is a vertical asymptote at $x = 0$, and the curve is above the horizontal $y = 2$ just to the right of 0. Choice A is the only possibility, but to be sure, use CALC/intersect to determine that the point of intersection is at $x = \dfrac{1}{3}$.

An alternative solution is to use the associated equation $\frac{|x-1|}{x}=2$ to find boundary values and then test points. Since the left side is undefined when $x = 0$, zero is one boundary value. Multiply both sides by x to get $|x - 1| = 2x$ and analyze the two cases for absolute value. If $x - 1 \geq 0$, then $x - 1 = 2x$ so $x = -1$, which is impossible because $x \geq 1$. Therefore, $x - 1 < 0$, so $1 - x = 2x$ or $x=\frac{1}{3}$ is the other boundary value. Testing points in the intervals $(-\infty,0)$, $\left(0,\frac{1}{3}\right)$, and $\left(\frac{1}{3},\infty\right)$ yields the correct answer, Choice A. [11]

* **45.** **(D)** Translating f 2 units right and 3 units down results in $g(x) = -(x - 2)^3 - 1$. Then $g(-1.2) \approx 31.77$. [12]

46. **(D)** The volume of the prism is area of base times height. The figure $EABC$ is a pyramid with base triangle ABC and height BE, the same as the base and height of the prism. The volume of the pyramid is $\frac{1}{3}$ (base times height), $\frac{1}{3}$ the volume of the prism. Therefore, the other solid, $EACFD$, is $\frac{2}{3}$ the volume of the prism. The ratio of the volumes is $\frac{1}{2}$. [15]

47. **(E)** For $x < 6$, the graph of f is a parabola whose vertex is at the point $(1, -2)$ with -2 as the minimum value. For $x \geq 6$, the value of $-2x + 5$ is less than or equal to $-2(6) + 5 = -7$. Therefore, $y \geq -2$ or $y \leq -7$. [1]

48. **(E)** Get the center axis form of the equation by completing the square:
$3x^2 - 6x + 2y^2 + 8y = 1$
$3(x^2 - 2x + 1) + 2(y^2 + 4y + 4) = 1 + 3 + 8 = 12$, which leads to

$$\frac{3(x-1)^2}{12}+\frac{2(y+2)^2}{12}=1 \text{ and finally to } \frac{(x-1)^2}{4}+\frac{(y+2)^2}{6}=1.$$

Thus, half the major axis is $\sqrt{6}$, making the major axis $2\sqrt{6}$. [13]

* **49.** **(D)** The probability that a student is a girl at this high school is 0.6. The probability that a student who plays a sport is a girl is 0.65. Therefore, the probability that a girl student plays a sport is $(0.6)(0.65) = 0.39$. [22]

* **50.** **(A)** According to the factor theorem, substituting 7 for x yields 0. Therefore,

$7^3 - 3(7)^2k^3 - 13(7) - 7 = 0$, or $k=\sqrt[3]{\frac{245}{147}}\approx 1.19$. [4]

Self-Evaluation Chart for Model Test 3 自评表

Subject Area	Questions and Review Section							Number Right	Number Wrong	Number Omitted
Algebra and Functions	1	2	3	4	7	10				
(24 questions)	2	4	—	1	3	9		____	____	____
	13	14	15	19	20	21				
	11	1	4	10	1	1		____	____	____
	29	30	31	32	35	37				
	1	9	8	4	1	1		____	____	____
	39	41	42	44	47	50				
	1	1	4	11	1	4		____	____	____
Trigonometry	5	8	12	22	23	26				
(7 questions)	7	7	7	6	7	7		____	____	____
	43									
	6							____	____	____
Coordinate and Three-Dimensional Geometry	6	9	11	27	38	45				
(8 questions)	15	12	15	15	15	12		____	____	____
	46	48								
	15	13						____	____	____
Numbers and Operations	16	17	18	24	25	34	36			
(7 questions)	20	16	19	19	17	19	16	____	____	____
Data Analysis, Statistics, and Probability	28	33	40	49						
(4 questions)	22	22	22	22				____	____	____
TOTALS								____	____	____

Evaluate Your Performance on Model Test 3 自评	
Rating	**Number Right**
Excellent	41–50
Very good	33–40
Above average	25–32
Average	15–24
Below average	Below 15

CALCULATING YOUR SCORE 估分

Raw score R = number right – $\frac{1}{4}$(number wrong), rounded = ______________

Approximate scaled score $S = 800 - 10(44 - R)$ = ______________

If $R \geq 44$, $S = 800$.

ANSWER SHEET
答题卡
Model Test 4
测试题4

1. Ⓐ Ⓑ Ⓒ Ⓓ Ⓔ	14. Ⓐ Ⓑ Ⓒ Ⓓ Ⓔ	27. Ⓐ Ⓑ Ⓒ Ⓓ Ⓔ	40. Ⓐ Ⓑ Ⓒ Ⓓ Ⓔ
2. Ⓐ Ⓑ Ⓒ Ⓓ Ⓔ	15. Ⓐ Ⓑ Ⓒ Ⓓ Ⓔ	28. Ⓐ Ⓑ Ⓒ Ⓓ Ⓔ	41. Ⓐ Ⓑ Ⓒ Ⓓ Ⓔ
3. Ⓐ Ⓑ Ⓒ Ⓓ Ⓔ	16. Ⓐ Ⓑ Ⓒ Ⓓ Ⓔ	29. Ⓐ Ⓑ Ⓒ Ⓓ Ⓔ	42. Ⓐ Ⓑ Ⓒ Ⓓ Ⓔ
4. Ⓐ Ⓑ Ⓒ Ⓓ Ⓔ	17. Ⓐ Ⓑ Ⓒ Ⓓ Ⓔ	30. Ⓐ Ⓑ Ⓒ Ⓓ Ⓔ	43. Ⓐ Ⓑ Ⓒ Ⓓ Ⓔ
5. Ⓐ Ⓑ Ⓒ Ⓓ Ⓔ	18. Ⓐ Ⓑ Ⓒ Ⓓ Ⓔ	31. Ⓐ Ⓑ Ⓒ Ⓓ Ⓔ	44. Ⓐ Ⓑ Ⓒ Ⓓ Ⓔ
6. Ⓐ Ⓑ Ⓒ Ⓓ Ⓔ	19. Ⓐ Ⓑ Ⓒ Ⓓ Ⓔ	32. Ⓐ Ⓑ Ⓒ Ⓓ Ⓔ	45. Ⓐ Ⓑ Ⓒ Ⓓ Ⓔ
7. Ⓐ Ⓑ Ⓒ Ⓓ Ⓔ	20. Ⓐ Ⓑ Ⓒ Ⓓ Ⓔ	33. Ⓐ Ⓑ Ⓒ Ⓓ Ⓔ	46. Ⓐ Ⓑ Ⓒ Ⓓ Ⓔ
8. Ⓐ Ⓑ Ⓒ Ⓓ Ⓔ	21. Ⓐ Ⓑ Ⓒ Ⓓ Ⓔ	34. Ⓐ Ⓑ Ⓒ Ⓓ Ⓔ	47. Ⓐ Ⓑ Ⓒ Ⓓ Ⓔ
9. Ⓐ Ⓑ Ⓒ Ⓓ Ⓔ	22. Ⓐ Ⓑ Ⓒ Ⓓ Ⓔ	35. Ⓐ Ⓑ Ⓒ Ⓓ Ⓔ	48. Ⓐ Ⓑ Ⓒ Ⓓ Ⓔ
10. Ⓐ Ⓑ Ⓒ Ⓓ Ⓔ	23. Ⓐ Ⓑ Ⓒ Ⓓ Ⓔ	36. Ⓐ Ⓑ Ⓒ Ⓓ Ⓔ	49. Ⓐ Ⓑ Ⓒ Ⓓ Ⓔ
11. Ⓐ Ⓑ Ⓒ Ⓓ Ⓔ	24. Ⓐ Ⓑ Ⓒ Ⓓ Ⓔ	37. Ⓐ Ⓑ Ⓒ Ⓓ Ⓔ	50. Ⓐ Ⓑ Ⓒ Ⓓ Ⓔ
12. Ⓐ Ⓑ Ⓒ Ⓓ Ⓔ	25. Ⓐ Ⓑ Ⓒ Ⓓ Ⓔ	38. Ⓐ Ⓑ Ⓒ Ⓓ Ⓔ	
13. Ⓐ Ⓑ Ⓒ Ⓓ Ⓔ	26. Ⓐ Ⓑ Ⓒ Ⓓ Ⓔ	39. Ⓐ Ⓑ Ⓒ Ⓓ Ⓔ	

Model Test 4 测试题4

Tear out the preceding answer sheet. Decide which is the best choice by rounding your answer when appropriate. Blacken the corresponding space on the answer sheet. When finished, check your answers with those at the end of the test. For questions that you got wrong, note the chapters containing the material that you must review. Also, if you do not fully understand how you arrived at some of the correct answers, you should review the appropriate chapters. Finally, fill out the Self-Evaluation Chart on page 299 in order to pinpoint the topics that give you the most difficulty.

50 questions: 1 hour

Directions: Decide which answer choice is best. If the exact numerical value is not one of the answer choices, select the closest approximation. Fill in the circle on the answer sheet that corresponds to your choice.

Notes:

(1) You will need to use a scientific or graphing calculator to answer some of the questions.
(2) You will have to decide whether to put your calculator in degree or radian mode for some problems.
(3) All figures that accompany problems are plane figures unless otherwise stated. Figures are drawn as accurately as possible to provide useful information for solving the problem, except when it is stated in a particular problem that the figure is not drawn to scale.
(4) Unless otherwise indicated, the domain of a function is the set of all real numbers for which the functional value is also a real number.

Reference Information. The following formulas are provided for your information.

Volume of a right circular cone with radius r and height h: $V = \frac{1}{3}\pi r^2 h$

Lateral area of a right circular cone if the base has circumference C and slant height is l: $S = \frac{1}{2}Cl$

Volume of a sphere of radius r: $V = \frac{4}{3}\pi r^3$

Surface area of a sphere of radius r: $S = 4\pi r^2$

Volume of a pyramid of base area B and height h: $V = \frac{1}{3}Bh$

MODEL TEST 4

USE THIS SPACE FOR SCRATCH WORK

1. If point (a,b) lies on the graph of function f, which of the following points must lie on the graph of the inverse f?

(A) (a,b)
(B) $(-a,b)$
(C) $(a,-b)$
(D) (b,a)
(E) $(-b,-a)$

2. Harry had grades of 70, 80, 85, and 80 on his quizzes. If all quizzes have the same weight, what grade must he get on his next quiz so that his average will be 80?

(A) 85
(B) 90
(C) 95
(D) 100
(E) more than 100

3. If L is a line through $(-1,3)$ and $(4,2)$, for what value of k is $(3,k)$ on L?

(A) -2
(B) 0
(C) 2.2
(D) 2.5
(E) 2.8

4. If $\log_b x = p$ and $\log_b y = q$, then $\log_b xy =$

(A) pq
(B) $p + q$
(C) $\frac{p}{q}$
(D) $p - q$
(E) p^q

5. The sum of the roots of $3x^3 + 4x^2 - 4x = 0$ is

(A) $-\frac{4}{3}$
(B) $-\frac{3}{4}$
(C) 0
(D) $\frac{4}{3}$
(E) 4

MODEL TEST 4

6. If $f(x) = x - \dfrac{1}{x}$, then $f(a) + f\left(\dfrac{1}{a}\right) =$

(A) 0

(B) $2a - \dfrac{2}{a}$

(C) $a - \dfrac{1}{a}$

(D) $\dfrac{a^4 - a^2 + 1}{a(a^2 - 1)}$

(E) 1

7. If $f(x) = \log(x + 1)$, what is $f^{-1}(3)$?

(A) 0.60
(B) 4
(C) 999
(D) 1,001
(E) 10,000

8. If $f(x) \geq 0$ for all x, then $f(2 - x)$ is

(A) ≥ -2
(B) ≥ 0
(C) ≥ 2
(D) ≤ 0
(E) ≤ 2

9. How many four-digit numbers can be formed from the numbers 0, 2, 4, 8 if no digit is repeated?

(A) 18
(B) 24
(C) 27
(D) 36
(E) 64

10. If $x - 1$ is a factor of $x^2 + ax - 4$, then a has the value

(A) 4
(B) 3
(C) 2
(D) 1
(E) none of the above

11. If 10 coins are to be flipped and the first 5 all come up heads, what is the probability that exactly 3 more heads will be flipped?

(A) 0.0439
(B) 0.1172
(C) 0.1250
(D) 0.3125
(E) 0.6000

USE THIS SPACE FOR SCRATCH WORK

USE THIS SPACE FOR SCRATCH WORK

12. If $i = \sqrt{-1}$ and n is a positive integer, which of the following statements is FALSE?

(A) $i^{4n} = 1$
(B) $i^{4n+1} = -i$
(C) $i^{4n+2} = -1$
(D) $i^{n+4} = i^n$
(E) $i^{4n+3} = -i$

13. If $\log_r 3 = 7.1$, then $\log_r \sqrt{3} =$

(A) 2.66

(B) 3.55

(C) $\frac{\sqrt{3}}{r}$

(D) $\frac{7.1}{r}$

(E) $\sqrt[r]{7.1}$

14. If $f(x) = 4x^2$ and $g(x) = f(\sin x) + f(\cos x)$, then $g(23°)$ is

(A) 1
(B) 4
(C) 4.29
(D) 5.37
(E) 8

15. What is the sum of the roots of the equation

$$\left(x-\sqrt{2}\right)\left(x^2-\sqrt{3}x+\pi\right)=0\ ?$$

(A) −0.315
(B) −0.318
(C) 1.414
(D) 3.15
(E) 4.56

16. Which of the following equations has (have) graphs consisting of two perpendicular lines?

I. $xy = 0$
II. $|y| = |x|$
III. $|xy| = 1$

(A) only I
(B) only II
(C) only III
(D) only I and II
(E) I, II, and III

MODEL TEST 4

17. If $f(x) = (4 - x)^2$ and $g(x) = \sqrt{x}$, then $(g \circ f)(x) =$

USE THIS SPACE FOR SCRATCH WORK

(A) $|4 - x|$
(B) $|2 - x|$
(C) $\sqrt{x(4-x)^2}$
(D) $\left(\sqrt{4-x}\right)^2$
(E) $x - 4$

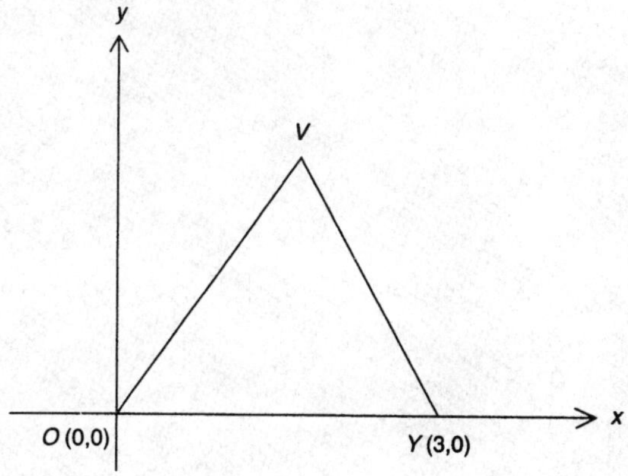

18. In the figure above, if $VO = VY$, what is the slope of segment VO?

(A) $-\sqrt{3}$

(B) $-\frac{\sqrt{3}}{2}$

(C) $\frac{\sqrt{3}}{2}$

(D) $\sqrt{3}$

(E) cannot be determined from the given information

19. A cylindrical bar of metal has a base radius of 2 and a height of 9. It is melted down and reformed into a cube. A side of the cube is

(A) 2.32
(B) 3.84
(C) 4.84
(D) 97.21
(E) 113.10

20. The graph of $y = (x + 2)(2x - 3)$ can be expressed as a set of parametric equations. If $x = 2t - 2$ and $y = f(t)$, then $f(t) =$

(A) $2t(4t - 5)$
(B) $(2t - 2)(4t - 7)$
(C) $2t(4t - 7)$
(D) $(2t - 2)(4t - 5)$
(E) $2t(4t + 1)$

USE THIS SPACE FOR SCRATCH WORK

21. The inverse of $y = \dfrac{2x+1}{3-x}$ is

(A) $y = \dfrac{-2x-1}{x-3}$

(B) $y = \dfrac{3-x}{2x+1}$

(C) $y = \dfrac{3x+1}{x-2}$

(D) $y = \dfrac{3x-1}{x+2}$

(E) $y = \dfrac{3x+1}{2-x}$

22. Rent-a-Rek has 27 cars available for rental. Twenty of these are compact, and 7 are midsize. If two cars are selected at random, what is the probability that both are compact?

(A) 0.0576
(B) 0.0598
(C) 0.481
(D) 0.521
(E) 0.541

23. If a and b are real numbers, with $a > b$ and $|a| < |b|$, then

(A) $a > 0$
(B) $a < 0$
(C) $b > 0$
(D) $b < 0$
(E) none of the above

24. If $[x]$ is defined to represent the greatest integer less than or equal to x, and $f(x) = \left|x - [x] - \frac{1}{2}\right|$, the maximum value of $f(x)$ is

(A) -1
(B) 0
(C) $\frac{1}{2}$
(D) 1
(E) 2

MODEL TEST 4

USE THIS SPACE FOR SCRATCH WORK

25. As x gets closer to 2, $\dfrac{x^3-8}{x^2-4}$ approaches

(A) 0
(B) 1
(C) 2
(D) 3
(E) ∞

26. A right circular cone whose base radius is 4 is inscribed in a sphere of radius 5. What is the ratio of the volume of the cone to the volume of the sphere?

(A) 0.222 : 1
(B) 0.256 : 1
(C) 0.288 : 1
(D) 0.333 : 1
(E) 0.864 : 1

27. If $x_0 = 1$ and $x_{n+1} = \sqrt[3]{2x_n}$, then $x_3 =$

(A) 1.260
(B) 1.361
(C) 1.396
(D) 1.408
(E) 1.412

28. The y-intercept of $y = \left|\sqrt{2}\csc 3\left(x + \dfrac{\pi}{5}\right)\right|$ is

(A) 0.22
(B) 0.67
(C) 1.41
(D) 1.49
(E) 4.58

29. If the center of the circle $x^2 + y^2 + ax + by + 2 = 0$ is point (4,–8), then $a + b =$

(A) –8
(B) –4
(C) 4
(D) 8
(E) 24

30. If $p(x) = 3x^2 + 9x + 7$ and $p(a) = 2$, then $a =$

(A) only 0.736
(B) only –2.264
(C) 0.736 or 2.264
(D) 0.736 or –2.264
(E) –0.736 or –2.264

MODEL TEST 4

USE THIS SPACE FOR SCRATCH WORK

31. If 2 is a root of the equation $x^4 + 2x^3 - 3x^2 + kx - 4 = 0$, then $k =$

(A) –12
(B) –10
(C) –8
(D) 4
(E) 8

32. If $\sin A = \frac{3}{5}, 90° \le A \le 180°, \cos B = \frac{1}{3}$, and $270° \le B \le 360°$, $\sin(A + B) =$

(A) –0.832
(B) –0.554
(C) –0.333
(D) 0.733
(E) 0.954

33. A family has three children. Assuming that the probability of having a boy is 0.5, what is the probability that at least one child is a boy?

(A) 0.875
(B) 0.67
(C) 0.5
(D) 0.375
(E) 0.25

34. If $\sec 1.4 = x$, find the value of $\csc(2 \tan^{-1} x)$.

(A) 0.33
(B) 0.87
(C) 1.00
(D) 1.06
(E) 3.03

35. The graph of $|y - 1| = |x + 1|$ forms an X. The two branches of the X intersect at a point whose coordinates are

(A) (1,1)
(B) (–1,1)
(C) (1,–1)
(D) (–1,–1)
(E) (0,0)

36. For what value of x between 0° and 360° does $\cos 2x = 2 \cos x$?

(A) 68.5° or 291.5°
(B) only 68.5°
(C) 103.9° or 256.1°
(D) 90° or 270°
(E) 111.5° or 248.5°

MODEL TEST 4

37. A data set has a mean of 12 and a standard deviation of 2. If 5 is added to twice each data value, the new data set has

(A) a mean of 24 and a standard deviation of 10
(B) a mean of 24 and a standard deviation of 15
(C) a mean of 29 and a standard deviation of 15
(D) a mean of 29 and a standard deviation of 4
(E) a mean of 29 and a standard deviation of 10

38. For each positive integer n, let S_n = the sum of all positive integers less than or equal to n. Then S_{51} equals

(A) 50
(B) 51
(C) 1,250
(D) 1,275
(E) 1,326

39. If the graphs of $3x^2 + 4y^2 - 6x + 8y - 5 = 0$ and $(x - 2)^2 = 4(y + 2)$ are drawn on the same coordinate system, at how many points do they intersect?

(A) 0
(B) 1
(C) 2
(D) 3
(E) 4

40. If $\log_x 2 = \log_3 x$ is satisfied by two values of x, what is their sum?

(A) 0
(B) 1.73
(C) 2.35
(D) 2.81
(E) 3.14

41. Which of the following lines are asymptotes for the graph of $y = \dfrac{3x^2 - 13x - 10}{x^2 - 4x - 5}$?

I. $x = -1$
II. $x = 5$
III. $y = 3$

(A) I only
(B) II only
(C) I and II
(D) I and III
(E) I, II, and III

USE THIS SPACE FOR SCRATCH WORK

MODEL TEST 4

USE THIS SPACE FOR SCRATCH WORK

42. If $\dfrac{3\sin 2\theta}{1-\cos 2\theta} = \dfrac{1}{2}$ and $0° \le \theta \le 180°$, then $\theta =$

(A) 0°
(B) 0° or 180°
(C) 80.5°
(D) 0° or 80.5°
(E) 99.5°

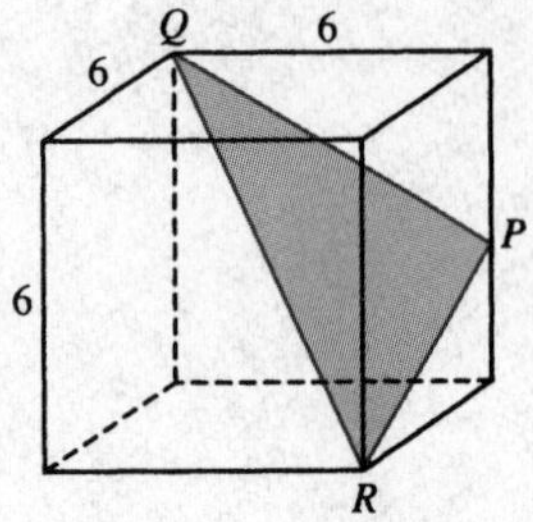

43. The cube in the figure above has edges of length 6. If point *P* is the midpoint of an edge, what is the perimeter of $\triangle QPR$?

(A) 13.41
(B) 14.28
(C) 17.10
(D) 21.90
(E) 23.81

44. Two positive numbers, *a* and *b*, are in the sequence 4, *a*, *b*, 12. The first three numbers form a geometric sequence, and the last three numbers form an arithmetic sequence. The difference $b - a$ equals

(A) 1
(B) $1\frac{1}{2}$
(C) 2
(D) $2\frac{1}{2}$
(E) 3

45. A sector of a circle has an arc length of 2.4 feet and an area of 14.3 square feet. How many degrees are in the central angle?

(A) 63.4°
(B) 20.2°
(C) 14.3°
(D) 12.9°
(E) 11.5°

46. The *y*-coordinate of one focus of the ellipse $36x^2 + 25y^2 + 144x - 50y - 731 = 0$ is

(A) −2
(B) 1
(C) 3.32
(D) 4.32
(E) 7.81

MODEL TEST 4

USE THIS SPACE FOR SCRATCH WORK

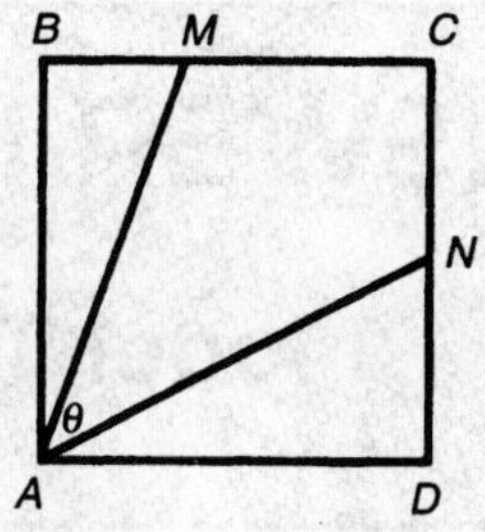

47. In the figure above, *ABCD* is a square. *M* is the point one-third of the way from *B* to *C*. *N* is the point one-half of the way from *D* to *C*. Then $\theta =$

(A) 50.8°
(B) 45.0°
(C) 36.9°
(D) 36.1°
(E) 30.0°

48. If f is a linear function such that $f(7) = 5, f(12) = -6$, and $f(x) = 23.7$, what is the value of x?

(A) –3.2
(B) –1.5
(C) 1
(D) 2.4
(E) 3.1

49. Under which of the following conditions is $\frac{x(x-y)}{y}$ negative?

(A) $x < y < 0$
(B) $y < x < 0$
(C) $0 < y < x$
(D) $x < 0 < y$
(E) all of the above

50. The binary operation * is defined over the set of real numbers to be $a * b = \begin{cases} a\sin\frac{b}{a} \text{ if } a > b \\ b\cos\frac{a}{b} \text{ if } a < b \end{cases}$

What is the value of 2 * (5 * 3)?

(A) 1.84
(B) 2.14
(C) 2.79
(D) 3.65
(E) 4.01

STOP

If there is still time remaining, you may review your answers.

MODEL TEST 4

ANSWER KEY
答案
Model Test 4
测试题4

1. **D**	14. **B**	27. **C**	40. **D**
2. **A**	15. **D**	28. **D**	41. **D**
3. **C**	16. **D**	29. **D**	42. **C**
4. **B**	17. **A**	30. **E**	43. **E**
5. **A**	18. **E**	31. **C**	44. **E**
6. **A**	19. **C**	32. **E**	45. **E**
7. **C**	20. **C**	33. **A**	46. **D**
8. **B**	21. **D**	34. **E**	47. **B**
9. **A**	22. **E**	35. **B**	48. **B**
10. **B**	23. **D**	36. **E**	49. **A**
11. **D**	24. **C**	37. **D**	50. **B**
12. **B**	25. **D**	38. **E**	
13. **B**	26. **B**	39. **C**	

ANSWERS EXPLAINED 答案解析

The following explanations are keyed to the review portions of this book. The number in brackets after each explanation indicates the appropriate chapter in the Review of Major Topics (Part 2). If a problem can be solved using algebraic techniques alone, [algebra] appears after the explanation, and no reference is given for that problem in the Self-Evaluation Chart at the end of the test.

An asterisk appears next to those solutions in which a graphing calculator is necessary or helpful.

1. **(D)** Since inverse functions are symmetric about the line $y = x$, if point (a,b) lies on f, point (b,a) must lie on f^{-1}. [1]

* 2. **(A)** Average $= \dfrac{70+80+85+80+x}{5} = 80$. Therefore, $x = 85$. [21]

3. **(C)** The slope of the line is $\dfrac{2-3}{4-(-1)} = -\dfrac{1}{5}$. Therefore, $\dfrac{k-2}{3-4} = -\dfrac{1}{5}$. Cross-multiplying yields $5k - 10 = 1$, so $k = \dfrac{11}{5} = 2.2$. [2]

4. **(B)** The bases are the same, so the log of a product equals the sum of the logs. [8]

* 5. **(A)** Plot the graph of $y = 3x^3 + 4x^2 - 4x$ in the standard window and use CALC/zero to find the three zeros of this function. Sum these three values to get the correct answer choice.

   An alternative solution is to first observe that x factors out, so that $x = 0$ is one zero. The other factor is a quadratic, so the sum of its zeros is $-\dfrac{b}{a} = -\dfrac{4}{3}$. [4]

6. **(A)** $f(a) = a - \dfrac{1}{a}$ and $f\left(\dfrac{1}{a}\right) = \dfrac{1}{a} - a$. Therefore, $f(a) + f\left(\dfrac{1}{a}\right) = 0$. [1]

7. **(C)** By the definition of f, $\log(x + 1) = 3$. Therefore, $x + 1 = 10^3 = 1{,}000$ and $x = 999$. [8]

8. **(B)** The $f(2 - x)$ just shifts and reflects the graph horizontally; it does not have any vertical effect on the graph. Therefore, regardless of what is substituted for x, $f(x) \geq 0$. [12]

9. **(A)** Only 3 of the numbers can be used in the thousands place, 3 are left for the hundreds place, 2 for the tens place, and only one for the units place. $3 \cdot 3 \cdot 2 \cdot 1 = 18$. [16]

10. **(B)** Substituting 1 for x gives $1 + a - 4 = 0$, and so $a = 3$. [4]

* 11. **(D)** The first 5 flips have no effect on the next 5 flips, so the problem becomes "What is the probability of getting exactly 3 heads in 5 flips of a coin?" $\binom{5}{3} = 10$ outcomes contain 3 heads out of a total of $2^5 = 32$ possible outcomes. $P(3\text{H}) = \frac{5}{16} \approx 0.3125$. [22]

12. **(B)** Powers of i repeat in groups of 4: $i^0 = 1, i^1 = i, i^2 = -1, i^3 = -i$. Then $i^4 = 1$, and so forth. Therefore, $i^{4n} = i^4 = 1$, so Choice A is true. $i^{4n+2} = i^2 = -1$, so Choice C is true. $i^{n+4} = i^n$ because the powers repeat in groups of 4, so Choice D is true. $i^{4n+3} = i^3$, so Choice E is true. However, $i^{4n+1} = i^1 = i$, so Choice B is *not* true. [17]

13. **(B)** Since $\sqrt{x} = x^{1/2}$, $\log_r \sqrt{3} = \log_r 3^{1/2} = \frac{1}{2}\log_r 3 = 3.55$. [8]

14. **(B)** The 23° is superfluous because $g(x) = f(\sin x) + f(\cos x) = 4\sin^2 x + 4\cos^2 x = 4(\sin^2 x + \cos^2 x) = 4(1) = 4$. [7]

* 15. **(D)** This is a tricky problem. If you just plot the graph of $y = \left(x - \sqrt{2}\right)\left(x^2 - \sqrt{3}x + \pi\right)$, you will see only one real zero, at approximately 1.414 ($\approx \sqrt{2}$). This is because the zeros of the quadratic factor are imaginary. Since, however, they are imaginary conjugates, their sum is real—namely twice the real part. Therefore, graphing the function, using CALC/zero to find the zeros, and summing them will give you the wrong answer.

   To get the correct answer, you must use the fact that the sum of the zeros of the quadratic factor is $-\frac{b}{a} = \sqrt{3} \approx 1.732$. Since the zero of the linear factor is $\sqrt{2} \approx 1.414$, the sum of the zeros is about $1.732 + 1.414 \approx 3.15$. [4]

16. **(D)** Graph I consists of the lines $x = 0$ and $y = 0$, which are the coordinate axes and are therefore perpendicular. Graph II consists of $y = |x|$ and $y = -|x|$, which are at ±45° to the coordinate axes and are therefore perpendicular. Graph III consists of the hyperbolas $xy = 1$ and $xy = -1$. Therefore, the correct answer choice is Choice D.

   There are two reasons why a graphing calculator solution is not recommended here. One is that equations, not functions, are given, and solving these equations so that they can be graphed involves two branches each. The other reason is that even with graphs, you would have to make judgments about perpendicularity. At a minimum, this would require you to graph the equations in a square window. [11]

17. **(A)** $(g \circ f)(x) = g(f(x)) = \sqrt{(4 - x)^2} = |4 - x|$. [1]

18. **(E)** Since the y-coordinate of the point V could be at any height, the slope of VO could be any value. [2]

* 19. **(C)** Volume of cylinder $= \pi r^2 h = 36\pi =$ volume of cube $= s^3$. Therefore, $s = \sqrt[3]{36\pi} \approx 4.84$. [15]

MODEL TEST 4

20. **(C)** Substitute $2t - 2$ for x. [10]

21. **(D)** Interchange x and y, and solve for y:

$$x = \frac{2y+1}{3-y}$$

$$3x - xy = 2y + 1$$

$$3x - 1 = 2y + xy$$

$$y(2 + x) = 3x - 1$$

$$y = \frac{3x-1}{x+2} \quad [1]$$

* 22. **(E)** The probability that the first car selected is compact is $\frac{20}{27}$. There are 26 cars left, of which 19 are compact. The probability that the second car is also compact is $\left(\frac{20}{27}\right) \cdot \left(\frac{19}{26}\right) \approx 0.541$. [22]

23. **(D)** Here, a could be either positive or negative. However, b must be negative. [algebra]

* 24. **(C)** Plot the graph of $y = \text{abs}(x - \text{int}(x) - 1/2)$ in a $[-5,5]$ by $[-2,2]$ window, and observe that the maximum value is $\frac{1}{2}$.

An alternative solution is to sketch a portion of the graph by hand and observe the maximum value. [11]

* 25. **(D)** Plot the graph $y = (x^3 - 8)(x^2 - 4)$ in the standard window. Using CALC/value, observe that y is not defined when $x = 2$. Therefore, enter 1.999 for x and observe that y is approximately equal to 3.

An alternative solution is to factor the numerator and denominator, divide out $x - 2$, and substitute the limiting value 2 into the resulting expression:

$$\lim_{x\to 2} \frac{x^3-8}{x^2-4} = \lim_{x\to 2} \frac{(x-2)(x^2+2x+2)}{(x-2)(x+2)}$$

$$= \lim_{x\to 2} \frac{(x^2+2x+4)}{x+2} = \frac{4+4+4}{2+2} = 3. \quad [9]$$

* 26. **(B)** A sketch will help you see that the height of the cone is $5 + 3 = 8$.

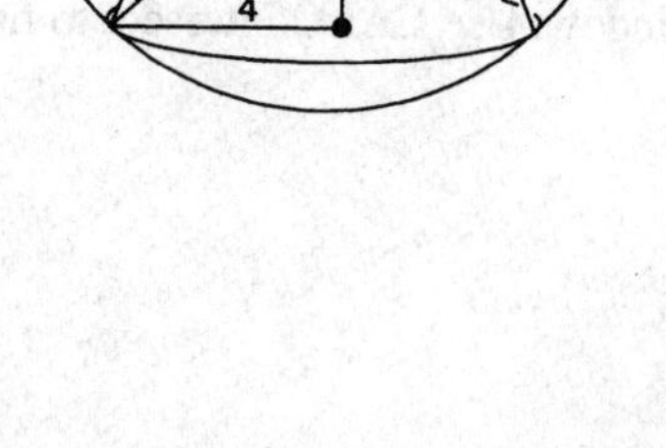

MODEL TEST 4

The volume of the cone is $V_c = \frac{1}{3}\pi r^2 h = \frac{1}{3}\pi(16)(8)$, and the volume of the sphere is

$V_s = \frac{4}{3}\pi r^3 = \frac{4}{3}\pi(125)$. The desired ratio is $V_c : V_s = 0.256:1$. [15]

∗ 27. (C) Enter 1 into your calculator. Then enter $\sqrt[3]{2\text{Ans}}$ three times, to accomplish three iterations that result in x_3 to get the correct answer, Choice C.

An alternative solution is to use the formula to evaluate x_1, x_2, and x_3, in turn. [19]

∗ 28. (D) With your calculator in radian mode, plot the graph of $y = \text{abs}\left(\sqrt{2}\left(1/\sin\left(x + \pi/5\right)\right)\right)$ in a [–1,1] by [0,5] window. Use VALUE/X = 0 to determine that the y-intercept is approximately 1.49. [7]

29. (D) The equation of the circle is $(x - 4)^2 + (y + 8)^2 = r^2$. Multiplying out indicates that $a = -8$ and $b = 16$, and so $a + b = 8$. [13]

30. (E) Since $p(a) = 2$, $3a^2 + 9a + 5 = 0$. Solve by using the Quadratic Formula to get the correct answer choice. [3]

31. (C) Use synthetic division to divide $x^4 + 2x^3 - 3x^2 + kx - 4$ by $x - 2$, and the remainder should be 0:

$$\begin{array}{r|rrrrr} 2 & 1 & 2 & -3 & k & -4 \\ & & 2 & 8 & 10 & 20+2k \\ \hline & 1 & 4 & 5 & k+10 & 16+2k \end{array}$$

Therefore, $16 + 2k = 0$, so $k = -8$. [4]

∗ 32. (E) First find $\sin^{-1}(3/5) \approx 36.87°$, the reference angle for angle A. Since A is in the second quadrant, $A \approx 180° - 36.87° = 143.13°$. Store 180-Ans in A. Similarly, find $\cos^{-1}(1/3) \approx 70.53°$, the reference angle for angle B. Since B is in the fourth quadrant, store 360-Ans in B. Then evaluate $\sin(A + B)$ to get the correct answer choice. [7]

∗ 33. (A) The probability that at least one is a boy is (1 – the probability that all 3 are girls) or $1 - (0.5)^3 = 0.875$. [22]

∗ 34. (E) Since $\sec 1.4 = x$, $\cos 1.4 = \frac{1}{x}$ or $x = \frac{1}{\cos 1.4}$. Therefore, $\csc(2\tan^{-1} x) = 1/\sin(2\tan^{-1}(1/\cos 1.4)) \approx 3.03$. [7]

∗ 35. (B) The equation $|y - 1| = |x + 1|$ defines two functions: $y = \pm|x + 1| + 1$. Plot these graphs in the standard window and observe that they intersect at (–1,1).

An alternative solution is to recall that the important point of an absolute value occurs when the expression within the absolute value sign equals zero. The important point of this absolute value problem occurs when $y - 1 = 0$ and $x + 1 = 0$, i.e., at (–1,1). [11]

∗ 36. (E) With your calculator in degree mode, plot the graphs of $y = \cos 2x$ and $y = 2\cos x$ in a [0,360] by [–2,2] window. Use CALC/intersect to find the correct answer, Choice E. [7]

37. **(D)** The new mean is 5 more than twice the old mean, or 2(12) + 5 = 29, but the new standard deviation is only twice the old one because adding a value to each data point does not affect the standard deviation. [21]

* 38. **(E)** Enter LIST/MATH/sum(LIST/OPS/seq(X,X,1,51)) to compute the desired sum.

An alternative solution is to observe that the sequence is arithmetic with $t_1 = 1$ and $d = 1$. Using the formula for the sum of the first n terms of an arithmetic sequence, $S_{51} = \frac{51}{2}(2+50\cdot 1) = 51\cdot 26 = 1{,}326$. [19]

* 39. **(C)** Complete the square in the first equation to get $3(x-1)^2 + 4(y+1)^2 = 12$. Solving this equation for y yields $y = \pm\sqrt{\frac{12-3(x-1)^2}{4}} - 1$. Solving for y in the second equation, $y = \frac{(x-2)^2}{4} - 2$. Plot the graphs of these three equations in the standard window to see that the graphs intersect in two places.

An alternative solution can be found by completing the square in the first equation and dividing by 12 to get the standard form equation of an ellipse, $\frac{(x-1)^2}{4} + \frac{(y+1)^2}{3} = 1$. The second equation is the standard form of a parabola. Sketch these two equations and observe the number of points of intersection. [13]

* 40. **(D)** Let $y = \log_x 2 = \log_3 x$. Converting to exponential form gives $x^y = 2$ and $3^y = x$. Substitute to get $3^{y^2} = 2$, which can be converted into $y^2 = \frac{\log 2}{\log 3} \approx 0.6309$. Thus, $y \approx \pm 0.7943$. Therefore, $3^{0.7943} = x \approx 2.393$ or $3^{-0.7943} = x \approx 0.4178$. Therefore, the sum of two x's is 2.81. [8]

41. **(D)** Factor the numerator and denominator: $\frac{(3x+2)(x-5)}{(x+1)(x-5)}$. Since the $x-5$ divide out, the only vertical asymptote is at $x = -1$. Since the degree of the numerator and denominator are equal, y approaches 3 as x approaches $\pm\infty$, so $y = 3$ is a horizontal asymptote. [9]

* 42. **(C)** With your calculator in degree mode, plot the graphs of $y = 1/2$ and $y = (3\sin(2x))/(1-\cos(2x))$ in the window [0,180] by [–2,2]. Use CALC/intersect to find the one point of intersection in the specified interval, at 80.5°.

An alternative solution is to cross-multiply the original equation and use the double angle formulas for sine and cosine, to get

$$6\sin 2\theta = 1 - \cos 2\theta$$

$$12\sin\theta\cos\theta = 1-(1-2\sin^2\theta) = 2\sin^2\theta$$

$$6\sin\theta\cos\theta - \sin^2\theta = 0$$

$$\sin\theta(6\cos\theta - \sin\theta) = 0$$

Therefore, $\sin\theta = 0$ or $\tan\theta = 6$. It follows that $\theta = 0°, 180°$, or $80.5°$. The first two solutions make the denominator of the original equation equal to zero, so 80.5° is the only solution. [7]

* 43. (E) By the Pythagorean theorem, QP and RP each equal $\sqrt{6^2+3^2} = \sqrt{45}$. Apply the Pythagorean theorem to find $SR^2 = 6^2 + 6^2$, and $QR^2 = 6^2 + 6^2 + 6^2$, so $QR = 6\sqrt{3}$. Therefore, the perimeter of $\triangle QPR = 2\sqrt{45} + 6\sqrt{3} = 23.81$. [15]

44. (E) From the geometric sequence, $b = a\left(\frac{a}{4}\right)$. From the arithmetic sequence, $b - a = 12 - b$, or $2b - a = 12$. Substituting gives $2\left(\frac{a^2}{4}\right) - a = 12$.

Solving gives $a = 6$ or -4. Eliminate -4 since a is given to be positive. Substituting the 6 gives $2b - 6 = 12$, giving $b = 9$. Therefore, $b - a = 3$. [19]

* 45. (E) Since $s = r\theta$, then $2.4 = r\theta$, which implies that $r = \frac{2.4}{\theta}$. $A = \frac{1}{2}r^2\theta$, and so $14.3 = \frac{1}{2}r^2\theta$, which implies that $r^2 = \frac{28.6}{\theta}$. Therefore, $\left(\frac{2.4}{\theta}\right)^2 = \frac{28.6}{\theta}$, which implies that $2.4^2 = 28.6\theta$. Therefore, $\theta = \frac{5.76}{28.6} \approx 0.2014$ radians $\approx 11.5°$. [7]

* 46. (D) Complete the square and put the equation of the ellipse in standard form:

$$36x^2 + 25y^2 + 144x - 50y - 731$$
$$= 36(x+2)^2 + 25(y-1)^2 - 900$$

$$\frac{(x+2)^2}{25} + \frac{(y-1)^2}{36} = 1$$

The center of the ellipse is at $(-2,1)$, with $a^2 = 36$ and $b^2 = 25$, and the major axis is parallel to the y-axis. Each focus is $c = \sqrt{a^2 - b^2}$ units above and below the center. Therefore, the y-coordinates of the foci are $1 \pm \sqrt{11} \approx 4.32$ and -2.32. [13]

* 47. (B) Because you are bisecting one side and trisecting another side, it is convenient to let the length of the sides be a number divisible by both 2 and 3. Let $AB = AD = 6$. Thus $BM = 2$, $MC = 4$, and $CN = ND = 3$. Let $\angle NAD = x$, so that, using right triangle NAD, $\tan x = \frac{3}{6} = 0.5$, which implies that $x = \tan^{-1} 0.5 \approx 26.6°$. Let $\angle MAB = y$, so that, using right triangle MAB, $\tan y = \frac{2}{6}$, which implies that $y = \tan^{-1}\frac{1}{3} \approx 18.4°$. Therefore, $\theta \approx 90° - 26.6° - 18.4° \approx 45°$. [6]

* 48. (B) The slope of the line is $\frac{-6-5}{12-7} = -\frac{11}{5}$. An equation of the line is therefore $y - 5 = -\frac{11}{5}(x - 7)$. Substitute 23.7 for y and solve for x to get $x = -1.5$. [1]

49. (A) You must check each answer choice, one at a time. In Choice A, $x < 0$, $y < 0$, $x - y < 0$, so the expression is negative. In Choice B, $x < 0$, $y < 0$, $x - y > 0$, so the expression is positive. At this point you know that the correct answer choice must be Choice A. [algebra]

* 50. (B) Put your calculator in radian mode: $5 * 3 = 5\sin\frac{3}{5} \approx 2.823$.

$2 * (5 * 3) = 2 * 2.823 \approx 2.823\cos\frac{2}{2.823} \approx 2.14$. [binary operation]

Self-Evaluation Chart for Model Test 4 自评表

Subject Area	Questions and Review Section							Number Right	Number Wrong	Number Omitted
Algebra and Functions (26 questions)	1	3	4	5	6	7	10			
	1	2	8	4	1	8	4	___	___	___
	13	15	16	17	18	20	21			
	8	4	11	1	2	10	1	___	___	___
	23	24	25	30	31	35				
	—	11	9	3	4	11		___	___	___
	40	41	43	48	49	50				
	8	9	15	1	—	—		___	___	___
Trigonometry (8 questions)	14	28	32	34	36					
	7	7	7	7	7			___	___	___
	42	45	47							
	7	7	6					___	___	___
Coordinate and Three-Dimensional Geometry (6 questions)	8	19	26	29	39	46				
	12	15	15	13	13	13		___	___	___
Numbers and Operations (5 questions)	9	12	27	38	44					
	16	17	19	19	19			___	___	___
Data Analysis, Statistics, and Probability (5 questions)	2	11	22	33	37					
	21	22	22	22	21			___	___	___
TOTALS								___	___	___

MODEL TEST 4

Evaluate Your Performance on Model Test 4 自评	
Rating	**Number Right**
Excellent	41–50
Very good	33–40
Above average	25–32
Average	15–24
Below average	Below 15

CALCULATING YOUR SCORE 估分

Raw score R = number right $- \frac{1}{4}$(number wrong), rounded = ______________

Approximate scaled score $S = 800 - 10(44 - R)$ = ______________

If $R \geq 44$, $S = 800$.

ANSWER SHEET

答题卡

Model Test 5

测试题5

1. Ⓐ Ⓑ Ⓒ Ⓓ Ⓔ	14. Ⓐ Ⓑ Ⓒ Ⓓ Ⓔ	27. Ⓐ Ⓑ Ⓒ Ⓓ Ⓔ	40. Ⓐ Ⓑ Ⓒ Ⓓ Ⓔ
2. Ⓐ Ⓑ Ⓒ Ⓓ Ⓔ	15. Ⓐ Ⓑ Ⓒ Ⓓ Ⓔ	28. Ⓐ Ⓑ Ⓒ Ⓓ Ⓔ	41. Ⓐ Ⓑ Ⓒ Ⓓ Ⓔ
3. Ⓐ Ⓑ Ⓒ Ⓓ Ⓔ	16. Ⓐ Ⓑ Ⓒ Ⓓ Ⓔ	29. Ⓐ Ⓑ Ⓒ Ⓓ Ⓔ	42. Ⓐ Ⓑ Ⓒ Ⓓ Ⓔ
4. Ⓐ Ⓑ Ⓒ Ⓓ Ⓔ	17. Ⓐ Ⓑ Ⓒ Ⓓ Ⓔ	30. Ⓐ Ⓑ Ⓒ Ⓓ Ⓔ	43. Ⓐ Ⓑ Ⓒ Ⓓ Ⓔ
5. Ⓐ Ⓑ Ⓒ Ⓓ Ⓔ	18. Ⓐ Ⓑ Ⓒ Ⓓ Ⓔ	31. Ⓐ Ⓑ Ⓒ Ⓓ Ⓔ	44. Ⓐ Ⓑ Ⓒ Ⓓ Ⓔ
6. Ⓐ Ⓑ Ⓒ Ⓓ Ⓔ	19. Ⓐ Ⓑ Ⓒ Ⓓ Ⓔ	32. Ⓐ Ⓑ Ⓒ Ⓓ Ⓔ	45. Ⓐ Ⓑ Ⓒ Ⓓ Ⓔ
7. Ⓐ Ⓑ Ⓒ Ⓓ Ⓔ	20. Ⓐ Ⓑ Ⓒ Ⓓ Ⓔ	33. Ⓐ Ⓑ Ⓒ Ⓓ Ⓔ	46. Ⓐ Ⓑ Ⓒ Ⓓ Ⓔ
8. Ⓐ Ⓑ Ⓒ Ⓓ Ⓔ	21. Ⓐ Ⓑ Ⓒ Ⓓ Ⓔ	34. Ⓐ Ⓑ Ⓒ Ⓓ Ⓔ	47. Ⓐ Ⓑ Ⓒ Ⓓ Ⓔ
9. Ⓐ Ⓑ Ⓒ Ⓓ Ⓔ	22. Ⓐ Ⓑ Ⓒ Ⓓ Ⓔ	35. Ⓐ Ⓑ Ⓒ Ⓓ Ⓔ	48. Ⓐ Ⓑ Ⓒ Ⓓ Ⓔ
10. Ⓐ Ⓑ Ⓒ Ⓓ Ⓔ	23. Ⓐ Ⓑ Ⓒ Ⓓ Ⓔ	36. Ⓐ Ⓑ Ⓒ Ⓓ Ⓔ	49. Ⓐ Ⓑ Ⓒ Ⓓ Ⓔ
11. Ⓐ Ⓑ Ⓒ Ⓓ Ⓔ	24. Ⓐ Ⓑ Ⓒ Ⓓ Ⓔ	37. Ⓐ Ⓑ Ⓒ Ⓓ Ⓔ	50. Ⓐ Ⓑ Ⓒ Ⓓ Ⓔ
12. Ⓐ Ⓑ Ⓒ Ⓓ Ⓔ	25. Ⓐ Ⓑ Ⓒ Ⓓ Ⓔ	38. Ⓐ Ⓑ Ⓒ Ⓓ Ⓔ	
13. Ⓐ Ⓑ Ⓒ Ⓓ Ⓔ	26. Ⓐ Ⓑ Ⓒ Ⓓ Ⓔ	39. Ⓐ Ⓑ Ⓒ Ⓓ Ⓔ	

Model Test 5 测试题5

Tear out the preceding answer sheet. Decide which is the best choice by rounding your answer when appropriate. Blacken the corresponding space on the answer sheet. When finished, check your answers with those at the end of the test. For questions that you got wrong, note the chapters containing the material that you must review. Also, if you do not fully understand how you arrived at some of the correct answers, you should review the appropriate chapters. Finally, fill out the Self-Evaluation Chart on page 321 in order to pinpoint the topics that give you the most difficulty.

50 questions: 1 hour

Directions: Decide which answer choice is best. If the exact numerical value is not one of the answer choices, select the closest approximation. Fill in the circle on the answer sheet that corresponds to your choice.

Notes:
(1) You will need to use a scientific or graphing calculator to answer some of the questions.
(2) You will have to decide whether to put your calculator in degree or radian mode for some problems.
(3) All figures that accompany problems are plane figures unless otherwise stated. Figures are drawn as accurately as possible to provide useful information for solving the problem, except when it is stated in a particular problem that the figure is not drawn to scale.
(4) Unless otherwise indicated, the domain of a function is the set of all real numbers for which the functional value is also a real number.

Reference Information. The following formulas are provided for your information.

Volume of a right circular cone with radius r and height h: $V = \frac{1}{3}\pi r^2 h$

Lateral area of a right circular cone if the base has circumference C and slant height is l: $S = \frac{1}{2}Cl$

Volume of a sphere of radius r: $V = \frac{4}{3}\pi r^3$

Surface area of a sphere of radius r: $S = 4\pi r^2$

Volume of a pyramid of base area B and height h: $V = \frac{1}{3}Bh$

USE THIS SPACE FOR SCRATCH WORK

1. $x^{2/3} + x^{4/3} =$

(A) $x^{2/3}$
(B) $x^{8/9}$
(C) x
(D) x^2
(E) $x^{2/3}(x^{2/3} + 1)$

2. In three dimensions, what is the set of all points for which $x = 0$?

(A) the origin
(B) a line parallel to the x-axis
(C) the yz-plane
(D) a plane containing the x-axis
(E) the x-axis

3. Expressed with positive exponents only, $\dfrac{ab^{-1}}{a^{-1} - b^{-1}}$ is equivalent to

(A) $\dfrac{a^2}{a-b}$
(B) $\dfrac{a^2}{a-1}$
(C) $\dfrac{b-a}{ab}$
(D) $\dfrac{a^2}{b-a}$
(E) $\dfrac{1}{a-b}$

4. If $f(x) = \sqrt[3]{x}$ and $g(x) = x^3 + 8$, find $(f \circ g)(3)$.

(A) 3.3
(B) 5
(C) 11
(D) 35
(E) 50.5

5. $x > \sin x$ for

(A) all $x > 0$
(B) all $x < 0$
(C) all x for which $x \neq 0$
(D) all x
(E) all x for which $-\dfrac{\pi}{2} < x < 0$

6. The sum of the zeros of $f(x) = 3x^2 - 5$ is

(A) 3.3
(B) 1.8
(C) 1.7
(D) 1.3
(E) 0

USE THIS SPACE FOR SCRATCH WORK

MODEL TEST 5

7. The intersection of a plane with a right circular cylinder could be which of the following?

I. A circle
II. Parallel lines
III. Intersecting lines

(A) I only
(B) II only
(C) III only
(D) I and II only
(E) I, II, and III

8. Two dice are tossed. What is the probability that the sum is 5?

(A) $\frac{1}{11}$

(B) $\frac{1}{9}$

(C) $\frac{1}{6}$

(D) $\frac{1}{4}$

(E) $\frac{1}{2}$

9. The graph of $f(x) = \frac{10}{x^2 - 10x + 25}$ has a vertical asymptote at $x =$

(A) 0 only
(B) 5 only
(C) 10 only
(D) 0 and 5 only
(E) 0, 5, and 10

10. When $P(x) = 2x^3 - 6x^2 + Kx$ is divided by $x + 2$, the remainder is -10. Then $K =$

(A) −30
(B) −15
(C) −6
(D) −1
(E) 6

USE THIS SPACE FOR SCRATCH WORK

11. Of the following lists of numbers, which has the largest standard deviation?

(A) 2, 7, 15
(B) 3, 7, 14
(C) 5, 7, 12
(D) 10, 11, 12
(E) 11, 11, 11

12. If $f(x)$ is a linear function and $f(2) = 1$ and $f(4) = -2$, then $f(x) =$

(A) $-\frac{3}{2}x+4$
(B) $\frac{3}{2}x-2$
(C) $-\frac{3}{2}x+2$
(D) $\frac{3}{2}x-4$
(E) $-\frac{2}{3}x+\frac{7}{3}$

13. The length of the radius of a circle is one-half the length of an arc of the circle. What is the radian measure of the central angle that intercepts that arc?

(A) 60°
(B) 120°
(C) 1^R
(D) 2^R
(E) π^R

14. If $f(x) = 2^x + 1$, then $f^{-1}(7) =$

(A) 2.4
(B) 2.6
(C) 2.8
(D) 3
(E) 3.6

15. Find all values of x that satisfy the determinant equation $\begin{vmatrix} 2x & 1 \\ x & x \end{vmatrix} = 3$.

(A) –1
(B) –1 or 1.5
(C) 1.5
(D) –1.5
(E) –1.5 or 1

16. The 71st term of 30, 27, 24, 21, . . . , is

(A) 5,325
(B) 240
(C) 180
(D) –180
(E) –183

17. If $0 < x < \frac{\pi}{2}$ and $\tan 5x = 3$, to the nearest tenth, what is the value of $\tan x$?

(A) 0.5
(B) 0.4
(C) 0.3
(D) 0.2
(E) 0.1

18. If $4.05^p = 5.25^q$, what is the value of $\frac{p}{q}$?

(A) –0.11
(B) 0.11
(C) 1.19
(D) 1.30
(E) 1.67

19. A cylinder has a base radius of 2 and a height of 9. To the nearest whole number, by how much does the lateral area exceed the sum of the areas of the two bases?

(A) 101
(B) 96
(C) 88
(D) 81
(E) 75

20. If $\cos 67° = \tan x°$, then $x =$

(A) 0.4
(B) 6.8
(C) 7.8
(D) 21
(E) 29.3

21. $P(x) = x^3 + 18x - 30$ has a zero in the interval

(A) (0, 0.5)
(B) (0.5, 1)
(C) (1, 1.5)
(D) (1.5, 2)
(E) (2, 2.5)

USE THIS SPACE FOR SCRATCH WORK

USE THIS SPACE FOR SCRATCH WORK

22. The lengths of the sides of a triangle are 23, 32, and 37. To the nearest degree, what is the value of the largest angle?

(A) 71°
(B) 83°
(C) 122°
(D) 128°
(E) 142°

23. If $f(x) = \dfrac{3}{x-2}$ and $g(x) = \sqrt{x+1}$, find the domain of $f \circ g$.

(A) $x \geq -1$
(B) $x \neq 2$
(C) $x \geq -1, x \neq 2$
(D) $x \geq -1, x \neq 3$
(E) $x \leq -1$

24. The overall average grade of a math course is based on homework (10%), quizzes (40%), and tests (50%). Ted has a 90 average for homework, 81 for quizzes, and 85 for tests. What is his overall average?

(A) 83
(B) 84
(C) 85
(D) 86
(E) 87

25. If $\sqrt{y} = 3.216$, then $\sqrt{10y} =$

(A) 321.6
(B) 32.16
(C) 10.17
(D) 5.67
(E) 4.23

26. What is the domain of the function $f(x) = \log\sqrt{2x^2 - 15}$?

(A) $-7.5 < x < 7.5$
(B) $x < -7.5$ or $x > 7.5$
(C) $x < -2.7$ or $x > 2.7$
(D) $x < -3.2$ or $x > 3.2$
(E) $x < 1.9$ or $x > 1.9$

27. A magazine has 1,200,000 subscribers, of whom 400,000 are women and 800,000 are men. Twenty percent of the women and 60 percent of the men read the advertisements in the magazine. What is the probability that a randomly selected subscriber reads the advertisements?

(A) 0.30
(B) 0.36
(C) 0.40
(D) 0.47
(E) 0.52

28. Let S be the sum of the first n terms of the arithmetic sequence 3, 7, 11, . . . , and let T be the sum of the first n terms of the arithmetic sequence 8, 10, 12, ... For $n > 1$, $S = T$ for

(A) no value of n
(B) one value of n
(C) two values of n
(D) three values of n
(E) four values of n

29. On the interval $\left[-\frac{\pi}{4}, \frac{\pi}{4}\right]$, the function $f(x) = \sqrt{1+\sin^2 x}$ has a maximum value of

(A) 0.78
(B) 1
(C) 1.1
(D) 1.2
(E) 1.4

30. A point has rectangular coordinates (3,4). The polar coordinates are $(5,\theta)$. What is the value of θ?

(A) 30°
(B) 37°
(C) 51°
(D) 53°
(E) 60°

31. If $f(x) = x^2 - 4$, for what real number values of x will $f(f(x)) = 0$?

(A) 2.4
(B) ±2.4
(C) 2 or 6
(D) ±1.4 or ±2.4
(E) no values

USE THIS SPACE FOR SCRATCH WORK

MODEL TEST 5

32. If $f(x) = x \log x$ and $g(x) = 10^x$, then $g(f(2)) =$

(A) 24
(B) 17
(C) 4
(D) 2
(E) 0.6

33. If $f(x) = x^{\sqrt{x}}$, then $f(\sqrt{2}) =$

(A) 1.4
(B) 1.5
(C) 1.6
(D) 2.0
(E) 2.7

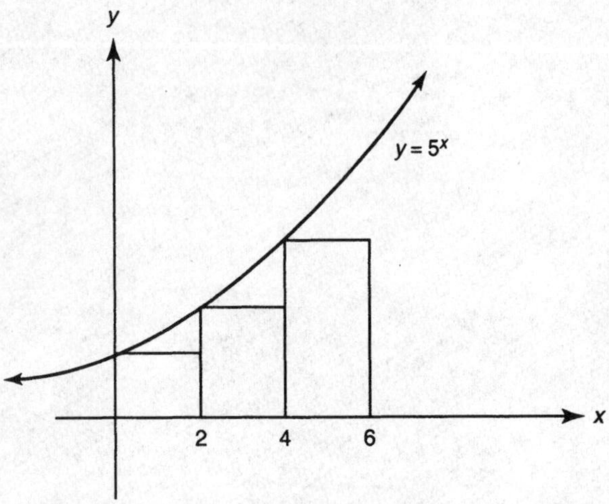

34. The figure above shows the graph of 5^x. What is the sum of the areas of the rectangles?

(A) 32,550
(B) 16,225
(C) 2,604
(D) 1,302
(E) 651

35. (p,q) is called a *lattice point* if p and q are both integers. How many lattice points lie in the area strictly between the two curves $x^2 + y^2 = 9$ and $x^2 + y^2 - 6x + 5 = 0$?

(A) 0
(B) 1
(C) 2
(D) 3
(E) 4

USE THIS SPACE FOR SCRATCH WORK

36. If $9^x = \sqrt{3}$ and $2^{x+y} = 32$, then $y =$

(A) $\frac{1}{2}$

(B) $\frac{3}{4}$

(C) $\frac{5}{2}$

(D) $\frac{11}{2}$

(E) $\frac{19}{4}$

37. For all real numbers $x, f(2x) = x^2 - x + 3$. An expression for $f(x)$ in terms of x is

(A) $2x^2 - 2x + 3$

(B) $4x^2 - 2x + 3$

(C) $\frac{x^2}{4} - \frac{x}{2} + 3$

(D) $\frac{x^2}{2} - \frac{x}{2} + 3$

(E) $x^2 - x + 3$

38. For what value(s) of k is $x^2 - kx + k$ divisible by $x - k$?

(A) only 0

(B) only 0 or $-\frac{1}{2}$

(C) only 1
(D) any value of k
(E) no value of k

39. If the graphs of $x^2 = 4(y + 9)$ and $x + ky = 6$ intersect on the x-axis, then $k =$

(A) 0
(B) 6
(C) –6
(D) no real number
(E) any real number

40. The length of the major axis of the ellipse $\frac{(x-3)^2}{16} + \frac{(y+2)^2}{25} = 1$ is

(A) 3
(B) 4
(C) 5
(D) 6
(E) 10

USE THIS SPACE FOR SCRATCH WORK

USE THIS SPACE FOR SCRATCH WORK

41. If $f_n = \begin{cases} \dfrac{f_{n-1}}{2} & \text{when } f_{n-1} \text{ is an even number} \\ 3 \cdot f_{n-1} + 1 & \text{when } f_{n-1} \text{ is an odd number} \end{cases}$

and $f_1 = 3$, then $f_5 =$

(A) 1
(B) 2
(C) 4
(D) 8
(E) 16

42. How many different rearrangements of the letters in the word CONTEST start with the two vowels?

(A) 120
(B) 60
(C) 10
(D) 5
(E) none of the above

43. Which of the following translations of the graph of $y = x^2$ would result in the graph of $y = x^2 - 6x + k$, where k is a constant greater than 10?

(A) left 6 units and up k units
(B) left 3 units and up $k + 9$ units
(C) right 3 units and up $k + 9$ units
(D) left 3 units and up $k - 9$ units
(E) right 3 units and up $k - 9$ units

44. How many positive integers are there in the solution set of $\dfrac{x}{x-2} > 5$?

(A) 0
(B) 2
(C) 4
(D) 5
(E) an infinite number

45. During the year 1995 the price of ABC Company stock increased by 125%, and during the year 1996 the price of the stock increased by 80%. Over the period from January 1, 1995, through December 31, 1996, by what percentage did the price of ABC Company stock rise?

(A) 103%
(B) 205%
(C) 305%
(D) 405%
(E) 505%

46. If $x_0 = 3$ and $x_{n+1} = x_n\sqrt{x_n + 1}$, then $x_3 =$

(A) 15.9
(B) 31.7
(C) 44.9
(D) 65.2
(E) 173.9

47. When the smaller root of the equation $3x^2 + 4x - 1 = 0$ is subtracted from the larger root, the result is

(A) −1.3
(B) 0.7
(C) 1.3
(D) 1.8
(E) 2.0

48. A committee of 4 is to be selected from a group of 7 women and 4 men. How many different committees of 2 men and 2 women can be formed?

(A) 22
(B) 24
(C) 126
(D) 128
(E) 789

49. If x, y, and z are positive, with $xy = 24$, $xz = 48$, and $yz = 72$, then $x + y + z =$

(A) 22
(B) 36
(C) 50
(D) 62
(E) 96

50. In radians, $\sin^{-1}(\cos 100°) =$

(A) −1.4
(B) −0.2
(C) 0.2
(D) 1.0
(E) 1.4

USE THIS SPACE FOR SCRATCH WORK

STOP

If there is still time remaining, you may review your answers.

ANSWER KEY
答案
Model Test 5
测试题5

1. **E**	14. **B**	27. **D**	40. **E**
2. **C**	15. **B**	28. **B**	41. **D**
3. **D**	16. **D**	29. **D**	42. **A**
4. **A**	17. **C**	30. **D**	43. **E**
5. **A**	18. **C**	31. **D**	44. **A**
6. **E**	19. **C**	32. **C**	45. **C**
7. **D**	20. **D**	33. **B**	46. **D**
8. **B**	21. **C**	34. **D**	47. **D**
9. **B**	22. **B**	35. **D**	48. **C**
10. **B**	23. **D**	36. **E**	49. **A**
11. **A**	24. **B**	37. **C**	50. **B**
12. **A**	25. **C**	38. **A**	
13. **D**	26. **C**	39. **E**	

ANSWERS EXPLAINED 答案解析

The following explanations are keyed to the review portions of this book. The number in brackets after each explanation indicates the appropriate chapter in the Review of Major Topics (Part 2). If a problem can be solved using algebraic techniques alone, [algebra] appears after the explanation, and no reference is given for that problem in the Self-Evaluation Chart at the end of the test.

An asterisk appears next to those solutions in which a graphing calculator is necessary or helpful.

1. **(E)** Factor out $x^{2/3}$, the greatest common factor of $x^{2/3} + x^{4/3}$, to get $x^{2/3} + x^{4/3} = x^{2/3}(1 + x^{2/3})$. [8]

2. **(C)** When $x = 0$, y and z can be any value. Therefore, any point in the yz-plane is a possible member of the set. [15]

3. **(D)** $\dfrac{\frac{a}{b}}{\frac{1}{a}-\frac{1}{b}} \cdot \dfrac{ab}{ab} = \dfrac{a^2}{b-a}$. [algebra]

* 4. **(A)** Enter f in Y_1 and g in Y_2, return to the home screen and enter $Y_1(Y_2(3))$ to get the correct answer choice. [1]

* 5. **(A)** Plot the graph of $y = x - \sin x$ and observe that the graph lies above the x-axis for all $x > 0$. [7]

* 6. **(E)** Plot the graph of $y = 3x^2 - 5$ in the standard window. The symmetry about the y-axis indicates that the zeros are opposites and therefore sum to zero.

An alternative solution is to use the fact that the zeros of a quadratic function sum to $-\dfrac{b}{a} = 0$. [3]

7. **(D)** If the plane is perpendicular to the axis of the cylinder, the intersection will be a circle, so I is possible. If the plane is parallel to the axis of the cylinder, the intersection will be parallel lines, so II is possible. It is impossible for the intersection of a plane and a cylinder to form intersecting lines because there are no intersecting lines on a cylinder. [15]

8. **(B)** Call the outcome of a roll (A,B). The sum of A and B is 5 for (1,4), (4,1), (2,3), and (3,2). There are 36 = (6)(6) possible outcomes. Therefore, the probability of a roll of 5 is $\dfrac{4}{36} = \dfrac{1}{9}$. [22]

* 9. **(B)** Plot f in a standard window and use TRACE to observe that y increases without bound on either side of $x = 5$.

An alternative solution can be found by observing that the denominator of f is $(x - 5)^2$, which equals zero only when $x = 5$. [9]

* **10.** **(B)** Perform synthetic division:

$$\begin{array}{r|rrrr} 2 & 2 & -6 & K & 0 \\ & & -4 & 20 & -2K-40 \\ \hline & 2 & -10 & K+20 & -2K-40 \end{array}$$

Since the remainder is -10, it follows that $-2K-40=-10$, so $K=-15$. [4]

11. **(A)** The standard deviation of a data set is a measure of the spread in the data. Of the five data sets presented, Choice A exhibits the greatest spread and therefore has the greatest standard deviation. [21]

12. **(A)** The slope of $f(x)=\frac{-2-1}{4-2}=\frac{-3}{2}$. Using the point-slope form, $f(x)-1=\frac{-3}{2}(x-2)$. Therefore, $f(x)=\frac{-3}{2}x+4$. [2]

13. **(D)** $s=r\theta$. $2r=r\theta$. $\theta=2$. [7]

* **14.** **(B)** Plot the graphs of $y=2^x+1$ in the standard window. Since $f^{-1}(7)$ is the value of x such that $f(x)=7$, also plot the graph of $y=7$. The correct answer choice is the point where these two graphs intersect.

An alternative solution is to solve the equation $2^x+1=7$: $x=\log_2 6=\frac{\log 6}{\log 2}\approx 2.6$. [1]

15. **(B)** Evaluate the 2 by 2 determinant to get $2x^2-x=3$. Then factor $2x^2-x-3$ into $(2x-3)(x+1)$ and set each factor to zero to get $x=\frac{3}{2}$ or $x=-1$. [18]

* **16.** **(D)** Use LIST/seq to construct the sequence as seq(30 – 3x,x,0,70) and store this sequence in a list (e.g., L_1). On the Home Screen, enter $L_1(71)$ for the 71st term, -180.

An alternative solution is to use the formula for the nth term of an arithmetic sequence: $t_{71}=30-(70)(3)=-180$. [19]

* **17.** **(C)** Put your calculator in radian mode: $5x=\tan^{-1}3\approx 1.249$. $x\approx 0.2498$. Therefore, $\tan x=0.255139\approx 0.3$. [7]

* **18.** **(C)** Take $\log_{4.05}$ of both sides of the equation, getting $p=\log_{4.05}5.25^q$, or $p=q\log_{4.05}5.25$. Dividing both sides by q and changing to base 10 yields

$$\frac{p}{q}=\frac{\log 5.25}{\log 4.05}\approx 1.19.\ [8]$$

* **19.** **(C)** Area of one base $=\pi r^2=4\pi$.
Lateral area $=2\pi rh=36\pi$.
Lateral area – two bases $=36\pi-8\pi=28\pi\approx 87.96\approx 88$. [15]

* **20.** **(D)** Put your calculator in degree mode and evaluate $\tan^{-1}(\cos 67°)$. [7]

* **21.** **(C)** Plot the graph of $y=x^3+18x-30$ in a [0,3] by [–5,5] window, and use CALC/zero to locate a zero at $x\approx 1.48$. [4]

*** 22.** **(B)** The angle opposite the 37 side (call it $\angle A$) is the largest angle. By the Law of Cosines, $37^2 = 23^2 + 32^2 - 2(23)(32)\cos A$.

$$\cos A = \frac{37^2 - 23^2 - 32^2}{-2(23)(32)} \approx \frac{-184}{-1{,}472} = 0.125.$$

Therefore, $A = \cos^{-1}(0.125) \approx 83°$. [6]

23. **(D)** The domain of g is $x \ge -1$ because $x + 1 \ge 0$. The domain of $f \circ g$ consists of all x such that $g(x)$ is in the domain of f. Since $g(3) = 2$ and 2 is not in the domain of f, 3 must be excluded from the domain of $f \circ g$. [1]

*** 24.** **(B)** Calculate the weighted average: $(0.1)(90) + (0.4)(81) + (0.5)(85) = 83.9$, which rounds to 84. [21]

*** 25.** **(C)** Since $\sqrt{y} = 3.216$, $y \approx 10.34$, and $10y \approx 103.4$, so $\sqrt{10y} \approx 10.17$. [algebra]

*** 26.** **(C)** Plot the graph of $y = \log\sqrt{2x^2 - 15}$ in the standard window and zoom in once. Use the TRACE to determine that there are no y values on the graph between the approximate x values of -2.7 and 2.7.

An alternative solution is to use the fact that the domain of the square root function is $x \ge 0$ and its range is $y \ge 0$. However, since the domain of the log function is $x > 0$, the domain of the function f must satisfy $2x^2 - 15 > 0$, or $x^2 > 7.5$. The approximate solution to this inequality is the correct answer, Choice C. [8]

*** 27.** **(D)** Twenty percent of 400,000 women is 80,000, and 60% of 800,000 men is 480,000. Altogether 560,000 subscribers read ads, or about 47%. [22]

28. **(B)** Equate S and T using the formula for the sum of the first n terms of an arithmetic series: $\frac{n}{2}[6 + (n-1)4] = \frac{n}{2}[16 + (n-1)2]$. This equation reduces to $n^2 - 6n = 0$, for which 6 is the only positive solution. [19]

*** 29.** **(D)** Plot the graph of $y = \sqrt{(1 + \sin(x)^2)}$ in a $\left[-\frac{\pi}{4}, \frac{\pi}{4}\right]$ by $[-2,2]$ window, and observe that the maximum value of y occurs at the endpoints. Return to the home screen, and enter $Y_1(\pi/4)$ to get the correct answer choice.

An alternative solution uses the fact that on the interval $\left[-\frac{\pi}{4}, \frac{\pi}{4}\right]$, the maximum value of $|\sin x| = \frac{\sqrt{2}}{2}$. Therefore, the maximum value of $f(x)$ is $\sqrt{1 + \frac{1}{2}} = \sqrt{\frac{3}{2}} \approx 1.2$. [7]

∗ **30.** **(D)** $\sin\theta = \frac{4}{5}$.

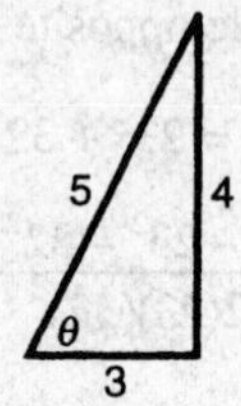

Therefore, $\theta = \sin^{-1}\left(\frac{4}{5}\right) \approx 53°$. [14]

∗ **31.** **(D)** Plot the graph of $f(f(x))$ in the standard window by entering $Y_1 = x^2 - 4$, $Y_2 = Y_1(x)$, and de-selecting Y_1. The graph has 4 zeros located symmetrically about the y-axis, making Choice D the only possible solution.
An alternative solution is to evaluate $f(f(x)) = (x^2 - 4)^2 - 4 = 0$ and solve by setting $x^2 - 4 = \pm 2$, or $x^2 = 6$ or 2, so $x = \pm\sqrt{6}$ or $\pm\sqrt{2}$. Again, Choice D is the only answer choice with 4 solutions. [1]

∗ **32.** **(C)** Enter f into Y_1 and g into Y_2. Evaluate $Y_2(Y_1(2))$ for the correct answer choice.
An alternative solution is to use the properties of logs to evaluate $f(2) = 2 \log 2 = \log 4$ and $g(\log 4) = 10^{\log 4} = 4$ without a calculator. [8]

∗ **33.** **(B)** $f\left(\sqrt{2}\right) = \left(\sqrt{2}\right)^{\sqrt{\sqrt{2}}} \approx 1.5$. [1]

∗ **34.** **(D)** The width of each rectangle is 2 and the heights are $5^0 = 1$, $5^2 = 25$, and $5^4 = 625$. Therefore, the total area is $2(1 + 25 + 625) = 1{,}302$. [8]

∗ **35.** **(D)** Plot the graphs of $y = \pm\sqrt{9 - x^2}$ and $y = \pm\sqrt{-x^2 + 6x - 5}$ in the standard window, but with FORMAT set to GridOn. The "grid" consists exactly of the lattice points. ZOOM/ZBox around the area enclosed by the two graphs, and count the number of lattice points in that area to be 3. The points (1,0) and (3,0) appear close to the boundary, but a mental check finds that (1,0) is on the boundary of the second curve, while (3,0) is on the boundary of the first. [15]

∗ **36.** **(E)** $9^x = (3^2)^x = 3^{2x}$, and $\sqrt{3} = 3^{1/2}$. Therefore, $2x = \frac{1}{2}$ and $x = \frac{1}{4}$. Since $32 = 2^5$, $x + y = 5$ so $y = \frac{19}{4}$. [8]

37. **(C)** $f(x) = f\left(2 \cdot \frac{x}{2}\right) = \left(\frac{x}{2}\right)^2 - \frac{x}{2} + 3 = \frac{x^2}{4} - \frac{x}{2} + 3$. [1]

38. **(A)** Using the factor theorem, substitute k for x and set the result equal to zero. Then $k^2 - k^2 + k = 0$, and $k = 0$. [4]

39. **(E)** If the graphs intersect on the x-axis, the value of y must be zero. Since the value of y is zero, it does not matter what k is. [4]

40. (E) This ellipse has its center at (3,–2). Since 25 > 16, the major axis is vertical, and its length is $2\sqrt{25}=10$. [13]

41. (D)

n	1	2	3	4	5
f_n	3	10	5	16	8

[19]

* 42. (A) There are 5 consonants, CNTST, but the two Ts are indistinguishable, so there are $\frac{5!}{2}=60$ ways of arranging these. There are two ways of arranging the 2 vowels in the front. Therefore, there are 2 • 60 = 120 distinguishable arrangements. [16]

43. (E) Complete the square on x^2-6x by adding 9. Then $x^2-6x+k=x^2-6x+9+k-9$ $=(x-3)^2+(k-9)$. This expression represents the translation of x^2 by 3 units right and $k-9$ units up. [12]

* 44. (A) Plot the graph of $y=\frac{x}{x-2}-5$ in the standard window and observe the vertical asymptote at $x=2$. $y>\frac{x}{x-2}-5$ where this graph lies above the x-axis, and there are no integer values of x in this interval.

An alternative solution is to solve the equation $\frac{x}{x-2}=5\ (x\neq 2)$: $x=5x-10$, or $x=\frac{5}{2}$.

If you test values in the intervals $(-\infty,2)$, $\left(2,\frac{5}{2}\right)$, and $\left(\frac{5}{2},\infty\right)$ you find that only the middle interval satisfies the inequality, but it contains no integers. [5]

45. (C) Let the starting price of the stock be \$100. During the first year a 125% increase means a \$125 increase to \$225. During the second year an 80% increase of the \$225 stock price means a \$180 increase to \$405. Thus, over the 2-year period the price increased \$305 from the original \$100 starting price. Therefore, the price increased 305%. [algebra]

* 46. (D) Enter 3 into your calculator. Then enter Ans $\sqrt{\text{Ans}+1}$ three times to accomplish three iterations that result in x_3 and the correct answer choice. [19]

* 47. (D) Substitute the values of a, b, and c into the Quadratic Formula to find the algebraic solutions; then subtract the smaller from the larger to find the decimal approximation to the answer:

$$x=\frac{-4\pm\sqrt{16+12}}{6}=\frac{-2\pm\sqrt{7}}{3};\ \frac{-2+\sqrt{7}}{3}-\frac{-2-\sqrt{7}}{3}=\frac{2\sqrt{7}}{3}\approx 1.8.\ [3]$$

∗ 48. (C) There are $\binom{4}{2} = \frac{4 \cdot 3}{2} = 6$ ways of selecting 2 men of 4 and $\binom{7}{2} = \frac{7 \cdot 6}{2} = 21$ ways of selecting 2 women of 7. Therefore, there are $\binom{4}{2}\binom{7}{2} = 6 \cdot 21 = 126$ ways of selecting a committee consisting of 2 men and 2 women. [16]

49. (A) First evaluate the ratio $\frac{xy}{xz} = \frac{y}{z} = \frac{24}{48} = \frac{1}{2}$. Cross-multiply to get $z = 2y$, and substitute in the third equation: $yz = y(2y) = 2y^2 = 72$. Therefore, $y = 6$, $z = 12$, and $x = 4$, and $x + y + z = 22$. [algebra]

∗ 50. (B) With your calculator in degree mode, evaluate $\sin^{-1}(\cos(100)) = -10°$ directly. To change to radians, return your calculator to radian mode and key in $-10°$ and multiply by $\frac{\pi}{180°}$. This will return $-0.17 \approx -0.2$ radians.

An alternative solution is to convert $-10°$ to radians by multiplying by $\frac{\pi}{180°}$. [7]

Self-Evaluation Chart for Model Test 5 自评表

Subject Area	Questions and Review Section							Number Right	Number Wrong	Number Omitted
Algebra and Functions	1	3	4	6	9					
(25 questions)	8	—	1	3	9			____	____	____
	10	12	14	18	21	23				
	4	2	1	8	4	1		____	____	____
	25	26	31	32	33	34	36			
	—	8	1	8	1	8	8	____	____	____
	37	38	39	44	45	47	49			
	1	4	4	5	—	3	—	____	____	____
Trigonometry	5	13	17	20	22	29	50			
(7 questions)	7	7	7	7	6	7	7	____	____	____
Coordinate and Three-	2	7	19	30	35	40	43			
Dimensional Geometry (7 questions)	15	15	15	14	15	13	12	____	____	____
Numbers and Operations	15	16	28	41	42	46	48			
(7 questions)	18	19	19	19	16	19	16	____	____	____
Data Analysis, Statistics,	8	11	24	27						
and Probability (4 questions)	22	21	21	22				____	____	____
TOTALS								____	____	____

Evaluate Your Performance on Model Test 5 自评	
Rating	**Number Right**
Excellent	41–50
Very good	33–40
Above average	25–32
Average	15–24
Below average	Below 15

CALCULATING YOUR SCORE 估分

Raw score R = number right $-\frac{1}{4}$(number wrong), rounded = ______________

Approximate scaled score $S = 800 - 10(44 - R)$ = ______________

If $R \geq 44$, $S = 800$.

ANSWER SHEET
答题卡

Model Test 6
测试题6

1. Ⓐ Ⓑ Ⓒ Ⓓ Ⓔ	14. Ⓐ Ⓑ Ⓒ Ⓓ Ⓔ	27. Ⓐ Ⓑ Ⓒ Ⓓ Ⓔ	40. Ⓐ Ⓑ Ⓒ Ⓓ Ⓔ
2. Ⓐ Ⓑ Ⓒ Ⓓ Ⓔ	15. Ⓐ Ⓑ Ⓒ Ⓓ Ⓔ	28. Ⓐ Ⓑ Ⓒ Ⓓ Ⓔ	41. Ⓐ Ⓑ Ⓒ Ⓓ Ⓔ
3. Ⓐ Ⓑ Ⓒ Ⓓ Ⓔ	16. Ⓐ Ⓑ Ⓒ Ⓓ Ⓔ	29. Ⓐ Ⓑ Ⓒ Ⓓ Ⓔ	42. Ⓐ Ⓑ Ⓒ Ⓓ Ⓔ
4. Ⓐ Ⓑ Ⓒ Ⓓ Ⓔ	17. Ⓐ Ⓑ Ⓒ Ⓓ Ⓔ	30. Ⓐ Ⓑ Ⓒ Ⓓ Ⓔ	43. Ⓐ Ⓑ Ⓒ Ⓓ Ⓔ
5. Ⓐ Ⓑ Ⓒ Ⓓ Ⓔ	18. Ⓐ Ⓑ Ⓒ Ⓓ Ⓔ	31. Ⓐ Ⓑ Ⓒ Ⓓ Ⓔ	44. Ⓐ Ⓑ Ⓒ Ⓓ Ⓔ
6. Ⓐ Ⓑ Ⓒ Ⓓ Ⓔ	19. Ⓐ Ⓑ Ⓒ Ⓓ Ⓔ	32. Ⓐ Ⓑ Ⓒ Ⓓ Ⓔ	45. Ⓐ Ⓑ Ⓒ Ⓓ Ⓔ
7. Ⓐ Ⓑ Ⓒ Ⓓ Ⓔ	20. Ⓐ Ⓑ Ⓒ Ⓓ Ⓔ	33. Ⓐ Ⓑ Ⓒ Ⓓ Ⓔ	46. Ⓐ Ⓑ Ⓒ Ⓓ Ⓔ
8. Ⓐ Ⓑ Ⓒ Ⓓ Ⓔ	21. Ⓐ Ⓑ Ⓒ Ⓓ Ⓔ	34. Ⓐ Ⓑ Ⓒ Ⓓ Ⓔ	47. Ⓐ Ⓑ Ⓒ Ⓓ Ⓔ
9. Ⓐ Ⓑ Ⓒ Ⓓ Ⓔ	22. Ⓐ Ⓑ Ⓒ Ⓓ Ⓔ	35. Ⓐ Ⓑ Ⓒ Ⓓ Ⓔ	48. Ⓐ Ⓑ Ⓒ Ⓓ Ⓔ
10. Ⓐ Ⓑ Ⓒ Ⓓ Ⓔ	23. Ⓐ Ⓑ Ⓒ Ⓓ Ⓔ	36. Ⓐ Ⓑ Ⓒ Ⓓ Ⓔ	49. Ⓐ Ⓑ Ⓒ Ⓓ Ⓔ
11. Ⓐ Ⓑ Ⓒ Ⓓ Ⓔ	24. Ⓐ Ⓑ Ⓒ Ⓓ Ⓔ	37. Ⓐ Ⓑ Ⓒ Ⓓ Ⓔ	50. Ⓐ Ⓑ Ⓒ Ⓓ Ⓔ
12. Ⓐ Ⓑ Ⓒ Ⓓ Ⓔ	25. Ⓐ Ⓑ Ⓒ Ⓓ Ⓔ	38. Ⓐ Ⓑ Ⓒ Ⓓ Ⓔ	
13. Ⓐ Ⓑ Ⓒ Ⓓ Ⓔ	26. Ⓐ Ⓑ Ⓒ Ⓓ Ⓔ	39. Ⓐ Ⓑ Ⓒ Ⓓ Ⓔ	

Model Test 6 测试题6

Tear out the preceding answer sheet. Decide which is the best choice by rounding your answer when appropriate. Blacken the corresponding space on the answer sheet. When finished, check your answers with those at the end of the test. For questions that you got wrong, note the chapters containing the material that you must review. Also, if you do not fully understand how you arrived at some of the correct answers, you should review the appropriate chapters. Finally, fill out the Self-Evaluation Chart on page 343 in order to pinpoint the topics that give you the most difficulty.

50 questions: 1 hour

Directions: Decide which answer choice is best. If the exact numerical value is not one of the answer choices, select the closest approximation. Fill in the circle on the answer sheet that corresponds to your choice.

Notes:

(1) You will need to use a scientific or graphing calculator to answer some of the questions.

(2) You will have to decide whether to put your calculator in degree or radian mode for some problems.

(3) All figures that accompany problems are plane figures unless otherwise stated. Figures are drawn as accurately as possible to provide useful information for solving the problem, except when it is stated in a particular problem that the figure is not drawn to scale.

(4) Unless otherwise indicated, the domain of a function is the set of all real numbers for which the functional value is also a real number.

Reference Information. The following formulas are provided for your information.

Volume of a right circular cone with radius r and height h: $V = \frac{1}{3}\pi r^2 h$

Lateral area of a right circular cone if the base has circumference C and slant height is l:

$S = \frac{1}{2}Cl$

Volume of a sphere of radius r: $V = \frac{4}{3}\pi r^3$

Surface area of a sphere of radius r: $S = 4\pi r^2$

Volume of a pyramid of base area B and height h: $V = \frac{1}{3}Bh$

1. If $10y - 6 = 3k(5y - 3)$ for all y, then $k =$

(A) $\frac{1}{2}$

(B) $\frac{2}{3}$

(C) $\frac{3}{2}$

(D) $\frac{5}{3}$

(E) 2

USE THIS SPACE FOR SCRATCH WORK

2. Two 6-sided dice are rolled. What is the probability that the sum of the faces showing up is less than 5?

(A) $\frac{1}{12}$

(B) $\frac{1}{6}$

(C) $\frac{7}{11}$

(D) $\frac{7}{10}$

(E) $\frac{5}{6}$

3. If (a,b) is a solution of the system of equations

$\begin{cases} 2x - y = 7 \\ x + y = 8 \end{cases}$, then the difference, $a - b$, equals

(A) −12
(B) −10
(C) 0
(D) 2
(E) 4

4. If $f(x) = x - 1$, $g(x) = 3x$, and $h(x) = \frac{5}{x}$, then $f^{-1}(g(h(5))) =$

(A) 4
(B) 2

(C) $\frac{5}{6}$

(D) $\frac{1}{2}$

(E) $\frac{5}{12}$

5. A sphere is inscribed in a cube. The ratio of the volume of the sphere to the volume of the cube is

(A) 0.79:1
(B) 1:2
(C) 0.52:1
(D) 1:3.1
(E) 0.24:1

6. Find y if the slope of the line containing the point $(-1, 3)$ and $(4, y)$ is 0.75.

(A) 0.75
(B) 1
(C) 6.75
(D) 8
(E) 9.67

7. The roots of the equation $3x^4 + 4x^3 + x - 1 = 0$ consist of

(A) three positive real numbers and one negative real number
(B) three negative real numbers and one positive real number
(C) one negative real number and three imaginary numbers
(D) one positive real number, one negative real number, and two imaginary numbers
(E) two positive real numbers, one negative real number, and one imaginary number

8. For what value(s) of k is $x^2 + 3x + k$ divisible by $x + k$?

(A) only 0
(B) only 0 or 2
(C) only 0 or -4
(D) no value of k
(E) any value of k

9. What number should be added to each of the three numbers 3, 11, and 27 so that the resulting numbers form a geometric sequence?

(A) 2
(B) 3
(C) 4
(D) 5
(E) 6

10. What is the equation of the set of points that are 5 units from point (2,3,4)?

(A) $2x + 3y + 4z = 5$
(B) $x^2 + y^2 + z^2 - 4x - 6y - 8z = 25$
(C) $(x - 2)^2 + (y - 3)^2 + (z - 4)^2 = 25$
(D) $x^2 + y^2 + z^2 = 5$
(E) $\frac{x}{2} + \frac{y}{3} + \frac{z}{4} = 5$

USE THIS SPACE FOR SCRATCH WORK

11. If $3x^{3/2} = 4$, then $x =$

(A) 1.12
(B) 1.21
(C) 1.34
(D) 1.49
(E) 1.53

12. If $f(x) = x^3 - 4$, then the inverse of $f =$

(A) $-x^3 + 4$
(B) $\sqrt[3]{x+4}$
(C) $\sqrt[3]{x-4}$
(D) $\frac{1}{x^3 - 4}$
(E) $\frac{4}{\sqrt[3]{x}}$

13. If f is an odd function and $f(a) = b$, which of the following must also be true?

I. $f(a) = -b$
II. $f(-a) = b$
III. $f(-a) = -b$

(A) only I
(B) only II
(C) only III
(D) only I and II
(E) only II and III

14. For all θ, $\tan\theta + \cos\theta + \tan(-\theta) + \cos(-\theta) =$

(A) 0
(B) $2\tan\theta$
(C) $2\cos\theta$
(D) $2(\tan\theta + \cos\theta)$
(E) 2

15. The period of the function $f(x) = k\cos kx$ is $\frac{\pi}{2}$. The amplitude of f is

(A) $\frac{1}{4}$
(B) $\frac{1}{2}$
(C) 1
(D) 2
(E) 4

USE THIS SPACE FOR SCRATCH WORK

MODEL TEST 6

USE THIS SPACE FOR SCRATCH WORK

16. If $f(x)=\dfrac{x+2}{(x-2)(x^2-4)}$, its graph will have

(A) one horizontal and three vertical asymptotes
(B) one horizontal and two vertical asymptotes
(C) one horizontal and one vertical asymptote
(D) zero horizontal and one vertical asymptote
(E) zero horizontal and two vertical asymptotes

17. At a distance of 100 feet, the angle of elevation from the horizontal ground to the top of a building is 42°. The height of the building is

(A) 67 feet
(B) 74 feet
(C) 90 feet
(D) 110 feet
(E) 229 feet

18. A sphere has a surface area of 36π. Its volume is

(A) 84
(B) 113
(C) 201
(D) 339
(E) 905

19. A pair of dice is tossed 10 times. What is the probability that no 7s or 11s appear as the sum of the sides facing up?

(A) 0.08
(B) 0.09
(C) 0.11
(D) 0.16
(E) 0.24

20. The lengths of two sides of a triangle are 50 inches and 63 inches. The angle opposite the 63-inch side is 66°. How many degrees are in the largest angle of the triangle?

(A) 66°
(B) 67°
(C) 68°
(D) 71°
(E) 72°

21. Which of the following is an equation of a line that is perpendicular to $5x + 2y = 8$?

(A) $8x - 2y = 5$
(B) $5x - 2y = 8$
(C) $2x - 5y = 4$
(D) $2x + 5y = 10$
(E) $y = \dfrac{2}{-5x+8}$

22. What is the period of the graph of the function $y = \dfrac{\sin x}{1+\cos x}$?

(A) 4π
(B) 2π
(C) π
(D) $\dfrac{\pi}{2}$
(E) $\dfrac{\pi}{4}$

USE THIS SPACE FOR SCRATCH WORK

23. For what values of k are the roots of the equation $kx^2 + 4x + k = 0$ real and unequal?

(A) $0 < k < 2$
(B) $|k| < 2$
(C) $|k| > 2$
(D) $k > 2$
(E) $-2 < k < 0$ or $0 < k < 2$

24. Minor defects are found on 7 of 10 new cars. If 3 of the 10 cars are selected at random, what is the probability that 2 have minor defects?

(A) 0.143
(B) 0.333
(C) 0.525
(D) 0.667
(E) 0.700

25. If $f(x) = 3x^2 + 24x - 53$, find the negative value of $f^{-1}(0)$.

(A) −58.80
(B) −9.80
(C) −8.23
(D) −1.87
(E) −0.21

26. If $\log_b x = 0.2$, and $\log_b y = 0.4$, what is the relationship between x and y?

(A) $y = 2x$
(B) $y = x^2$
(C) $y = \sqrt{x}$
(D) $xy = 0.6$
(E) $xy = \dfrac{\log 0.6}{\log b}$

MODEL TEST 6

27. If $7^{x-1} = 6^x$, find x.

(A) −13.2
(B) 0.08
(C) 0.22
(D) 0.52
(E) 12.6

USE THIS SPACE FOR SCRATCH WORK

28. A red box contains eight items, of which three are defective, and a blue box contains five items, of which two are defective. An item is drawn at random from each box. What is the probability that one item is defective and one is not?

(A) $\frac{17}{20}$
(B) $\frac{5}{8}$
(C) $\frac{17}{32}$
(D) $\frac{19}{40}$
(E) $\frac{9}{40}$

29. If $(\log_3 x)(\log_5 3) = 3$, find x.

(A) 5
(B) 9
(C) 25
(D) 81
(E) 125

30. If $f(x) = \sqrt{x}, g(x) = \sqrt[3]{x+1}$, and $h(x) = \sqrt[4]{x+2}$, then $f(g(h(2)))$ =

(A) 1.2
(B) 1.4
(C) 2.9
(D) 4.7
(E) 8.5

31. In $\triangle ABC$, $\angle A = 45°$, $\angle B = 30°$, and $b = 8$. Side a =

(A) 6.5
(B) 11
(C) 12
(D) 14
(E) 16

MODEL TEST 6

32. The equations of the asymptotes of the graph of $4x^2 - 9y^2 = 36$ are

(A) $y = x$ and $y = -x$
(B) $y = 0$ and $x = 0$
(C) $y = \frac{2}{3}x$ and $y = -\frac{2}{3}x$
(D) $y = \frac{3}{2}x$ and $y = -\frac{3}{2}x$
(E) $y = \frac{4}{9}x$ and $y = -\frac{4}{9}x$

USE THIS SPACE FOR SCRATCH WORK

33. If $g(x - 1) = x^2 + 2$, then $g(x) =$

(A) $x^2 - 2x + 3$
(B) $x^2 + 2x + 3$
(C) $x^2 - 3x + 2$
(D) $x^2 + 2$
(E) $x^2 - 2$

34. If $f(x) = 3x^3 - 2x^2 + x - 2$, and $i = \sqrt{-1}$ then $f(i) =$

(A) $-2i - 4$
(B) $4i - 4$
(C) $4i$
(D) $-2i$
(E) 0

35. If the hour hand of a clock moves k radians in 48 minutes, $k =$

(A) 0.3
(B) 0.4
(C) 0.5
(D) 2.4
(E) 5

36. If the longer diagonal of a rhombus is 10 and the large angle is 100°, what is the area of the rhombus?

(A) 37
(B) 40
(C) 42
(D) 45
(E) 50

37. Let $f(x) = \sqrt{x^3 - 4x}$ and $g(x) = 3x$. The sum of all values of x for which $f(x) = g(x)$ is

(A) −8.5
(B) 0
(C) 8
(D) 9
(E) 9.4

MODEL TEST 6

38. How many subsets does a set with n distinct elements have?

(A) n^2
(B) 2^n
(C) $\frac{(2n)!}{2(n!)}$
(D) n
(E) $n!$

39. If $f(x) = 2^{3x-5}$, find $f^{-1}(16)$.

(A) 1
(B) 2
(C) 3
(D) 4
(E) 5

40. For what positive value of n are the zeros of $P(x) = 5x^2 + nx + 12$ in ratio 2:3?

(A) 0.42
(B) 1.32
(C) 4.56
(D) 15.8
(E) 25

41. If $f(-x) = -f(x)$ for all x and if the point $(-2, 3)$ is on the graph of f, which of the following points must also be on the graph of f?

(A) $(-3, 2)$
(B) $(2, -3)$
(C) $(-2, 3)$
(D) $(-2, -3)$
(E) $(3, -2)$

42. A man piles 150 toothpicks in layers so that each layer has one less toothpick than the layer below. If the top layer has three toothpicks, how many layers are there?

(A) 15
(B) 17
(C) 20
(D) 148
(E) 11,322

43. If the circle $x^2 + y^2 - 2x - 6y = r^2 - 10$ is tangent to the line $12y = 60$, the value of r is

(A) 1
(B) 2
(C) 3
(D) 4
(E) 5

USE THIS SPACE FOR SCRATCH WORK

MODEL TEST 6

USE THIS SPACE FOR SCRATCH WORK

44. If $a_0 = 0.4$ and $a_{n+1} = 2|a_n| - 1$, then $a_5 =$

(A) –0.6
(B) –0.2
(C) 0.2
(D) 0.4
(E) 0.6

45. If $5.21^p = 2.86^q$, what is the value of $\frac{p}{q}$?

(A) –0.60
(B) 0.55
(C) 0.60
(D) 0.64
(E) 1.57

46. The matrix $A = \begin{bmatrix} -3 & x \\ 4 & 2/3 \end{bmatrix}$ does **not** have an inverse. Find the value of x.

(A) $-\frac{2}{3}$
(B) $-\frac{1}{2}$
(C) 0
(D) $\frac{3}{4}$
(E) 1

47. There is a linear relationship between the number of chirps made by a cricket and the air temperature. A least-squares fit of data collected by a biologist yields the equation:

temp (°F) = 22.8 + (3.4)(#chirps/min)

What is the estimated increase in temperature that corresponds to an increase of 5 chirps per minute?

(A) 3.4°F
(B) 17.0°F
(C) 22.8°F
(D) 26.2°F
(E) 39.8°F

48. If the length of the diameter of a circle is equal to the length of the major axis of the ellipse whose equation is $x^2 + 4y^2 - 4x + 8y - 28 = 0$, to the nearest whole number, what is the area of the circle?

(A) 28
(B) 64
(C) 113
(D) 254
(E) 452

USE THIS SPACE FOR SCRATCH WORK

49. The force of the wind on a sail varies jointly as the area of the sail and the square of the wind velocity. On a sail of area 50 square yards, the force of a 15-mile-per-hour wind is 45 pounds. Find the force on the sail if the wind increases to 45 miles per hour.

(A) 135 pounds
(B) 225 pounds
(C) 405 pounds
(D) 450 pounds
(E) 675 pounds

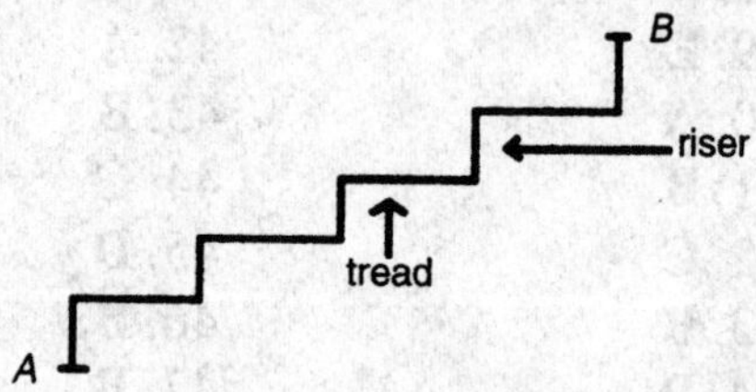

50. If the riser of each step in the drawing above is 6 inches and the tread is 8 inches, what is the value of $|AB|$?

(A) 40 inches
(B) 43.9 inches
(C) 46.6 inches
(D) 48.3 inches
(E) 50 inches

STOP

If there is still time remaining, you may review your answers.

ANSWER KEY
答案
Model Test 6
测试题6

1. **B**	14. **C**	27. **E**	40. **D**
2. **B**	15. **E**	28. **D**	41. **B**
3. **D**	16. **C**	29. **E**	42. **A**
4. **A**	17. **C**	30. **A**	43. **B**
5. **C**	18. **B**	31. **B**	44. **C**
6. **C**	19. **A**	32. **C**	45. **D**
7. **D**	20. **C**	33. **B**	46. **B**
8. **B**	21. **C**	34. **D**	47. **B**
9. **D**	22. **B**	35. **B**	48. **C**
10. **C**	23. **E**	36. **C**	49. **C**
11. **B**	24. **C**	37. **E**	50. **B**
12. **B**	25. **B**	38. **B**	
13. **C**	26. **B**	39. **C**	

ANSWERS EXPLAINED 答案解析

The following explanations are keyed to the review portions of this book. The number in brackets after each explanation indicates the appropriate chapter in the Review of Major Topics (Part 2). If a problem can be solved using algebraic techniques alone, [algebra] appears after the explanation, and no reference is given for that problem in the Self-Evaluation Chart at the end of the test.

An asterisk appears next to those solutions in which a graphing calculator is necessary or helpful.

1. (B) Divide both sides by $5y-3$ to have the k-term on its own, $\frac{10y-6}{5y-3}=3k$. Factor out 2 from the numerator and then divide common terms, $\frac{2(5y-3)}{5y-3}=2=3k$.

   Divide both sides by 3 to get $k=\frac{2}{3}$. [algebra]

2. (B) There are 36 possible outcomes when two dice are rolled. The possible rolls can be represented by ordered pairs, where the first entry is the outcome of one die and the second is the outcome of the other. Thus, the 36 pairs are (1 and 1), (1 and 2), . . . , (1 and 6), (2 and 1), (2 and 2), . . . , (2 and 6), . . . , (6 and 1), (6 and 2), . . . , (6 and 6). Six pairs have sums less than 5: (1 and 1), (1 and 2), (1 and 3), (2 and 1), (2 and 2), (3 and 1). Therefore, the probability that the sum is less than 5 is $\frac{6}{36}=\frac{1}{6}$. [22]

3. (D) Adding the equations gives $3x=15$. $x=5$ and $y=3$. $a-b=2$. [2]

4. (A) $h(5)=1$. $g(1)=3$. Interchange x and y to find that $f^{-1}(x)=x+1$, and so $f^{-1}(3)=4$. [1]

* 5. (C) Diameter of sphere = side of cube.

   Volume of sphere $=\frac{4}{3}\pi r^3$.

   Volume of cube $=s^3=(2r)^3=8r^3$.

$$\frac{\text{Volume of sphere}}{\text{Volume of cube}}=\frac{\frac{4}{3}\pi r^3}{8r^3}=\frac{\pi}{6}\approx\frac{3.14}{6}\approx\frac{0.52}{1}.\ [15]$$

6. (C) The desired slope is $\frac{y-3}{4+1}=\frac{3}{4}$. Cross-multiply and solve for y: $4y-12=15$, so $y=6.75$. [1]

* 7. (D) Plot the graph of $y=3x^4+4x^3+x-1$ in the standard window. Observe that the graph crosses the x-axis twice—once at a positive x value and once at a negative one. Since the function is a degree 4 polynomial, there are 4 roots, so the other two must be complex conjugates. [4]

8. (B) If x^2+3x+k is divisible by $x+k$, then $(-k)^2+3(-k)+k=0$, or $k^2-2k=0$. Factoring and solving yields the correct answer choice. [4]

MODEL TEST 6

9. **(D)** If x is the number, then to have a geometric sequence, $\frac{11+x}{3+x}=\frac{27+x}{11+x}$. Cross-multiplying yields $121 + 22x + x^2 = 81 + 30x + x^2$, and subtracting x^2 and solving gives the desired solution.

An alternative solution is to backsolve. Determine which answer choice yields a sequence of 3 integers with a common ratio. [19]

10. **(C)** The set of points represents a sphere with equation $(x-2)^2 + (y-3)^2 + (z-4)^2 = 5^2$. [15]

*** 11.** **(B)** Plot the graph of $y = 3x^{3/2} - 4$ in the standard window and use CALC/zero to find the correct answer choice.

An alternative solution is to divide the equation by 3 to get $x^{3/2}=\frac{4}{3}$ and then raise both sides to the $\frac{2}{3}$ power: $x=\left(\frac{4}{3}\right)^{2/3}\approx 1.21$. [8]

12. **(B)** Let $y = f(x) = x^3 - 4$. To get the inverse, interchange x and y and solve for y. $x = y^3 - 4$. $y=\sqrt[3]{x+4}$. [1]

13. **(C)** Use the definition of an odd function. If $f(a) = b$, then $f(-a) = -b$. Only III is true. [1]

14. **(C)** Tangent is an odd function, so $\tan(-\theta) = -\tan\theta$, and cosine is an even function, so $\cos(-\theta) = \cos\theta$. Therefore, the sum in the problem is $2\cos\theta$. [7]

15. **(E)** Period $=\frac{2\pi}{k}=\frac{\pi}{2}$. $k = 4$. Amplitude = 4. [7]

*** 16.** **(C)** Plot the graph of $y=\frac{x+2}{(x-2)(x^2-4)}$ in the standard window and observe one vertical asymptote ($x = 2$) and one horizontal asymptote ($y = 0$). [9]

*** 17.** **(C)** Tan 42° $=\frac{x}{100}$, so $x = 100 \tan 42 \approx 90$. [6]

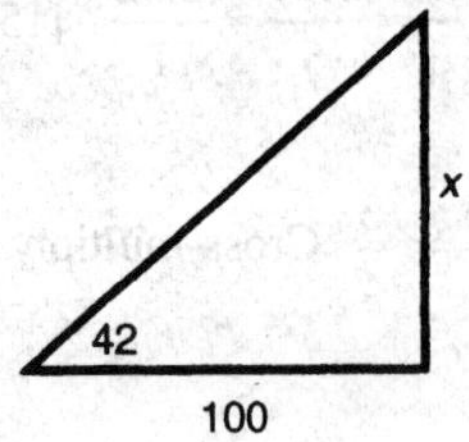

*** 18.** **(B)** $4\pi r^2 = 36\pi$. $r^2 = 9$. $r = 3$. $V=\frac{4}{3}\pi r^3 = 36\pi \approx 113$. [15]

*** 19.** **(A)** There are six ways to get a 7 and two ways to get an 11 on two dice, and so there are $36 - 8 = 28$ ways to get anything else. Therefore, P(no 7 or 11) =

P(always getting something else) $=\left(\frac{28}{36}\right)^{10}\approx 0.08$. [22]

MODEL TEST 6

∗ 20. **(C)** Use the law of sines: $\frac{\sin B}{50} = \frac{\sin 66°}{63}$. $\sin B = \frac{50 \sin 66}{63} \approx \frac{45.68}{63} \approx 0.725$.

$B = \sin^{-1}(0.725) \approx 46°$ and $\angle A = 180 - 46 - 66 = 68°$. [6]

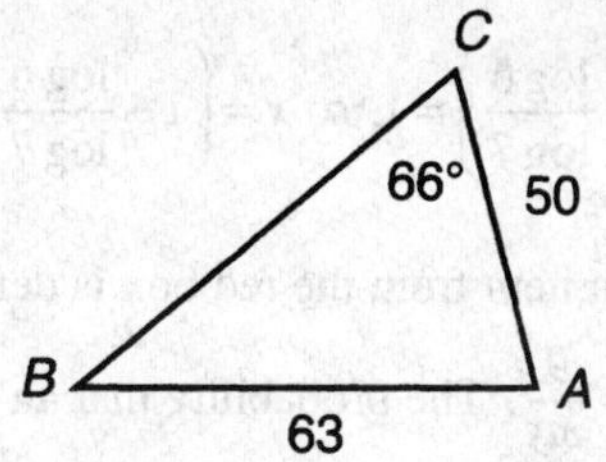

21. **(C)** Solve the equation for y to find the slope of the line is $-\frac{5}{2}$. The slope of a perpendicular line is $\frac{2}{5}$. Inspection of the answer choices yields Choice C as the correct answer. [2]

22. **(B)** With your calculator in radian mode, plot the graph of $y = \sin x/(1 + \cos x)$ and observe that the period is 2π.

An alternative solution is to use the identity $\tan\frac{x}{2} = \frac{\sin x}{1+\cos x}$ and the fact that the period of $\tan x$ is π to deduce the period of $\tan\frac{x}{2}$ as $\frac{\pi}{1/2} = 2\pi$. [7]

23. **(E)** $b^2 - 4ac > 0$. $b^2 - 4ac = 16 - 4k^2 > 0$. $4 > k^2$. So $-2 < k < 2$. However, $k \neq 0$ because if $k = 0$, there would no longer be a quadratic equation. [3]

24. **(C)** The denominator of the probability is ${}_{10}C_3 = 120$, the number of ways 3 cars can be chosen from 10. There are ${}_7C_2 = 21$ ways of choosing 2 defective cars of 7, and ${}_3C_1 = 3$ ways of choosing 1 nondefective car of 3. Therefore, there are $(21)(3) = 63$ of choosing 2 defective and 1 nondefective cars, and the probability of this is $\frac{63}{120} \approx 0.525$. [22]

∗ 25. **(B)** Find $f^{-1}(0)$ means to find a value of x that makes $3x^2 + 24x - 53 = 0$. Enter the left side of the equation into Y_1, and key 2nd Trace (CALC) to find the zero -9.80. [3]

26. **(B)** Since $\log_b x = 0.2$ and $\log_b y = 0.4$, it follows that $x = b^{0.2}$ and $y = b^{0.4}$. Therefore, $x^2 = (b^{0.2})^2 = b^{0.4} = y$. [8]

* 27. **(E)** Enter 7^(*x* – 1) – 6^*x* into Y_1, and generate an Auto table with TblStart = –14 and ΔTbl = 1. Scan through values of x and observe a change in the sign of Y_1 between $x = 12$ and $x = 13$. Thus, Choice E is the correct answer choice.

An alternative solution is to take $\log_7$ of both sides to get $x - 1 = \log_7 6^x = x \log_7 6 =$

$x\dfrac{\log 6}{\log 7}$. Therefore, $x\left(1-\dfrac{\log 6}{\log 7}\right)=1$, so $x=\left(1-\dfrac{\log 6}{\log 7}\right)^{-1}\approx 12.6$. [8]

28. **(D)** The probability that an item from the red box is defective and an item from the blue box is good = $\dfrac{3}{8}\cdot\dfrac{3}{5}=\dfrac{9}{40}$. The probability that an item from the red box is good and that an item from the blue box is defective = $\dfrac{5}{8}\cdot\dfrac{2}{5}=\dfrac{10}{40}$. Since these are mutually exclusive events, the answer is $\dfrac{9}{40}+\dfrac{10}{40}=\dfrac{19}{40}$. [22]

* 29. **(E)** By the change-of-base theorem, $\log_3 x = \dfrac{\log_5 x}{\log_5 3}$. Therefore, $\log_5 x = 3$ and $x = 5^3 = 125$. [8]

* 30. **(A)** Enter f into Y_1; g into Y_2; and h into Y_3. Then return to the Home Screen and evaluate $Y_1(Y_2(Y_3(2)))$ to get the correct answer choice.

An alternative solution is to evaluate each function, starting with h in turn:

$\sqrt{\left(\sqrt[3]{\sqrt[4]{2+2}+1}\right)}+\sqrt{((4)^\wedge(1/4)+1)^\wedge(1/3)}\approx 1.2$. [1]

* 31. **(B)** Use the law of sines: $\dfrac{\sin 45°}{a}=\dfrac{\sin 30°}{8}$. Therefore $a=\dfrac{8\sin 45°}{\sin 30°}\approx 11$. [6]

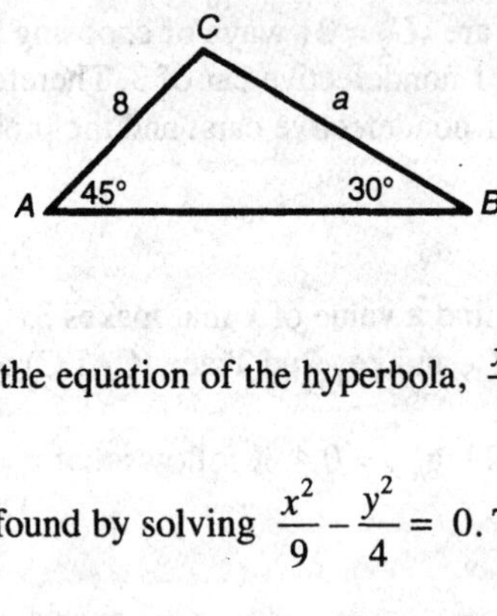

32. **(C)** From this form of the equation of the hyperbola, $\dfrac{x^2}{9}-\dfrac{y^2}{4}=1$, the equations of the asymptotes can be found by solving $\dfrac{x^2}{9}-\dfrac{y^2}{4}=0$. Thus, $y=\pm\dfrac{2}{3}x$. [13]

33. **(B)** Since $x = (x + 1 - 1)$, $g(x) = g((x + 1) - 1) = (x + 1)^2 + 2 = x^2 + 2x + 3$. [12]

* 34. **(D)** Evaluate $f(i) = 3i^3 - 2i^2 + i - 2 = -2i$ on your graphing calculator. [17]

* 35. (B) In 1 hour, the hour hand moves $\frac{1}{12}$ of the way around the clock, or $\frac{2\pi}{12} = \frac{\pi}{6}$ radians. $\frac{48}{60} \cdot \frac{\pi}{6} = \frac{2\pi}{15} \approx \frac{6.28}{15} \approx 0.4$. [7]

* 36. (C) Diagonals of a rhombus are perpendicular; they bisect each other, and they bisect angles of the rhombus. From the figure below, $\tan 40° = \frac{x}{5}$, $x = 5 \tan 40° \approx 4.195$.

$A = \frac{1}{2}d_1d_2 = \frac{1}{2}(10)(2)(4.195) \approx 42$. [6]

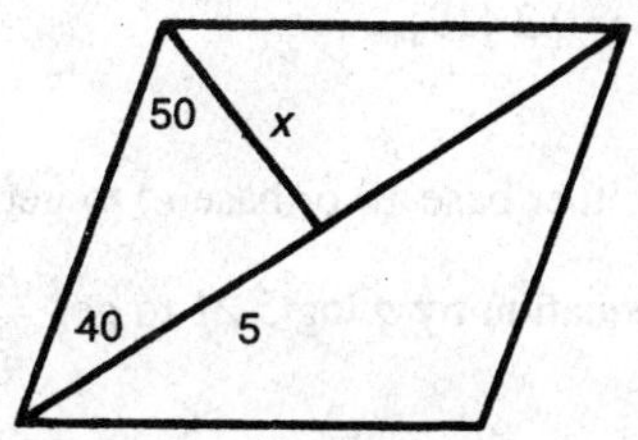

* 37. (E) Plot the graphs of f and g in a [–10,15] by [–10, 50] window. One point of intersection is the origin. Find the other by using CALC/intersection to get the correct answer choice.

An alternative solution is to set $\sqrt{x^3 - 4x} = 3x$, square both sides, and factor out x to get $x(x^2 - 9x - 4) = 0$. Use the Quadratic Formula with the second factor to find the solutions $x \approx -0.4, 9.4$, and observe that the first does not satisfy the original equation. Thus, the two solutions are 0 and 9.4, resulting in the correct answer choice. [1]

38. (B) Each element is either in a subset or not, so there are 2 choices for each of n elements. This yields $2 \times 2 \times \cdots \times 2$ (n factors) $= 2^n$ subsets. [16]

39. (C) This problem is most readily solved by substituting each answer choice into f to determine which produces the value 16. Since $f(3) = 16$, $f^{-1}(16) = 3$. [8]

* 40. (D) If the zeros of $P(x)$ are in the ratio 2:3, they must take the form $2k$ and $3k$ for some value k, and $(x - 2k)(x - 3k) = x^2 - 5k + 6k^2 = 0$. Dividing $P(x)$ by 5 and equating coefficients yields $\frac{n}{5} = -5k$ and $\frac{12}{5} = 6k^2$. Therefore, $k = \pm\sqrt{\frac{2}{5}}$. Since the problem asks for a positive value of n, we use $k = -\sqrt{\frac{2}{5}}$, so $n = -25k \approx 15.8$. [3]

41. (B) The function f is odd, so it is symmetrical about the origin. If (–2, 3) is on the graph of f, (2, –3) must also be on the graph.

An alternative solution is to conclude $f(-2) = 3$ since (–2, 3) is on the graph of f. Therefore, $f(2) = -3$, so the point (2, –3) is also on the graph. [1]

42. (A) This is an arithmetic series with $t_1 = 3$, $d = 1$, and $S = 150$. $150 = \frac{n}{2}[6 + (n-1)\cdot 1]$. $n = 15$. [19]

∗ 43. (B) Complete the square in the equation of the circle: $(x-1)^2 + (y-3)^2 = r^2$. The center of the circle is at (1,3). If the circle is tangent to the line, then the distance between (1,3) and the line $y = 5$ is the radius of the circle, r. Therefore, $r = 2$. [15]

∗ 44. (C) Enter 0.4 into your calculator, followed by 2|Ans| – 1 five times to get $a_5 = 0.2$.

An alternative solution is to evaluate each a_i in turn:

$$a_1 = 2|0.4| - 1 = -0.2$$
$$a_2 = 2|a_1| - 1 = 2|-0.2| - 1 = -0.6$$
$$a_3 = 2|a_2| - 1 = 2|-0.6| - 1 = 0.2$$
$$a_4 = 2|a_3| - 1 = 2|0.2| - 1 = -0.6$$
$$a_5 = 2|a_4| - 1 = 2|-0.6| - 1 = 0.2 \ [19]$$

∗ 45. (D) Take the logarithms (either base 10 or base e) to get $p \log 5.21 = q \log 2.86$.

Divide both sides of this equation by $q \log 5.21$ to get $\frac{p}{q} = \frac{\log 2.86}{\log 5.21} \approx 0.64$. [8]

46. (B) Since matrix A doesn't have an inverse, $\det A = |A| = 0$. Therefore,

$(-3)\left(\frac{2}{3}\right) - 4x = 0$, so $x = -\frac{1}{2}$. [18]

∗ 47. (B) Temperature increases by 3.4°F for each additional chirp. Therefore, 5 additional chirps indicate an increase of 5(3.4) = 17.0°F. [21]

∗ 48. (C) Complete the square on the ellipse formula, and put the equation in standard form: $x^2 - 4x + 4 + 4(y^2 + 2y + 1) = 28 + 4 + 4$. $\frac{(x-2)^2}{36} + \frac{(y+1)^2}{9} = 1$. This leads to the length of the major axis: $2\sqrt{36} = 12$. Therefore, the radius of the circle is 6, and the area $= 36\pi \approx 113$. [13]

49. (C) Since the velocity of a 45-mile-per-hour wind is 3 times that of a 15-mile-per-hour wind and the force on the sail is proportional to the square of the wind velocity, the force on the sail of a 45-mile-per-hour wind is 9 times that of a 15-mile-per-hour wind: $9 \cdot 45 = 405$. [1]

∗ 50. (B) Total horizontal distance traveled = (4)(8) = 32. Total vertical distance traveled = (5)(6) = 30. If a coordinate system is superimposed on the diagram with A at (0,0), then B is at (32,30). Use the program on your calculator to find the distance between two points to compute the correct answer choice. [2]

MODEL TEST 6

Self-Evaluation Chart for Model Test 6 自评表

Subject Area	Questions and Review Section						Number Right	Number Wrong	Number Omitted
Algebra and Functions	1	3	4	6	7	8			
(24 questions)	—	2	1	1	4	4	____	____	____
	11	12	13	16	21	23			
	8	1	1	9	2	3	____	____	____
	25	26	27	29	30	37			
	3	8	8	8	1	1	____	____	____
	39	40	41	45	49	50			
	8	3	1	8	1	2	____	____	____
Trigonometry	14	15	17	20	22	31			
(8 questions)	7	7	6	6	7	6	____	____	____
	35	36							
	7	6					____	____	____
Coordinate and Three-Dimensional Geometry	5	10	18	32	43	48			
(6 questions)	15	15	15	13	15	13	____	____	____
Numbers and Operations	9	33	34	38	42	44			
(7 questions)	19	12	17	16	19	19	____	____	____
	46								
	18						____	____	____
Data Analysis, Statistics, and Probability	2	19	24	28	47				
(5 questions)	22	22	22	22	21		____	____	____
TOTALS							____	____	____

Evaluate Your Performance on Model Test 6 自评	
Rating	**Number Right**
Excellent	41–50
Very good	33–40
Above average	25–32
Average	15–24
Below average	Below 15

CALCULATING YOUR SCORE 估分

Raw score R = number right – $\frac{1}{4}$(number wrong), rounded = ____________

Approximate scaled score $S = 800 - 10(44 - R)$ = ____________

If $R \geq 44$, $S = 800$.

Summary of Formulas 公式汇总

CHAPTER 2: LINEAR FUNCTIONS 第2章 线性函数

General form of the equation: $Ax + By + C = 0$

Slope-intercept form: $y = mx + b$, where m represents the slope and b the y-intercept

Point-slope form: $y - y_1 = m(x - x_1)$, where m represents the slope and (x_1, y_1) are the coordinates of some point on the line

Slope: $m = \dfrac{y_1 - y_2}{x_1 - x_2}$, where (x_1, y_1) and (x_2, y_2) are the coordinates of two points

Parallel lines have equal slopes.

Perpendicular lines have slopes that are negative reciprocals.

If m_1 and m_2 are the slopes of two perpendicular lines, $m_1 \cdot m_2 = -1$.

Distance between two points with coordinates (x_1, y_1) and $(x_2, y_2) = \sqrt{(x_1 - x_2)^2 + (y_1 - y_2)^2}$

Coordinates of the midpoint between two points =

$$\left(\frac{x_1 + x_2}{2}, \frac{y_1 + y_2}{2}\right)$$

Distance between a point with coordinates (x_1, y_1) and a line $Ax + By + C = 0 = \dfrac{|Ax_1 + By_1 + C|}{\sqrt{A^2 + B^2}}$

If θ is the angle between two lines, $\tan\theta = \dfrac{m_1 - m_2}{1 + m_1 m_2}$ where m_1 and m_2 are the slopes of the two lines.

CHAPTER 3: QUADRATIC FUNCTIONS 第3章 二次函数

General quadratic equation: $ax^2 + bx + c = 0$

General quadratic formula: $x = \dfrac{-b \pm \sqrt{b^2 - 4ac}}{2a}$

General quadratic function: $y = ax^2 + bx + c$

Coordinates of vertex: $\left(-\dfrac{b}{2a}, c - \dfrac{b^2}{4a}\right)$

Axis of symmetry equation: $x = -\dfrac{b}{2a}$

Sum of zeros (roots) = $-\dfrac{b}{a}$

Product of zeros (roots) = $\dfrac{c}{a}$

Nature of zeros (roots):

If $b^2 - 4ac < 0$, two complex numbers
If $b^2 - 4ac = 0$, two equal real numbers
If $b^2 - 4ac > 0$, two unequal real numbers

CHAPTER 6: TRIANGLE TRIGONOMETRY 第6章 三角几何

$$\sin\theta = \frac{\text{opposite}}{\text{hypotenuse}} \qquad \cos\theta = \frac{\text{adjacent}}{\text{hypotenuse}}$$

$$\tan\theta = \frac{\text{opposite}}{\text{adjacent}} \qquad \cot\theta = \frac{\text{adjacent}}{\text{opposite}}$$

$$\sec\theta = \frac{\text{hypotenuse}}{\text{adjacent}} \qquad \csc\theta = \frac{\text{hypotenuse}}{\text{opposite}}$$

In any $\triangle ABC$:

Law of sines: $\frac{\sin A}{a} = \frac{\sin B}{b} = \frac{\sin C}{c}$

Law of cosines: $a^2 = b^2 + c^2 - 2bc\cos A$

$b^2 = a^2 + c^2 - 2ac\cos B$

$c^2 = a^2 + b^2 - 2ab\cos C$

Area $= \frac{1}{2}bc \cdot \sin A$

CHAPTER 7: TRIGONOMETRIC FUNCTIONS 第7章 三角函数

$$\pi^R = 180^\circ$$

Length of arc in circle of radius r and central angle θ is given by $r\theta$. (θ in radians)

Area of sector of circle of radius r and central angle θ is given by $\frac{1}{2}r^2\theta$.(θ in radians)

1. $\sin^2 x + \cos^2 x = 1$
2. $\tan^2 x + 1 = \sec^2 x$
3. $\cot^2 x + 1 = \csc^2 x$

} Pythagorean identities

4. $\sin 2A = 2\sin A\cos A$
5. $\cos 2A = \cos^2 A - \sin^2 A$
6. $\quad = 2\cos^2 A - 1$
7. $\quad = 1 - 2\sin^2 A$
8. $\tan 2A = \frac{2\tan A}{1 - \tan^2 A}$

} double-angle formulas

CHAPTER 8: EXPONENTIAL AND LOGARITHMIC FUNCTIONS

第8章 指数函数与对数函数

Exponents

$x^a \cdot x^b = x^{a+b}$ $\qquad \frac{x^a}{x^b} = x^{a-b}$

$(x^a)^b = x^{ab}$

$x^0 = 1$ $\qquad x^{-a} = \frac{1}{x^a}$

Logarithms

$\log_b(pq) = \log_b p + \log_b q$

$\log_b p^x = x\log_b p$

$\log_b p = \frac{\log_a p}{\log_a b}$

$\log_b\left(\frac{p}{q}\right) = \log_b p - \log_b q$

$\log_b 1 = 0$

$\log_b b = 1$

$b^{\log_b p} = p$

$\text{Log}_b N = x$ if and only if $b^x = N$

CHAPTER 11: PIECEWISE FUNCTIONS 第11章 分段函数

Absolute Value

If $x \geq 0$, then $|x| = x$.
If $x < 0$, then $|x| = -x$.

Greatest Integer Function

$[x] = i$, where i is an integer and $i \leq x < i + 1$

CHAPTER 13: CONIC SECTIONS 第13章 圆锥截面

Standard Equation of a Circle

$(x - h)^2 + (y - k)^2 = r^2$
with center at (h,k) and radius $= r$

Standard Equation of an Ellipse

$\frac{(x-h)^2}{a^2} + \frac{(y-k)^2}{b^2} = 1$, major axis horizontal

$\frac{(x-h)^2}{b^2} + \frac{(y-k)^2}{a^2} = 1$, major axis vertical,

where $a^2 = b^2 + c^2$

Standard Equation of a Hyperbola

$\frac{(x-h)^2}{a^2} - \frac{(y-k)^2}{b^2} = 1$, transverse axis horizontal

$$\frac{(y-k)^2}{a^2}-\frac{(x-h)^2}{b^2}=1$$, transverse axis vertical,

where $c^2 = a^2 + b^2$

CHAPTER 14: POLAR COORDINATES
第14章 极坐标

$x = r\cos\theta \qquad y = r\sin\theta$

$x^2 + y^2 = r^2$

CHAPTER 15: THREE-DIMENSIONAL GEOMETRY
第15章 三维几何

Distance between two points with coordinates

(x_1,y_1,z_1) and (x_2,y_2,z_2) =

$$\sqrt{(x_1-x_2)^2+(y_1-y_2)^2+(z_1-z_2)^2}$$

Distance between a point with coordinates (x_1,y_1,z_1) and a plane with equation

$$Ax + By + Cz + D = 0 = \frac{Ax_1+By_1+Cz_1+D}{\sqrt{A^2+B^2+C^2}}$$

Cylinder Formulas

Volume = $\pi r^2 h$

Lateral surface area = $2\pi rh$

Total surface area = $2\pi rh + 2\pi r^2$

In all formulas, r = radius of base, h = height

Cone Formulas

Volume = $\frac{1}{3}\pi r^2 h$

Lateral surface area = $\pi r\sqrt{r^2+h^2}$

Total surface area = $\pi r\sqrt{r^2+h^2}+\pi r^2$

In all formulas, r = radius of base, h = height

Sphere Formulas

Volume = $\frac{4}{3}\pi r^3$

Surface area = $4\pi r^2$

In all formulas, r = radius

CHAPTER 16: COUNTING
第16章 计算

Permutations

$${}_nP_r = \frac{n!}{(n-r)!}, \text{ where } n! = n(n-1)(n-2)\cdots 3\cdot 2\cdot 1$$

Combinations

$${}_nC_r = \binom{n}{r} = \frac{n!}{(n-r)!r!} = \frac{{}_nP_r}{r!}$$

CHAPTER 17: COMPLEX NUMBERS
第17章 复数

$i^0 = 1, i^1 = i, i^{-2} = -1, i^3 = -i, i^4 = 1, \ldots$

$|a + bi| = a^2 + b^2$

CHAPTER 18: MATRICES
第18章 矩阵

Determinants of a 2 × 2 Matrix

$$\begin{vmatrix} a & b \\ c & d \end{vmatrix} = ad - bc$$

CHAPTER 19: SEQUENCES AND SERIES
第19章 数列与级数

Arithmetic Sequence (or Progression)

nth term = $t_n = t_1 + (n-1)d$

Sum of n terms = $S_n = \frac{n}{2}(t_1 + t_n)$

$= \frac{n}{2}[2t_1 + (n-1)d]$

Geometric Sequence (or Progression)

nth term = $t_n = t_1 r^{n-1}$

Sum of n terms = $S_n = \frac{t_1(1-r^n)}{1-r}$

If $|r| < 1$, $S_\infty = \lim_{n\to\infty} S_n = \frac{t_1}{1-r}$

CHAPTER 20: VECTORS

第20章　向量

If $\vec{V} = (v_1, v_2)$ and $\vec{U} = (u_1, u_2)$,

$\vec{V} + \vec{U} = (v_1 + u_1, v_2 + u_2)$

$\vec{V} \cdot \vec{U} = v_1 u_1 + v_2 u_2$

Two vectors are perpendicular if and only if $\vec{V} \cdot \vec{U} = 0$.

CHAPTER 21: STATISTICS

第21章　统计

Mean $\bar{x}$ of $x_1, x_2, \ldots, x_n$: $\bar{x} = \frac{1}{n}\sum_{i=1}^{n} x_i$

Standard deviation s_x of $x_1, x_2, \ldots, x_n$:

$$s_x = \sqrt{\frac{1}{n}\sum_{i=1}^{n}(x_i - \bar{x})^2}$$

CHAPTER 22: PROBABILITY

第22章　概率

$$P(\text{event}) = \frac{\text{number of ways to get a successful result}}{\text{total number of ways of getting any result}}$$

Independent events: $P(A \cap B) = P(A) \cdot P(B)$

Mutually exclusive events: $P(A \cap B) = 0$ and $P(A \cup B) = P(A) + P(B)$

Index 索引